Western Technology and Soviet Economic Development 1917 to 1930

By

ANTONY C. SUTTON

HOOVER INSTITUTION ON WAR, REVOLUTION AND PEACE
STANFORD UNIVERSITY, STANFORD, CALIFORNIA

To

Mum and Dad

Hoover Institution Publications [76]
© 1968 *by the Board of Trustees of the Leland Stanford Junior University*
All rights reserved
Library of Congress Catalog Card Number: 68-24442
Printed in the United States of America
Second Printing 1970
Third Printing 1972
Reprint Edition 2023

Preface

By far the most significant factor in the development of the Soviet economy has been its absorption of Western technology and skills. Previously this technological transfer has not been treated in detail; hence the data that comprise Part I of this study are thoroughly documented. Without such documentation, the argument of Part II would appear less than credible. The reader may, however, wish to pass on to Part II after briefly satisfying himself with the general content of Part I. Chapter two discussing Soviet oil, and chapter eleven, on electrical equipment, are representative of the empirical treatment of key sectors in Soviet industry.

The primary sources for data are the U.S. State Department Decimal File and the German Foreign Ministry Archives, supplemented by journals in half a dozen languages from a dozen countries. Of these, the journals published by Soviet trade representatives abroad were of particular help.

Grateful appreciation is due the Relm Foundation for funds to purchase several hundred thousand microfilmed documents. Acknowledgment is also due to California State College at Los Angeles and to the Economic Opportunity Program for secretarial and research assistance. The National Archives, the Library of Congress, and the Hoover Institution library were unfailingly responsive and remarkably adept at interpreting requests for information. Without their sympathetic aid, this study could have been neither attempted nor completed. In addition, Dr. Stefan Possony of the Hoover Institution was very helpful in making research suggestions which, in the final analysis, turned out to be of fundamental importance. The Hoover Institution also accepted the considerable burden of preparing the manuscript for publication; particular thanks is due London G. Green for his capable and understanding work as editor.

Finally, acknowledgment is made to F. W. B. Coleman, resident United States Minister in Riga, Lativa, during the 1920s. Riga was the main American 'listening post' of this time, and dispatches by Coleman to Washington, D.C., suggest a deep understanding of events in the Soviet Union. These detailed and accurate reports were of major help in this study.

It is especially important in a study which breaks substantially new ground in a controversial area to point out that any criticism concerning the interpretation of data must fall squarely on the shoulders of the writer, and not on his sources. Such criticism is, of course, to be welcomed.

A. C. S.

Pasadena, California
April 1, 1966

Contents

Contents

Contents

Tables

CHARTS AND MAPS

Glossary

Artel:	Collective labor group
Basmach:	Counter-revolutionary bandit
Bedniak:	'Poor' peasant
Centrosoyuz:	Central Union of Consumers Co-operatives
Chervonetz:	Ten ruble bank note
Dessiatin	2.7 acres
Glavk:	Central board or committee
Glavkontsesskom:	Chief Concessions Committee
Geolro:	State Commission for Electrification
Gosbank:	State Bank
Gosplan:	State Planning Commission
Guberniia:	Province
Hectare:	2.47 acres
Kolkhoz:	Collective farm
Kopeck:	Small coin, 1/100 of a ruble
Koustarny:	Home industry, handicraft wares
Krai:	Region
Kroner:	Swedish monetary unit
Kulak:	Literally 'fist' (term applied to 'rich' peasant)
Oblast':	Province
Pood:	36.1128 pounds
Rayon:	District (of an oblast')
Ruble, gold:	Ruble valued in gold at 0.222168 grams
Sazhen:	2.3333 yards
Seredniak:	'Middle' peasant
Usufruct:	Legal term for operation of an economic activity without ownership rights
Uyezd:	District
Verst:	0.6629 miles

Glossary

VSNKh (Vesenkha):	Vysshyi Sovet Narodnogo Khozaistva—Supreme Council of National Economy
Zemstvos	Elected rural councils in tsarist Russia
Zolotnik	0.15 of an ounce (4.265 grams)

PART ONE

An Empirical Examination of Foreign Concessions and Technological Transfers

CHAPTER ONE

Introduction

ECONOMIC DEVELOPMENT AND THE INTERNATIONAL TRANSFER OF TECHNOLOGY

It is accepted that a significant factor in the economic growth of those countries undergoing rapid development during the twentieth century is the 'advantage of coming late.' Advanced industrial and agricultural technology can be effectively transferred, reducing the latecomer's investment in research and development. Indeed, continuing investment in technology by advanced countries has generally made for a dramatic decrease in capital-output ratios, during the last sixty years.[1]

Massell[2] argues, with empirical support, that the productivity increase in United States manufacturing between 1919 and 1955 is attributable far more to technological change than to increased capital investment. Traditionally it has been assumed that capital investment exceeds technological advance as the major factor in economic development. According to Massell however, 90 percent of the increase in the U.S. output per man-hour is to be attributed to technological improvement and only 10 percent to increases in capital investment. Improvement in labor skills is included as technological advance.

In the sphere of Soviet development, other things being equal, we would then look for technology as a contributing factor of some significance. Development literature in the West omits this factor, although recognition of its importance is implicit in the Soviet emphasis on technological advance.

---

[1] Paul S. Anderson, 'The Apparent Decline in Capital-Output Ratios,' *The Quarterly Journal of Economics,* LXXV, No. 4 (November 1961), 629.

[2] B. F. Massell, 'Capital Formation and Technological Change in United States Manufacturing,' *Review of Economics and Statistics,* XLII (May 1960), 182–8.' In economic terminology, the change in productivity is due to a shift of the production function to the right rather than a deepening in capital intensity and a movement along the production function. Other writers have arrived at similar conclusions. Massell's conclusions coincide with those of Solow and Fabricant, who use different data and methodology.

Considerable evidence will be presented to show that Soviet technology was completely dependent on the West in the decade of the 1920s. Thus we can argue that a major portion of Soviet economic development would have been dependent on the technological contribution of Western enterprises even had there been no capital transfers. There were, however, such capital transfers— of at least sufficient magnitude to support the transfer of technology.

The argument of this study hinges indeed on the contribution of Western technology to Soviet economic development. As technology in the period between 1917 and 1930 originated in the West and not in the Soviet Union, it is concluded that the Western contribution was decisive in Soviet economic development during this period. The essential technology can usually be acquired for significantly less than the cost of the overall project. For example, the total cost of the Volkhov hydroelectric project was 90 million rubles, the major part of which was absorbed by the construction of the dam, the access roads, and the supporting buildings, while only 6 million was spent on imported equipment. However, it was the imported equipment—the turbines, generators, and switchgear—that determined the technical success of the project.

This, of course, is not to argue that technology is the only factor in economic development. Political, social and psychological factors play their respective roles. This interplay is particularly interesting in the Soviet example but is, unfortunately, outside the scope of this study.

THE SOVIET UNION AND THE TRANSFER OF TECHNOLOGY

A study of the influence of Western technology upon the early stages of Soviet economic development may then be a profitable field for research and, in fact, may change our view of those forces allegedly 'released' by socialism and traditionally held responsible for Soviet economic growth. No rigorous analysis of this technological transfer has yet been attempted, although its existence has been noted within the Western world.[3]

The mechanisms for this transfer were in fact many and varied, and include some not found elsewhere in world economic development. First, there was a carryover of internal capital investment from prerevolutionary industrial Russia.[4] This industrial structure was but slightly affected by the Revolutions and subsequent Civil War; evidence to be developed in this study indicates

---

[3] Werner Keller, *Ost minus west=null* (Munich: Droemersche Verlagsanstalt, 1960).

[4] Anton Crihan, *Le capital étranger en Russie* (Paris: Pichon, 1934). P. V. Oll, *Les capitaux étrangers en Russie* (Petrograd: 1922), estimated this capital, expropriated by the Soviet government, to be over $1 billion, a figure quoted in S. N. Prokopovitch, *Histoire Economique de l'U.R.S.S.* (Paris: Flammarian, 1952), p. 281.

that the popular story of substantial physical destruction is, except in the case of the Don Basin, a myth. More damage was done to Russian industry by the ineptitudes of War Communism than by World War I, the Revolutions, the Civil War, and the Allied Intervention combined. Many of the largest plants worked at full capacity right through the Revolutions and Civil War under their 'capitalist' managers. Others, with equipment intact, were placed in a state of 'technical preservation' until managers with skills requisite to recommence operations could be found.

Second, the New Economic Policy (NEP) denationalized certain economic activities and restored some measure of free enterprise to both foreign and domestic capitalists. Internally, the relaxation of controls affected retailing, wholesaling, and small industries employing less than twenty persons. However, the 'commanding heights' of the economy (iron and steel, electrical equipment, transportation, and foreign trade) were retained under Communist control and grouped into trusts and syndicates. Foreign capital and technology were then invited into these units through concessions and mixed joint-stock companies, both with and without domestic private and state participation. The concession, in its varying forms, was the most significant vehicle for the transfer of foreign technology.

At the beginning of the NEP, the emphasis was on concessions to Western entrepreneurs. In the middle and last years of the decade the concession was replaced by technical-assistance contracts and the import of complete plants and equipment. After the acquisition of a specific technology, by either concession, purchase, or confiscation, came duplication in Soviet plants. Major acquisitions were supplemented by the purchase or appropriation of designs, plans, patents, and prototypes. This process extended even to agriculture. For instance, the purchase of pedigreed stock provided for rapid multiplication—equivalent in its way to the reproduction of technical processes.[5]

A third transfer vehicle was the employment of individual Western engineers and experts and the corresponding dispatch of Soviet engineers and workers to training positions in foreign plants. When foreign assistance was required on a substantial and continuing scale, the technical-assistance contract was utilized. The study trip abroad by Soviet engineers was used both as prelude

---

[5] Numerous examples are given in detail below. One interesting importation of Western agricultural technology was the acquisition of Australian and American stud merinos. In 1929, the Soviet government purchased between 20,000 and 30,000 pedigreed breeding sheep. In order to maintain Australian flocks, the Australian government placed an embargo, still maintained today, on the export of sheep for breeding purposes. (House of Representatives, Commonwealth of Australia, *Parliamentary Debates*, 12th Parliament, 1st Session, p. 315.)

to a technical-assistance contract and when minor foreign training or technical help was required.[6]

The transfer of technical knowledge sometimes took forms easily overlooked. For example, the number of subscriptions taken out by the Soviet government for American technical and scientific publications jumped dramatically as the industrialization process got under way.[7]

The penetration of early Soviet industry by Western companies and individuals was remarkable. Western technical directors, consulting engineers, and independent entrepreneurs were common in the Soviet Union. In retrospect, perhaps the most surprising examples were the directorships held by General Electric affiliates on the boards of Soviet electrical trusts.[8]

Although the technological transfer took many forms, dictated by political and economic circumstances, the central mechanism was the concession, around which this study is built. The concession was also interrelated with other mechanisms and the very small amount of internally originated research, development, and innovation. It is true that after 1930 the importance of the concession declined greatly as other forms of technological transfer came into use but for the period from 1917 to 1930 the concession is central.

THE ROLE OF THE FOREIGN CONCESSION, 1917 TO 1930

The use of concessions was suggested in December 1917 at the first All Russian Congress of Councils of the National Economy. After extensive debate it was agreed that concessions were desirable for the restoration of the Russian economy. Subsequent negotiations with American, German, French, and British capital however, were temporarily halted by the Allied Intervention and Civil War.

In 1920, when political conditions were more stabilized, Lenin issued a decree allowing concessions to be granted by simple departmental permission. However, negotiations with Urquhardt, a British financier and well-known capitalist in prewar Russia, ended in failure; and so ended the second attempt to establish foreign concessions. Urquhardt sensed the likelihood of con-

---

[6]   A partial list is in Saul G. Bron, *Soviet Economic Development and American Business* (New York: Horace Liveright, 1930), pp. 144–6. Bron was chairman of the Amtorg Trading Corporation in New York.

[7]   In 1925 the Soviet government held 200 subscriptions to United States technical journals, in 1926–7 about 1,000, in 1927–8 about 8,000, and in 1928–9 more than 12,000, as noted in Amtorg Trading Co., *Economic Review of the Soviet Union* (New York: 1928), III, 383.

[8]   The General Electric Co. was represented on the board of Electroexploatsia, which was responsible for new electrical power stations and systems construction. Swedish General Electric (ASEA) was a 'founder and a principal shareholder' of Electroselstroi, responsible for electrification of rural areas, as noted in *Annuaire Politique et Économique*, (Moscow: N.K.I.D., 1926), p. 25 (rear).

fiscation and would not embark without ironclad guarantees. An agreement between Krassin and Urquhardt was rejected by Lenin, who had problems with the more unrealistic members of the Party, who refused to accept a return of foreign capital under any guise.

A third, successful, attempt stemmed from the decree of March 8th, 1923, replaced by the law of August 21, 1923, which was further amended in December 14, 1927 and supplemented by special ordinances of May 23, 1926 and April 17, 1928. The August 1923 law established a Chief Concessions Committee (Glavkontsesskom) and the legal structure for the conduct of negotiations and the transfer of Russian property to foreign enterprises.[9]

A pure concession is an economic enterprise in which a foreign company enters into a contract with the host country to organize, equip, and exploit a specific opportunity, under the legal doctrine of *usufruct*. In return for the burden of development, exploitation, and production, the foreign company receives a non-contractual surplus or profit, usually taxed by the host country. The Soviets even considered the foreign commune, wherein foreign settlers entered the U.S.S.R. with their tools and equipment, as an agreement 'in lease *usufruct*.'[10] A variant of the pure concession found in Soviet development is the credit or contract concession. Here the foreign firm has the function of organization and finance, but operation is by a Soviet organization. Mixed companies are of this nature, and are still utilized in Soviet economic relations with satellite countries. Technical-assistance contracts are sometimes viewed as concession operations by the Soviets but rarely by the West. The return allowed to the foreign participant in a technical-assistance agreement is usually determined by contract and is not merely a surplus accruing to the entrepreneur. On the other hand, not all economic agreements lacking contractual payment features can be described as concessions. The design competitions, such as the Locomotive Design Competition of 1927, had non-contractual rewards but were not concessions, although they had elements of technological transfer.

The mixed corporation was also used in agriculture, as were credit and contract concessions financed by foreign firms but operated by Soviet organizations. In addition, technical-assistance contracts were used to acquire advice on particular agricultural problems, and in some cases concessions participated in the financing of equipment purchases.

Concessions, however, operated within all sectors of the economy, although the largest single group numerically was in raw materials development. Indus-

---

[9] The Concession Law of 1923 is reprinted in the *Journal of the Workmen-Peasant Government of the U.S.S.R.*, No. 13, 1923. The amendment is reprinted in *Collection of Laws of the U.S.S.R.* (Moscow: 1927), Part I, No. 69.

[10] The Imkommune Uhlfeld (Austria) is a good example. See page 129.

trial concessions formed a smaller but, as will be seen, strategically important group. Although concessions were offered in housing and public utilities, they were not, with the exception of a few housing developments, attractive to foreign investors.

In size, concessions ranged from the gigantic Lena Goldfields, Ltd., of the United Kingdom, operating thirteen separate industrial complexes and valued, after Soviet expropriation, at over $89 million, to small factories manufacturing pencils (the Hammer concession) or typewriter ribbons (the Alftan concession).

The Soviet definition of a concession is sometimes broader than that used in the West, and to avoid confusion the broader definition is utilized in this study. Concessions are here categorized in three ways; each category refers to a distinct organizational type.

The 'pure' concession (or Type I) was an agreement between the U.S.S.R. and a foreign enterprise whereby the foreign firm was enabled to develop and exploit an opportunity within the U.S.S.R., under the legal doctrine of *usufruct*, i.e., without acquiring property rights. Royalty payments to the U.S.S.R. were an essential part of the agreement, and in all cases the foreign enterprise was required both to invest stipulated capital sums and to introduce the latest in Western technology and equipment.

The 'mixed' company concession (or Type II) utilized a corporation in which Soviet and foreign participation were on equal basis (at first 50:50 but later 51 : 49), with a Soviet Chairman of the Board who had the deciding vote in cases of dispute. Normally the foreign company invested capital and technology or skills and the Soviets provided the opportunity and the location. Labor, both skilled and unskilled, was partly imported, and profits were to be split.

Whereas the first two types are clearly recognized as concessions, the technical-assistance contract (or Type III concession) has not usually been so designated, except in the U.S.S.R. Probably the Soviets were well aware of the negligible marginal cost to Western companies of supplying technical knowledge, patents, designs, and similar technological vehicles. In essence, Type III was a 'reverse technical concession,' in that the Soviets were making payments to exploit foreign technological resources; the Western company was not, in this case, making payment to exploit Russian natural resources or opportunities.

All known concessions can be grouped into these three categories, as table 1–1 demonstrates. The common link is that each type, in its own way, acted as a mechanism for the transfer of Western technology and skills, although only Types I and II involved the transfer of capital.

Table 1-1   CONCESSION APPLICATIONS AND
AGREEMENTS, 1921–30

Year	Applications[1]	Number of agreements Types I and II[1]	Type III[2]
1921–2	224	18	0
1922–3	579	44	1
1923–4	396	55	0
1924–5	256	103	4
1925–6	482	110	7
1926–7	263	Not available	13
1927–8	200	Not available	17
1928–9	270	Not available	33
1929–30	Not available	Not available	59
Total	2,670 (to 1928–9)	330 (to 1925–6)	134 (to 1929–30)

Sources: [1] A. A. Santalov and L. Segal, *Soviet Union Yearbook, 1930* (London: Allen and Unwin, 1930), p. 206.

[2] U.S.S.R. Chamber of Commerce, *Economic Conditions in the U.S.S.R.* (Moscow: Vneshtorgizdat, 1931), p. 162.

THE PLACE OF THE CONCESSION IN THE ECONOMIC HISTORY OF THE U.S.S.R.

Analyses of Soviet economic growth and the processes by which it has been attained have been restricted by lack of accurate data and firsthand knowledge of decision-making processes. The Soviets have, in fact, continually attempted to disguise the true rate and process of this economic growth.

It has been almost universally accepted that the foreign concessions policy of the 1920s and 30s did *not* aid the industrial development of the U.S.S.R. Certainly this interpretation has been propagated by the Soviets. N. Liubimov, former professor of economics at the University of Moscow, argues:

> Any discussion of concessions in the Union of Soviet Socialist Republics must emphasize their relative unimportance in Soviet activity. . . .[11]

Western writers, whether Marxist or non-Marxist in orientation, have taken a similar viewpoint. For instance, Maurice Dobb, a Marxist, argues that:

> . . . the policy of granting concessions on a larger scale to foreign companies had little success, apart from one or two special cases, while the concessions which were granted were more often in the sphere of foreign trade than in production.[12]

[11] 'The Soviets and Foreign Concessions,' *Foreign Affairs*, IX, No. 1 (October 1930), 95.

[12] *Soviet Economic Development since 1917* (5th ed.; London: Routledge and Kegan Paul, 1960), p. 142.

Then he adds:

> The policy of granting concessions to foreign firms to undertake trading
> and industrial ventures was unsuccessful in yielding more than about 10
> million rubles (gold) of foreign capital in the first years of the concession
> policy.[13]

This is a meaningless statement unless the period in question is indicated.
Several concessions contributed much more than 10 million rubles of investment apiece.

Soviet sources, which would hardly overstate the investment of concession
capital, give figures for 1927 and 1928 indicating an investment, at least five
times greater than that given by Dobb. Nevertheless, Dobb continues:

> In the early '20s' an attempt had been made to invite the aid of foreign
> capital on a limited scale in the form of concessions grants. But we have
> seen that the policy did not meet with any great success. . . . [14]

Dobb's conclusions are, in fact, unsound and unsupported by the available
concessions data.

Non-Marxist writers have also assigned a minor role to the foreign concession. A. Baykov[15] does not mention concessions. A. Yugoff[16] holds that they
had only a slight effect on economic development. Their ineffectuality, he
argues, was due mainly to a prohibitive currency policy and restrictions on
the free export of foreign bills of exchange. On this basis, Yugoff generally
discounts the technological and economic impact of the concession.

M. Hwang Jen[17] ignores restrictions on export of proceeds mentioned by
Yugoff, and instead argues that export of proceeds was a source of loss to
the Soviets, and that generally the concession was an inefficient vehicle for
the transfer of either capital or technology. Jen is impressed with the ingenuity
of the concession but concludes that it was unrealistic as a method of development.

There has been some difference of opinion within the executive branch of
the United States government on the importance of the concession in Soviet
economic development. The State Department has not considered the concession particularly important.[18]

---

[13] *Ibid.*, p. 150.
[14] *Ibid.*, p. 180.
[15] *The Development of the Soviet Economic System* (New York: Macmillan, 1947).
[16] *Economic Trends in Soviet Russia* (New York: R. Smith, 1930), pp. 221–3.
[17] *Le Régime des Concessions en Russie Soviétique* (Paris: Gamber, 1929).
[18] The importance of the concession has been in general toned down. For example,
     in submitting advice to Professor Raymond T. Bye for a speech before the American
     Economic Association, the State Dept. suggested that 'a few large concessions' be
     re-stated as 'one large concession' (316–109–807). (Numeral references to U.S.
     archival material are explained in Appendix A.)

On the other hand, United States Military Intelligence (MID) arrived at conclusions closer to the theme of this study:

> The lack of capital, the failure of the New Economic Policy to stimulate actively trade and production, and the exhaustion of raw material stocks have influenced the leaders to look outside of Russia for aid in bringing about economic recovery.[19]

and:

> By September 1927, Soviet authorities are reported to have granted 156 concessions, embracing practically all branches of national economy. In February 1928 there were 110 concessions in operation.[20]

In brief, despite the single contrary estimate mentioned, the concession has generally been regarded, in the West and in Russia, as a negligible factor in Soviet economic development. Further, it has been suggested that supportive data is unavailable. Keller claims concession operation records are buried in the files of each firm and that the Soviets will not release their data.[21]

In the light of this almost universal conclusion that the concession was insignificant as a development mechanism, certain essential questions must be clearly answered. Can the data on concessions and transfers be assembled? Is such data reliable? Does the assembled data support the current assumption of a negligible role for the concession? Finally, what was the contribution of the concession to Soviet technological and economic development?

METHODOLOGY OF THE STUDY

A simple but consistent methodology is utilized in this study. Our objective is to estimate in a quantitative manner the impact of Western technology on early Soviet economic development. Each plant in this fairly primitive economy is identified and the origin of its equipment and technical processes traced. Because many of the plants were operated by Western concession operations, the major research task has been to obtain extensive and accurate data on concession operations. This was a complex and time-consuming task, involving a search in sources originating in a dozen countries. The data generally comes from one of five sources distinguished by varying degrees of reliability. This variety however, allows for comparison and informed interpretation of data from different sources on many similar problems.

---

[19] U.S. War Dept., *Soviet Russia; on Economic Estimate*, March 18, 1928, p. 4319–h (U.S. State Dept. Decimal File, 316–110–306).

[20] *Loc. cit.* The estimate of 156 concessions is not inconsistent with table 1–1. MID probably counted only Type I concessions, while table 1–1 col. 2 includes Types I and II.

[21] Keller, *op. cit.*, p. 219.

The primary sources of data are the United States State Department Decimal File and the German Foreign Ministry Archives for 1917 to 1930. These are a superlative source of detail not available elsewhere; yet a few concessions were not recorded by their respective home governments. In general, concessions and similar agreements were noted in Western news media, but with scanty detail; it is rare that the German or American archives provide data on a concession unmentioned in some newspaper; about 10 percent are recorded only in the archives. Most concessionaires were reluctant to provide details, and considering the shabby treatment the majority received from the Soviets, it is unlikely they wanted to publish the amount of their losses. However Western governments were interested in the progress of concessions, and instructions went out to consular and other officials to acquire data. The U.S. Riga (Latvia) consulate was very active in this collection process.

The State Department Archives contain a number of firsthand reports of visits to Soviet plants made by United States company officials in search of business. In some cases, however, such as the W. A. Harriman manganese concession, the State Department had to glean its information from indirect sources such as European newspapers.[22] Archival sources are, then, incomplete. They have to be utilized concurrently with data from the four other sources.

The second source of data is Western news media and in general consists of voluntary information releases from those companies desiring to publicize their operations. During the 1920s fear of public opinion curbed news concerning the concessions of many companies.[23] Indeed, some concessions known from other sources, are not recorded at all in Western news media. The problem with this second group of sources is incompleteness of detail and possible corporate bias to protect a 'public image.'[24]

The third source of data, and a surprisingly lucrative source, consists of publications of Soviet trade representatives in Western countries. These sources have been treated with the same circumspection as data originating within the Soviet Union. However, it has been found that data from this source usually agrees with news media reports, with specific exceptions noted in the text. The major exception occurs in explanations for liquidation of concessions; official Soviet explanations often diverge considerably from the versions of the expropriated corporation. The explanation for the existence of detailed information in Soviet sources lies in the intent of the publications: to encourage further investment by Western companies. The information

---

[22]   U.S. State Dept. Decimal File, 316–138–17/19.

[23]   *New York Times*, August 17, 1925, p. 3, col. 5.

[24]   The most useful Western newspapers are the *Times* (London), the *New York Times*, *L'Information* (Paris), and the *Russian Daily News* (Harbin, China).

had to be reasonably accurate—it could be checked, and the greatest problem of the Soviets then, as now, was to instill confidence. There was, however, no requirement to publish adverse information. Although these publications were used to print 'explanations' by some Western businessmen for the expropriation or failure of other concession enterprises, the 'explanations' were consistently pro-Soviet.[25]

A fourth source consists of data originating within the U.S.S.R., particularly in *Pravda*, *Izvestia*, and *Ekonomicheskaya Zhizn*. A series of five maps (dated 1921) suggests the vast plans, involving thousands of projected concessions, which characterized early Soviet thinking. These are reproduced in U.S. State Department Archives (130–1207/1234). An atlas of available concessions was also published in 1926 by the Central Concessions Committee *(Karty kontsessionnykh ob'ektov S.S.S.R.)* together with a few little booklets describing available concessions. These are useful as an indicator of the technological state of the plants being offered.

Soviet sources are viewed here in the light of the 1927 decree making the transmission of economic information prejudicial to Soviet concessions policy a crime against the state. Concessions and foreign companies working within the U.S.S.R. felt the sting of a decree against actions considered criminal only in the Communist world. Representatives of the Swedish firms Alfa Laval and Diabolo-Separator, manufacturers of dairy equipment (particularly cream separators) were accused of economic espionage in 1928 because they determined the probable future requirements of Soviet trusts for cream separators and reported the results of the market survey back to their respective firms in Sweden. The three defendants who worked for the Swedish firm were given five to eight years each in prison. Eight employees of Soviet trusts and commercial organizations, together with a German citizen named Bartsch, were given from one to three years each for accepting bribes and abetting economic espionage.[26] Consequently, after 1927, the flow of data from both the West and from the Soviet internal and external press declined substantially. Whereas detailed reports exist on industrial conditions up to 1927, few are found for the period from 1927 to 1930.[27]

The fifth source consists of a collection of miscellaneous material in several languages, including books written by engineers, consultants, and others who

[25] Amtorg Trading Co. *Economic Review of the Soviet Union* (New York: 1928), III, 373.

[26] Based on article in *Vossische Zeitung* (Berlin), July 1928, as reported by the American Legation in Berlin, Report No. 3750 of July 24, 1928 (U.S. State Dept. File, 316–109–754/5). Bartsch was promptly released.

[27] The report by M. Klemmer, a Western Electric Co. engineer, to the U.S. State Dept. (U.S. State Dept. Decimal File, 316–141–628) is clearly economic espionage within the Soviet meaning of the term. See also chap. 11.

worked in the U.S.S.R., and statistical summaries and handbooks published by Soviet representatives abroad.

In general, the problem of interpretation of Soviet data is not acute, although it is time-consuming. Data distortion had not at this time reached the quagmire stage; the major problem is incompleteness and the pervasive Soviet habit of omitting unfavorable facts and figures.

Use of data from several sources enabled cross-checking. As a general rule, data from Soviet and Western sources had to be consistent before it was utilized (exceptions to this rule are noted). Such a method avoids the problem of choosing between contradictory statements and statistics. For example, statements concerning the condition of the electrical equipment industry in 1922 can be found in the Soviet press which lead to the conclusion that it was, on the one hand, healthy and profitable,[28] and, on the other, in a state of near-collapse.[29] Evidence was also found that the electrical trusts were approaching foreign companies for help.[30] Subsequently foreign engineers entered the U.S.S.R. and their survey reports found their way into Western government archives.[31] With this support, the second conclusion could be accepted as reasonably factual.

Omission, at times, assumed significant proportions. Acceptance of the mineral production figures for 1927–8 published by the Leningrad Academy of Science Geological Committee would lead one to believe that neither gold nor platinum was produced in the U.S.S.R., and that the Lena Goldfields, Ltd., concession produced only limestone, dolomite, and quartz, whereas, in fact, it produced almost 40 percent of Soviet gold, 80 percent of Soviet silver, and significant proportions of copper, lead, zinc, and iron.[32] Similarly, the concession agreement with International Barnsdall Corporation omitted all reference to the specific geographic area covered by the agreement, although

---

[28] 'Experience proved that the electrical industries had improved very much under Government control. They were working satisfactorily and even giving profit to the State.' *Izvestia*, October 9, 1921 (paraphrased).

[29] Three months before the October 9 statement above, half the electrical plants in Petrograd had been closed due to a fuel crisis and the others drastically slowed, according to *Izvestia*, July 12, 1921. Eight months after the October 9 statement, the industry is described as having no working capital, no credits, no payments, ' . . . the position is a very difficult one . . . electric lamps and cables can only be obtained by force . . .' according to *Ekonomicheskaya Zhizn*, No. 124, June 7, 1922.

[30] Electro-Technical Trust (GET) letter to International General Electric Inc., May 2, 1922 (U.S. State Dept. Decimal File, 316–139–58).

[31] Examples are the B. W. Bary report (1921) (U.S. State Dept. Decimal File, 316–139–11); and the Reinke report (1923) (U.S. State Dept. Decimal File, 316–108–672).

[32] V. I. Kruglyakova (ed.), *Sbornik statisticheskikh svedenii po gornoi i gornozavodsk promyshlennosti S.S.S.R. za 1927/8 gg.* (Moscow: 1930) pp. 60, 74, 90, 102, 106, 146, 150, 152. Limestone and quartz were used as a flux for the (statistically non-existent) Lena Goldfields gold-smelting operations.

the W. A. Harriman manganese concession agreement had its geography spelled out in minute detail.[33] A healthy dose of skepticism has proved to be an invaluable research tool.

[33] Reasons for omission in the case of Barnsdall are significant and are outlined in chap. 2.

CHAPTER TWO

Caucasus Oil Fields—
The Key to Economic Recovery

THE Caucasus oil fields are a major segment of Russian natural resource wealth. Baku, the most important field, was developed in the 1870s. In 1900 it was producing more crude oil than the United States, and in 1901 more than half of the total world crude output. The Caucasus oil fields survived the Revolution and Intervention without major structural damage and became a significant factor in Soviet economic recovery, generating about 20 percent of all exports by value; the largest single source of foreign exchange. The process by which the oil economy recovered from impending disaster and acquired modern refinery operations in a brief four or five years is the topic of this chapter.

COLLAPSE OF OIL FIELD DRILLING

Caucasian fields require continuous drilling to maintain an oil flow from producing wells. Therefore, oil production in this area is directly proportional to the amount of drilling undertaken. Before the Revolution, drilling averaged in excess of 35,000 feet per month, and had been as high as 50,000 feet in Baku alone.

The Bolsheviks took over the Caucasus in 1920-1, and until 1923 oil field drilling almost ceased. During the first year of Soviet rule ' . . . not one single new well has started giving oil'[1] and even two years after Soviet occupation, no new oil-field properties had been developed. In addition, deepening of old wells virtually ceased. As a result, water percolated into the wells, and the flow of crude oil became first a mixture of oil and water and finally a flow of oily water.

---

[1] U.S. State Dept. Decimal File, 316–137–221.

Table 2-1   AVERAGE MONTHLY DRILLING IN RUSSIAN
OIL FIELDS, 1900–21

1900	*1913*	*1920*	*1921*	
48,496 ft.*	36,665 ft.	780 ft.	Jan.	336 ft.*
			Feb.	406 ft.*

Sources: 1900—A. Beeby Thompson, *The Oil Fields of Russia* (London: Lockwood, 1908), p. 120.

1913—G. Ghambashidze, *The Caucasian Petroleum Industry and Its Importance for Eastern Europe and Asia* (London: Anglo-Georgian Society, 1918), p. 9.

1920–21—*Ekonomicheskaya Zhizn*, May 20, 1921.

* Baku only.

Drilling records are an excellent indicator of the state of oil field maintenance, development, and production. The complete collapse after the Soviet takeover is clearly suggested in Table 2–1. In 1900, Russia had been the world's largest producer and exporter of crude oil; almost 50,000 feet of drilling per month had been required in Baku alone to maintain this production. By early 1921, the average monthly drilling in Baku had declined to an insignificant 370 feet or so (0.7 percent of the 1900 rate), although 162 rigs were in working order. This drilling was concentrated in only eight holes due to lack of steel pipe.[2]

The result was that, by 1922, half of the Baku wells were idle and the remainder were producing increasing quantities of water. In the Grozny field a greater portion of the wells were idle; only eight were in process of drilling, and the Old Grozny section was completely shut down. Smaller fields at Emba and Kuban were in similar chaos; both had received extensive drilling in 1915; consequently there were forty to fifty producing wells in 1922 but no new or maintenance drilling was in progress.[3]

The reasons for the catastrophic decline in oil-field production were four. First the number of available oil-field workers declined from about 40,000 in 1915 to less than 10,000 in 1920–1; coupled with this was the growing technical inefficiency of the remaining workers. Second, there was a breakdown in railroad transportation and a decline in pipeline capacity, because of lack of maintenance. Third, new oil-field supplies and equipment, including repair facilities were almost nonexistent. Last, there was a breakdown in the oil field electrical supply system. One of the largest Baku powerhouses, for example, had twenty-two water tube boilers, none were in operation in 1922.[4]

[2]   U.S. State Dept. Decimal File, 316–137–442.
[3]   The decline of the Caucasus oil fields is covered in detail in *Ekonomicheskaya Zhizn* for 1921–2.
[4]   *Ekonomicheskaya Zhizn*, December 24, 1922 and February 10, 1923.

The paradox was the collapse of one of the few industries capable of generating sufficient foreign exchange for an industrial revival. Serebrovsky, Chairman of Azneft, put forward the program for recovery in a *Pravda* article. The plan for 1923 was to increase oil-well drilling to 35,000 sazhens per year (245,000 feet). This would require 35 rotary drills (to drill 77,000 feet) and 157 percussion drills (to drill 130,000 feet). Serebrovsky pointed out that Azneft had no rotary drills, and that Russian enterprise could not supply them. Rotary drilling, however, was essential for the success of the plan. He then announced:

> But just here American capital is going to support us. The American firm International Barnsdall Corporation has submitted a plan. . . . Lack of equipment prevents us from increasing the production of the oil industry of Baku by ourselves. The American firm . . . will provide the equipment, start drilling in the oil fields and organize the technical production of oil with deep pumps.[5]

During the next few years International Barnsdall, together with the Lucey Manufacturing Company[6] and other major foreign oil-well equipment firms, fulfilled Serebrovsky's program. Massive imports of equipment came from the United States. International Barnsdall inaugurated the rotary drilling program, initiated Azneft drilling crews into its operational problems, and reorganized oil-well pumping with deep-well electrical pumps.

INTERNATIONAL BARNSDALL CORPORATION

Numerous British, Swedish, Dutch, Greek, German, and American oil-field concessions were rumored from 1919 onward, but there is no evidence that any were granted and implemented, in spite of many extravagant claims, before the three Barnsdall concessions in 1921–2.

The first International Barnsdall concession was signed in October 1921,[7] and was followed in September of 1922 by two further agreements. There is no doubt that Barnsdall did work under the first agreement. *Pravda* reported groups of American oil-field workers on their way to the oil fields,[8] and a couple of months previously the United States Constantinople Consulate had reported that Philip Chadbourn, the Barnsdall Caucasus representative, had passed through on his way *out* of Russia.[9] In particular, the U.S. State Department Archives contain an intriguing quotation from Rykov (unfortunately with no stated source), dated October 1922:

[5] *Pravda*, September 21, 1922.
[6] Captain J. F. Lucey, founder of the Lucey Manufacturing Co., was the first Chairman of the Committee on Standardization of Rotary Drilling Equipment, organized by the United States petroleum industry in 1926.
[7] *New York Times*, March 29, 1922, p. 24, col. 2.
[8] October 22, 1922.
[9] U.S. State Dept. Decimal File, 316–130–1201/2.

The one comparatively bright spot in Russia is the petroleum industry, and this is due largely to the fact that a number of American workers have been brought into the oil fields to superintend their operation.[10]

MAP 2-1

FOREIGN OIL DRILLING CONCESSIONS IN THE CAUCASUS, 1921-8

Legend: 1. British Petroleum Co. Ltd., Gouria concession (1923, Type I)
2. International Barnsdall Corp., Baku concession (1921-2, Type III)
3. Duverger Baku concession (1923, Type I)
4. Duverger Emba concession (1923, Type II)
5. Società Minere Italo-Belge di Georgia, Shirak concession (1923, Type I)
6. F. Storens concession in Busachi (1925, Type I)

---

[10] *Ibid.*, 316-107-1167.

In September 1922, two extensive agreements were signed by Serebrovsky, representing Azneft, and Mason Day, president of the International Barnsdall Corporation, a New York-based oil company.[11] Barnsdall agreed to drill for oil in the 'Baku district in the Balakhani oil-field area (sic)'[12] within an area of 400 dessiatins, or 1,080 acres. The work was to consist of deepening old oil wells and drilling new wells under the supervision of a mixed commission containing both Soviet and American members. The maximum depth of these wells was to be 450 sazhens (3,150 feet) with a starting diameter of at least 20 inches and a finishing diameter of not less than 4 inches. Barnsdall agreed to import tools and equipment for the simultaneous drilling of 20 wells; and to drill at least 10,000 feet in the first year, no less than 20,000 in the second, and no less than 30,000 annually thereafter. Electric power, derricks, water, clay, timber, cement, and workshops (without equipment) were to be supplied by Azneft.

Barnsdall imported equipment at its own risk, with cost plus 5 percent to be repaid by Azneft on arrival at the drilling site. Azneft had the option of paying in either gold rubles or oil and oil products at market price. Each oil well drilled was paid for on a schedule based on 80,000 gold rubles per each sazhen (7 feet) drilled for the first 100 feet in each hole, and 10,000 gold rubles for each additional sazhen. As in the case of the equipment, payment could be made either in gold rubles or in oil or oil products, at the option of Azneft. A royalty of 20 percent in oil was paid to Barnsdall on either new or deepened wells, and the term of the agreement was set at fifteen and a half years.

The second Azneft-Barnsdall agreement was an oil-well-pumping contract under which International Barnsdall undertook to install modern pumps in both shut-down and watered wells and in new wells drilled under the first contract.

There was a specific requirement in the pumping contract for electrical deep pumps to be installed in all wells except fountains, gushers, and those requiring air-lift. During the first year, sufficient equipment was to be imported by Barnsdall to develop deep pumping in a minimum of 40 wells, with a further 100 pumps to follow each year for the 15-year term of the agreement. Electrical power was to be supplied free by Azneft.

No payment was made by Azneft for the pumping equipment, which was to pass to the Soviets at the expiration of the agreement. A royalty payment of 15 percent of the gross crude output of each well was assigned to International Barnsdall, with free tank storage at Baku.

---

[11] The Barnsdall agreements were not published. Mason Day, after some pressure, supplied a copy to the U.S. State Dept. This copy is now in the Archives, and is the basis for this section. Mason Day later joined forces with Sinclair and was convicted in the Teapot Dome oil scandal. Barnsdall financing was by Blair and Co., of New York.

[12] U.S. State Dept. Decimal File 316–137–510.

OIL FIELD PROPERTIES COVERED BY THE
BARNSDALL AGREEMENT

To assess the impact of Western technology on the development of the Caucasus oil industry, it is necessary to determine the areas of the Baku fields covered by the Barnsdall agreements. The technological impact was in two forms: the direct oil-field work undertaken by Barnsdall engineers and crews; and the installation by Azneft engineers of equipment supplied by the Lucey Manufacturing Company, Metropolitan-Vickers, Ltd., and other companies and only partly under the technical supervision of Barnsdall.[13]

The geographical area to be covered by the agreement was deliberately obscured not only to the Western public but also to the U.S. State Department. There were major discrepancies in the statements of Mason Day and the Soviet press concerning the actual area placed under development.

The property rights of the prerevolutionary owners and lessees of Baku oil lands were in question, and the probability existed that these claimants would restrict Barnsdall and other Western company operations by legal action. It was therefore important for the U.S.S.R. to convey the impression that all Barnsdall work was being done on land formerly owned by the Crown, so that former private owners and lessees would have no cause for injunctive action in Western courts.

The contract clearly states that the area covered by the first, or drilling, contract, was 400 dessiatins in the Balakhani area of the Baku oil fields, with the option of extension to Sabunchi and Ramuni. A dessiatin is 2.7 acres. In talks with the U.S. State Department, Day used a conversion factor of 1 dessiatin = 7/8 acre, and Barnsdall press releases talked about 400 acres rather than 400 dessiatins. In other words, there was a deliberate attempt on the part of Barnsdall to make the area covered by the agreement appear considerably smaller.

The area covered was, in fact, 1,080 acres, and as the location of previously privately-owned and leased property in the Balakhani section was known, it was concluded by the U.S. State Department that:

> There can be no doubt . . . that the vested rights of private owners or lessees will be infringed on from the very outset under either the first or the second contract.[14]

---

[13] International Barnsdall obtained $1.5 million credit in the United States from Lucey Manufacturing for oil-field equipment. In addition, Lucey obtained a substantial order directly from Azneft. Hill Electrical Drills, EMSCO (Los Angeles), and Metropolitan-Vickers, among others, secured significant orders for oil-field equipment. [W. A. Otis, *The Petroleum Industry of Russia*, U.S. Dept. of Commerce, Trade Information Bulletin No. 263, p. 24. Also *EMSCO Derrick and Equipment Company* (Los Angeles: Banks Huntley, 1929), pp. 26–7].

[14] Memorandum, Durand to Herter, February 1923 (316–137–586).

The substance of the State Department assessment was that it would be difficult, if not impossible, to find 400 dessiatins *not* previously operated or leased by private persons or companies.

A comparison of the four sections of the Baku oil field supports this position.

Table 2–2 DISTRIBUTION OF CRUDE OIL PRODUCTION AND
PROPERTY OWNERSHIP IN THE BAKU OIL FIELDS, 1915

Baku Oil Field Section	Percent Total Production	Percent Previously Owned or Leased
Balakhani	19.5%	93.0%
Sabunchi	41.7	100.0
Ramuni	15.7	100.0
Bibi-Eibat	23.1	100.0

Source: Memorandum, Lewery to Durand (316–137–580/3).

The Sabunchi, Ramuni, and Bibi-Eibat sections had been completely under private ownership or leasing arrangement at the time of the Revolution. The Balakhani section was the only section with some open state land, but this amounted to only 7 percent of the total oil land in the section. The area of this unworked Crown land, which would not be subject to private claims, was less than 45 dessiatins. The balance of this section and the other three sections would all have been subject to injunctive action if worked by International Barnsdall.

The agreement stated that work was to be done on the Balakhani section, i.e., the only section with some Crown land, but contained an option to extend the work to the Sabunchi and Ramuni sections under instruction from Azneft. It was also verbally understood to extend to the Bibi-Eibat section.[15] The technical-assistance and pumping agreements covered all sections of the Baku field; so did the equipment sold by Lucey and other suppliers to Azneft.

In brief, the news releases attendant upon the International Barnsdall contract limited public discussion to 400 acres or less in the Balakhani field for good reason: to avoid legal action in Western courts.

> Whatever may be the purpose of the Barnsdall group, the contract reads as if the Russian authorities expected and intended to assign them for improvement and pumping wells which have been confiscated from former private owners, mostly foreigners.[16]

[15]   U.S. State Dept. Decimal File, 316–137–581.
[16]   Memorandum, Durand to Herter, February 8, 1923 (316–137–587).

The agreement was intended to cover the whole of the Baku field. Both the Soviets and International Barnsdall, considered it prudent to misrepresent the area covered by the contract.[17]

EXTENT OF BARNSDALL DRILLING

Barnsdall was required to undertake a minimum of 10,000 feet of drilling in the first year of operations and additional amounts in subsequent years, under the direction of a mixed committee, which included Azneft representatives. There is substantial reason to believe that Barnsdall undertook more drilling than the minimum required by the contract, which again may have camouflaged a private agreement. There was certainly substantial financial incentive for Barnsdall to exceed the minimum.

Analysis of drilling reports suggests a rate in excess of 180,000 feet per year. In the month after the arrival of the first group of engineers (June 1923), Barnsdall put down 15 wells in the Kirmaku area of northwest Balakhani.[18] Given an average depth of 1,000 feet for Baku wells, this equalled 15,000 feet a month, or 180,000 feet a year.[19] Also, Barnsdall had six American engineers in Baku, a number hardly warranted by a drilling rate of only 10,000 feet a year. One drilling agreement was in operation for two years. International Barnsdall was 'driven out' of the U.S.S.R. in 1924 after incurring 'very important material losses.'[20] Louis Fischer says the agreement lapsed 'by mutual consent' in 1924.[21]

CHANGES IN DRILLING TECHNOLOGY AT BAKU

Although the exact area and footage drilled will probably never be known, a complete change in Soviet drilling technology has been recorded. The old labor-intensive percussion methods gave way completely to the United States-developed rotary drilling techniques. This changeover is summarized in table 2–3.

---

[17] Morris, Chief of the Petroleum Division, U.S. Dept. of Commerce, made the succinct comment, ' . . . the Russians knew exactly what they were doing when they assigned Barnsdall's territory' (316–137–584). Lucey Manufacturing later confirmed to the State Dept. that Barnsdall was working throughout the Baku area irrespective of former ownership (316–137–745).

[18] Otis, *op. cit.*, p. 25.

[19] This would be equivalent to sinking 180 wells averaging 1,000 feet each. Scheffer noted that 300 wells were put down in Baku between October 1923 and October 1924 [Paul Scheffer, *Seven Years in Soviet Russia*, (New York: Macmillan, 1932), p. 94].

[20] W. Kokovtzoff, 'Le gouvernement des soviets et les concessions aux étrangers,' *Revue des Deux Mondes*, XXXV Sept. 1, 1926, 158–81.

[21] *Oil Imperialism* (New York: International, 1926), p. 169.

There was no substantial rotary drilling in the U.S.S.R. before 1923.[22] However, in the five years following, the percussion method was almost completely abandoned and the American rotary method substituted. By 1928 the percussion method accounted for only 2 percent of drilling (against 100 percent in 1913) and rotary drilling accounted for 81 percent (against none in 1923). The cable technique had brief use but was abandoned in favor of rotary methods. It should be noted that the Soviet-developed turbine drill had an early but insignificant utilization, and did not gain wide acceptance until later in the 1930s.[23]

Table 2–3   OIL-DRILLING TECHNIQUE,
PERCENTAGE UTILIZATION BY AZNEFT (BAKU), 1913–28

| Year | OIL-DRILLING TECHNIQUE | | | |
	Rotary	Cable	Percussion	Turbine
1913	—	—	100.0%	—
1924	36.0%	8.0%	56.0	—
1925	54.3	7.7	37.2	0.8%
1926	62.6	20.6	16.2	0.6
1927	71.3	19.7	7.3	1.7
1928	81.3	14.0	2.1	2.6

Source: Adapted from Alcan Hirsch, *Industrialized Russia* (New York: Chemical Catalog Co., 1934), p. 146. Hirsch was Chief Consulting Engineer to Chemtrust.
Note: These figures are supported by less detailed data in *Le Pétrole Russe* (Paris: Editions de la Représentation Commerciale de l'U.R.S.S. en France, 1927) No. 6, p. 5, where the following figures are given for rotary drilling:

1923–4: 34.7%   1924–5: 54.2%   1925–6: 63.7%   1926–7: 71.0%

The insignificant turbine drilling is confirmed in Kruglyakova, *op. cit.*, p. 120. It is stated that, of a total 367,480 meters drilled, 7,164 meters (or 1.9 percent) were turbine-drilled. Of this, 5,685 meters were drilled at an experimental hole at location No. 24, Surachanskaya.

The substitution of rotary drilling for the old percussion methods increased speed of drilling by a factor of ten and reduced costs by more than one half between 1924 and 1928.[24]

Neftsyndicat provides more detailed data which is consistent with Hirsch's statement. In 1920–1, when no rotary drilling was utilized, average drilling rates were 6.8 meters per drill-month. This jumped to 69.8 meters in 1925–6,

[22]   A Russian mining engineer, Adiassevich, imported a rotary drilling rig and tools from California and completed a few 22-inch holes between 1913 and 1915 (316–137–210).

[23]   These percentages contrast with those of the 1960s. By denying the Soviets Western rotary drills and drill pipe, we have forced them to utilize the turbine and electric drill techniques and to incur the cost of both development and a less efficient technique. The final cost to their oil economy has been substantial.

[24]   Alcan Hirsch, *Industrialized Russia* (New York: Chemical Catalog Co., 1934), p. 146.

with a maximum figure of 640 meters. The same source suggests that a 600–700 meter hole required in 1927 only 70-80 days for drilling, whereas under the old drilling system it had required one year. In terms of cost, the advantages were just as significant. In one year, from 1923–4 to 1925–6, drilling costs fell from 413 rubles to 218 rubles per meter, and the number of workers required for one drill-month of operations fell from 49 to 30.[25]

CHANGES IN PUMPING TECHNOLOGY AND OIL FIELD ELECTRIFICATION

There was a parallel revolution in pumping technology. In 1922 oil-well pumping was undertaken by bailing (a primitive, inefficient technique) or by air-lift. About 10 percent of production was free-flowing and did not require mechanical assistance. A small portion was collected by surface methods. There was no deep-well electrical pumping in 1922, and no oil field pumps were produced in the U.S.S.R. until the initiation of the Maschinenbrau A-G technical-assistance agreement with Mosmash,[26] in the mid-1920s.

Table 2–4   CRUDE OIL EXTRACTION TECHNOLOGY
IN BAKU OIL FIELDS, 1921–2 AND 1927–8

Method of Extraction		*1921–2*	*1927–8*
Bailing	} OLD	49.3%	0.0%
Air-lift		40.3	27.9
Gushers		9.8	26.0
Pumping	} NEW	0.0	44.8
Surface		0.6	1.3
		100.0%	100.0%

Source: 1921–2, Otis, *The Petroleum Industry of Russia*, p. 19
1927–8, U.S. State Dept., Decimal File, 316–137–1130.

On the other hand, electrical deep-pumping was at this time in general use in the United States and elsewhere and was considerably cheaper than the more primitive extraction methods. The second part of the Barnsdall contract required installation of deep-well pumps in Barnsdall-developed wells; pumps were also purchased from the United States and Germany for Soviet operations. Acquisition of pumps was so rapid that four years after the signing of the Barnsdall contract, 45 percent of Baku crude oil was being pumped rather than bailed.

[25] *Le Pétrole Russe* (Paris: Editions de la Représentation Commerciale de l'U.R.S.S. en France) No. 6 (1927), p. 6.
[26] See page 35.

The change in extraction technology in the Baku fields is summarized in table 2–4. Bailing declined from 49.3 percent in 1921–2 to zero in 1927–8, while pumping increased from zero in 1921–3 to 44.8 percent of output in 1927–8. The other significant change was the increase in production from free-flowing wells (gushers) from 9.8 percent to 26.0 percent, reflecting the increase in new well-drilling activity by International Barnsdall, in Type I concessions, and in newly equipped and trained drilling crews of Azneft. In absolute numbers, there were only 38 wells equipped with modern pumps in May 1924; one year later, in July 1925, over 500 wells had modern pumps.[27]

The general operation of the Baku oil fields was electrified in the same period; by September 1928, of 3,312 oil wells in operation, about 3,212 (97 percent) had pumping powered by electricity, 3 by steam engines, and 96 by gasoline engines. This compares to only 30 percent electrification in 1913. The oil-field electrification program, including the supply of some switch-gear and other equipment, was undertaken by Metropolitan-Vickers, Ltd. (United Kingdom), a subsidiary of Westinghouse,[28] while between 1927 and 1930,

> . . . large quantities of General Electric products began to furnish the motive power for drilling oil wells and for pumping oil in the rich fields of Baku and Grozny.[29]

Details in *Le Pétrole Russe* suggest that the electrification program was also concentrated into a very few years and in old wells involved a substitution of electric for gasoline and steam engines rather than just the introduction of electric motors.

Table 2–5   ELECTRIFICATION OF THE GROZNY OIL
FIELDS, 1923–7

	Number of Engines (by Type) on Oct. 1				
	1923	*1924*	*1925*	*1926*	*1927*
Steam engines	145	137	127	91	31
Gasoline engines	37	31	27	22	21
Electric motors	76	126	192	276	396
Total	258	294	346	389	448
Percent electric motors	29.5	42.9	55.5	71.0	88.3

Source: Le Pétrole Russe, No. 6, p. 6.

[27] *Financial Times* (London), May 25, 1923.
[28] This was one of the largest of the Metropolitan-Vickers contracts with the U.S.S.R. The breach of relations between the United Kingdom and Soviet Russia in 1927 (following the 'Arcos affair') did not disturb Metropolitan-Vickers. The company worked continually in the U.S.S.R. on a substantial scale from 1921 until after the trials of 1933, when six of their engineers were accused of sabotage and expelled.
[29] *Monogram* (Schenectady: General Electric Co.), November 1943, p. 16.

In Grozny, for example, the number of oil-field motors increased from 258 in 1923 to 448 in 1927. Electric motors formed only 29 percent of the total in 1923 but 88 percent in 1927. During the same period steam engines were virtually eliminated and the number of gasoline engines reduced by almost half.

The same change took place in Baku. At the beginning of 1925–6 there were 1,821 electric and 175 steam engines in Baku. By August 1927 there were 2,810 electric motors and only 27 steam engines.

This technological substitution greatly reduced the cost of producing oil. In 1913 the Baku fields used 1.3 million tons of crude oil (about 15 percent of the total produced) as fuel in the oil fields. By September 1925 this total had fallen to 8.4 percent; and by July 1927 to 3.9 percent. In brief, the substitution of electricity for oil reduced operating costs and also released considerable quantities of crude oil for export.

This export of Western technology—primarily American—was first concentrated in the Baku fields, and later in the Grozneft and Embaneft regions. The lag in regional application is supported by the statistics. In the Azneft field 36 percent of the drilling was done by the rotary method in 1924, but a comparable percentage (35 percent) was not attained by Grozneft until 1927. Whereas Azneft had 54 percent rotary drilling in 1925, Grozneft did not attain this percentage until 1928.

Neither Grozny nor Emba had specific technical-assistance contracts for crude oil production. Their production problems, much less acute, were overshadowed by those of transportation and marketing. Consequently the three-year transfer lag was not of major importance.

Although the first, International Barnsdall was not the only vehicle for technological transfer in the oil fields. This transfer was designed to modernize the most prolific of the oil fields (which was also the field with the most serious production problems) by developing new wells and instituting a rational organizational and technical structure for deepening old wells. The transfer was a complete success.

THE 'PURE' OIL CONCESSIONS

Another transfer vehicle used, outside the Baku field, was the pure (Type I) concession. The fields offered for pure concessions were more remote or smaller, or in less-developed areas. Although Baku, Grozny, and Emba were offered on this basis, there were no serious negotiations for pure concessions after 1925. A typical offering for a pure concession was the Cheleken Island field in the Caspian Sea. As early as 1830, there were more than 3,000 hand-dug oil wells up to 250 feet deep, and production continued until the Revolution. By 1923 only 12 wells were still producing; the rest were inoperative. The field was then offered for concession.[30] There were at least five operating concessions of this type between 1922 and 1928.[31]

In February 1925 the Chief Concessions Committee concluded an agreement with F. Storens, a Norwegian firm, for the industrial and mineral exploitation of the Busachi Peninsula in the Caspian Sea. The area covered 12,000 square versts on the eastern part of the peninsula. Storens was required to make an expenditure of 800,000 rubles on exploration work within five years. The life of the concession was set at 40 years, although the Soviet government had the option to buy out Storens in 30 years. All equipment was imported duty-free, but unstated dues and fees were payable, including 5 percent of any metals output and 15 percent of any oil produced (50 percent if a gusher). A deposit of 50,000 rubles was accepted as a guaranty of the execution of the contract.[32] [33]

At the end of 1923, a concession agreement was concluded between the Società Minere Italo-Belge di Georgia of Turin, Italy, and the Chief Concessions Committee, under which the company agreed to conduct oil exploration on 50,000 acres of the Shirak Steppes near Tiflis. The Società was given the right to explore and drill for three years, and production concessions could be subsequently granted for 30 years, the U.S.S.R reserving the right to buy out the undertaking after 20 years. During the exploration period the grantees paid the Soviet government a royalty for each dessiatin explored. At the end of the exploration period, the company was required to make a report and hand over equipment and all oil produced to the Soviets.

The company was also required to pay a percentage on gross product, pay export taxes, and comply with Soviet law on taxation and labor. At the end of

[30]   Amtorg, *op. cit.*, II, No. 24 (December 15, 1927): 'Cheleken Oil Field proposed for concession,' p. 6.

[31]   These were Storens, Italo-Belge, British Petroleum, the Japanese Sakhalin, and the French Duverger group. Others were rumored. At one time the Chief Concessions Committee was considering 62 applications for oil concessions, but little has been recorded concerning their operation. The Comparre Oil Company of New Jersey was formed by W. Averell Harriman specifically for a Baku oil concession.

Type II (mixed company) concessions were not common in oil operations; apart from the Dutch-Soviet trading company mentioned in the text, there was only Duverger and the Turkestan Co. for Raw Materials Preparation, jointly operated by Sorgagen A-G (Germany) and Neftsyndikat (316–111–819).

[32]   *Ekonomicheskaya Zhizn*, No. 33, February 10, 1925.

[33]   'One of the most important and largest concessions granted is that for mining and oil concessions given to the Norwegian Company Storen. . . . According to the geological reports, this area is very rich in oil. Considering that it has never been worked before and operations will be more difficult than usual, the concessionaire was given many special privileges.' [L. Segal and A. A. Santalov, *Soviet Union Year Book: 1926* (London: Allen and Unwin), p. 165.] According to *Karty Kontsessionnykh ob'ektov S.S.S.R.* (Moscow: 1926) the Busachi Peninsula oil deposits were known but not worked or delineated at this time.

the concession period, the entire property reverted to the Soviets without compensation. A bond was required from the grantees, who were also required to introduce the latest methods of drilling and oil production.[34]

An extension of the agreement was applied for and granted in September 1926. Preliminary work was completed, and the area for development was increased from the original 415 to 1,515 hectares. The extension was granted with the stipulation that the company sink four oil wells, each at least 500 meters deep.[35]

In 1923 an agreement was signed between the Gouria Petroleum Corporation, Ltd. (United Kingdom), and the Chief Concessions Committee covering the development and exploitation of 1,100 square miles in Gouria, on the Black Sea, between Poti and Batum. A 40-year concession stipulated that rental payments and part of the production were to be assigned to the Soviets, who also had an option to purchase the whole output.[36]

The Duverger group (France) obtained oil concessions in 1923 in both the Baku and the Emba fields. The lease of 'state' lands in Baku was subject to an annual percentage of profits or oil payable to the U.S.S.R. The concessionaires had full management control. The Emba concession was a Type II mixed company arrangement for exploitation of the fields between Samar and Tashkent. The initial capitalization required payment of five million francs.[37]

OIL DEVELOPMENT IN THE SOVIET FAR EAST[38]

Protocol B of the January 1925 convention between the U.S.S.R. and Japan contained the conditions under which petroleum and coal concessions were granted to Japan in North Sakhalin. In effect, these replaced the 1922 Sinclair Exploration Company concessions, cancelled by the U.S.S.R.

The petroleum concessions gave the Northern Sakhalin Petroleum Company (Kita Sagaren Sekio Kigio Koumiay, succeeded by Kita Karafuto Sekio Kabushiki Kasha) the exclusive right to explore and exploit half of the two known oil fields for a period of forty-five years. The other half of each field remained in the hands of the Soviets. In addition to the original area of 2,200 dessiatins, a further area was later granted for exploration work, on the under-

---

[34] *Corriere Diplomatico e Consolare*, February 10, 1924, and *Ekonomicheskaya Zhizn*, No. 62, December 13, 1923. Oil seepages had been known in the area for many years, but prerevolutionary exploration had not been profitable.

[35] U.S. Consulate in Riga, Report, September 10, 1926 (316–137–991/3).

[36] 'The concessionaire company is extremely reticent concerning the details of the arrangement and the London press has . . . referred to the matter only in a cursory way.' (U.S. Embassy in London, Report No. 14817, March 23, 1923.)

[37] *New York Times*, July 19, 1923, p. 23, col. 2.

[38] This section is based on evidence in the U.S. State Department Decimal File (Rolls 137, 176 and 177 of Microcopy 316).

standing that half of any oil field discovered was to be transferred to the U.S.S.R. for Soviet operation. A royalty was payable on all output, ranging from 5 percent for production not in excess of 30,000 tons per year up to 15 percent for production in excess of 630,000 tons. A royalty of from 15 to 45 percent was payable on gushers depending on yield. For natural gas the royalty ranged from 10 to 35 percent, depending on the composition of the gas. Foreign skilled labor was allowed to the extent of 50 percent of the total labor force and unskilled to 25 percent of labor force. All disputes were subject to the law and courts of the U.S.S.R.

Soviet Far Eastern oil development was completely dependent on Japanese concessions and technical assistance. Beginning in 1925, the Japanese began exploring and developing the extensive oil strata of North Sakhalin.

Table 2–6   NORTH SAKHALIN OIL PRODUCTION, 1926–31

Year	METRIC TONS PRODUCED			*Percent Produced by Japanese Concessions*
	Japanese Concessions	*Soviet Production*	*Total Production*	
1926	29,829	—	29,829	100.0
1927	78,700	—	78,700	100.0
1928	104,000	17,000	121,000	85.9
1929	187,000	26,065	213,065	87.8
1930	195,040	96,268	291,308	66.9
1931	275,000	133,172	408,172	67.4

Source: V. Conolly, *Soviet Trade from the Pacific to the Levant* (London: Oxford 1935), p. 43.

The Soviets started work in 1928, after obtaining the necessary credits and technical assistance from the Japanese.[39] As the areas were divided into checkerboard development plots, the Soviet plots alternating with the Japanese, the Soviets were able first to develop their plots by obtaining credits and aid from the Japanese. When the Japanese concessions were expropriated, the whole area came under Soviet control.

OIL EXPLORATION TECHNOLOGY

The adoption of electrical well-logging, one of several methods of well-logging, is an excellent example of the priority given to the acquisition of

[39] 'It is characteristic that in the first place the Russians had to seek a three year credit from Japan, so as to obtain the necessary boring materials, pipes, etc. to start work. . . .' [V. Conolly, *Soviet Trade from the Pacific to the Levant* (London: Oxford, 1923), p. 43.] Conolly refers to a one-million-yen loan granted in 1928 and repaid in crude oil. [*Oil News* (London), September 1, 1928.]

the latest in Western science and technology. Schlumberger and coworkers started working on this technique in France in 1922, and, although he was joined by other researchers throughout the world, this group played an essential and primary role in its development. The first use of electrical well-logging is reported by Schlumberger from France in 1927. A company was formed—the Société de Prospection Electrique Procédés Schlumberger—which almost immediately made a technical-assistance agreement with Azneft to introduce electrical prospecting and subsurface techniques into the U.S.S.R. It appears that Azneft, along with Venezuela, was used as a test field.[40] By 1933 the U.S.S.R. had eighteen electrical well-logging crews in the field, compared to four in the United States and five in Venezuela.

Azneft concluded another contract, with the Radiore Company of Los Angeles, for technical assistance in electrical prospecting (presumably using magnetometer and gravimetric techniques), but no further data is available.[41]

Similarly, well-cementing techniques (Perkins) and core and rock bit manufacturing technology were introduced in the same period.

PIPELINE CONSTRUCTION, 1925-8

Production problems at Baku were, by 1924-5, well on the way to solution. Rotary drilling and deep-well electrical pumps had revolutionized oil-field technology. The bottleneck now became transportation: particularly the means to move an increasing flow of crude oil to the Black Sea ports for export. The pipeline program initiated in 1925 as the solution to this problem is an excellent example of the intricate interlocking of foreign technologies and skills utilized in Soviet economic development. In this sector we find Type I, II, and III concessions with foreign firms and individuals, in addition to the import of equipment, supplies, training skills, supervisory ability, semi-manufactured materials, and oil-field services for cash, credit, or a share in anticipated oil profits.

After the occupation of the Caucasus, two pipelines were available for oil shipments. The 560 miles from Baku on the Caspian Sea to Batum on the Black Sea were spanned by an eight-inch kerosene line built in 1905 by the Nobel interests. Capacity was about 600,000 tons a year, but by 1921 the line operated only at about 50 percent of capacity and was in need of substantial overhauling. By 1922 shipments were only 22 percent of capacity, and half

[40] In September 1931, the following instructions were issued to the Schlumberger field personnel: 'The results in Russia and Venezuela are remarkable. It has been decided to run the SP surveys in all wells.' [American Petroleum Institute, *History of Petroleum Engineering* (New York: 1961) p. 535.] Schlumberger used electrical well-logging at Baku as early as 1929.

[41] U.S.S.R. Chamber of Commerce, *Economic Conditions in the U.S.S.R.* (Moscow: Vneshtorgizdat, 1931), p. 226.

of Azneft oil was moving to Black Sea ports on the overcrowded, badly maintained rail system which paralleled the pipeline.[42]

Table 2–7   RUSSIAN OIL PIPELINES BEFORE 1930

Pipeline	Km	Diameter in inches	No. of Stations	Years Completed	Service
Baku-Batum	883	8	16	1896–1906	Kerosene
Grozny-Petrovsk	162	8	4	1910–13	Kerosene
Tukha-Krasnodar	102	8	6	1910–11	Crude oil
Grozny-Tuapse	649	10	7	1926–8	Crude oil
Baku-Batum	834	10	13	1927–30	Crude oil

Source: Robert E. Ebel, *The Petroleum Industry of the Soviet Union* (New York: American Petroleum Institute, 1961), p. 143.

The Grozny oil field was linked to Petrovsk on the Caspian Sea by a 110-mile line, used in 1921 only for fuel oil and residues, and operating at about 70 percent of capacity. At Grozny the problem was even more one of transportation than production. Recovery had been aided in 1923–4 by two large gushers. When these ceased in 1926, however, output was cut back by 65 percent.[43] Grozneft's main requirement was a pipeline to the Black Sea, rather than to the Caspian, to connect with European markets.

In brief, the essential problem in 1925 was to get Caucasus oil to the Black Sea ports. This was not within the technical scope of either Azneft or Grozneft; the railways were operating at capacity and were themselves in need of reorganization and new equipment. The rails and ballast were in need of replacement and the tank cars 'in bad shape.'[44]

The position was critical. Over 37 miles of line required replacement on the Baku-Batum line, as well as 18 new diesel pumping engines. It was estimated that repairs to restore prewar capacity would require $1 million. On several occasions between 1923 and 1925, both the Baku and Grozny fields were shut down, as the oil storage tanks at the terminals were full and no transport existed to move the crude oil.[45]

In 1915 Royal Dutch Shell had proposed a Grozny-Novorossisk pipeline, this proposal, together with one to build a 10-inch Baku-Batum line, was later revised. It was decided to build first a 10-inch crude line from Grozny to Tuapse (near Novorossisk) on the Black Sea, then a 10-inch crude line from

[42]   U.S. State Dept. Decimal File, 316–137–744.

[43]   U.S. State Dept. Decimal File, 316–137–977.

[44]   U.S. State Dept. Decimal File, 316–137–1059.

[45]   Dobb, *op. cit.*, p. 168, suggests, incorrectly, that the shutdown was part of the general 'sales crisis' afflicting Russian industry in 1922–3. The oil was needed in fact, to fulfill foreign purchase contracts.

Baku to Batum, and then to rebuild the existing 8-inch Baku-Batum pipeline. These lines were put into construction in 1925–6 and scheduled for completion by 1928.

The construction of a pipeline may be broken into a standard sequence of operations. Assuming that the route is surveyed and cleared, the first operation is trenching, followed by welding and inserting the pipes, and finally by covering them. The critical skilled functions are those of welding, trenching, and covering. The major inputs are the steel pipe itself, welding equipment, and skilled welding labor. Engines are required for installation at pumping stations along the route. Table 2–8 lists these operations for the two pipe-lines built between 1925 and 1928, together with the enterprise undertaking each operation.

Table 2-8 SOVIET CONSTRUCTION OF THE GROZNY-TUAPSE AND BAKU-BATUM PIPELINES, 1925-8

Sequence	Construction of Operation	Undertaken By
1.	Manufacture of line pipe	German pipe mills under Russgertorg contract*
2.	Supervision of pipe transportation	Otto Wolff Co.*
3.	Purchase of trenching equipment	Purchased in United States
4.	Training of welders	J. I. Allen Co. (Los Angeles)
5.	Purchase of welding equipment	Purchased in United States by Ragaz (Russian-American Compressed Gas Co.)**
6.	Welding of pipeline	Ragaz**
7.	Supervision of welding	J. I. Allen Co. (Los Angeles)
8.	Purchase of line pumping engines	9 provided by Crossley Co. (United Kingdom) and 30 Mann engines made by Gomza***

Sources: * See chap. 16.
** See chap. 12.
*** Gomza had a Type III concession agreement with Mann A-G (Germany). See chap. 10.

The 10-inch steel pipe required for the lines was bought in Germany by Russgertorg[46] on five-year credit terms. Twenty ships were required to transport the total quantity of 51,000 tons of pipe from Germany to the Black Sea, and German transportation specialists were hired by Wolff to ensure safe arrival of the cargo at Poti, on the Black Sea.[47]

[46] The Otto Wolff Trading Concession (Russgertorg) is covered in detail in chap. 16. Soviet trusts were also trying to get the order for pipe, but their prices were higher (3.85 rubles/pood versus 2.71 rubles/pood), and quality was far inferior to that of the German pipe.

[47] U.S. State Dept. Decimal File, 316–137–1082.

The critical task of welding the line was handled by the Russian-American Compressed Gas Company (or Ragaz) a Type II concession owned jointly by the International Oxygen Corporation of Newark, New Jersey, and Metalosindikat.[48] One of the seven plants manufacturing compressed gases established by Ragaz was at Baku and produced the large quantities of welding gases required for construction. The $100,000 worth of welding and electrical equipment necessary for this operation was purchased by Ragaz in the United States.[49] Automatic thyratron and ignition welding equipment was later manufactured in the U.S.S.R. with the technical assistance of General Electric.[50] The 150 Russian welders were trained by the J. I. Allen Company of Los Angeles. The latter then supervised work on the site under the general contract supervision of Ragaz.[51] It does not appear that either of the two special schools established by Ragaz for the training of welders was used for the pipeline welders. The trenching equipment was purchased in the United States.[52]

Table 2–9 COMPARATIVE PRICE AND DELIVERY SCHEDULES
FOR 300-HP DIESEL ENGINES FOR BAKU-BATUM PIPELINE

	Germany	*Russia* (Gomza)
Delivery	8 within 6 months	8 within 14 months
	All within 18 months	All within 27 months
Price	87 rubles per hp.	180–186 rubles per hp.

Source: Adapted from Confidential Report No. 5419 of Polish Consul General, Tiflis, May 25, 1928.

Azneft wanted to purchase all pumping engines for the line stations from abroad and cited lower costs to support its case. A comparison between the relevant German and Russian offers is summarized in table 2–9; Azneft was instructed by Gosplan and Vesenkha, after nine engines had been ordered in the United Kingdom, to purchase the balance of thirty from Gomza (the Soviet State Machine Building Trust).

Thirty Mann-type 300 horsepower diesel engines were finally supplied by the Gomza works and nine by the Crossley Company (United Kingdom). The pumps were supplied by the Moscow machine-building trust, built under

[48]   The concession agreement between Metalosindikat and the International Oxygen Corp. was signed in January 1926 and is discussed in detail below.
[49]   Amtorg, *op. cit.*, III, No. 14–15 (August 1, 1927).
[50]   *Monogram*, November 1943.
[51]   *New York Times*, April 9, 1928, p. 5, col. 2.
[52]   U.S. State Dept. Decimal File, 316-137-1082.

license and the technical supervision of German companies, operating under Type III concession agreements.[53]

REFINERY CONSTRUCTION[54]

Prerevolutionary refineries were small units, located primarily at Baku and producing fuel oil, kerosene, and lubricating oils.

The Soviet objective of utilizing crude oil as a means to generate foreign exchange for industrial development required a different approach to refining. Refining had to produce those oil products in demand in the Western world, at a cost reasonably close to that of Western refineries. There was no refinery technology within Russia in the 1920s to design plants of this type;[55] this technology could be found only in Germany and in the United States. There were no cracking units in the U.S.S.R. before 1928. Of nineteen refineries and cracking plants built between the Revolution and 1930, only one had some units manufactured in the U.S.S.R. and even that was under British technical supervision, using the United States Winkler-Koch process.

Although the first United States patent had been granted for a cracking process in 1860 (United States Patent No. 28,246, to L. Atwood), it is usually accepted that 1926 was the year in which it was universally recognized that gasoline from the cracking process was better than that produced by straight distillation.[56] The United States was far ahead of foreign producers in 1926, with more than 2,500 cracking process patents issued, some 26 processes in

[53] Both the state machine-building trust (Gomza) and the Moscow machine-building trust (Mosmash) had technical-assistance agreements with German companies. Gomza had an agreement with Maschinenfabrik Augsburg-Nürnberg A-G to build under license and with technical assistance both two- and four-cycle motors, with and without compressors, and Mann-type diesel motors. Mosmash was formed from nine large prerevolutionary machine-building works in Moscow, including those of the Bromley Brothers, Danhauer and Kaiser, and other Russian, British, French, and German companies. Mosmash had several Type III technical-assistance agreements, and one with Maschinenbrau A-G of Saarbrucken included the manufacture of pumps. See chap. 10 for details.

[54] The refinery section is based extensively on the monthly *Le Pétrole Russe* (a supplement to *La Vie Economique des Soviets*), published by the Neftsyndikat representative in Paris between 1927 and 1930. Although the principal objective of the journal was to further Soviet penetration of Western oil markets, the 22 issues published contain a wealth of detail on Soviet oil-field development and refinery construction. The only complete set in the United States is in the Hoover Institution, Stanford University.

[55] A sample examination of *Neftianoe Khozaistvo*, a Soviet monthly devoted to the oil industry, for 1928 suggests that the problems receiving research attention were those of applying foreign technology to the U.S.S.R., the examination of domestic oil deposits, and the structure of world oil markets. Nothing, except the development turbine drill, suggests any Soviet contribution to world oil technology.

[56] Cracking is a process of breaking down and rearranging oil molecules by high temperatures and pressures. The older straight-run distillation process could produce only a limited amount of gasoline, but cracking enables fuel oil, for example, to be converted into gasoline.

commercial operation, and another 28 in experimental or demonstration pilot plants. There was an enormous American investment in these processes—not only in those utilized commercially but also in those that fell by the wayside.

Russian crudes have gasoline fractions running only 5–10 percent, but the gas-oil fractions are greater, averaging 35–40 percent; consequently cracking is very important for the Soviet petroleum industry. Until the installation of the refinery complexes in 1927–8, only straight-run distillation was used, and this resulted in both a small total production of gasoline and low recovery percentages. To increase both production and recovery percentages, some form of cracking process was vital.

Exports of crude oil had begun again in 1922, and in 1926 an extensive program of refinery and cracking plant construction was begun to upgrade the products exported. Two locations on the Black Sea were selected (Batum and Tuapse) and two in the oilfields (Baku and Grozny) as initial sites for refinery complexes. These complexes were built entirely by Western companies, with the exception of some minor equipment and the partial duplication of a Baku refinery by Azneft in 1929.

Batum, on the Black Sea, was the site of the largest development. Three petroleum refineries, two cracking plants, an asphalt plant, and a kerosene plant were built between 1923 and 1930.

In April 1927 construction was begun on the first petroleum refinery. This utilized the latest United States technology, with a capacity of 1,600,000 tons a year of petroleum products. At the same time two other refineries, duplicates of the first, were placed on order.

The first Batum refinery was built by Craig, Ltd. (United Kingdom), for ten million rubles, advanced on six-year credit terms.[57] The other two units, built by German companies (Heckmann, Wilke and Pintsch) were financed from a 1926 revolving credit of 300 million marks from the German government. A large part of the amount was used for oil-field equipment. These units were financed on four-year credit terms.[58]

The units listed in table 2–10 were fabricated abroad and erected in the U.S.S.R. by Western engineers, some of whom worked on behalf of their own companies and some of whom were employed by Azneft as consultants. Between 1926 and 1929 more than $20 million was expended in the United States alone for oil-field and refinery equipment—by far the greater part on long-term credits.[59] A substantial portion of the 1925–6 German credits was also used for oil-field and refinery equipment. The Batum petroleum refineries utilized the latest United States continuous sulphuric acid process,

[57]   U.S. State Dept. Decimal File, 316-137-1031.
[58]   U.S. State Dept. Decimal File, 316-137-980.
[59]   Alcan Hirsch, *op. cit.*, p. 152.

Table 2-10   CONSTRUCTION OF THE
                             BATUM REFINERY COMPLEX, 1927-30

Unit	Construction by	Capacity*
Refinery I (1928)	Craig Co. (United Kingdom)	1,600,000 tons per year crude oil
Refinery II (1928)	Heckmann (Germany)	1,600,000 tons per year crude oil
Refinery III (1929)	Wilke, Pintsch (Germany)	1,600,000 tons per year crude oil
Cracking Plant I (1928)	Winkler-Koch system (manufactured by Graver Corp.)	Not available
Cracking Plant II (1929)	Winkler-Koch system (manufactured by Graver Corp.)	Not available
Kerosene Plant (1927)	Standard Oil Co. of New York	150,000 long tons per year

Sources: Le Pétrole Russe, various issues, 1927.
          U.S. State Dept. Archives.
          Amtorg, op. cit.

* Refinery capacities are approximate only; several figures exist for each unit. These
  are maximal. Columns 1 and 2 are confirmed by several sources.

although built by British and German companies.[60] The four gasoline cracking units were built by the Graver Corporation of Chicago as part of an order for ten units valued at $2 million and supplied on long-term credit for installation at Batum, Tuapse, and Yaroslavl. Graver also had a technical-assistance agreement with the U.S.S.R. which covered petroleum refineries.[61] The cracking units utilized the Winkler-Koch and Cross systems of cracking, and the Winkler-Koch Engineering Company, of Wichita, Kansas, also had a technical-assistance agreement with the U.S.S.R. to facilitate the transfer of its cracking technology.

The 150,000-ton kerosene plant was built in 1927 by the Standard Oil Company of New York and then leased back by Azneft. Standard operated the plant under a three-year, Type II contract, loading company tankers with kerosene at Batum for shipment to Middle East and Far East markets.[62]

[60] Azneft ' . . . a choisi le procédé américain de raffinage du pétrole par l'acide sulfurique, en les mélangeant d'une façon uninterrompue par le moyen d'injecteurs.' [Le Pétrole Russe, No. 2 (Oct. 5, 1927), p. 15.] Also, Amtorg, op. cit., IV, No. 1 (January 1, 1929), and Ekonomicheskaya Zhizn, No. 161, July 17, 1929.

[61] The usual claims of prior discovery were made for the cracking process: ' . . . the eminent constructor Choukhov' discovered the process long before the Americans. Why the Choukhov process was not utilized is left unanswered. (Le Pétrole Russe, No. 12, May 5, 1928, p. 18.)

[62] At least ten photographs were traced of a Standard Oil of New York unit at Batum. These were dated between 1927 and 1930, but the unit was described variously as a refinery, kerosene plant, fuel oil plant, etc. It is presumed, but not known with certainty, that there was only one Standard unit—a kerosene plant. While Standard

This was the first United States investment in Russia since the Revolution. There is no evidence that Azneft constructed or fabricated parts for any of the Batum refineries; there was complete reliance on imported technology, supervision, and equipment.

Tuapse, on the Black Sea north of Batum, was the site of the second refinery complex oriented to Western oil products markets. This complex was run by Grozneft, the Grozny oil trust.

Table 2–11   CONSTRUCTION OF THE
                               TUAPSE REFINERY COMPLEX, 1927–30

Unit	Construction by	Capacity
Refinery I	Heckmann*	1,000,000 tons per year
Refinery II	Heckmann*	1,000,000 tons per year
Cracking Plant I	Cross system (Graver Corp.)	Not available
Cracking Plant II	Cross system (Graver Corp.)	Not available

Source: Le Pétrole Russe, various issues, 1927–9.
* The refinery construction is known to be German, but the firm is not precisely known; it was probably Heckmann.

The equipment for the refineries at Tuapse came from Germany, and the two cracking units were manufactured and installed by the Graver Corporation, of Chicago. The Burrell-Mase Engineering Company (United States) reorganized, modernized, and expanded the overall gas and petroleum production and refining facilities for Grozneft, and between 10 and 20 Burrell-Mase engineers were occupied with the project for a period of two years. One interesting comparison between refinery construction at Tuapse and Batum involves the length of time required to build a refinery under Soviet conditions. Burrell points out that a refinery which could be built in five months in the United States took two years to build in the Soviet Union under Grozneft.[63] On the other hand, a Standard Oil construction engineer, Tompkins, building the Standard-leased Batum refinery for Azneft, is quoted as saying that the company was able to complete construction in only three months 'in light of the complete assistance of Soviet authorities.'[64] This comparison supports

---

of New York was thus aiding Soviet development at Batum, Soviet agents were busy in the Far East endeavoring to undermine its market position, with the lavish use of bribery and threats. [Naval Intelligence Report No. 159, May 11, 1928 (316–137–1084/5).]

[63] George A. Burrell, *An American Engineer Looks at Russia* (Boston: Stratford, n.d.), p. 269. Burrell has 37 publications in the field of gas and petroleum engineering listed in the Library of Congress card catalog, and was an outstanding expert in the field.

[64] Amtorg, *op. cit.*, II, No. 18 (September 15, 1927), 5.

the observation made elsewhere that Azneft under Serebrovsky was a far more efficient concern in this period than either Grozneft or Embaneft. Serebrovsky was later shifted by Stalin to the gold trusts, to repeat his Azneft success.

Foreign equipment was used throughout these complexes, including even American fire extinguisher equipment and such auxiliary facilities as machine shops.[65] Electrical equipment for refineries, i.e., pumps, compressors, and control apparatus, was largely supplied by the General Electric Company.[66]

Table 2-12   CONSTRUCTION OF THE
                SOVIET INLAND REFINERIES, 1927–30

Unit	Constructed by	Capacity
Baku		
Refinery I	United Kingdom technical supervision in Baku	470,000 tons per year
Cracking Plant I	Winkler-Koch system (United Kingdom)*	—
Cracking Plant II	Winkler-Koch system (United Kingdom)*	—
Heavy Oil Plant	Steinschneider (Germany)	3,600,000 tons per year
Grozny		
Refinery I	Borman (Germany)	365,000 tons per year
Refinery II	Pintsch (Germany)	365,000 tons per year
Cracking Plant I (3 Units)	2 Dobbs (Germany); Sakhanov & Tilitchev (Germany)	—
Emba		
Vara Refinery (lubricants)	Borman (Germany)	128,000 tons per year

Source: Le Pétrole Russe, various issues, 1927–9.
* Probably by Vickers.

In both Tuapse and Batum other American corporations—in particular the Foster-Wheeler Corporation of New York, E. B. Badger and Sons of Boston, and the Winkler-Koch Corporation of Wichita—played an important part in the design and construction of cracking units.[67]

The inland refineries at Baku depended more on German and United Kingdom construction aid; but two new factors are apparent. The refinery

---

[65] The only manufacturer of fire extinguisher equipment in the U.S.S.R. was the concession Boereznsky (Lithuania).

[66] *Monogram*, November 1943.

[67] The Winkler-Koch Corp. of Wichita, had a technical-assistance agreement with Neftsyndikat for the construction of cracking plants. [American-Russian Chamber of Commerce, *Economic Handbook of the Soviet Union* (New York: 1931), p. 101.]

at Baku was partly built by Azneft under a British technical supervisor, but the tuyères and some of the other pipe work were built by Azneft—the only case of Soviet oil-field construction in that decade. In addition, the cracking plant at Grozny was partly Soviet-designed by Sakhanov and Tilitchev but constructed by German companies. These are the same procedures noted in other industries. Soviet construction was at first limited to the simple and the straightforward (i.e., pipework) in less strategic locations (the inland refineries) and then gradually moved into more complex and more important functions at more important locations. Either Soviet designs were first made abroad or prototypes were made both abroad and in the U.S.S.R., presumably for comparison purposes, before complete development was tackled in the U.S.S.R. However, Soviet design and technology were almost nonexistent, and such examples as we have may have been no more than the 'Sovietization' of an existing Western technology; this name-changing was typical in the electrical equipment industry.

ACQUISITION OF FOREIGN MARKETS FOR PETROLEUM PRODUCTS

The technological revolution in oil-field production, construction of new pipelines, repair of pre-Revolutionary pipelines, and the refinery construction program on the Black Sea coast put the Soviets in a position to collect on their investments and development strategy.

Production of crude oil almost tripled from 1923 to 1928, and exports followed a similar development, from 185,000 tons in 1922 to 1.9 million tons in 1927–8. The refinery program enabled a greater proportion of oil derivatives, of higher value (especially gasoline) to be exported. Before 1923 no gasoline had been exported, and most petroleum product exports consisted of kerosene and oils.

In 1923 almost half of Soviet oil exports consisted of kerosene, or heating oil, which could be produced by prewar straight-run distillation refineries. By 1928, as a result of the new refinery and cracking-unit construction programs, the proportion of kerosene dropped to less than one-quarter, and gasoline now made up more than one-quarter of total exports. There was also a significant increase in total petroleum exports, from 430,000 tons to almost 2.75 million tons—a sixfold increase. Light oil fractions figured among the 1928 exports but not in 1923 exports.

In brief, table 2–13 indicates both a very substantial increase in the quantity of oil exported and an increase in the product quality. Both factors resulted directly from the refinery construction program. By 1928, the value of oil exports was 124 million rubles, or 19.1 percent of the value of all Soviet exports, and the largest single earner of foreign exchange.

Table 2-13   COMPOSITION OF SOVIET OIL EXPORTS,
1923 AND 1928

Product	1923 Tons	1923 Percent	1928 Tons	1928 Percent
Crude oil	35,000	8.1	244,542	8.9
Gasoline	50,000*	11.6	725,840	26.5
Kerosene	200,000	46.5	680,360	24.9
Fuel oil	—	—	640,822	23.4
Gas oil	—	—	191,787	7.0
Solar oil	—	—	49,145	1.8
Light oil	—	—	22,472	0.8
Lubricating oil	100,000	23.3	179·861	6.6
Other types	45,000	10.5	—	—
Totals	430,000	100.0	2,734,829	99.9

Source: Imperial Institute, *The Mineral Industry of the British Empire and Foreign Countries, 1928–30* (London: H.M.S.O., 1931).

* These early (1923) gasoline exports were derived from a German process utilizing natural gas, natural gasoline, and straight-run distillation.

In May–June 1923, coinciding with the start of the Barnsdall drilling and pumping work, a mixed or Type II, agreement was made with Sale and Company of London, for the immediate sale of 30,000 tons of crude oil and follow-on sale of 100,000 tons of kerosene per year. The company was capitalized at £250,000 sterling; both Sale and Company and the Soviets held an equal number of directorships. Neftsyndicat reserved the right to buy out all shares of the company after ten years, no doubt looking forward to the time when they would be strong and knowledgeable enough to establish their own distribution network in the United Kingdom.[68] This appears to have been the first major breach in the solid front presented by the world oil companies against the purchase of Russian oil, or 'stolen oil' as it was called in contemporary business terminology. Royal Dutch Shell then argued that self-interest dictated the purchase of 30,000 tons (and an option for a further 170,000).[69] The Soviet estimate of oil products available for export in 1923 was 430,000 tons; these two sales alone made a sizeable contribution to the re-entry of the U.S.S.R. into the world oil markets.

[68] *Izvestia*, No. 104, May 12, 1923.

[69] Standard Oil in the United States, British, French, and Italian companies had been buying Soviet oil on a minor scale before the 1923 contracts. Vlessing in Holland acted as the agent for continental Europe. It would be difficult to match the hypocrisy displayed by both major oil groups. Sir Henri Deterding, of Royal Dutch Shell, was blasting Standard of New York for buying 'stolen oil' while himself buying it in large quantities and negotiating for a monopoly arrangement with the U.S.S.R. Standard switched dramatically from an anti-Soviet to a pro-Soviet stand in 1927, and its public relations man, Ivy Lee, put out a sycophantic *U.S.S.R. —a World Enigma* (London: Benn, 1929) to reinforce its position. This got Standard of New York into a conflict with Standard of New Jersey.

This breach was followed by the formation of a Dutch-Soviet mixed company for the export of Soviet oil, under an agreement signed on May 11, 1923 between Royal Dutch Shell and the U.S.S.R. Capital participation was 50:50, with £1.25 million sterling being subscribed. The head office was in London and the company sold Soviet oil abroad through exclusive dealerships. The agreement lasted for ten years, and the company earned a 10 percent commission.[70]

In 1924 Royal Dutch Shell was purchasing oil via this mixed company on behalf of Standard, the purchases being split between the two major oil groups. This, however, presented a united front to Neftsyndicat and the trade organization—a front which offset the bargaining power of the Soviet trade monopoly. Since 1924 the Soviets have vehemently protested the formation of such foreign trade groups.

The first goal in the expansion of oil exports at this time was to establish trading relations with existing distributors in each foreign market. The Standard Oil Company handled the Near and Far East markets, and the Blue Bird Motor Company and British-Mexican Petroleum Company handled imports into the United Kingdom and cracked Soviet kerosene in the United Kingdom until refineries were built later in the U.S.S.R. Asiatic Petroleum bought oil for distribution in India and Ceylon. Turkey and Spain bought large quantities (532,000 tons in 1928) for distribution through their government monopoly networks. A five-year agreement in 1925 between Neftsyndicat and Bell Pétrole covered delivery of Grozny crude to France.

Later, when the acceptance of Soviet petroleum had been established, the Soviets began to establish their own distribution networks. Russian Oil Products (ROP), owned jointly by Arcos and Neftsyndicat, was founded in the United Kingdom. By 1925 ROP had established a chain of oil depots in the United Kingdom and was engaged in extensive price warfare with existing distributors. In the mid-1920s the Soviets canceled their agreements with German distributors and established their own subsidiary, the Deutsche-Russische Naptha Company, which established the Derop chain of gasoline service stations in Germany. In Sweden, the Nordiska Bensin Aktiebolaget was established and promptly drove prices down 30 percent to gain entry into the market. Gradually by the end of the decade the Soviets controlled their own distribution networks in most of their major markets, although they still relied on Standard Oil for distribution in the Middle and Far East, while in Spain a mixed company arrangement with the Argus Bank of Barcelona had exclusive rights for Spain, Portugal, and their colonies, with Neftsyndicat receiving 25 percent of the profits and the losses. The export of petroleum

[70]   *Handelsblad*, May 12, 1923 (quoted in 316–137–844).

products to Persia was handled through the Persian-Azerbaidjian Naptha Company (a subsidiary founded by Azneft) and Shark (the Russian-Persian Import and Export Company), a Type II concession.[71]

Several very large orders were placed directly by Western governments for Soviet oil. The Italian Navy bought 150,000 tons in 1927, the French Navy bought 33,300 tons in 1927, and the United States Shipping Board bought 200,000 tons—at a time when there were no official diplomatic or trade relations between the two countries.

SUMMARY OF SOVIET OIL DEVELOPMENT, 1917-30

No new oil fields were developed in the 1920s; all the producing fields had been developed by prerevolutionary operators. This inheritance was intact in 1921, when the Caucasian oil fields were occupied by the Soviet armies, but world technological advances, primarily American, put these fields and their products at a distinct competitive disadvantage. Further, the early Bolsheviks had no ability in oil-field operation, and production rapidly declined by 1922-3.

Serebrovsky, Chairman of Azneft, was instrumental in focusing Soviet attention upon foreign oil production techniques and within seven years the Soviet oil fields were modernized: two new pipelines were completed, and three distinct refinery complexes, comprised of nineteen major identifiable units, had been put into operation. Exports by 1926-7 were double those of 1913.

It is overwhelmingly obvious from the preceding discussion that the importation of foreign oil-field technology and administration, either directly or by concession, was the single factor of consequence in this development. Statements that this achievement was 'without foreign assistance and capital'[72] are obviously propagandistic nonsense. Development of an indigenous oil technology comparable to the contemporaneous American technique was not a useful alternative. The only available elements for an indigenous technology were the turbine drill and the Choukov cracking process, and these were more or less dismissed from consideration by the Soviets.[73] The development of domestic technology would have been costly in both time and expense,

---

[71] U.S. State Dept. Decimal File, 316–137–900.

[72] Such statements may be found in Louis Fischer, *Oil Imperialism* (New York: International, 1926), p. 110; and in T. Gonta, *The Heroes of Grozny, How the Soviet Oil Industry Fulfilled the Five Year Plan in Two and a Half Years* (Moscow: 1932).

[73] The turbine drill did a small percentage of drilling; the Choukov process has never been used. The Export Control Act of 1949 forced the Soviets to develop the less efficient turbine drill (it overheats below about 8,000 feet) and so incur some of the costs of development.

and the oil fields were in no condition to wait; they were rapidly watering, and maintenance operations were nonexistent.

The only rational solution from the Soviet viewpoint was to introduce American rotary drilling and electrical deep-well pumping, while continuing the tsarist oil-field electrification program. This, together with refinery complex construction, was implemented, except in the case of the tuyères of one Baku refinery, by Western firms, engineers, and consultants with Western skills and equipment. This alternative cost far less than developing an oil-field technology from scratch. The marginal cost of supplying refining and cracking units by Western firms to the U.S.S.R. was insignificant, as the research and development cost had already been recouped from units built in the West. Any return in excess of direct costs was profit.

There was no domestic Russian demand for gasoline, and little for light fractions, but there was an urgent demand for foreign exchange to finance the industrialization program.[74] With the installation of modern cracking plants, penetration of Western markets became possible. This overall development strategy was so successful that the declining petroleum industry of 1922–3 was able by 1928 to contribute 20 percent of Soviet foreign exchange. The Soviets developed a completely up-to-date refining and cracking industry within a few years of the United States—an industry destined to play a great role in the Soviet industrialization drive of the early 1930s.

[74] There was no production of automobiles or trucks in the U.S.S.R. until the implementation of the Fiat and Ford Motor Co. agreements of 1928–9. There were very few imported automobiles and trucks, and no motor buses at all until after 1924. The internal demand for oil products was for heating and lighting oils; i.e., fuel oil and kerosene.

CHAPTER THREE

Coal and Anthracite Mining Industries

YEARS OF CRISIS AND STAGNATION

THE most productive Russian coal fields are in the Donetz Basin (Donbas). In 1910 these supplied more than 18 million tons of a total of 24 million tons of coal and anthracite produced in Russia. This prerevolutionary industry was highly labor-intensive, employing 123,000 workers in coal mines and 19,000 in anthracite pits, with little mechanical equipment apart from primitive hand-propelled mine cars. About 4.6 million tons of coal and coke were imported.

From the Revolutions until the mid-1920s, the coal and anthracite mining industries endured a series of crises involving over-production, severe under-production, bad quality, lack of skilled labor, and general technical backwardness. The blame for these crises was laid at a bewildering number of doors: the Revolution, the Civil War, the Intervention, flooding of the mines, housing shortages, food shortages, labor shortages, bad attendance and sickness, lack of bread, 'central authorities,' lack of fireproof bricks, lack of technical materials, non-payment for output, reorganization, inefficient railroads, lack of shipping, technical backwardness, and non-payment of wages all received their share of the blame.

Looking at the situation as a whole one sees two factors that stand out as prime causes for the catastrophic crises: first, the attempt to transform a capitalist system into a socialist system without a clear understanding of the operation of either system; and second, the very low level of technical and economic knowledge of those who assumed the burden of transformation. The causes listed in the contemporary Soviet press were generally no more than symptoms of an imperfect transformation.

These difficulties led to a policy of concentration and a subsequent reduction in the number of operating coal mines. In 1921 there were 1,816 coal mines in the Donbas of which 857 (47 percent) were closed. Of the remaining 959 mines, some 387 (or 41 percent) were leased to former operators or peasants.[1] The 572 state operated shafts were reduced to 202 shafts in 1922, and after several crises further reduced to 175 in mid-1922 and to 36 by mid-1923.[2] These 36 nationalized collieries produced 78 percent of the total Donbas output, 16 percent being produced by other state and railroad trusts and 6 percent by private leased coal pits. An attempt to export coal to earn foreign exchange through an organization formed specifically for the purpose (Exportugol) also failed.

Lack of the technical facilities to produce coal was only part of the problem. Although the mines were not mechanized, the conveyor and mine rail equipment was, according to *Ekonomicheskaya Zhizn*, 80 percent in order.[3] The output per worker was, on the other hand, miserably low; about 5 tons per worker *per month* compared to about 48 tons per worker in the United States. This was barely sufficient to supply enough coal to keep the pits operating, and at one point in 1921 the Donbas mines produced only enough coal for themselves and had no surplus production for shipment. This was due partly to the lack of mechanization and to inefficient organization, and partly to problems created by the attempt to impose 'socialist organization' on a technically backward enterprise. Together they resulted in chaos. Average daily shipments of coal from the Donbas dropped to 57 carloads in the summer of 1921, normally the most advantageous season for mining and transportation. Coal was imported into the Donbas from both the United Kingdom and the United States in 1921–3: truly a case of 'carrying coals to Newcastle.'[4]

From 1923 onward, efforts were made to lease more coal mine operations and smaller pits to private individuals, artels and joint-stock companies, and an effort was made to induce foreign concessionaires into the coal regions.

UNION MINIÈRE AND THE DONETZ BASIN COAL MINES

The major effort in coal mine mechanization was handled under Type III technical-assistance agreements with United States companies between 1927 and 1930, but there were also a number of pure Type I concessions. With one exception, these were on the more distant borders of the U.S.S.R.—those areas more difficult to develop.

[1] P. Zuev, *Ugol'nya Promyshlennost' i ee Polozhenie* (Moscow: 1921), p. 9.
[2] *The Engineer*, November 16, 1923, p. 529.
[3] *Ekonomicheskaya Zhizn*, No. 66, March 21, 1924.
[4] 'In 1870 they produced 9 million poods . . . so we have gone back to the conditions of 50 years ago.' *Pravda*, October 28, 1921.

The single exception was the operation of coal mines in the Donbas by the Union Minière group. Before 1917 part of the Donbas output had been controlled by a French company, Union Minière du Sud de la Russie, whose properties were expropriated after the Bolshevik Revolution. It was reported

Table 3-1 OPERATING FOREIGN CONCESSIONS IN THE U.S.S.R.
COAL AND ANTHRACITE MINING INDUSTRY, 1922-30*

Concession Holder	*Country of Origin*	*Concession Type*	*Work Undertaken in U.S.S.R.*
Companies			
Union Minière Group	France	I Production	Opening Krivoi Rog mines
Anglo-Russian Grumant Co., Ltd.	United Kingdom	I Production	Operating Spitzbergen mines
Polar Star Concession	Unknown	I Production	Operating coal mines Spitzbergen, railroad in Murmansk
Kita Karafuto Sekio	Japan	I Production	Opening Sakhalin coal mines
Mitsui Shakeef	Japan	I Production	Opening Sakhalin coal mines
Lena Goldfields, Ltd.	United Kingdom	I Production	Opening Kuzbas coal mines and anthracite mines
Bryner and Company, Ltd.	United Kingdom	I Production	Operating Far East coal mines (Tetiukhe)
American Industrial Corp.	United States	II Production	Operating Kemerovo coal mines
G. Warren, Inc.	United States	II Trade	Importing anthracite to United States
Roberts & Schaefer, Inc.	United States	III Technical assistance	Reorganizing Donbas coal mines
Allen & Garcia, Inc.	United States	III Technical assistance	Reorganizing Donbas coal mines
Stuart, James and Cooke, Inc.	United States	III Technical assistance	Reorganizing Donbas coal mines
Thyssen A-G	Germany	III Technical assistance	Sinking shafts in Donbas coal mines
Stein A-G	Germany	III Technical assistance	Sinking shafts
Goodman Manufacturing, Inc.	United States	III Technical assistance	Providing technical assistance on manufacture of coal cutters
Hilaturas Casablancas S.A.	Spain	III Technical assistance	Providing technical assistance on manufacture of coal cutters
American Commune	United States	Commune	Operating mine No. 2, Donbas
Individual consultants			
J. W. Powell	United States	III Technical assistance	Providing assistance to Giproshaft
T. G. Hawkins	United States	III Technical assistance	Providing assistance to Giproshaft
C. Pierce	United States	III Technical assistance	Providing assistance to Giproshaft.

Source: See text.

* This table contains the important concession agreements. It does not include agreements for supply of equipment, which also included training and installation clauses, such as the Krupp and Sullivan contracts for supply, installation, and operator training for heavy coal cutters.

in December 1923 that an 'extremely valuable' concession to exploit the Donetz Coal Basin had been granted to a French group, and evidence points to the operation of these mines by Union Minière. In the statistical annual for 1927–8, eleven very large coal mines in Makeevka were listed as 'Union' and two in Ekaterinovsk were listed as 'Franco-Russky.'[5] Given the proclivity of the Bolsheviks to propagandize, it is unlikely these shafts would have continued for ten years under their prerevolutionary name except for a specific reason. On the other hand, there was every reason for the Union Company to have completely obscured public knowledge of a concession. There were some two million tsarist shares and bonds held in France, with active representative organizations fighting for total settlement of prewar debts. This was a parallel to the International Barnsdall situation.

THE KUZBAS PROJECT OF THE AMERICAN INDUSTRIAL COLONY

This project is of more than purely historical interest; it enables us quantitatively to establish the effect of United States management methods on a backward Soviet enterprise of the early NEP period. The Kuzbas operation counters any argument that it was lack of equipment alone, or the ravages of the Revolution, that delayed economic development. The removal of socialist methods of operation and substitution of profit-oriented methods, even by a group ideologically sympathetic to the Soviet 'experiment,' brought about an immediate and significant upward change in output. Within six months of the take-over of Kemerovo mines by American workers, output of coal, coke, and sawmill products almost doubled; this occurred *before* the injection of modern equipment.[6] Rutgers, director of the Kuzbas project, held that the Soviets looked upon Kuzbas as a Soviet state enterprise run on American lines and 'unfortunately' needing Americans, strongly implying that counter-revolutionary activity at least hindered Soviet development, but that American labor discipline and organizational methods were required ahead of the

---

[5]   V. I. Kruglyakova, *op. cit.*, p. 175. The original report was in the *New York Times*, November 14, 1923. It was also announced by the Soviet Embassy in Berlin in December 1923 (569–3–150) and confirmed by the United States Consulate in Riga (569–3–155). A hint that the concession operated for at least two years is in a *Times* (London) report of March 30, 1926: 'Following consultation of representatives of all the big French enterprises in Russia, among them. . . . Union Minière du Sud de la Russie . . .'

[6]   'These mines were lying almost idle when they were taken over by the Americans . . . the presence of the Americans has a stimulating effect upon the Russian workmen, there is already a tendency to increase production.' *Ekonomicheskaya Zhizn*, No. 19, January 28, 1923. The 'stimulating effect' is rather overstated, as the Russian workers were, at the least, hostile to these new foreign elements.

machinery itself.[7] A similar situation was reported from the Donbas. A group of American miners near Youzovka nearly trebled former production.[8]

In early 1922 a concession agreement was concluded between the U.S.S.R. and a group of American workers represented by Bill Haywood and an 'American Organization Committee,' formed in New York by the Society for Technical Aid to Soviet Russia, which had the objective of persuading American skilled workers to go to the U.S.S.R. This unit was to exploit the 'almost idle' plants of the Nadejdinsky and Kuznetsk regions. The concession included iron ore and coal mines, forests, and auxiliary industries in Nadejdinsky, and the coal mines, chemical by-products plant, and supplementary industries at Kemerovo. In addition, the unit operated brick kilns, a leather-shoe factory at Tomsk, the Jashkinsky cement plant, Guriev Zavod (pig iron) and other enterprises.

According to the terms of the agreement,[9] the group undertook to import 2,800 fully qualified workers to Kemerovo and 3,000 to Nadejdinsky. A capital subscription was required by the Soviet government of $100 in machinery and $100 in food per worker. These were imported along with the workers. The Committee was responsible for organizing the purchase of machinery and raw materials abroad. The U.S.S.R. undertook to pay expenses and buy machinery to the value of $300,000. The total product of the concession was the property of the U.S.S.R, but some surpluses of coal, wood, bricks, and agricultural produce accrued to the settlers.

In January 1923, five groups of colonists arrived and began work under skilled mining engineers. The total population ultimately reached 400 Ameri-

Table 3-2   EFFECT OF UNITED STATES MANAGEMENT
IN KEMEROVO (KUZNETSK) COAL MINES, 1923

	Average Output Per Month	
	Aug. 1, 1922 to Feb. 1, 1923 (*Soviet management*)	*Feb. 1, 1923 to Aug. 1, 1923* (*United States management*)
Coal produced	6,950 metric tons	10,657 metric tons
Coke produced	160 metric tons	288 metric tons
Sawmills	16,800 cubic feet	29,600 cubic feet

Source: Nation, August 8, 1923, p. 146.

---

[7]   R. E. Kennell, 'Kuzbas: A New Pennsylvania,' *Nation*, May 2, 1923. The American Industrial Colony published its own journal, *Kuzbas*. Only issue No. 3 of Vol. I appears to have survived in the United States (at the Hoover Institution Library, Stanford University).

[8]   *Pravda*, No. 246, October 31, 1922.

[9]   Complete text is in U.S. State Dept. Decimal File, 316-111-1270.

cans and 2,000 Russians. S. J. Rutgers was the chief director; Grindler, the chief engineer; and A. Pearson, technical director, at the Kemerovo project. Despite local opposition from 'counterrevolutionaries,' the group took over full management control on February 1, 1923.

The effect of introducing American skills and methods of organization was both immediate and substantial (table 3–2). One of the first steps was to reduce the number of employees by 20 percent and simultaneously increase output per worker. The Colony installed three sawmills, re-equipped the coal mines, built fifty coke ovens, new bridges, and railroads, and after a year in operation had set up a completely autonomous industrial colony.

Those colonists (the 'White Feather Groups') who, disillusioned with the 'socialist paradise,' made efforts to leave Russia were treated harshly. It took all winter for some to get out of Russia; they were stranded periodically and finally reached Riga, Latvia, destitute and hungry. A graphic and moving story by one of these colonists, a young woman, written at the request of the the United States Consulate in Riga is in the U.S. State Department files.[10]

PURE CONCESSIONS IN REMOTE AREAS

The Anglo-Russian Grumant Company continued to operate its coal concession in the 'no-man's land' of Spitzbergen. Another concession was made in 1923 to the Polar Star Company to operate other mines on Spitzbergen Island and railroads in the Murmansk area. Lena Goldfields operated a Kiselev coal mine and two Yegushin anthracite mines (numbers 1 and 5) in Siberia as part of its 1925 concession.

The Tetyukhe (Bryner) concession operated coal mines in the Far East, as did Japanese concession operators. Only twenty coal mines were in operation in the Far East in 1924; of these six were state-owned enterprises, six operated by Japanese concessionaires on Sakhalin Island, and one operated as a concession by Bryner and Company near Vladivostock.[11] In 1924 the state mines in the Far East produced about 46 percent of total output of coal and lignite while the privately operated concessions (Japanese and Bryner) produced about 54 percent.

The two Japanese Sakhalin coal concessions granted under Protocol B of the 1925 U.S.S.R.-Japanese convention became an important export source later in the 1920's, their export rising from 4,000 metric tons in 1925 to

[10]　U.S. State Dept. Decimal File, 316–110–795/801. However, the autonomous industrial colony (AIK) at Kuzbas was not broken up until late 1927, when few of the original Americans remained (316–108–391).

[11]　U.S. Embassy in Tokyo, Report 13, March 1925. This last concession is of interest in relation to the 'arm's length hypothesis.' One of the partners was suspected of being in the pay of the Soviets (Decimal File 861.00/11270).

115,500 in 1929.[12] However, total Far East coal and lignite output was only about 3 percent of the total Soviet production.

In 1920 the independent Georgian government concluded an agreement for the operation of the Tkwarozly region coal mines with the Italian company ILVA Alti Forni e Acciaierie d'Italia s.p.a. The Soviet government offered ILVA a renewal of the agreement, but this was not taken up by the company. The mines, although investigated by several commissions, remained dormant until at least 1928.[13]

TECHNICAL ASSISTANCE FROM GERMANY

Pure technical-assistance (Type III) agreements for the coal mines and particularly Donugol, were sought prior to any others. In the latter half of 1925, a commission of Ruhr industrialists and economic experts began examining the Donbas coal mines. This commission was invited by the U.S.S.R.,

> . . . because it wanted objective economists to make a report to industrialists in Germany on the exact conditions in the Don district . . . and to confer . . . on the basis for collaboration between the two countries.[14]

Dr. Rechlin, a member of the commission, argued that such collaboration was entirely possible because the coal deposits of the two countries were similar from the geological and physical viewpoints; consequently the same type of coal-cutting machines could be used in the Donbas as in the Ruhr. By 1926, Thyssen A-G and other coal-machinery-making firms in Germany were receiving orders for equipment, and coke ovens had been ordered from Koppers A-G in Essen. The anticipated purchase of the Rhenish-Westphalian Metal Products and Machine Company, manufacturers of locomotives in Dusseldorf, by the U.S.S.R. did not materialize.

The Soviets were not completely satisfied with German techniques and in 1926 appointed a commission to make an extensive study of comparative coal mining methods in Germany, France, England, and the United States. 'The result was a victory for American methods and engineers. . . . '[15]

TECHNICAL ASSISTANCE CONTRACTS
WITH STUART, JAMES AND COOKE, INC.

In early 1927, Amtorg reported that American coal-mining methods and a major emphasis on mechanization were to be adopted throughout Soviet coal mines. Concurrently with this announcement, Charles E. Stuart, of Stuart,

[12] Amtorg, *op. cit.*, V, 354; and *Times* (London), January 11, 1926. The agreement on Sakhalin coal concessions is in U.S. State Dept. Decimal File, 316–176–426.
[13] U.S. Legation in Warsaw, Report 1699, April 23, 1928 (316–136–1244).
[14] U.S. Embassy in Berlin, Report 1407, August 17, 1926 (316–136–1232).
[15] Amtorg, *op. cit.*, II, No. 7, p. 2.

James and Cooke, Inc., coal-mining consultants in the United States, was making a preliminary inspection of Soviet coal mines:

> . . . with a view to their mechanization in accordance with the most modern American practice and methods. Mr. Stuart stated that several shafts will be operated under the direction of the firm to serve as model mines for the purpose of gradually extending the methods and systems.[16]

Between 1927 and 1930, Stuart, James and Cooke, Inc., signed four technical-assistance contracts with Soviet trusts. Two of these were with coal trusts (Donugol and Moskvugol), the latter for technical assistance in the reorganization of the Dubovaya Balka and October Revolution coal mines in the Moscow area.

Charles E. Stuart was an active promoter of American assistance to the Soviet Union. In a speech before the 1928 annual convention of mining engineers, he stressed '. . . . the traditional friendship between the two countries,' and suggested that 'America will surely play the foremost part in the rehabilitation of Russia.'[17]

A year later, after the four technical-assistance contracts had been implemented, Stuart was even more generous in his praise of Soviet officials. In 1928 he was allowed to make a 10,000-mile trip throughout the U.S.S.R. and recorded it on movie film later shown to the American Association of Mining Engineers.[18]

The Stuart Company drafted a complete five-year reorganization plan for Donugol, modernizing equipment, layout, and working methods. Twelve American engineers, sent to Kharkhov in 1927 to implement the program, were supplied with Russian assistants, clerks and draftsmen. One year later the staff of Russian engineering assistants was arrested by the OGPU. Despite this demoralizing episode, the rationalization continued through the late 1920s and 1930s. At first German and then American coal mining equipment was utilized. Later Soviet-made equipment, manufactured under the Goodman, the Casablancas, and similar technical-assistance agreements, was used. A similar three-year reorganization plan was implemented by the Stuart company for the Moskvugol coal fields, in the Moscow sub-basin.[19]

---

[16]   Amtorg, *op. cit.*, II, No. 7, p. 2.

[17]   *New York Times*, February 23, 1928. Although there were no diplomatic relations between the two countries, the Soviets were allowed to operate *Amtorg* in New York, supposedly to facilitate trading relations. Saul Bron was the president of Amtorg.

[18]   *New York World*, March 3, 1929. Stuart was hardly a prophet concerning Soviet intentions. For example, he stated: 'The prevailing opinion in the United States that the U.S.S.R. while endeavoring to bring foreign capital into its enterprises has the intention of seizing those enterprises in the future, is entirely wrong.'

[19]   *Torgovo-Promyshlennaya Gazeta*, No. 246, October 24, 1929. *Izvestia*, No. 128, June 8, 1927. Stuart, James and Cooke, Inc., had similar contracts with Yurt, the

ROBERTS & SCHAEFER AND ALLEN & GARCIA
CONTRACTS

In mid-1929 a Type III technical-assistance agreement was signed between Donugol and Roberts & Schaefer, mining consultants and engineers of Chicago. The agreement was to sink five new coal shafts in the Donbas to be completed within thirteen months, and to provide a production of 3.5 million tons per year. The firm manufactured the equipment, installed it in the mines, and brought the mines into operation. For this purpose engineers were sent from Chicago to the Donbas, and a number of Donugol engineers were sent to the United States for training.[20]

Another United States firm of mining consultants, Allen & Garcia, was given a three-year contract with Donugol in late 1927 to plan and build new coal pits in the Donetz Basin, including both surface buildings and shafts.[21] Two years later, in 1929, the firm received a second contract with Donugol to plan and build three new coal pits within three years. The firm provided thirty-five United States mining engineers and accepted ten Soviet engineers per year for training in the United States.[22]

In addition to contracts between American consulting firms and Donugol, there were a number of individual contracts between specialist American engineers and Giproshaft, the Institute for Designing Coal Mines, and Kuzbastrust.

In 1929, under the reorganization plan of the Donetz coal trust, three new large capacity shafts were sunk, with an aggregate output of 1.65 million tons of coal. The one in the Gorlov district had a capacity of 650,000 tons, the one in the Dolzhansk area an annual capacity of 600,000 tons, and the one in the Krindachev area a capacity of 400,000 tons per annum.

For the year 1929–30, some fourteen new shafts were planned, the largest with an output of 1.6 million tons per year. Brukh, chief engineer of Stein A-G coal mine in Germany, designed the 1.6-million-ton shaft in the Scheglov district, and Thyssen A-G designed a similar shaft in the Gorlov district, under the supervision of engineer Drost. Another million-ton shaft was designed by Stuart, James, and Cooke, Inc.[23]

---

southern ore Trust; Kiseltrust, a Urals mining trust, and the Kuzbastrust, in the Kuzbas coal fields. The company apparently viewed these undertakings as pure concessions (316–136–372).

When Stuart, James and Cooke, Inc., issued their report on the reorganization of the coal mines in 1931, V. I. Mezhlauk ordered 10,000 copies to be printed and distributed to all executives down to foreman level in the coal and related industries. [E. M. Friedman, *Russia in Transition* (London: Allen & Unwin, 1933).]

[20] *Ekonomicheskaya Zhizn*, No. 143, June 26, 1929.
[21] U.S. State Dept. Decimal File, 316–136–1242.
[22] *Pravda* (Leningrad), No. 246, October 25, 1929.
[23] *Bank for Russian Trade Review*, II, No. 7 (July 1929), p. 10.

Lomov, a member of the Central Executive Committee, pointed out in 1929 that reconstruction of the Donetz Coal Basin was impossible without outside aid, as only 350 trained Russian engineers existed for 275 coal and anthracite shafts. The gap would have to be made up with foreign engineers, whom '. . . we are trying to employ on a large scale.'[24] He added that shafts were being designed by two German firms (Thyssen and Stein) and a number of American firms, and that an agreement was about to be concluded with an American firm to develop anthracite shafts. 'In this way we shall be able to solve the problem facing the Donetz Basin.'[25]

RESULTS OF THE MECHANIZATION
OF COAL MINES

Russian coal mines before 1923 were highly labor-intensive; there was little, if any, mechanization even of an elementary nature. In 1923 the Donetz Coal Trust imported a few Sullivan coal cutters,[26] followed by seventeen in 1925 and another forty-five in 1926.

In August 1923, the purchase and installation of mining machinery from the United States was placed on a more formal and, from the Soviet viewpoint, more satisfactory basis. J. A. Meyerovitch, who represented in the U.S.S.R. a group of Milwaukee and Chicago equipment manufacturers including Sullivan and Allis-Chalmers, informed the United States Riga Legation that a concession had been concluded between the group and the U.S.S.R. Under this agreement the group was to arrange the export of Russian mineral products and to supply American mining equipment on a matching basis. However, Meyerovitch had the distinct impression that the Soviets were more interested in political recognition than in trade.[27]

Coal-mining equipment purchases were stepped up in 1925–6 and included a significant number of German and American heavy (178) and light (125) coal cutters, conveyors (30), hoists (32), and electric and gasoline tractors and chargers. Both the Sullivan Company and Krupp, the leading sellers, sent engineers to install and introduce the equipment to Soviet miners. Westinghouse installed electric tractors, and Jeffry front-end loaders, while Soviet purchasing commissions visited the United States.[28]

---

[24] 'Debates on the Five Year Plan,' *Pravda* (Moscow), April 28, 1929.

[25] *Ibid.*

[26] The contract was arranged by Meyerovitch, the Sullivan Co. representative in the U.S.S.R. It involved $210,000 worth of coal mining machinery, on terms of two-thirds cash and one-third in four months, one of the earliest trade credits granted by a Western company (316–130–1274).

[27] U.S. State Dept. Decimal File, 316–131–719. See also chap. 16 on RAITCO.

[28] Amtorg, *op. cit.*, II, No. 16 and No. 19.

Table 3-3   INTRODUCTION OF THE MANUFACTURE
OF COAL MINING MACHINERY

Item No.*	Description	Production (Units) 1927–8	1928–9	First Soviet Output
Group A:	First produced in 1928–9			
26	Coal cutting machines:			
	Heavy	None	11	1928–9
	Light	None	48	1928–9
28	Pick hammers	None	29	1928–9
29	Mine ventilators (stationary)	None	206	1928–9
Group B:	First produced in 1930 and after			
13	Motors for electric mine locomotives	None	None	1932
17	Motors for coal cutting machines	None	None	1931
30	Mine ventilators (mobile)	None	None	1933
32	Mine safety lamps	None	None	1931
39	Grizzly screens for coke	None	None	1930
142	Belt conveyors	None	None	1930

Source: A. Gershenkron, *A Dollar Index of Soviet Machinery Output, 1927–8 to 1937,* (Santa Monica: RAND Corp., 1951).
* Refers to the category of machinery given in Gerschenkron.

There was no production of any type of coal mining machinery in the U.S.S.R. until the end of the decade. Priority was then given to the establishment of coal-cutter and underground-drill production, and Type III agreements were made with two Western companies: Goodman Manufacturing, Inc. of Chicago and Hilaturas Casablancas S.A. of Spain.[29] Production

Table 3-4   EARLY MECHANIZATION OF THE
DONETZ COAL BASIN, 1922–8

Year	Number of Machines in Use* (all imported)	Metric Tons of Coal Production per Machine (per year)	Production per Worker (per month)
1922–3	32	6,264	5.8
1923–4	36	7,541	7.2
1924–5	48	10,682	8.7
1925–6	90	13,007	10.5
1926–7	225	14,196	11.5
1927–8	348	14,300	12.4

Source: L. Liberman, *Trud i Byt Gorniskov Donbassa* (Moscow: 1929), pp. 97–8.
* Heavy coal cutters only.

[29] *Pravda*, No. 246, October 25, 1929.

of electric motors was undertaken after 1930 (Group B) to a General Electric design described by them as unique and used only in Soviet-made coal cutters.[30]

The effect of imported and Soviet-made coal-cutting machinery was significant. In the Donetz Basin the number of coal-cutting machines in operation increased from none in 1921 to 348 in 1927–8, the last year in which the U.S.S.R. was completely dependent on imported equipment. In the peat mining industry reliance was completely on imported drag lines, and it was not until the 1930s that the hydro-peat method, using specially designed General Electric motors, was introduced.[31]

Increase in production per machine from 6,264 metric tons in 1922–3 to 14,300 metric tons per machine in 1927–8 (table 3–4) testifies to the success of the Stuart, James and Cooke rationalization scheme and to the efficient training of workers and installation of equipment by Western manufacturers. In terms of output-per-worker, the increase was also significant: from 5.8 tons per worker *per month* to 12.4 tons in 1927–8, compared to the United States average of 48 tons per worker per month.

Table 3–5 DONETZ BASIN: CHANGES IN NUMBER OF SHAFTS, TOTAL OUTPUT AND MINE AVERAGES, 1913 TO 1926–7

Date	Number of Shafts	Production (in millions of metric tons)	Average per Mine (in metric tons)
1913	1,200	25.3	21,083
1921–2	954	7.2	7,547
1922–3	577	8.1	14,038
1923–4	591	12.2	20,642
1924–5	238	12.5	52,521
1925–6	377	19.6	51,989
1926–7	480	24.5	51,042

Sources: 1913 to 1926–7 U.S. State Dept. Decimal File, 316–136–1304 (based on Central Statistical Office data). Not available after 1926–7.

The effect of Type III technical-assistance agreements can be traced very clearly in table 3–5 covering Donetz Basin output from 1913 to 1926–7. In 1913, 1,200 shafts produced a total of 25 million tons of coal, an average of 21,083 metric tons per shaft per year. The catastrophic decline in production through 1921–2 is followed by the policy of concentration; coincident with introduction of the American and German equipment and training in 1923, there is a climb in output to 12 million tons. The reduction of shafts from 591 to

[30] *Monogram,* November 1943.
[31] *Ibid.*

238 in the same period that output was increasing was due to concentration of the newly imported equipment into comparatively few mines, increasing the output per mine while ruthlessly closing down the non-mechanized mines. In 1925, beginning with German reorganization assistance and continuing with large imports of mechanical coal cutters and conveyors, output increased; and the number of operating shafts increased as the mechanization program spread. The dramatic rise in mine output accompanies the first introduction of mechanical equipment, and the output stabilizes at 51,000 tons per shaft at this date, indicating a methodical program of mechanization and training in an increasing number of mines.

Whereas in 1922–3 only 200,000 tons of coal were mined by machine in the Donbas by 1928–9 about 30 percent (or 7.6 million tons) were machine-mined; and the U.S.S.R. had not at that time begun to manufacture coal cutters.

The Warren Coal Corporation, coal distributors of Boston, concluded an agreement with Amtorg in May 1929 covering the distribution of 160,000 tons of Soviet anthracite per year in the United States. Warren became sole distributor for Russian anthracite in New York and the New England States.[32]

In critical stagnation at the beginning of the decade, the coal mines, technically backward and with inefficient, unskilled labor, were reorganized according to United States coal-mining procedures utilizing first German and later American coal-mining equipment. At the very end of the decade, arrangements were made with Spanish and American companies for technical assistance in the manufacture of coal-mining equipment, all of which had been previously imported. Pure concessions were not of major importance in the aggregate, except that Union Minière operated a number of large Donbas mines at a time when the majority of these mines were either closed or being re-equipped by German (later American) engineers. However, more remote mines, in the Kuzbas and the Far East were extensively operated by foreign concessionaires.

---

[32] Agreement is in U.S. State Dept. Decimal File, 316–136–1285.

CHAPTER FOUR

Early Development of the Soviet Metallurgical Industry

THE metallurgical industry, *primus inter pares* of the 'commanding heights' of the economy, was kept well within the control of the planning organs and the Party. The decade of the 1920s, which has been called by Clark the 'restoration period'[1] to distinguish it from the massive new metallurgical construction of the 1930s, suggests that only limited technical and economic advances could be made without Western technical assistance.

THE SOUTHERN ORE TRUST (YURT)

Yurt controlled iron ore in Krivoi Rog and manganese in the Nikopol deposits. After 1924 there was an agreement with Rawack and Grunfeld, of Germany, for the operation of these manganese and iron ore mines. Rawack and Grunfeld also held a monopoly for the sale of all South Russian iron ore and manganese in foreign markets. In 1924–5 the company sold 21 million poods of iron and manganese ores to Germany, Italy, Belgium, and the United Kingdom.[2] The Port of Nikolaev was equipped with ore loaders by the company to handle the export of these ores.

Only six mines were operated at the beginning of the year. The major restoration of the Krivoi Rog iron ore and manganese mines took place after 1925 under predominantly German technical assistance. In December 1925, fourteen iron ore and three manganese mines were reopened; these were tsarist mines closed since the Revolution. The mining equipment was purchased in the United Kingdom and Germany by Yurt, on nine months' credit. Company engineers from the United Kingdom and Germany assembled the equipment and put it into operation.

---

[1] M. Gardner Clark, *The Economics of Soviet Steel* (Cambridge: Harvard, 1956), p. 65.
[2] U.S. Consulate in Hamburg, Report 360, October 12, 1925 (316-108-1544).

At this point the mines at Krivoi Rog and Nikopol were inspected by a German industrial delegation headed by Steinitz, of Rawack and Grunfeld, which expressed the opinion that the newly equipped mines could produce 500 million poods of iron ore and 150 million poods of manganese within five years and that the members of the delegation were prepared to provide assistance to reach that objective. Its opinion was that new equipment to fulfill the five-year program need only consist of electrical mining equipment; Yurt was instructed by Vesenkha to consider the German suggestions, which were later implemented. It was also agreed that credit would be advanced by Germany to Yurt on the basis of the proceeds from the anticipated export of manganese ore from Nikopol.[3]

In October 1927 Yurt concluded a technical-assistance contract with Stuart, James and Cooke, Inc., for the further preparation of projects and consulting services.[4]

RECONSTRUCTION IN THE METALLURGICAL SECTOR

The position of the Russian iron and steel industry in 1920 was almost unbelievably bad. In 1913 there had been 160 blast furnaces operating in Russia; but in 1920 only 12 were operating intermittently. In 1913 there had been 168 Martin steel furnaces; but in 1920 only 8 were operating intermittently. Production of iron ore was 6 million poods, compared to 551 million poods in 1913. Production of cast iron was 6 million poods, compared to 231 million in 1916 and 6.6 million poods in 1718 under Peter the Great.

Production of rolled iron was 6.4 million poods, compared to 222 million in 1916, and so on. Of sixty-six cast-iron foundries available, only two were in production. However, employment had not fallen in the same proportion: whereas 257,000 were employed in metal works in 1913, there were 159,000 so employed in 1920 despite the catastrophic decline in output.[5]

The metallurgical sector, however, received comparatively few concessions until the Type III technical-assistance agreements of 1927-9, which were a prelude to the Five-Year Plan construction. Although, production had partially recovered by the late 1920s, technologically the industry had remained at the level of the tsarist era. Independently attempted technical advances backfired and forced the Soviets to seek out Western assistance—another proof that Soviet development and technical progress in the twenties were essentially dependent on Western technical aid. Soviet-originated projects

[3]   U.S. Consulate in Hamburg, Report 417, December 12, 1925 (316–108–1582).
[4]   *Torgovo-Promyshlennaya Gazeta*, No. 229, October 7, 1927.
[5]   These figures taken from a confidential report in U.S. State Dept. Decimal File (316–107–359). Also see report from General Wrangel's staff, December 1921 (316–107–569).

MAP 4-1   METALLURGICAL PLANTS IN SOUTH RUSSIA, 1926

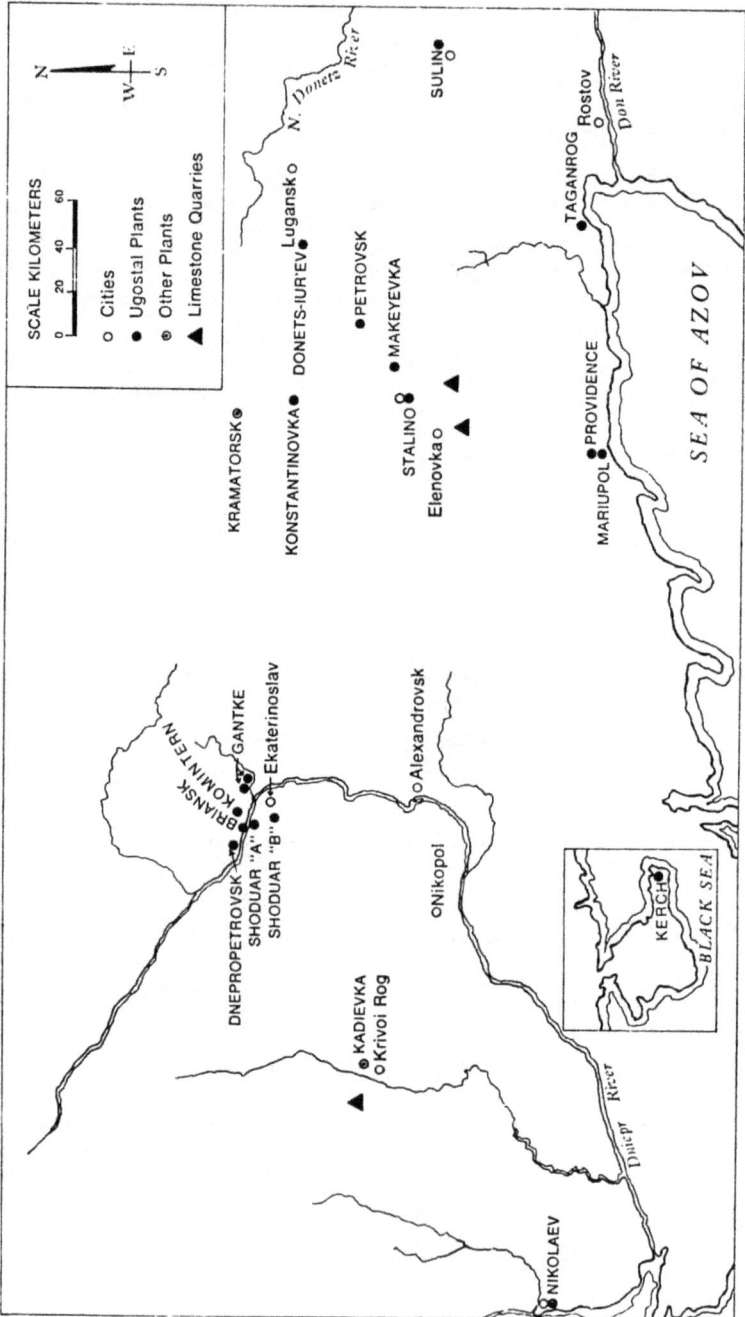

were fumbling and technically inept, and made little contribution to reconstruction or development. The only successful Soviet work of the period was
the restoration of seven small blast furnaces—not a particularly difficult
task—and these, as Clark points out,

> . . . are almost never mentioned in Soviet technical or metallurgical
> literature. Perhaps the Soviets are ashamed of these first attempts, which
> certainly look like pygmies beside the giants built during the First Five
> Year Plan.[6]

The Donbas sector is by far the most important of the iron- and steel-
producing regions. As shown in figure 4–1, Ugostal (Southern Steel Trust),
formed in 1923, divided the inherited plants into four groups: the Donetz
group proper, at the east end of the basin; the Ekaterinoslav group, at the
western end of the basin and north of the iron-ore fields of the Krivoi Rog;
the southern group of plants on the Sea of Azov; and the Kramatorsk and
Hartman locomotive plants.

The Donetz group metallurgical industry was in a sorry state in 1921. All
plants were closed except for Makeevka and Petrovsk. The latter had no
blast furnaces in operation, and rolling was limited to available steel slab
stocks. Whereas more than 233 million poods had been produced in all Russia
in 1916, only 7 million poods were produced in 1920[7] (i.e., about 3 percent),
and much of this was too bad in quality for use. In the Donetz area the position
was even worse, with production less than .5 percent of the prewar level.

Contraction of the metallurgical industry continued into mid-1922. Most
of the Donbas steel plants remained closed, reportedly because of a lack of
purchase orders and working capital. Only South Briansk and Chaudoir
operated on a continuous basis; Petrovsk, the largest, continued with one
furnace working continually and the others either intermittently or not at all.
Makeevka was partially closed in 1922.

In early 1923, the mines supplying Petrovsk became idle, as did the open-
hearth steel-making plant. The plant was in fair condition technically but now
lacked skilled labor. Makeevka was completely closed, although the workers
were retained.

---

[6] Clark, *op. cit.*, p. 82. Soviet restoration was limited to the simplest of repair work;
even furnace lining (a skilled but simple task) was difficult for them. For example,
the Perin and Marshall engineers stated that in 1926 the unfinished No. 5 blast
furnace at Petrovsk required only a 'comparatively small expenditure' to complete.
The furnace had been under construction prior to 1914 and 'nearly all of the metal
work (had) been erected for the furnace proper, stoves and skip bridge,' but 'much
of the piping' was still lying on the ground where it had rested since 1914. The
inference is that completion was beyond the technical capabilities of Ugostal.
[Perin and Marshall, *Report on Improvement of the Ugostal Steel Plants of South
Russia* (New York: 1926), p. 42.] Petrovsk No. 5 was not working as late as October
1928. (Kruglyakova, *op. cit.*, p. 70.)

[7] *Ekonomicheskaya Zhizn*, No. 106, May 18, 1921. Numerous articles in this and
other journals in the period 1920–2 indicate a pitiable condition.

Table 4-1   UGOSTAL (SOUTHERN STEEL TRUST) PRODUCTION, 1913–28, DONETZ GROUP

Plant Name		Output (metric tons)						
		1913			1923-4			1927-8
Prerevolution	Ugostal	Pig Iron	O.H. steel	Rolled steel	Pig Iron	O.H. steel	Rolled steel	Pig Iron
Neurissiche A-G	Stalino	276,230	231,290	208,680	154,282	92,179	69,861	302,924
Briansk-Alexander	Petrovsk	348,200	315,165	279,040	—	—	—	296,293
Société Minière et Metallurgique 'Union'	Makeevka	229,940	154,835	128,790	—	12,604	12,017	200,881
Alchevsk	Donetz-Iur'ev	246,990	250,245	212,160	—	—	—	223,841
Société des Tuileries	Frunze	60,110	63,170	60,210	—	—	—	58,316

Sources:

1. Perin and Marshall, *Report on Improvement of the Ugostal Steel Plants of South Russia* (New York: 1926).
2. ——, *Report on the Steel Industry of South Russia* (New York: 1926).

One widely held view was that Ugostal should be disbanded and all the South Russian steel works closed. The area was being worked at a loss. There were few orders; most were being placed abroad. However, the trust employed 27,000 people: sufficient argument to keep the mills in intermittent operation! A compromise was reached by formally closing Makeevka and discharging one half of the workers while transferring the other half to the Ugostal coal mines.[8]

In the next three or four years, several blast furnaces were rebuilt, with Western assistance and by 1927-8 pig-iron output was increased in four of the ten plants which constituted the prewar Donetz group. The Donetz group now produced more than 1 million tons of pig iron (compared to 1.6 million in 1913), including output from blast furnaces at Briansk-Alexander, the Donetz-Iur'ev works, and the Frunze (old Société des Tuileries) works. In 1928 all output from the Donetz section of Ugostal, the largest single group of metallurgical works, was from pre-Revolutionary plants which had been put back into operation.

The second group of works forming the Ugostal trust was in the Ekaterinoslav area, at the western end of the Donbas and to the northeast of the Krivoi Rog iron-ore deposits. This group comprised six prerevolutionary plants, only three of which (Dnieprovsk, Briansk, and Gdantke) had been pig-iron producers with blast furnaces. Of these three only Briansk was producing pig-iron in 1923-4; neither the Dnieprovsk or the Gdantke were operating as pig-iron producers. Consequently in 1923-4 only one of the six works situated near the Krivoi Rog iron ore deposits was producing any pig iron.

Two works, the Dnieprovsk and the Lenin (formerly the Shoduar 'A') were producing small quantities of open-hearth steel and rolled steel products.

In sum, this group was only producing about 140,000 tons of rolled steel products in 1923-4, compared to almost 826,000 tons in 1913.

The third group of Ugostal metallurgical works was the Azov Sea group of four prerevolutionary plants which produced 400,000 tons of pig iron in 1913. No blast furnaces in this group were operating in 1923-4, and only two produced any rolled steel: Zhdanov and Taganrog. As Taganrog produced no slab steel, it was probably importing slabs from the Zhdanov works (formerly the Marioupol), (table 4-3).

The old Providence works was first merged with the Zhdanov, a few miles to the South, and then closed down.

The Kertch works was first built by French and Belgian capital in 1900, but the owners had closed it down as unprofitable after a few years.[9] The

[8] *Pravda*, No. 48, March 3, 1923.
[9] Clark, *op. cit.*, p. 157.

Table 4–2 UGOSTAL (SOUTHERN STEEL TRUST) PRODUCTION, 1913–28, EKATERINOSLAV GROUP

Plant Name		Output (metric tons)						
		1913			1923–4			1927–8
Prerevolution	Ugostal	Pig Iron	O.H. steel	Rolled steel	Pig Iron	O.H. steel	Rolled steel	Pig Iron
Dnieprovsk	Dzerzhinsk	417,165	386,660	330,270	—	13,305	17,433	426,225
Briansk	Petrovsk	408,975	325,370	259,530	132,899	81,523	79,143	466,964
Shoduar 'A'	Lenin	—	100,730	39,205	—	51,084	17,385	—
Shoduar 'B'	Comintern	—	—	47,305	—	—	—	—
Gdantke	Karl Liebknecht	—	—	—	—	—	17,391	—
Krivoi Rog	Krivoi Rog	75,595	—	—	—	—	—	—

Sources: Perin and Marshall, *Report on Improvement of the Ugostal Steel Plants of South Russia* (New York: 1926); V. I. Kruglyakova (ed.), *Sbornik statisticheskikh svedenii* . . ., pp. 70–71.

Table 4-3   UGOSTAL (SOUTHERN STEEL TRUST) PRODUCTION, 1913–28, AZOV GROUP

Plant Name		Output (metric tons)								
		1913			1923–4			1927–8		
Prerevolution	Ugostal	Pig Iron	O.H. steel	Rolled steel	Pig Iron	O.H. steel	Rolled steel	Pig Iron	O.H. steel	Rolled steel
La Providence Russe Providence	} combined	165,670	173,695	145,180	None	None	None	None	None	None
La Providence Russe Zhdanov		69,675	78,230	53,750	None	56,746	28,650	180,648	None	None
Société Metallurgique de Taganrog	Taganrog (Andreev)	154,480	171,105	144,350	None	None	3,269	None	57,000	49,828
Société Metallurgique de Taganrog	Kertch (Voikov)	9,925	815	—	None	None	None	None	None	None

Source: Perin and Marshall, *Report on Improvement of the Ugostal Steel Plants of South Russia* (New York: 1926).

equipment had survived until 1925 in good condition, and the Soviets reopened the works according to plans drawn up by German and American engineers. The first blast furnace was ready for blowing-in by 1929. The cost of reconstruction, however, greatly exceeded even the most pessimistic estimates, and a search was put under way for the 'criminals' who had miscalculated. The major problem was that the furnaces would not smelt local iron ores.

> The failure of the Kertch works is typical of the actual conditions of the new industrial enterprises which have been organized by inexperienced and inefficient persons for the sake of political propaganda and without any regard of the conditions under which the new plant will have to work.[10]

By late 1929 only two of the projected three blast furnaces had been built, and capital costs already had exceeded 66 million rubles—far in excess of the 18 million originally estimated for the whole project. The operating costs were also significantly greater as local Lipetsk 40-percent-iron ore required additional fuel, which had to be transported from the Donbas. Use of this ore required an additional nine rubles a ton for transportation.[11]

THE STRUCTURE OF UGOSTAL IN 1929

At the end of the decade, Ugostal consisted of eight plants constructed before the Revolution and one reconstructed plant, the Kertsch, whose problems have already been discussed. These plants had produced 3.2 million metric tons of pig iron in 1913, whereas in 1929 they produced less than 2.5 million, with labor productivity about 50 percent below the prewar level. Real wages had declined heavily because of the many compulsory contributions required of the plant workmen.[12]

Several smaller works were included in the trust, including the former Handtke plant, producing iron pipes, and the former Sirius and Taganorog plants, producing railroad equipment.

Although a few American and Polish engineers worked on the Ugostal plants, the bulk of the rehabilitation was carried out by German engineers working under the post-Rapallo economic-cooperation contracts between Germany and the Soviet Union.

[10]   U.S. State Dept. Decimal File, 316–139–252/8. The American and German engineers said their calculations were correct, but they had failed to take political considerations into account (316–133–858).

[11]   U.S. State Dept. Decimal File, 316–139–252/8.

[12]   Based on report from Polish Consulate General in Kharkov, June 5, 1929, from information supplied by a Polish engineer working for Ugostal and believed to be 'absolutely reliable' (316–139–251).

CONCESSION OFFERS IN METALLURGICAL CONSTRUCTION

Large new metallurgical projects and the rehabilitation of prerevolutionary plants were offered as concessions under the broadened post-1927 concessions policy.

The possibility of using the iron-ore reserves of Magnitogorsk with the extensive coking coal deposits of Kuznetsk had been discussed in Russia since the nineteenth century. The Magnitogorsk concession proposal was for a 656,000-ton-capacity plant (rolled products), to produce pig iron, together with steel-making and rolling facilities.[13] The rolling capacity of the suggested plant was planned as follows:

Heavy rails	245,000 tons
Large stanchions (structurals) . . .	33,000 tons
Medium commercial iron and pit rails .	65,500 tons
Small commercial iron products . .	230,000 tons
Casting iron	27,500 tons
	601,000 tons

A preliminary outline of the technical requirements was published. The plant was scheduled to include four blast furnaces, open-hearth and Bessemer furnaces, and rail and continuous blooming mills of American design. Three basic requirements repeatedly emphasized were that the plant had to operate on coke, that the coking had to be undertaken at Magnitogorsk from Kuznetsk coal, and that coke by-products were to be utilized. This emphasis is interesting as it relates to the basic economic weakness of the Magnitogorsk-Kuznetsk project and the technical weakness of the Soviets in coke by-products production.[14]

Given the long haul for coking-coal, transport costs were the major factor in determining profitability. Early discussion, beginning in the 1890s and continuing through the 1920s, had revolved around this point. As late as 1927, I. G. Feigin had stated that 'transportation of raw material and fuel for 2,000 kilometers is completely irrational.'[15] But the official party line was that transportation costs could not be a determinant of location in a Socialist economy, this being bourgeois Weberian theory.

The concession was offered a supply of coking coal from Kuznetsk, then being planned by Freyn and Company, Inc., at a rate of 0.38 kopecks per

---

[13]   P. I. Egorev, *The Magnitogorsky (Magnet Mountain) Metallurgical Works* (Moscow: Glavnyi Kontsessionnyi Komitet, 1929). This was the same technical arrangement suggested by Perin and Marshall two years earlier and rejected as 'technically inadequate.'

[14]   See chap. 12.

[15]   Clark, *op. cit.*, p. 215.

ton-kilometer. Consequently, any concessionaire with the temerity to under-take construction of Magnitogorsk and install coking facilities dependent on Kuznetsk coal would have been completely at the mercy of the Soviet govern-ment. By merely raising transport rates to equal costs, the Soviets could have forced the concessionaire to abandon the project. This was in addition to the immense difficulties which could have been imposed on the concessionaire as a result of the single-track, inadequate, and overcrowded railway already straining under the weight of increased coal tonnages. It will be recalled that the major problem in getting American and British relief to this part of Russia had been a heavily overburdened and inadequate rail system which required several weeks for journeys of a few hundred miles, even though large segments of the population were starving.[16]

The estimated cost of building Magnitogorsk was 171 million rubles. The plant was to employ 6,216 people and return a profit of 10 percent. The concessionaire was given the option either to operate the plant for a number of years as a pure concession and then turn it over to the Soviet government, or to operate it as a credit concession in which erection and operation would be undertaken by the Soviets and the foreign company would grant a ten-to-twelve-year credit.

Clark states that the basic rate of 0.38 kopecks, also used in the argument over the construction of the shuttle under the Five-Year Plan, was about one-third the rate charged for coal hauled the same distance in the general rate schedule. The Magnitogorsk concession lay outside the control of potential concessionaires; one could have fulfilled an agreement, stayed within the cost estimates given, and yet within a few months or years been forced to abandon the concession operation.

Whether this was the intent or not is debatable. The history of other concessions gives support to the probability that this was indeed an aim of concession policy. Chernomordik, referring to the special discount or subsidy given to the Magnitogorsk-Kuznetsk shuttle says,

> The Soviet freight-rate system, based on the principle of costs, includes the use of freight rates as a lever of economic policy.[17]

In brief, the proposed Magnitogorsk concession could have operated only with a subsidy from the Soviet government to the foreign operator. It is unlikely this subsidy would have been long continued.

The restoration of other large metallurgical complexes was offered to foreign capital.

---

[16]   H. H. Fisher, *The Famine in Soviet Russia* (New York: Macmillan, 1927), p. 173.
[17]   D. Chernomordik, 'Toward a Theory of Railroad Freight Rates,' *Voprosy Ekono-miki*, No. 9, 1948, p. 32.

The Nadejdinsky Metallurgical Works in the Urals, founded in 1894, battered in the Revolution and Civil War, subsequently operated by the American Industrial concession, and still in a bad state of repair, was one such project. The works comprised the iron ore mines about 90 kilometers away, and the Bogoslovsky brown-coal mine about 50 kilometers away, together with extensive forest properties for the manufacture of charcoal, and both narrow- and wide-gauge railroads.

Production in 1929 was less than half of 1913 output, and the ore and coal mines had received little new equipment since 1899–1907, when the plant had first been placed in operation.

The equipment was out of date. The air and gas blowers dated from between 1905 and 1913. The six rail- and sheet-rolling mills dated from the mid-1890s and were classified in 1929 as only 50-percent fit (three mills), 70-percent fit (two mills) and 90-percent fit (one mill). Even if restored to normal operation, they would have been be well below current engineering standards. The blast-furnace plant operated on a fuel comprising a mixture of brown coal, charcoal, and wood; and occasionally one furnace operated on imported Siberian coke.[18]

Employment in 1929 was over 20,000 workers, producing about 163,000 tons of pig iron per year and converting this into 155,000 tons of steel.

The product totals produced by the plant in 1929 were:

> 59,600 tons rails
> 4,600 tons roofing iron
> 2,500 tons commercial iron
> 4,000 tons pit rails (light rails).

The concession offered required the prospective concessionaire to drop rail and tire production and rebuild the plant for roofing-iron production only. In effect, this involved the construction of a completely new plant (at a cost of between 47 and 52 million rubles) which, it was claimed, would produce 11.7 to 13.0 percent return on investment.[19]

The Taganrog Metallurgical Works dated from 1895, and was in a very poor state of repair.[20] The furnaces were oil-fired and produced just over 57,000 tons of steel ingots in 1927–8. Of six rolling mills, only the roofing mill was described as satisfactory. The electrical equipment dated from the period 1895–1907.

---

[18] I. N. Kostrow, *The Nadejdinsky and Taganrog Metallurgical Works* (Moscow: Glavnyi kontsessiony komitet, 1929).

[19] *Ibid.*, p. 21.

[20] *Ibid.*, p. 30. The four Martin furnaces are described as 'exceedingly worn out and of obsolete type.' The three Thomas converters are described as 'partly demolished . . . very much out of date.'

A concession was offered to produce 160,000 tons of roofing iron per year, with the stipulation that coke ovens were to be built together with a plant for the manufacture of chemical by-products. Profit was estimated at 10 percent.

There are interesting parallels between these metallurgical concession offers. Each stipulated (Magnitogorsk and Taganrog) or involved (Nadejdinsky) the construction of coke ovens and the utilization of coke as a fuel. Without control of coking-coal deposits the concessionaire could not have controlled the operation of the metallurgical plant. Using the weapon of transport costs, the Soviets could have squeezed out the concessionaires without violating the letter of the agreement.

The profit estimates, from 10 to 13 percent, indicate a rather naïve concept of the degree of inducement required to enter a new line of endeavor. Even without political risk, as in the United States or Great Britain, an estimated annual return of 20 percent would have been more suitable.

PURE (TYPE I) CONCESSIONS IN THE METALLURGICAL INDUSTRY

Pure concessions were not a major factor in the development of the iron and steel industry, the Soviets were obviously unwilling to allow Western elements to operate freely in the most strategic of the 'commanding heights.'

The Russian-American Steel Works was established in the Soviet Union by emigrant American workers in 1921. They were able to double output in the first year and then ran into problems; insufficient orders were forthcoming from the trust, and the works was diverted into supplying small orders for private firms and repairing automobiles and tools. There were insufficient raw materials—about 30 percent of the steel received was unfit for use—and shortages of oil and coal.[21]

An early Type I concession, perhaps better described as a commune, was granted to 3,000 emigrant American workers about 1922. The Nadejdinsky mines, in Perm okrug, and later part of the Uralmed trust was reportedly being operated along with associated coal mines and forests. They were granted 20,000 dessiatins of land for agricultural use and a loan (at 7 percent) of 350,000 gold rubles for working capital. Each worker was required to bring $100 in cash and $100 worth of tools. The government purchased 50 percent of production and the balance accrued to the concession.[22]

At least two metallurgical works were leased to Russian concessionaires. The Randrun foundry, at Omsk, was leased back to its former owner in

---

[21]   *Pravda*, No. 79, April 12, 1923.
[22]   Haywood contract with the Soviet of Labor and Defense (316–111–1270). See chap. 3 for details of the Haywood (American Industrial Corp.) contract.

October 1921 on condition that he undertake the necessary repairs to get it back into production. As soon as the foundry was back in operation, the former owner was again ejected and the Soviets took over operations.[23]

Another large works, the Goloborodov—part of the Eketerinslav group in southeast Russia—was leased for five years with a rent based on output.[24]

In 1924 the Viksun Metal Works, in the Urals, nominally part of the Gomza trust, was leased for forty years to the German firm, Bergman, on a pure concession basis. Bergman was required to restore the equipment and put the plant in operating condition before May 1925. Forests, mineral rights, and mines over a 250-square-verst area were handed over to Bergman for exploitation. The company had the right to hire and fire, with the restriction that foreign personnel were not to comprise more than 25 percent of workmen, 45 percent of foremen, and 75 percent of technical personnel. The only assistance from the Soviets was to provide labor. The concessionaire was required to make payments, beginning in 1928, to comprise 30 percent of the final manufactures (heavy machinery, etc.) or semi-manufactured materials and minerals output in the lease years three through ten. A minimum conversion of five million poods of ore into metal was required, with a corresponding manufactured output. The concessionaire was required to manufacture heavy machinery and various metal goods including guns, shells, and small arms.[25]

The Lena concession operated the blast furnaces and steel works at Sissert and Revda, in the Urals. The company first renovated seven iron ore mines, three limestone quarries, and two quartz quarries in Polevskoi rayon, installed new iron works plant at the Seversky blast furnace, and renovated the Revda iron and steel works. By 1927 the annual combined output of these works was 100,000 tons of roofing iron, almost 30,000 tons of wire, 1,400 tons of nails, and 3,000 tons of cast iron shapes. This was achieved in a plant producing nothing when taken over in 1925 by Lena, who spent more than $2.5 million on imported equipment for these works.

The available evidence indicates that foreign labor was not generally utilized—apart from that in these pure concessions—before about 1927. The Polish Foreign Ministry concluded as late as mid-1929 that:

---

[23] U.S. State Dept. Decimal File, 316–107–203.

[24] U.S. State Dept. Decimal File, 316–107–52.

[25] The agreement contained a clause that military production could be exported, so it may be assumed that this agreement was part of the wider German-Russian military co-operation of the 1920s. This was not one of the GEFU shell-making plants (316–139–191).

There was also a report from the United States Riga Consulate in late 1923 to the effect that a number of the Krivoi Rog coal and iron ore mines had been turned over to the munitions firm Crouardi for the production of armaments. (U.S. State Dept. Decimal File, 569–3–99.)

Very few foreigners are among the technical personnel of the JUGOSTAL; but such foreigners as are employed are engineers or skilled workmen from Germany or Czechoslovakia, and occasionally Poles.[26]

The Perin and Marshall report[27] on the reconstruction of the South Russia iron and steel industry was centered around reconstruction and enlargement of one works, the Petrovsk, while including the Stalino, Makeevka, and Donetz-Iur'ev works in a subsidiary role; the others were scheduled to be closed down.

In essence, the Perin and Marshall report proposed three new 750-ton skiploaded blast furnaces and completion of an existing 600-ton furnace to replace smaller hand-fed units. Steel was to be made in three departments: an open-hearth plant with three modern open hearths replacing four obsolete furnaces, a new Bessemer plant, and a duplex plant to make steel from an all hot-metal charge (to overcome the scrap shortage).

The major technological change suggested by Perin and Marshall was installation of a powerful blooming mill to break large ingots into slabs before rolling them into finished products—a very successful process in the United States but not then introduced in Europe or Russia.

> The (consequent) large supply of relatively cheap billets and blooms will permit the small and medium shape, merchant and sheet mills of the Donbass steel works to be remodeled so as to reduce the amount of work which these mills must do with a reduction in labor and an increase in tonnage.[28]

The report pointed out that these proposals would not interfere with existing Ugostal plans but would generate a substantial increase in capacity at reasonable cost. The metallurgy of the duplex process lent itself to the high-sulfur coking coal available. Semi-skilled labor could be used, as was typical in the United States.

A contract was concluded in October 1927 between Percival Farquhar (an American financier) and the Soviet government to develop the Donetz Basin. The contract was based on the findings of the Perin and Marshall report.

[26]   Report of the Polish Consul General at Kharkov, June 5, 1929 (316–139–255/8). This was reasonably accurate for the period before 1929; T. H. McCormick had a two-year contract as technical director of the Poltava steel mills for 1928–1930, and the Frank Chase Company, Inc., had a contract in 1928 to reorganize the foundry department of the Podolsk plant, but no others, except the Freyn-Gipromez technical agreements, have been traced at this time.

[27]   Perin and Marshall, *Report on Improvement of the Ugostal Steel Plants of South Russia* (New York: 1926). This was one of three reports prepared for Percival Farquhar in his negotiations for a large concession based on the Don railroad and metallurgical industries. The Farquhar documents covering these negotiations are in the Hoover Institute Library, Stanford University.

[28]   *Ibid.*, pp. 59–60.

In order to implement this agreement, Farquhar proposed the formation of a Delaware company, the United American German Corporation, which would administer the contract. The capital was to be $2 million: one half subscribed by Percival Farquhar, Ingersoll-Rand Company, and Dillon Reed, and the other half by Vereinigte Stahlwerke and Otto Wolff in Germany.

The contract consisted of two parts: first, a definite agreement to construct a large, modern one-million-ton-capacity iron and steel mill with all ancillary equipment 'according to American standards, specifications and patents in the coal and iron ore district of South Russia';[29] and second, optional for the company, was the reconstruction of the railroad transportation system of the Don 'on American standards,' together with the construction of iron ore concentration plants at Krivoi Rog and elevators, docks and shipyards at Stalingrad.

Under the first part of the contract, the United American German Corporation was to receive drafts from the Soviet State Bank to the amount of $40 million, bearing 6 percent interest, amortizable over a period of six years. The Corporation would then sell in the United States $20 million worth of 6-percent debentures 'guaranteed unconditionally (as to) principal and interest by the German Government.' The balance of the capital would be provided by manufacturers' and bankers' credits. This was not acceptable to the State Department or to the Treasury Department, on the grounds that the benefits would accrue to Germany rather to the United States, and that the transaction would be, in effect, Russian financing and the employment of American credit for the purpose of making an advance to the Soviets. It was held to differ only in form, not in substance, to previous unacceptable proposals.

Subsequent to the failure of this move, an agreement was signed between the Farquhar-Otto Wolff group and the Soviets involving a $40 million credit for the reorganization of the Makeevka metallurgical trust, on a six-year-loan basis. This was a straight credit arrangement involving neither concessions nor sale of the property.[30][31]

In 1928, Gipromez, staffed by the Freyn Company, rejected the Farquhar proposal for Makeevka as containing serious defects. It was argued that costs were underestimated. Technical defects were found in the rolling-mill arrangement, the equipment selection was not justifiable on either technical or economic grounds, and the project contained no provision for either internal

---

[29] Based on memorandum submitted to Secretary of State Kellogg by P. Farquhar, dated October 5, 1927 (316–131–975/6). The contract is in U.S. State Dept. Decimal File, 316–131–977/92.

[30] Those readers wishing to explore the Soviet-Farquhar contract in more detail should examine the four boxes of Farquhar's personal papers at the Hoover Institution, Stanford University.

[31] German Foreign Ministry Archives (quoting a Tass report of January 21, 1928), T120–3032–H109353.

transport or power supply. The connection between the rejection of the Farquhar project, the subsequent conclusion of a technical-assistance agreement with Dr. Kuppe (a well-known German rolling-mill specialist), and the earlier agreement between Gipromez and Freyn, under which planning assistance was given to new iron and steel projects, is unknown. It would be reasonable to assume that the events were not disconnected. There is no hard evidence of active competition between the American and German concessionaires and planners, but such competition was certainly not beyond the realm of possibility.[32]

TECHNICAL-ASSISTANCE AGREEMENTS WITH GIPROMEZ

The agreement between Vesenkha (Supreme Council of the National Economy) and the Freyn Company, Inc., of Chicago, signed in August 1928, was the first milestone in the transfer of Western metallurgical technology. This was an extension of an earlier agreement, signed in 1927, under which Freyn gave technical assistance in reconstructing existing metallurgical plants and construction of new plants in the U.S.S.R., and was especially concerned with the design of the new Kuznetz iron and steel plant, estimated to cost $50 million and planned as a key element in the forthcoming Five-Year Plan, and the reconstruction of the old Telbiss iron and steel mill. The second 1928 agreement enabled Gipromez (the State Institute for Planning Iron and Steel Works) to create a new metallurgical section staffed by 'the most prominent' Freyn engineers, twelve of whom took up permanent residence in the U.S.S.R.[33] At the same time, six Gipromez design engineers went to the United States for three to four months, 'visiting American plants and consulting American engineering authorities.'[34] In addition, access was now given to Freyn archives

---

[32]   The real reason for turning down the proposal was that the Soviets were not too assured Farquhar could raise the required capital, and in any event they objected to the sale of 'German machinery at American prices.' He was paid $600,000 for his technical services. (316–131–1088/9, U.S. Embassy in Berlin, Report 4121, November 19, 1928.)

See also Charles A. Gauld, *The Last Titan: Percival Farquhar* (Stanford: Stanford University, Institute of Hispanic American and Luzo-Brazilian Studies, 1964). Gauld makes the point that the Soviets are impressed by those capitalists who suffered their losses in silence. Farquhar lost about $100,000 on the Donetz project but said nothing publically: 'Farquhar's silence impressed the Kremlin . . . (he) was surprised when later the Soviet planners, on resuming the Donetz project, invited him to return to help co-ordinate it. But he had had enough of semi-Asiatic dealings with Soviet 'state capitalism.' He declared 'I learned that capitalists cannot do business with amoral, cynical Communists' (p. 205). Farquhar's impression was not typical—see W. Averell Harriman's adventures, pp. 89–91 below.

[33]   'American Technique Assists Soviet Metallurgy,' *Ekonomicheskaya Zhizn*, No. 182, August 8, 1928, and Clark, *op. cit.*, p. 65. Gipromez was founded April 10, 1926 and was comprised of a council of 237 professors and engineers. The utilization of Freyn designs will be traced in Vol. II.

[34]   Amtorg, *op. cit.*, II, No. 14 (July 15, 1927).

and standard metallurgical drawings; and all Soviet project planning was transferred from the United States, where it had been conducted to that time, to the U.S.S.R. In other words, the design and technical experience of the leading United States steel works designer was now at the disposal of Gipromez. The first basic 'Soviet' blast furnace design resulting from this agreement was, according to Clark, used for twenty-two blast furnaces, each with a capacity of 930–1,000 cubic meters and an output of 1,000 tons or more a day—substantially larger than that of any previous Russian furnace.

Under the second agreement, Freyn contracted to plan and supervise the reconstruction of forty metallurgical plants and the building of eighteen completely new iron and steel plants, at an estimated total expenditure of over $1 billion.[35] These plants were to form the basic structure for the Five-Year Plan. In addition to the Freyn assistance, Dr. Kuppe, a prominent German steel-rolling specialist, acted as a consultant to Gipromez.[36]

Amtorg was able to conclude in 1928 that although the U.S.S.R. lagged behind in iron and steel, the 'enormous technical advances made during recent years in . . . the United States and other countries are now being incorporated in the new plants under construction in the U.S.S.R.'[37]

Thus Russia was able to utilize wide-strip mills, a fundamental innovation in iron and steel technology, within six or seven years of their introduction in the United States and at least two years *before* utilization in Europe.[38]

[35] Amtorg, *op. cit.*, IV, No. 6 (March 15, 1929).

[36] U.S. State Dept. Decimal File, 316–131–1075.

[37] Amtorg, *op. cit.*, III, No. 2 (January 15, 1928) p. 24.

[38] The first wide-strip mill in the United States was installed in 1926; the first in Europe was the Richard Thomas, Ltd., mill at Ebbw Vale, South Wales, completed in 1937. German continuous mills of the 1920s were not able to produce steel strip wider than 30 inches.

CHAPTER FIVE

Non-ferrous Metal Mining and Smelting; The Manganese Concessions

LEAD-ZINC MINING AND SMELTING

ZINC, lead, silver, and copper production, both in the form of mined ore and smelted metals, are examined in this chapter separately, although in practice they are mined jointly and smelters produce separate metals, as well as by-products.

Some lead-zinc ores were mined and exported in tsarist times, but no smelting on a sizeable scale developed until the 1910 opening, by the British Urquhardt (Ridder) concession, of lead-zinc mines in East Kazakhstan, near the Chinese border. The company installed 120 kilometers of narrow-gauge railroad and the Altai smelting plant. The immediate post-revolutionary history of this complex was unhappy:

> When the Bolsheviks took over the mines, they spent enormous sums for new equipment, much of which deteriorated or was completely ruined through ignorance and deliberate sabotage. From the viewpoint of waste it might have been better . . . if the mines had been developed by foreign capital.[1]

The Ridder mines covered an area of 15,000 square miles and were reopened after the Revolution by the Lena Goldfields, Ltd., Type I concession with the long-term financial assistance of the Deutsche Bank.[2]

The Ridder lead-zinc-silver smelting plant established by the Urquhart concession was not let out to concession after the Revolution, although extensive negotiations took place between the Russo-Asiatic Company and

---

[1] J. D. Littlepage and D. Bess, *In Search of Soviet Gold* (New York: Harcourt Brace, 1938), p. 266.

[2] *Times* (London), November 20, 1928. V. I. Kruglyakova, *op. cit.*, omits all mention of either the mining or smelting of lead, zinc, or silver ores by Lena Goldfields, Ltd. However, Soviet sources (see page 96 below) confirm Lena operations.

the Soviets toward this end.[3] In 1924, the Ridder smelter became part of the Altai Polymetal Trust, which was formed in lieu of the rejected Urquhardt concession. A commission under the direction of a Professor Gubkin approved a plan for reorganization of the non-ferrous mining and smelting industry submitted by an engineer, van der Better;[4] however, apart from uniting the copper smelters at Kyshtim, Tanalyk, and Kalat with the lead-zinc smelter at Ridder under the same organizational roof, no significant development of mines and smelters was undertaken until the Altai Polymetal Trust made a technical-assistance agreement with Frank E. Downs, who became Technical Director (at $20,000 per year) in 1928.[5]

A New York corporation held the Belukha concession for mineral prospecting in the southern Altai mountains from 1925 to 1927.[6]

Table 5-1 summarizes the sources of metallic zinc production for 1926-32. In 1926 the only operating zinc smelter was the old Sadon-Buron (Alagir), built by a prerevolutionary French concessionaire and operated by Zvetmetzoloto (the Non-Ferrous Metals Trust) but fed with ore mined by 'concessions.'[7] Sadon-Buron produced 1,888 metric tons of metallic zinc—the total Soviet production. By 1932, production had risen, with the help of foreign engineers, to 4,892 metric tons: just under 36 percent of total Soviet zinc metal production.

The Lena Goldfields concessions of 1925 included the construction of a new lead-zinc smelter at Altai, fed with ore from the prewar Ridder mines. The new Altai smelter was built more or less on schedule, started, and expropriated in 1930. In 1932 the plant produced 4,578 metric tons of zinc metal, or almost 34 percent of Soviet production.[8]

---

[3] The agreement signed by Krassin and Urquhardt, and later rejected by Lenin, covered an extraordinarily large territory in Siberia, including twelve developed metal mines, coal mines, four non-ferrous smelters, a refinery, iron and steel mills, twenty sawmills, the Ridder lead-zinc mines and smelter, the Spassky copper mines, Karaganda coal mines, and other mine and smelting properties in the Altai and Urals regions. (*Le Petit Parisien*, October 27, 1922.) The significance for this study is that all the properties *were in good technical condition and ready to be operated.* [U.S. Embassy in London, Report 1717, September 26, 1922, in U.S. State Dept. Decimal File, 316-136-172/5).]

[4] *Izvestia*, No. 32, February 8, 1924.

[5] U.S. Embassy in Berlin, Report 3114, January 21, 1928 (316-136-512). In 1927-8 the Altai Polymetal Trust was able to smelt only 67 kgs of silver. (Kruglyakova, *op. cit.*, p. 152.)

[6] U.S. State Dept. Decimal File (316-136-1240).

[7] Kruglyakova, *op. cit.*, p. 152, reports the ore was mined by a concession (unnamed). It is inferred that this was the Siemens-Schukert concession.

[8] Liubimov, *op. cit.*, states that the smelter was *not* built. Amtorg, *op. cit.*, IV, 1929, p. 33, and other Soviet sources make clear, however, that it was in fact completed in 1929-30. *The Engineering and Mining Journal*, October 1936, has photographs of the smelter and supporting operations.

Table 5-1   SOURCES OF ZINC METAL PRODUCTION IN U.S.S.R., 1926–32

Operator	Ore Mines	Smelter	1927–8[1]	1929	1930	1932	Percent (1932)
				(in metric tons)			
Polymetal Trust	North Caucasus	Sadon-Buron (prewar Alagir)	2,246	N.A.*	N.A.	4,892	35.9
Tetyukhe Mines, Ltd.	Far East	Belovo (1930)	—	—	Startup	4,152	30.5
Lena Goldfields, Ltd.	Ridder	Altai (1928)	Startup	1,600	N.A.	4,578	33.6
Altai Polymetal Trust	Ridder	Ridder (prewar)	Startup	N.A.	N.A.	N.A.	N.A.
Total zinc metal production			2,246			13,622	100.0 (excluding Ridder)
Percentage produced by concessions			100.0				64.1

Source: 1. Kruglyakova, *Sbornik statisticheskikh svedenii* . . ., p. 152.

* Not available.

The Tetyukhe mines (Bryner and Company), another Type I concession, made a significant contribution to Soviet foreign exchange earnings from 1927 to 1930 by the export of zinc concentrates. The company re-established the mines, and until the smelter was ready to produce zinc metal, the zinc ore was beneficiated and exported. Conolly gives the exports as 9,000 tons in 1927, 15,000 tons in 1928, and 18,000 tons in both 1929 and 1930. Exports dropped to 6,000 tons in 1931 as the new smelter came into production.[9] The Tetyukhe (Bryner) concession, signed in 1924, exceeded its annual quota of 20,000 tons of zinc and 10,000 tons of lead concentrate by 1928. The plant was equipped with the latest imported equipment in the flotation mill. The company then proceeded to build the Belovo zinc smelter to produce 5,000 tons of lead metal and 10,000 kilograms of silver per year, by 1932 producing 30 percent of Soviet zinc metal.[10]

In 1927-8 lead ore was mined and concentrated at five locations. The Ridder mines of the Altai Polymetal Trust produced 3,699 tons, and the prerevolutionary Alagir mines produced a little in excess of 2,000 tons of lead concentrates. The Auli-Atinski mines of the Atbassvetmet produced just over 1,000 tons of concentrate. The Tirinski Development Company, a privately leased operation, produced just under 150 tons, and the Igergol mine of the Svintsovii Artel produced 16 tons.[11] In brief, these were small operations incapable by themselves of supporting a large-capacity smelter,

Table 5-2 SOURCES OF LEAD METAL PRODUCTION, 1927-8

Smelter Name	Method of Organization	Origin of Smelter	1927-8 Production (in metric tons)
Alagir	Polymetal Trust	(prewar)	939
Igergol	Artel	—	5
Tirinski	Joint Stock Co.	—	96
Ridder	Altai Polymetal Trust	(prewar)	1,225
Auli-Atinski	Atbassvetmet	(prewar)	327
Lena-Altai	Lena Goldfields, Ltd.	(prewar and new)	2,300
Belovo	Tetyukhe Mines, Ltd.	(new)	—
Total lead metal production			4,892
Percentage produced by concessions			47.0%
Percentage produced by concessions and prewar smelters			100.0%

Source: Kruglyakova, *Sbornik statisticheskikh svedenii* . . ., pp. 148-9.

[9] Conolly, *op. cit.*, p. 7.
[10] *Bank for Russian Trade Review*, II, No. 1 (January 1929), 7.
[11] Kruglyakova, *op. cit.*, pp. 148-9.

but able to produce comparatively small quantities of metallic lead from local smelters, as shown in table 5–2.

A concession was also granted in December 1925 to operate the Priamur Mines, developed in the Far East during the tsarist period. The concession was set up to last for thirty-six years, the first three of which were to be spent prospecting—at a cost of 400,000 rubles—in Primorska Gubernia. A land rental of 1.25 rubles per hectare and a royalty on production were payable; the concessionaire undertook to build a port and establish a smelter.[12] Production did not begin before 1930.

COPPER MINING AND SMELTING INDUSTRY; SILVER

Copper ore mines flourished in prerevolutionary Russia in the Urals, the Caucasus, the Khighiz Steppes, and Siberia. These mines were high-grade operations and did not beneficiate low-grade ores; the Atlas Mines, for example, operated on 10–20 percent copper ore and the Spassky on 7–22 percent ore. Geographical isolation required completely self-supporting operation; and all the mining complexes made iron products and owned and operated forests for charcoal. Most of them also operated coal mines, power facilities, and communications. The Kyshtim mine even operated a boot and shoe factory to supply its miners with work boots. All had granaries and food stores.

Tsarist Russia was almost self-sufficient in copper metal production. Output in 1910 was 22,000 tons and in 1912 about 33,000 tons of smelted copper, of which a small quantity was exported. Imports consisted only of electrolytic copper, of which production was insignificant.

Mining operations collapsed with the Revolution. In 1921–2 only an insignificant 13,266 tons of copper ore was mined from the single operating mine, the Korpushinsk, which was part of the Kalatinsk smelter complex in the Urals. A shipment of copper ore in 1922 enabled the Kalatinsk smelter to smelt the first copper metal since 1918, but as *Pravda* said, 'All other copper establishments in Russia are now in a state of technical preservation.'[13] Between 1922 and 1925 only the Kalatinsk smelter was in operation.[14]

Uralmed (the Urals Copper Trust) was formed in December 1921 and took over operation of copper mines in the Verkh-Isset, Revdinsk, and Syssert districts, together with the Kalatinsk, Lower Kyshtim, Kishmino-Kluchevsk,

---

[12]   *Ekonomicheskaya Zhizn*, No. 188, August 20, 1924; and U.S. State Dept. Decimal File, 316–136–357.

[13]   No. 184, August 17, 1922.

[14]   The Soviets claimed that copper smelters were in a state of 'technical preservation' because there was no demand for copper. However, copper metal imports in 1913 were only 1,150 tons, whereas they were 5,325 tons in 1925–6, 10,921 tons in 1926–7, and 23,087 tons in 1927–8. About one-half of the imports came from the United States. (*Ekonomicheskaya Zhizn*, No. 161, July 17, 1929.)

and Karabash copper-smelting works. Most of the mines and all four smelters were in working order.

Similarly, the Caucasus mines and smelters, the Spassky and Atlas works in the Kirghiz, and the Julia mine in the Yeniseisk region were closed.

Briefly, in 1925, some eight years after the Revolution, of the half-dozen smelters and the dozen copper mines which had survived more or less intact, only the Kalata smelter in Uralmed was producing any copper metal at all: 2,807 tons of copper metal in 1923–4 and 5,588 tons in 1924–5. The missing ingredient for production was the technical ability to get existing mines and smelters into production. This ingredient was provided by the Lena and Siemens concessions and by Type III technical-assistance agreements.

Considerable emphasis was placed by the U.S.S.R. on the development of its non-ferrous potential, clearly for strategic reasons. By the end of the 1920s, the non-ferrous mining and smelting industry (lead, zinc, copper, and silver) employed 65 engineers and 157 technicians from the United States alone.[15] The overall plan for reconstruction was developed by an engineer, van der Better, under the auspices of Uralsvetmet,[16] which united the copper smelters in the Urals with the lead-zinc complex at Ridder. Capital sums of $5 million were then allocated to Kyshtim and Ridder and $1.5 million to Kalata.

The component sectors of the copper mining and smelting industry are divided (table 5–3) into seven groups. The largest in terms of 1927–8 production was the Kalata-Karabash combine (Group I), consisting of numerous mines and smelters developed before the Revolution. The chief engineer for this group was Littlepage,[17] and with the aid of American engineers the group rebuilt ore tonnages and copper smelting substantially after 1925. Group II also consisted of Urals mines and smelters, and was taken over by the Lena Goldfields concession in 1925. The tsarist-era Gumishev copper smelter was restarted, and a new much larger smelter, the Degtiarka, was completed by 1930. By 1927 Lena had the new smelter, including a 500-ton-per-day concentrating plant, under construction. This was the first use in the U.S.S.R. of selective flotation of ferrous sulphides in copper production.[18] The mines to feed Gumishev and the new smelters were reorganized tsarist mines at Soyuzelski and Degtiarinskii. In 1928 these were also producing 53,000 tons of sulphur pyrites—the first production of pyrites in the U.S.S.R.[19] By the end

[15] V. Karmashov, 'Non-Ferrous Metal Industry of Soviet Russia,' *Engineering and Mining Journal*, CXXX, July 24, 1930. Karmashov was employed in the Technical Bureau of the industry. These engineers, such as Woods who supervised copper mining for Armmed, and Lerva, an engineer at Uralmed, were hired on renewable two-year contracts (316–136–512).

[16] *Izvestia*, No. 32, February 8, 1924.

[17] Littlepage and Bess, *op. cit.*, p. 108.

[18] *Torgovo-Promyshlennaya Gazeta*, No. 221, September 28, 1927.

[19] Kruglyakova, *op. cit.*, p. 150.

Table 5-3   COPPER ORE MINES AND SMELTERS, PRODUCTION 1923-4 TO 1927-8

Group	Mine Number	Mine Name	Combinat/Trust	Smelter Supplied	1923-4[1]	1927-8[2]
					Metric tons of ore mined	
I			*Uralsvetmet*			
	1	Belorachenskii	Kalata Combinat	Kalata		15,455
	2	Kalatinskii	Kalata Combinat			67,690
	3	Korpushinski	Kalata Combinat		167,004	62,070
	4	Obnovlennie	Kalata Combinat			21,768
	5	Pervomaiski	Karabash Combinat	Karabash		97,424
	6	Rykovski	Karabash Combinat			131,969
	7	Stalinski	Karabash Combinat			43,160
II	8	Sissert (Polesvski)	Lena Goldfields	Polevski (Degtiarsky)	—	28,212
	9	Dagtiark (Pourvouplosk)	Lena Goldfields		—	6,285
III	10	Kompaneiski (Bogomolstroi)	Kalata Combinat	Bogomolstroi	—	51,061
	11	Levichinski	Uralsvetmet		—	18,450
	12	Third International	Tagilsk Combinat		—	15,870
IV	13	Tubinski	Bashgortrest	Bashgortrest (South Urals)	—	9,280
	14	Julia	Bashgortrest		—	11,795
	15	Siberski	Bashgortrest		—	4,868
V	16	Djerkasganski	Atbastvetmet (1929)	Kazakh	—	269
VI	17	Lenin (Kovart)	Armmed	Zanguezour (Red November)	—	48,541
	18	Lenin (Bashkend)	Armmed		—	5,078
	19	Allarverdy	Armmed	Bambak (Karl Marx)	—	60,230
	20	Shamblugski	Armmed		—	60,230
VII	21	Kedabekski	Agespromcombinat		—	598

Sources: 1. *Ekonomicheskaya Zhizn*, No. 236 (October 15, 1925).
2. Kruglyakova, *Sbornik statisticheskikh svedenii . . .*, p. 102.

of 1927, Lena Goldfields engineers had blocked out more than six million tons of 2.5-percent copper ore at these mines.

The Group III mines were developed by the Kalata combine to feed the $38 million Bogomol copper smelter. This latter was brought into production in the Five-Year Plan and also built by Western companies. Groups V and VII were in the development stage, and mines in Group IV, including the tsarist Julia mine, were being developed to feed the new Bashgortrest smelter, also built after 1930.

The Caucasus smelters and supporting mines were renovated (one with the aid of a Siemens-Schukert concession) and later grouped into the Armmed trust. The Zanguezour district group of copper mines, including the Kovart and Bashkend mines, which had been in operation since 1840, were renamed the Lenin Group and put into the Armmed trust. It is known that they came through the Revolution in good operating condition and required only to be placed into production. In 1927–8 they produced 53,619 tons of copper ore. This ore was shipped to the old prerevolutionary Ougourchaisk copper smelter, renamed the 'Red November', and yielded 665 tons of black fired copper metal, or about 75 percent the prewar capacity.[20]

The Atbastvetmet trust, in the Kazakh area, did not make its contribution until late in the 1920s. This trust included the Karsak Pai 5,000-ton smelter, with a 250-ton-per-day flotation plant which had been begun as a prerevolutionary enterprise and was completed at the end of the 1920s, and also included mines opened up before the Revolution.[21]

Two trusts were completely new: the Bogomolstroi and the Bashgortrest, in the South Urals. These were extensively aided by Western companies, particularly the Southwestern Engineering Corporation and Arthur E. Wheeler of the United States.[22]

The reconstruction and expansion of the copper-mining and smelting industry can be divided, then, into three segments. There was the reconstruction, somewhat delayed, of the prerevolutionary copper smelters in the Urals (Kalata and Karabash complexes) and the Caucasus. Second, and quite distinct from these operations were the Type I pure concession operated by Lena Goldfields in the Urals around the old Gumishev and Polevsky smelters and the new 12,000-ton Degtiarka smelter (which replaced Gumishev), and

---

[20] *Ibid.*, p. 104; and U.S. State Dept. Decimal File, 316–136–1066.
[21] J. W. Wardell, *In the Kirghiz Steppes* (London: Galley Press, 1961); and letter from Wardell (manager of the prewar operation at Karsak-Pai) to the writer, 1965.
[22] Southwestern Engineering Corp., of Los Angeles, had a technical-assistance agreement with the Non-Ferrous Metals Trust for the design, construction, and operation of non-ferrous metal plants. Archer E. Wheeler and Associates, of New York, had a technical-assistance agreement with the same trust for equipment of the plants. [American-Russian Chamber of Commerce, *Economic Handbook of the Soviet Union* (New York: 1931), p. 101.] See Vol. II.

Table 5–4   CAPACITY, PRODUCTION AND TECHNICAL ASSISTANCE OF SOVIET COPPER SMELTERS, 1929

Smelter	1929 Capacity Copper Metal[1] (in metric tons)	Production of Black Fired Copper[2] (in metric tons)	Origin[3]	Foreign Assistance
Karsak Pai	5,000	—	Partly built prewar by United Kingdom concession. Finished 1928–9.[3]	See col. four.
Degtiarsky Polevski-Gumishev	3,000	2,950	New and reconstructed.[4] Completed 1929.	Lena Goldfields, Ltd.
Bashkirtrest	3,000	1,747	New.	South Western Engineering, Inc.
Kalata	12,000	5,569	Prewar reconstructed.	United States engineers.
Karabash	15,000	2,629	Prewar reconstructed.	United States engineers.
Armmed	3,000	2,038	Reconstructed.	Siemens-Schukert concession and United States mining engineers.

Sources:

[1] V. Karmashov, 'Non-Ferrous Metal Industry of Soviet Russia,' *Engineering and Mining Journal*, CXXX (July 24, 1930), 67.

[2] Kruglyakova, *op. cit.*, p. 106; and Amtorg, *op. cit.*, III, 34.

[3] Wardell, *op. cit.*, and letter of April 1965.

[4] Amtorg, IV, 33.

the Siemens-Schukert Type I concession at the Arhaham mine, south of Batum, in the Caucasus. Third, construction of three new smelting plants began within this period, but these had little impact on copper metals output until the early 1930s. They included the completed Karsak Pai smelter, begun before the Revolution, and two new smelters: the Bogomolstroi and the Bashkirtrest, in the South Urals.

Although technical-assistance agreements (Type III) were successfully utilized for construction of copper smelters, it is not clear that agreements made for assistance to the copper mines were equally successful before 1930. Chief engineer Goncharov of Bogomol, while on a study visit to the United States in 1927, invited an American engineer, McDonald, to work at Uralmed, the Urals copper trust responsible for new copper-mine development. MacDonald was installed as manager of all underground mining and adviser on planning mine extensions, particularly for the Kompaneisky group—the largest of those supplying Bogomol. There was overt hostility on the part of Russian mining engineers, and McDonald apparently beat a retreat back to the United States without achieving very much in the way of planning.[23]

At the end of the decade, these trusts were absorbed, along with the gold industry, into Svetmetzoloto, and two further technical-assistance agreements were then made, with the W. A. Wood Company and with Norman L. Wimmler, both of the United States; but these had no impact within this decade.[24]

In 1928 the Lena Goldfields Company produced 80 percent of Russian silver. The Tetyukhe concession, in the Far East, was required to produce 6,000 kilograms of silver per year. It was reported in 1928 that Tetyukhe was fulfilling its agreement. Thus in 1928 all Russian silver was produced by foreign concession.

Even if the technical competence to operate the zinc, lead, silver, and copper mines had been available, the Soviets would have faced enormous difficulties in attempting to restart operations without Western help. These mines had been operated by Western companies before the Revolution, and records of some twenty-five years of work—most importantly of drilling experience and the solution of metallurgical problems—was stored in the home offices. This accumulated knowledge was required to make rational progress, certainly in underground operations.[25] Without it the Soviets could perhaps at some point have restarted the mines and smelters, but only at an enormous cost.

[23] *Pravda*, No. 239, October 16, 1929.
[24] American-Russian Chamber of Commerce, *op. cit.*, p. 101.
[25] Urquhardt estimated that the complete records of 100,000 feet of drilling in Siberia, Caucasus, and the Urals, together with the geological evaluation of thousands of Russian ore deposits, were stored in London and unavailable to the Soviets. [*Times* (London), October 24, 1922.]

A NON-COLLUSIVE DUOPSONY;
THE MANGANESE CONCESSIONS

The Soviets acquired modern mining and transportation facilities for their manganese deposits at Chiaturi and Nikopol, acquired foreign exchange, and finally shattered American foreign policy concerning loans to the U.S.S.R., in a series of astute business agreements with the Harriman-Guaranty Trust group in the United States and the Rawack and Grunfeld group in Germany.[26]

In 1913, tsarist Russia supplied 52 percent of world manganese, of which about 76 percent, or one million tons, was mined from the Chiaturi deposits in the Caucasus. Production in 1920 was zero, and by 1924 had risen only to about 320,000 tons per year. The basic problem was

> that further development was seriously retarded by the primitive equipment, which was considered grossly inadequate even according to prewar standards.[27]

The Chiaturi deposits, situated on high plateaus some distance from Batum, were mined in a primitive manner, and the ore was brought on donkeys from the plateaus to the railroads. There was a change of gauge en route, and the manganese had to be transshipped between the original loading point and the port. When at the port the ore was transferred by bucket: a slow, expensive process.

The other deposits of manganese were at Nikopol in the Ukraine and, although somewhat smaller than those at Chiaturi, were significant. These deposits were reopened, before the Rapallo Treaty, by a group of German companies, through a joint-stock company, Tschemo A-G., with a 30-year monopoly grant. The Soviets then demanded a 55-percent share of Tschemo A-G., and, when refused, nationalized the company. They then began negotiations with W. Averell Harriman and the Deutsche Bank, and the Rawack and Grunfeld group.[28]

On July 12, 1925, a Type I concession agreement was made between the W. A. Harriman Company of New York and the U.S.S.R. for exploitation of the Chiaturi manganese deposits and the extensive introduction of modern mining and transportation methods. In the first full year of operation, the Harriman syndicate was able to extract 762,000 tons of ore.

---

[26]   As this study is concerned with the impact of technology on the economy, the Harriman negotiations are not described. The interested reader is referred to over 300 pages of documents in the U.S. State Dept. Decimal File, 316–138-12/331, and the German Foreign Ministry Archives. Walter Duranty described the Harriman contract as 'utterly inept' and von Dirksen of the German Foreign Office as 'a rubber contract.' The full contract was published [Vysshii sovet narodnogo khoziaistva, *Concession Agreement Between the Government of the U.S.S.R. and W. A. Harriman & Co. Inc. of New York* (Moscow: 1925)].

[27]   Amtorg, *op. cit.*, II, No. 23 (December 1, 1927), 8.

[28]   U.S. State Dept. Decimal File, 316–138-50.

Harriman was associated with Gelsenkirchner Borgwerke A-G. and the Disconte Gesellschaft, to whom a royalty of $1 per ton of manganese ore was payable as settlement for prerevolutionary interests. As the result of a London conference on June 29, 1925, this group obtained 25 percent, 51 percent remaining with Harriman, and the balance going to other interests, including an English group.[29]

Under the Harriman concession agreement, $4 million was spent on mechanizing the mines and converting them from hand to mechanical operation. A washer and reduction plant were built; and a loading elevator at Poti with a two-million-ton capacity and a railroad system were constructed, together with an aerial tramway for the transfer of manganese ore. The expenditure was approximately $2 million for the railroad system and $1 million for mechanization of the mines.[30]

After the conclusion of the Harriman agreement, the Soviets negotiated with Rawack and Grunfeld A-G. for the exclusive sales and export rights for the Nikopol deposits. The latter also mechanized the mines with German technical assistance.[31] The Nikopol-Nikolaev loading equipment was rebuilt by German engineers, using German and British equipment, at a cost of two million rubles on nine months' credit.[32]

Table 5-5 MANGANESE PRODUCTION IN U.S.S.R., 1913–29

Year	Chiaturi (Harriman)	Nikopol (Rawack and Grunfeld)	Total U.S.S.R. Production	Percent Produced by Concessions
		(in metric tons)		
1913	970,000	270,000	1,240,000	N.A.***
1922–3	52,177	22,000	74,177	none
1923–4	320,132	173,531	493,663	none
1924–5	335,994*	382,223	676,000**	24
1925–6	772,000	415,000	1,334,000	100
1926–7	775,700	527,000	1,109,000	100
1927–8	540,000	615,000	766,000	100
1928–9	644,300	612,500	1,415,000	100

Source: A. A. Santalov and L. Segal, 'Concessions production,' *Soviet Union Yearbook, 1930* (London: George Allen and Unwin, 1931), p. 135.

* 160,000 tons of the 1925 output produced by the Harriman concession.

** Between 1926 and 1929 the total U.S.S.R. production does not equal the sum of the outputs from Chiaturi and Nikopol. A reconciliation would require taking account of stockpiles, ore fines, transport losses, and the small Urals output.

*** N.A. Not available.

[29] U.S. Embassy in Berlin, Report 334, July 14, 1925 (316–138–12/331).
[30] U.S. Embassy in Berlin, Report 300, June 25, 1925 (316–138–12/331).
[31] U.S. Embassy in Berlin, Report 1775, December 9, 1926 (316–138–12/331).
[32] U.S. Consulate in Hamburg, Report 149, December 12, 1925 (316–138–12/331).

By the end of 1925, the Soviets had thus made agreements on both their major manganese deposits. In both instances they had previously pushed production as far as possible, given the primitive state of mines. To increase production they then had to turn to Western technical assistance and equipment. The agreements differed. Whereas Harriman and his German associates were committed to make specific royalty payments whether or not the output was sold, and also to undertake major capital improvements, the Rawack and Grunfeld group was acting as a sales agent and was paid for its technical assistance. However, so far as the world market was concerned, the Soviets had now placed both concessionaires in a competing position. Table 5–5 indicates that both concessions were able to raise output; this was also their undoing. Prices began to fall, and both concessionaires got into trouble with rising costs and declining returns.[33]

Walter Duranty, writing in the *New York Times* considered the original Harriman contract to be 'utterly inept,' and said that after three years of a 'checkered and unprofitable existence, (it was) about to expire quietly.'[34]

At the time of the Harriman withdrawal it was suggested that a fall in world manganese prices made continued mining of the Chiaturi concession unprofitable; the Soviets certainly utilized the Harriman price policy as its reason for the failure of the concession.[35]

Although market prices for manganese ore dropped in the late 1920s, the decrease was hardly sufficient to force a well-managed mining company out of business. In 1927–8 manganese quotations fell about 2 cents per long ton unit, from the 40-cent average for 1926. Prices in 1929 touched 35 cents toward the end of the year, but it will be noted that this reasonably steep decline came *after* the surrender of the concession. Most metal prices fluctuate, and a fluctuation of 2 cents to 5 cents per long-ton unit is not of major consequence.

Even if some actual contract prices in 1928 were below quoted market price—not an unusual occurrence—they would be reflected fairly quickly in the open market quotations.

Essentially the reasons for failure appear to be threefold:

1. The harsh treatment by the local Georgian government, and the unfavorable attitude of the Soviet government soon after the signing of the agreement in 1925. In one year the concession had to endure visits and inspections from various control commissions on 127 working days.

---

[33]   U.S. Consulate in Hamburg, Report 12, January 16, 1927 (316–138–12/331).

[34]   *New York Times*, June 17, 1927, III, p. 3, col. 5. Also see J. E. Spurr, 'Russian Manganese Concessions,' *Foreign Affairs*, V, No. 3 (April 1927), 507. Spurr considers that the terms of the Harriman concession were too hard in the face of world competition.

[35]   *Bank for Russian Trade Review*, No. 14, December 1928, p. 15.

2. High production costs. The 'professional proletarians' were constantly demanding more wages.

3. Weaknesses in the original contract: particularly the requirement to pay between $3.00 and $4.00 royalty per ton of ore irrespective of tonnage removed.

THE IMPLICATIONS OF THE HARRIMAN FAILURE

The Harriman negotiations had begun in the United States at the end of 1924 with unofficial representatives of the Soviet government. The State Department was unaware of the negotiations, and Harriman did not inform them.[36] The first word of the agreement reached the State Department via a speech made by Prime Minister Ramsay MacDonald in the House of Commons and reported back by the American Embassy in London.

As word of the negotiations spread, Western governments protested and inquired whether there was a change in United States government trade policy.[37] The British government, for example, pointed out that other companies had been trying to get the concession and that the Soviets desired an agreement for political purposes only:

> Viz., for the purpose of establishing the fact that a big American concern had taken the properties which belonged to foreign concerns and thereby recognizing the right of the Soviet Government to nationalize property.[38]

The Harriman negotiations caused some confusion in the State Department, which for reasons not clearly established by the files did not wish to initiate an investigation, although obviously disturbed by the whole affair.[39]

Harriman was not the first businessman to attempt to circumvent United States policy on trade with the U.S.S.R. There were attempts throughout the 1920s, and the policy had in fact been substantially eroded by 1929. Policy up to 1927 was to view long-term loans and credits with disfavor if they

---

[36] U.S. State Dept. Decimal File, 316-138-17/19, Washington to London Embassy: 'The memorandum transmitted by you embodies the first information received by the Department concerning the concession other than that which has appeared in the public press.'

[37] The protests of the German, Belgian and Georgian (exile) governments are in the U.S. State Dept. Decimal File, 316-138-17/20/41/84. The German Foreign Office Archives contain a letter from von Dirksen to the United States Embassy in Berlin concerning the effect of the Harriman concession on German firms and, in diplomatic language, implying a breach of agreement.

[38] U.S. State Dept. Decimal File, 316-138-18. Memorandum from U.S. Embassy in London dated October 28, 1924.

[39] Such a move, i.e., to initiate an investigation, was held to be 'very unwise.' (Memorandum, State Dept. to Commerce Dept., U.S. State Dept. Decimal File, 316-138-28.)

involved floating a loan in the United States or using American credit for the purpose of making advances. The State Department stated their policy on three occasions during the 1920s, each time as the result of an attempt of American financiers to utilize a German front group to advance credit to the U.S.S.R.

On July 15, 1926, the State Department informed the New York Trust Company that it would view with disfavor an arrangement to discount certain Russian obligations endorsed by German firms (40 percent) and the German government (60 percent), the discounting to be carried out by American banks, and the financing of Soviet purchases of equipment to be completed in Germany.

On October 14, 1927 Percival Farquhar was informed by the State Department that a scheme to sell $20 million of bonds in the United States in order to place the proceeds at the disposal of the Soviet government for the purchase of goods and materials in Germany would not be viewed with favor.

It must be made clear the State Department argument in these cases did not rest upon non-recognition of the U.S.S.R., but upon the fact that the benefits of the loan would accrue to German rather than United States manufacturers. The State Department had not interposed, for example, when Chase National in 1925 arranged a short-term credit for cotton shipments destined for the U.S.S.R., nor in the provision of loans by the International Harvester Company.

Their position was reviewed in the case of the American Locomotive proposal in October 1927 and weakened to the extent that no objection was raised to American manufacturers of railway equipment granting long-term credit to the Soviets for the purchase of locomotives, cars, and other railroad materials from the United States.[40]

The only position not breached in late 1927 was that on long-term *loans* to the Soviet government. The Harriman concession was utilized by the Soviets to give the coup de grace to what was left of American trade policy with Russia. Harriman was induced to accept long-term bonds as compensation for expropriation.

Discussion between the Harriman interests and Soviet representatives in July and August 1928 led to an agreement to cancel the concession, and the Soviets agreed to repay Harriman the estimated $3,500,000 investment. However, Harriman was 'to arrange a commercial loan for the Soviet authorities to develop the manganese industry.' The acceptance by Harriman of a

---

[40] This was apparently decided at the Presidential level. There is the following hand-written notation by RFK (Kelley of Division of Eastern European Affairs) on the file copy of the letter to American Locomotive: 'Drafted after discussion of the matter by Secretary with Mr. Mellon, Mr. Hoover and the President.'

long-term credit arrangement and position as Soviet fund-raiser as compensation for expropriation was the final breach in the American policy of restriction on trade with the U.S.S.R.[41]

According to the United States Commercial Attaché in Prague, after the Harriman collapse the Soviets went about Europe bragging they could borrow money from Harriman at 7 percent; therefore their credit must be good.[42]

With the departure of Harriman, the Soviets had two sizeable manganese deposits, both with up-to-date mining and loading equipment supplied on credit terms. In addition, they had Rawack and Grunfeld to continue operating the Nikopol deposits, take over operation of the Chiaturi deposits, and continue as exclusive sales agent for the U.S.S.R. on the world market. As Rawack and Grunfeld now controlled output from both deposits, they were no longer in the position of duopolists competing price down to zero, although they still had to face competition from newly opened deposits in Brazil and West Africa. It is also very interesting to note that *one-half* of the 1927–8 output of Chiaturi was from the Perevessi Hill deposit,[43] the high-grade area which had been left out of the Harriman concession. In other words, Harriman had been induced (on top of all else) to mechanize production of the *low-grade* deposits and install loading facilities so that the Soviets could take advantage of these low-cost loading facilities to ship high-grade, almost surely low-cost, ore.

Sales of manganese ore were further facilitated in 1929 by the negotiation of a five-year contract with United States Steel Corporation for an annual supply of between 80,000 and 150,000 tons.[44]

[41] This was the State Dept. assessment (316–124–45). Harriman's recollection is subtly different: 'In 1926 I was back there on business, representing a group that was mining manganese in the Caucasus. I found Stalin and Trotsky in disagreement about foreign concessions like ours. I talked to Trotsky for four hours, concluded that we should give up the concession and got our money out—paid in full with interest and with a small profit.' ('How Harriman "Earned a Dinner" from Khruschev', *Life*, August 9, 1963, p. 29.)

[42] The interested reader is directed to the four-page report from the attaché, which summarizes very well the impossibility of normal commercial dealings with the Communists, although, as the attaché pointed out, 'Harriman and Company are not saying very much.' (316–138–332/5.)

[43] Kruglyakova, *op. cit.*, p. 100.

[44] *Ekonomicheskaya Zhizn*, No. 182, August 10, 1929.

CHAPTER SIX

Gold Mining, Platinum, Asbestos, and Minor Mineral Concessions

GOLD MINING AND FOREIGN CONCESSIONS

RUSSIA has excellent gold ore reserves. In tsarist times the Lena River gold mining area in Siberia, reputedly one of the richest in the world, measured by both extent of reserves and metal content of the ore, was operated by concessionaires. In 1913 there were 39 foreign and Russian companies operating 770 mines in the Lena River area; of these 121 were actually producing gold and employed over 10,000 workers. 'These mines had excellent equipment, full electrification and large hydroelectric installations. . . .'[1]

British companies held several concessions from the tsarist government, including some for development of the Siberian gold and platinum mines in the Lena River region. These were developed as self-supporting industrial entities complete with iron and steel plants, smelters, and agricultural and small-consumer goods manufacturing works. The departure of the Western owners with the Revolution significantly reduced Russian gold production.

There was a catastrophic decline in the condition of the Siberian gold fields, of which Lena-Vitim was the most important, from about 1921 onward. The Urals' 1913 gold production of 25,700 pounds dropped to just over 8 pounds in 1921, the West Siberian output from 7,200 pounds in 1913 to 33 pounds in 1921, the East Siberian output from 103,000 pounds in 1913 to 8 pounds in 1921, and the Yenessei output from 5,000 pounds in 1913 to 140 pounds in 1922.[2]

The Siberian Revolutionary Council suspended operations in the Lena-Vitim area in early 1921, with the arguments that the labor force of 9,000 was producing significantly less than before the war and that it was costing

---

[1] *Ekonomicheskaya Zhizn*, No. 196, September 2, 1922.
[2] *Izvestia*, No. 213, September 22, 1922.

two zolotniks of gold to produce one zolotnik. However, the Council was overruled by the Soviet of Labor and Defense, and the fields were ordered to continue working. Shortly thereafter, the 1920 decree which had forbidden private interests from mining gold was replaced by a decree authorizing special concessions for gold and platinum operations. This was followed by the organization of the Lenzoloto trust in December 1921. This trust had the exclusive right to mine gold on the right bank of the Lena River, although individual prospectors continued working both elsewhere and for Lenzoloto itself on a contract basis.

It was argued in *Ekonomicheskaya Zhizn* that the mines had suffered from two years of civil war in the Urals, were badly equipped, and were exhausted by 200 years of continual mining.[3] However, the report which formed the basis for the foundation of Lenzoloto gives a more detailed and substantially different picture. In substance, the gold mining equipment was in good operating condition.[4] However, the reasons for conversion into a trust are obvious from the catastrophic decline in output.

> Mining of gold by prospectors almost ceased in 1921, as it was impossible to send supplies to the prospectors and also there were persistent attempts on the part of local organs to turn prospectors into ordinary State workmen, who receive payment in money and goods regardless of the amount of gold they find.[5]

Conditions did not improve much in 1922–3. Employment dropped to just under 5,000 men because of lack of food and supplies; there were financial difficulties and equipment needed repair. It was believed that the richer gold areas would only last another seven to eight years. Dredges, not manufactured in Soviet Russia, were required to develop the low-grade areas on a profitable basis. The average gold content was 65 zolotniks per cubic sazhen, while the average of the extensive poorer area was in the neighborhood of 44 zolotniks per cubic sazhen. An article in *Ekonomicheskaya Zhizn* recommended turning part of the Lena fields over to private enterprise in accordance with the 1921 decree and also recommended the purchase of foreign dredges to operate poorer areas.[6]

Conditions apparently had not improved much one year later. Only the Feodosyer placer among the hydraulic operations was working, and underground production was curtailed. There were the perennial financial problems, and no move had been made to obtain the 17-foot Bucyrus dredge, ordered from the United States in 1916 and stored at San Francisco. It was estimated

[3] *Ekonomicheskaya Zhizn*, No. 172, August 4, 1922.
[4] *Ekonomicheskaya Zhizn*, No. 196, September 2, 1922.
[5] *Ekonomicheskaya Zhizn*, No. 172, August 4, 1922.
[6] *Ekonomicheskaya Zhizn*, No. 196, September 2, 1922.

it would take two years and another $1.5 million to move it to Siberia. Later in the year the government speeded up payments to Lenzoloto to relieve the financial crisis but refused to import the dredge, as low gold reserves would not warrant the expenditure.[7] However, dredging was the only solution to the long term Siberian gold problem.

The situation was so abysmally bad that in a 1923 report on Soviet gold mines in *Ekonomicheskaya Zhizn*, it was seriously suggested that it was no longer worthwhile to continue working the deposits. Production was too small and the costs too high to justify the expenditures of materials and labor. An almost unbelievable cost-revenue ratio of 25:1 was quoted. A dredge was considered to be the only solution.[8]

In mid-1923, a French mining expert, Professor E. N. Barbot-de-Marni, was hired by the Soviets to make a report on the Siberian mines, including those in the prewar Lena group. The report stated that there had been no illicit digging of gold, but that work had been concentrated in high-grade mines, while low-grade mines were ignored. The equipment was prewar and utilized in an inefficient manner. Barbot-de-Marni pointed out that, although the Lena mines possessed the most advanced drilling equipment in Russia (forty steam drills of the Keystone type), no exploration and development work was in progress. In brief, the higher-grade properties were working and so could work at a profit, whereas lower-grade properties and exploration work required for future development were ignored. Barbot-de-Marni's recommendation was for state assistance to get development under way.

In mid-1923, thirty-four leasing contracts were made with private individuals and enterprises in the Lena-Vitim area. There were seventeen contracts in the platinum mining areas of Semipalatinsk. Nine mines were leased in the Northern Yenessei and five in the Southern Yenessei district, together with eleven gold mines in the Altai Mountains.[9]

After 1925, gold began to assume its key role in Soviet development as a major earner of the foreign exchange required to pay for imports of foreign equipment and technology utilized in the industrialization program. Gold mining was, consequently, put in the vanguard of the Soviet mineral exploitation program: an effort characterized by Shimkin as 'the merciless and insatiable Soviet quest for gold.'[10]

---

[7]   *Ekonomicheskaya Zhizn*, January 16, 1923. The original cost of the dredge was $495,367, of which $432,135 was paid before the Revolution. However, spares, freight, customs, and assembly required an estimated total expenditure of $1,532,836.

[8]   *Ekonomicheskaya Zhizn*, February 20, 1923.

[9]   *Ekonomicheskaya Zhizn*, No. 143, June 29, 1923.

[10]   Demitri B. Shimkin, *Minerals: A Key to Soviet Power* (Cambridge: Harvard, 1953), p. 172.

The Lena Goldfields, Ltd. (United Kingdom), concession was concluded on April 30, 1925. It was to extend for a period of thirty years in the Lena gold mines and for fifty years in the Ural and Altai Mountain districts. The area included in the concession was that previously leased from the tsarist government and operated by a Russian subsidiary, the Lensky Zolotopromish-lennoie Tovarichestvo. In the 1925 agreement the properties of the former Sissert copper mines and the Altai District Mining Company were also operated by Lena Goldfields.

The Lena concession therefore, covered the following properties:[11]

1. The Sissert copper mines (described in chapter 5).
2. The Nikolopavdinsky platinum mines, reportedly. However, nothing has been traced of any post-revolutionary development of this property by Lena Goldfields.
3. The copper, lead, and zinc deposits on the Irtish River (discussed in chapter 5).
4. The north Kuznetsk (Kiselov) coal mines (discussed in chapter 3).
5. The anthracite mines at Yegoshin in the Urals (discussed in chapter 3).
6. Gold mines on the Lena-Vitim Rivers in Siberia. This is the only development covered in this chapter, and a major part of the Lena complex.
7. The Zirianovsky, Zmeynogorsky, and Pryirtishky districts (discussed in chapter 5).
8. The copper and iron smelters at Sissert and Revdinsky (discussed in chapters 4 and 5).
9. The Degtiarinsky copper mines (discussed in chapter 5.)
10. The Gumeshevsky copper smelter (discussed in chapter 5).
11. Wire- and nail-making factories in the Urals (discussed in chapter 13).
12. The Bodaibo railroad in the Lena-Vitim area, the Degtiarinsk railroad in the Urals, and the shipping system on the River Lena, under a separate agreement with the People's Commissariat of Ways and Communications.

The concession did not include Soviet participation in either operations or management, but the Soviet government received a royalty equal to 7 percent of the total output of gold, and the concessionaire received the right to export any surplus duty-free.

The company was granted unrestricted freedom of hiring and firing labor, and, in regard to social insurance and railroad rates, treatment equal to that afforded government trusts.

---

[11] Based on an interview with Lyman Brown by the United States Consulate at Riga, Latvia in May 1925 (316-136-419). There is some doubt whether the Nikolopav-dinsky platinum mines were operated by the Lena concession, but they were part of the tsarist-granted prerevolutionary concession.

Arbitration of disputes was to be by an arbitration court composed of an equal number of representatives from both sides, with an umpire selected from either the faculty of the Freiburg Mining School, in Saxony or the King's Mining School, in Stockholm.

The agreement was a departure from previous agreements in that it permitted extensive industrial and commercial operations without the joint management of the Soviet government, and in addition gave the concessionaire practically unlimited control of real property (at least on paper), although title was not established, together with control of labor and the right of unrestricted export.[12]

In 1928 the Lena Goldfields Company was producing 35 percent of all the gold mined in the Soviet Union.[13] It was also by far the most efficient producer.[14]

Table 6-1   SOURCES OF GOLD PRODUCED IN THE
SOVIET UNION, 1913–28

Year	Kilograms of Gold Produced By:		% Produced by Lena Concession
	U.S.S.R.	Lena Concession	
1913	—	11,728	—
1921	—	966*	—
1922–3	11,179	2,588*	—
1923–4	20,000	4,734*	—
1924–5	25,258	6,749*	—
1925–6	25,149	8,364**	33
1926–7	23,152	8,552**	37
1928	27,965	7,953**	28

Sources: 1913–24: B. P. Torgashev, *The Mineral Industry of the Far East* (Shanghai: Chali, 1930), p. 102.

1925–28: Amtorg, *Economic Review of the Soviet Union*, III, 34.

* Operated by Soyuszoloto.

** Operated by Lena Goldfields Co. This production is in excess of the 6,500 kg. annual production required by the concession agreement.

---

[12]   Based on interview between Lyman Brown, representing the concession, and F. W. B. Coleman, the United States Consul at Riga, Latvia, printed in Report No. 2838, May 12, 1925. Coleman makes pointed comment on the value of the concession, and history was to bear him out almost exactly: 'While my opinion may be a passing one and gratuitous, I think that Mr. Brown is too optimistic and that nothing will come out of the agreement in the shape of profits. Asked what security he had that the party of the first part would fulfill the terms of their contract, Mr. Brown said that they 'could not afford to do otherwise: which, in view of the past records, is adjudged very slim security.' (316–136–426.)

[13]   *Times* (London), September 3, 1930, p. 13. The Soviet estimate is also 35 precent. (Amtorg, *op. cit.*, III, 116.)

[14]   The Lena Co. employed 8,000 workers and was producing 2.73 kgs of gold per worker per year. The Soviet national average was between 0.44 and 0.59 kgs of gold per worker per year. (Amtorg, *op. cit.*, III, 285.)

Lena Goldfields fulfilled its agreement to produce more than 6,500 kilograms of gold per year. Both Soviet and Western sources agree on this point. Reference to table 6–1 indicates that, during the life of the concession, Lena consistently exceeded the agreed gold output, and averaged more than one-third of Soviet gold production between 1925 and 1928.

According to Soviet sources, Lena also fulfilled the other requirements of the concession.[15] A summary of the first three years of operations (1925–8) stated that Lena had installed a 17-foot dredge in the Bodaibo section of the Lena-Vitim fields 'before the time set in the agreement.' This in itself was a massive undertaking, as a large, complex piece of equipment had to be moved from the United States to the far interior of Siberia, installed, and put into operation. Special roads and equipment were built, and the dredge was put into operation in July 1928. A yearly average 8,000 kilograms of gold was produced between 1925 and 1928, with a slight drop at the end of 1928 because of the changeover from hand to machine methods. It was estimated that the dredge alone, apart from re-equipment of the underground mines operated by Lena, would double Soviet gold production almost immediately.[16]

By March 1929, Lena had invested, according to *Izvestia*,[17] over eighteen million rubles in new equipment, and in addition had restored old plants to operation. However, the Lena Goldfields honeymoon was not to last for long. In April 1928, just as the dredge was being finally readied for production, an article by I. Maisel in *Ekonomicheskaya Zhizn* entitled 'It must be ended' began the harassment which was to culminate in the expulsion of Lena in 1930. Maisel argued that Lena had turned exploitation over to starateli (private prospectors) and to artels comprised of former hired laborers. That this was the arrangement also used by the Aldenzoloto trust was not mentioned. The article cataloged alleged complaints against the operation and specifically stated that the company was 'manifesting a quite unjustified and inadmissible intolerance and stubborness' in relation to the miners' economic provisions: i.e., social insurance payments and allotments for cultural needs. The crux of the argument was, however, the organization of artels, the company preferring a

15 Amtorg, *op. cit.*, IV (February 1929), 33.

16 The dredge was one of four placer dredges built for Russia by the Bucyrus Co. (United States) in 1916–7. Of these, two were delivered and one canceled. The fourth was the Lena dredge, a massive piece of equipment, as high as a six-story building. It was delivered to Lena in 1927 after being moved from South Milwaukee to Baltimore on seventy-five flat cars, to Murmansk by steamer and to Irkutsk by rail, then 200 miles on a mountain trail by wagon and sledge, and then to Kachuca by barge on the River Lena. At Kachuca it was reloaded on small boats for a 700-mile trip up the River Vitim to Bodaibo, just 11 miles short of its final destination. Delivery and assembly took 18 months. [*Designed for Digging: The First 75 Years of Bucyrus-Erie Company* (Evanston: Northwestern University Press, 1955), p. 156.]

17 *Izvestia*, March 26, 1929.

simple association of miners while the Miners' Union wanted an organization similar to labor artels under which the artel also became a contractor. The time was picked well—the start of the gold-mining season—and the union called for a revision of company policy, irrespective of a concession agreement which clearly gave the Lena company a clear option in this aspect of labor relations.

This article was followed eighteen months later by one in *Izvestia* of October 22, 1929, which made a derisive attack on the profits being made by Lena: 'The profits of the concessionaire are growing—what a victory.' As the Lena concession got into full operation, it was attacked as a 'weed in the socialist system' which required attention. Two months later the GPU searched the company offices and arrested several Lena employees.

Continual Soviet interference with production by labor strikes, management fines, and similar harassment slowed output after 1928.[18] The Soviets then claimed that the reduced output was non-fulfillment of paragraph 39 of the concession agreement, *ergo* the agreement 'has lost its validity owing to the one-sided and unlawful action of the Lena Goldfields. . . .'[19] Liubimov was thus enabled to make the statement that gold production was 'below agreement,'[20] although previously published Soviet figures (table 6–1) had indicated a production well in excess of the agreement.

In February 1930 it was reported that the Soviet government had given notice of its intention to annul the Lena concession in the first week of April 1930. Lena denied the validity of this report on the basis that the Soviet government had no authority under the concession agreement to give any such notice or to annul the concession.

The labor disturbances had started in earnest in January, and on January 30 the Soviet courts sentenced the Lena manager to eight months' forced labor and a fine of $62,500 for alleged late payment of wages.

On February 12, 1930, Lena sent the Soviet government a telegram asking for arbitration and nominated Sir Leslie Scott as its representative. There was no direct reply to the telegram, but on February 28 the Soviets agreed to arbitration via *Izvestia*, which published a long indictment of the Lena Company alleging that:

(*a*) The company had insufficient capital to undertake the program.

(*b*) It had failed to reach its production and construction program in the last year.

(*c*) It had failed to utilize the latest technical methods.[21]

---

18   *Times* (London), September 3, 1930, p. 13.
19   *Documents Concerning the Competence of the Arbitration Court Set Up in Connection with the Questions Outstanding Between the Lena Goldfields Company Limited and the U.S.S.R.* (Moscow: Glavnyi kontsessionnyi komitet, 1930), p. 32.
20   Liubimov, *op. cit.*, p. 139.
21   *Izvestia*, March 6, 1930.

The article alleged failure to meet foreign obligations and breakdowns in the dredge and the Urals copper smelter as evidence of the validity of these charges.

Three weeks later, four Russian employees of the concession were placed on trial on charges of espionage and sabotage, and on May 9 all four were jailed.

In the meantime, the Arbitration Court had been established in Berlin with Professor Stutzer as Chairman. On May 10, Moscow recalled its delegate to the Court. Stutzer decided to continue hearings and stated that the concession could be abrogated only by a decision of the Court. At the end of May, the Soviet government instructed the Commissariat of Transportation to take over the steamships and other transportation property of the Lena concession.

On August 7 the Special Court of Arbitration opened its hearing with the Soviets absent. It was established without question that Lena had fulfilled the terms of the agreement. Whereas the agreement called for an expenditure of $11 million in seven years, Lena had actually spent $17.5 million in four and a half years. Evidence of adequate financing was presented. On the other hand, extensive evidence was presented that after 1929 the Soviets had started to use physical pressure against Lena, first by cutting off supplies, and then by ejecting the company from the Sissertsky limestone deposits by armed force. (Limestone was essential as a flux in the Lena smelter operations.) An independent arbitrator valued the Lena property at more than $89 million.

The Soviets did not put in an appearance; the Court found for Lena, but the concession passed into the pages of history. A booklet was published by the U.S.S.R. in both German and English, as a rather superficial attempt to explain what was clearly completely unjustifiable expropriation.[22]

In retrospect, there can be no other conclusion than that the Soviets deliberately enticed Lena into the U.S.S.R. to get the massive dredge installed and also as much else as they could along the way. It is, in the light of history, a clear case of premeditated industrial theft on a massive scale.

Before Lena Goldfields entered the Siberian gold fields, some 75 percent of all Russian gold output was being produced by hand methods, and there was no mechanical equipment. Consequently, output per worker was both very low and fluctuating: ' . . . even the record of the most efficient producer, the foreign concession at the Lena Goldfields, was unimpressive.'[23] With the

---

[22] *Materialien zur Frage der Zustaendigkeit des Schiedsgerichts in Sachen 'Lena Gold-fields'—Union d.S.S.R.* (Moscow: Glavnyi kontsessionnyi komitet, 1930), published in English as *Documents Concerning the Competence of the Arbitration Court Set Up in Connection with the Questions Outstanding Between the Lena Goldfields Company Limited and the U.S.S.R.* Also see, for the Soviet side, S. A. Bernstein, *The Financial and Economic Results of the Working of the Lena Goldfields Limited* (London: Black-friars, n.d.). This title must be a classic among misnomers. The booklet contains not a single statistic concerning 'results.'

[23] Shimkin, *op. cit.*, p. 168.

introduction of the Lena dredge, however, the stage was set for a massive increase in production at a much lower production cost, and the field of operations could be extended into the low-grade-ore-bearing areas. By 1928 Herbert Guedella (Chairman of Lena) in his annual report to shareholders reported that the results of capital expenditures were beginning to show. There had been an intense reorganization of production during the previous three years; large orders for plant equipment had been placed (in addition to the dredge), and these had been financed with the aid of the Deutsche Bank in Germany.[24] In brief, by 1930 the technical reorganization was almost complete. In addition, the Soviets decided to utilize American technology. Consequently, Lena, held predominantly by British interests, could be expropriated without fear that political repercussions would affect further technical acquisitions.

THE LESSER GOLD CONCESSIONS

Smaller gold-mining and exploration concessions were located in the Far East, in the Amur River basin, Okhotsk, and Northwest Siberia.

Table 6–2　LESSER SOVIET GOLD MINING CONCESSIONS LEASED TO FOREIGN OPERATORS, 1921–8

Concessionaire	Country of Origin	Location	Years	Investment	Work
Vint concession	United States	Amur Basin	1921–8	N.A.*	Mining
Far Eastern Prospecting Co. Inc. (formerly Smith concession)	United States	Amur Basin	1923–4	125,000 rubles	Prospecting
Ayan Corporation, Ltd.	United Kingdom	Okhotsk	1925–7	400,000 rubles	Prospecting
Yotara Tanaka	Japan	Kamchatka	1925–?	N.A.	Mining
Shova Kiuka Kabushiki Kaisia	Japan	Far East	1925–?	N.A.	Mining
D.A. Hammerschmidt	United States	Amur Basin	1926–8	$375,000	Prospecting

Source: U.S. State Dept. Decimal File, see text.
* Not available.

The first such concession was granted to J. C. Vint in 1921 and was followed by at least five others. Apart from direct concessions, there were also attempts by the Soviets to get Chinese capital and labor for the Okhotsk and Amur fields.[25] As late as 1928, when the trust Dalzol (Far East Gold Trust) had been

[24] *Times* (London), November 20, 1928.
[25] *Harbin Daily News*, May 27, 1924.

organized to operate the Amur River mines, the Soviets had agents in Harbin, China, to recruit 3,000 coolies and were also utilizing United States gold mining machinery and mining specialists.[26]

The Vint gold mining concession, granted in December 1921 for 20 years, covered 1,600 dessiatins along the River Smirtak, in the Amur Region of the Far East, and gave Vint the right to exploit prerevolutionary mines at Ftoroi, Blagovestchensky, Petrovsky, Zaharievsky, Novopoktovsky, Beregovi, Evdo-kievsky, and Codachny, and the placer deposits in the Smirtak River valley for two versts upstream from the Codachny gold mine. As late as 1923 this concession represented 'practically the only organized effort either in Russia or Siberia to produce gold.'[27] Vint was required to install a dredge, with a capacity of not less than 2 cubic feet, not later than June 1, 1922. Extra dredges had to be installed before July 15, 1925 to excavate not less than 50 cubic sazhens per day.[28]

In lieu of the deposit of 35,000 gold rubles required in the concession agreement, Vint was allowed to purchase a dredge already on the Smirtak River.

Vint had both British and American partners and raised capital in the United States, Britain, Belgium, and China at various times during the life of the concession, which lasted at least until 1927.

The Vint concession is especially interesting from the viewpoint of the heavy tax burden placed upon more successful concessionaires. According to information given in an interview with the U.S. State Department, Vint was subjected to the following taxes:

1. A 'dessiatin tax' of one gold ruble per year for each of the 1,600 dessiatins in the concession.
2. A land tax of 0.75 ruble per dessiatin.
3. A workmen's insurance tax equal to 10 percent of the wages paid.
4. A workmen's association tax equal to 2 percent of wages paid.
5. An assessment of 10 gold kopecks per dessiatin for the 'gold miners' association.'
6. A 6-percent tax on turnover in the general merchandise store which Vint was required to operate as part of the concession.
7. A local tax not in excess of 30 percent of the total state tax (items 1 through 4 above).
8. The cost of providing a school for the miners' children.

[26] 'The Soviet mining officials are unable to work these mines without foreign mining experts and without the labor of Chinese coolies who work more efficiently and with less wages than do Russian laborers.' [U.S. Consulate in Harbin, China, Report, July 23, 1928 (316–136–675).]

[27] U.S. Consulate in Riga, Report 1480, November 20, 1923.

[28] There is a copy of the Vint agreement in the U.S. State Dept. Decimal File, 316–136–348, with other data scattered throughout 136.

9. A 5-percent royalty on gross output to the government, which in any event reserved the right to fix the price of gold and required all production to be delivered to government laboratories.

Vint held that he was unable to make the proposition pay and that taxes were continually raised—eventually to the point of eliminating profits. Apart from that, he argued that locally concluded agreements were not always honored in Moscow, and that on taking a local agreement to Moscow for ratification he would be 'chipped down' even further. Although the concession may have been profitable from Vint's viewpoint in 1923, continuing tax pressure made it unprofitable from about 1924 until its demise some time after 1927.

C. Smith, a mining engineer and former employee of the Inter-Allied Railway Commission, in Siberia, was the operator of a gold mining concession in the River Karga area of the Amur Basin. The concession, granted in November 1923, was for the exploration and production of gold. One year was allowed for initial prospecting, during which all gold had to be turned over 'without payment,' and a further twenty-three years was allowed to mine any prospects discovered in the initial prospecting period. The agreement contained the usual terms: customs-free import of machinery and equipment, a land rental fee and 5–8 percent output tax, together with state and local taxes. At the end of the concession period, all equipment and properties were to be turned over to the Soviet government in good condition.

It is certain that Smith did some work. He brought in a mining engineer, three American drilling specialists, and fifty Russian laborers. The concession was transferred to a United States registered company, the Far Eastern Exploration Company.[29] Drills and supplies ordered through this company were shipped to the Drazhud gold fields. At this point the history of the concession becomes vague. It was reported that more than $125,000 was spent in the first nine weeks of exploration, but that the expenditure was made in looking at oil-well borings and that the imported drills were not used. It can reasonably be assumed that the concession lasted only a short while—probably less than one year—and that it made an insignificant contribution to Soviet gold fields development in the Far East.[30]

[29] *New York Times*, October 30, 1923, p. 8, col. 2, reported that the Far Eastern Exploration Company, headed by Henry T. Hunt, had received concession prospecting rights to 3,500 square miles of placer fields in the Amur Basin; there was no mention of C. Smith.

[30] U.S. State Dept. Decimal File, 316–131–147. The Smith concession is more interesting in relation to the 'arm's length hypothesis' discussed in chap. 17. Smith was suspected by the U.S. State Dept. of being in the pay of the Soviet Union, was a member of the Peasant International, and later, in 1926, became Moscow representative for the American-Russian Chamber of Commerce, which had such prestigous members as Westinghouse, International General Electric, and Deere.

In early 1925, a gold prospecting and mining concession was granted to the Ayan Corporation, Ltd., of the United Kingdom. The company acquired the right to prospect for, and mine, gold in the Okhotsk uyezd, Kamchatka. The concession had a nominal life of thirty-six years; during the first four years the company was required to expend 600,000 rubles in prospecting work, deposit 100,000 rubles as security, and purchase all buildings and existing physical property at market value. Modern prospecting and mining techniques were to be imported by the concessionaire, who was also required to build roads and communications, with the right to run aerial communications if desired.

The entire gold output was to be delivered to government laboratories for purchase by the Soviet government. A rental was paid on land explored, a 5-percent royalty on the total output of gold, and an overall 5-percent tax. The company organized food stores and was required to abide by the labor laws and to hand over all buildings and property intact at the end of the thirty-six years.[31]

After two years the concession was cancelled at the request of the Ayan Company, in the light of unpromising prospecting results.[32]

A protocol of the 1925 Treaty of Friendship and Recognition between Japan and the U.S.S.R. made provision for gold concessions in Kamchatka and Okhotsk. The Kamchatka concession was taken up by two Japanese firms, Yotara Tanaka and Shova Kiuka Kabushiki Kaisia.

The D. A. Hammerschmidt concession to prospect and mine gold in the Amur Basin was signed on November 12, 1926. The American concessionaires were required to transfer not less than $375,000 capital to a joint-stock company, and the founder members were to be subject to the approval of the Soviet government. The initial prospecting period was to expire on March 31, 1928 and the mining period on March 21, 1948. During the initial period, Hammerschmidt and his associates were required to undertake 2,000 meters of drilling and do trenching on an exploratory basis. Any gold mined was to be deposited with the Soviet government, and the concession was to be voided if mining did not commence before March 31, 1928. A royalty of 3 percent was to be paid to the U.S.S.R., in addition to an annual land rent, plus 4 percent of the gold mined, in lieu of national and local taxes. The mine was to be turned over to the U.S.S.R. at the end of the concession period.

The concession was subject to the Labor Code, and the lessee 'agreed to admit . . . for purposes of study, Soviet geologists, engineers and technical personnel.'[33]

[31]   *Izvestia*, No. 103, May 8, 1925.
[32]   U.S. State Dept. Decimal File, 316–136–667.
[33]   *Ekonomicheskaya Zhizn*, No. 275, November 27, 1926.

These smaller concessions did not have the same magnitude of capital investment as Lena Goldfields, but they were required to introduce modern mining and exploration equipment and techniques.

Those gold mines that did not come within the sphere of concessionary activity were equipped with modern equipment, and Western mining engineers were hired to establish and plan future production. The Kockar gold mine, in the Southern Urals, previously a French concession, was the first to be equipped in this manner, in 1928. According to Littlepage, who was in a position to have accurate data, by the end of the 1920s *each* gold mine, outside the concessions, had four or five United States mining engineers and employed 'thousands of foreign workers.'[34]

It is estimated, therefore, that in 1928 about 40 percent of Soviet gold was being produced directly by foreign concessions utilizing modern dredges and ore-crushing and sorting plants. This estimate is indirectly confirmed by other data from Soviet sources. It was reported in 1928, for example, that 56 percent of gold was being produced by 'individual prospectors and purchased from them by the large companies'—presumably Soyuszoloto and the other gold trusts. The balance of 44 percent was being produced by 'organizations using hired labor'—presumably Lena and the smaller concessions.[35]

DISCOVERY AND DEVELOPMENT OF THE ALDEN GOLD FIELDS

In 1924 a rich gold field was discovered and exploited in Northwest Siberia: the Alden. There are two features worth noting about this discovery: first, this was the initial gold discovery under Soviet rule and the only major discovery in the 1920s, and second, it was not opened up to foreign concessions for development. The question then logically arises: how is such a development, remote from Western influence, consistent with the hypothesis of this study?

Under the 1922 decree, private leasing and exploration had been restored in gold and platinum mining. The Alden discovery was made in 1923 by Kuzmin, a private digger working on his own account and not employed by a State organization.[36] The report of the discovery spread rapidly, and the response was a typical Western-style gold rush. Thousands of prospectors flocked into the Alden area, under the inducements offered in newspaper

[34]   J. D. Littlepage and D. Bess, *In Search of Soviet Gold* (New York: Harcourt Brace & Co., 1937), pp. 68, 87–8. Littlepage was chief production inspector for the Soviet Gold Trust at this time; he later became deputy chief engineer of the same trust.

[35]   The heavy reliance on individual prospectors or 'Russian concessionaires' is confirmed by Littlepage and Bess, *op. cit.*, p. 121.

[36]   *Izvestia*, No. 1, January 1, 1927

publicity.[37] The result was a decrease in the working force of the Far Eastern province mines from 12,238 in 1923 to 8,222 in 1924, as workers moved to the Northwest.[38] The field was then closed to private claims, and in mid-1925 the 12,000 or so workers who had moved to Alden were organized into artels. A trust, Aldenzoloto, was then created and a few months later the Yakut Autonomous Socialist Soviet Republic was closed to outsiders.[39]

In brief, this remarkably rich deposit was prospected and initially developed by individual 'Russian concessionaires,' as Littlepage calls them, rather than foreign concessionaires. The state trust was formed three years after the initial discovery and development.

The extraordinary inefficiency of the state trust (even the best-run) has been described by Littlepage, who was in a position to observe. The Soviet Gold Trust was run by Serebrovsky, the best of the trust directors in the 1920s. Serebrovsky hired Littlepage as his technical administrator, but the difficulty of efficient administration is seen in the examples given by Littlepage. The Alaska Juneau gold mine, one of the largest in the world, had five people in the office and could provide figures promptly. Littlepage describes the typical trust gold mine with 150 in the mine office, and a fraction of the United States output. It could take weeks or months to get comparable figures.[40]

PLATINUM EXPORTS

Before World War I, the Urals provided almost all the world's supply of the platinum group metals. Production of platinum in 1901 was 14,000 pounds and in 1914 10,700 pounds. In general, the platinum producing areas escaped the ravages of war and revolution, and demand was certainly stimulated between 1917 and 1919 by vigorous pre-emptive buying on the part of the Allies to prevent platinum from falling into German hands. The provisional Omsk government required sale to government sources but little else of a restrictive nature. The area was occupied by the Soviets in 1919 and within two years production dropped to between 700 and 1,000 pounds per year.

> The condition of the platinum industry appears to be no better than that of the gold industry. All the events which caused the collapse of the gold industry . . . refer as well to the platinum industry.[41]

By 1921, production had fallen to 360 pounds, concentrated in three areas along the River Isse. Apparently some production was on an 'irregular' basis,

[37]   *Harbin Daily News*, December 7, 1924.
[38]   *Ekonomicheskaya Zhizn*, No. 355, December 9, 1924.
[39]   *Izvestia*, No. 23, January 29, 1926.
[40]   Littlepage and Bess, *op. cit.*, p. 216.
[41]   *Ekonomicheskaya Zhizn*, No. 173, August 4, 1922.

and platinum was exported to the West through Latvia in substantial quantities until choked off by more effective Soviet border patrols in 1925.[42]

From about 1923 to 1926, Rusplatina used the London chemical firm of Johnson, Mathey and Company as a world distributing agent, although at rare intervals platinum was also shipped via the Compagnie de la Platine, in Paris. This trade was on the basis of a yearly renewable contract. In 1926 Johnson, Mathey and Company became a little high-handed and the Soviets established Edelmetall Verwertungs Gesellschaft in Berlin, which apparently had the effect of bringing the London firm back into line.

This was followed by an active campaign of price cutting to regain the prewar share of the market. In order to accomplish this, the industry had been reorganized and equipped with imported modern electric shovels. This meant that platinum could be mined profitably where the ore content was as low as 1/30 pennyweight platinum content per ton, in contrast to the requirement for 1/10-pennyweight per ton under earlier conditions. By 1926, production was restored to 5,800 pounds per year, all of which was exported. However, this was hardly a major contribution to foreign exchange earnings, as the price of platinum had been forced down from $112–$120 in 1925 to $62 per ounce in 1927.

Two platinum-refining works had been started by the Russian government in 1914 under the pressure of changing wartime conditions. These plants were started again in the early 1920s, with the assistance of Professor L. Duparc (France), described as 'the greatest platinum expert in Europe.'[43]

BAUXITE AND THE ALUMINUM COMPANY OF AMERICA

A Type I concession agreement was signed in April 1926 between the U.S.S.R. and the Aluminum Company of America (ALCOA) which gave the latter the right to explore for bauxite, the raw material for aluminum, throughout Russia during a period of two years. Although no details were published concerning this agreement, representatives of ALCOA were interviewed from time to time by U.S. State Department officers, and it appears that nine ALCOA engineers prospected for bauxite in several locations—mainly south of Tikhvin.

The Tikhvin area blocked out by ALCOA contained four deposits of Grade I bauxite, estimated to contain 2.8 million tons of 'probable' ore, together with additional tonnages of 'possible' ore. The ore had a high silica content,

---

[42]   The figures for 'irregular exports' are available, as Latvia produces no platinum and Latvian platinum exports for this period are all of 'irregular' Russian platinum. Export figures for 'regular' platinum are not available, but these were approximately 40,000 oz. per year, compared to just under 10,000 oz. for 'irregular' exports.

[43]   *Annuaire, op. cit.,* page XI.

together with iron oxide (an impurity), and the project was abandoned at the end of 1927, as the engineers considered the deposits not of commercial value and unworthy of further development.[44]

The Soviets did not give up. Tikhvin was their best bauxite deposit, and they were determined to build an aluminum industry. In 1929 the German firm Vereinigte Aluminumwerke A-G., which had perfected a reduction process applicable to the Russian bauxite grades, reported that the Soviets had been attempting ' . . . for some time to secure the patent rights for Russia or at least operating rights to this process, but the negotiations have remained negative due to the failure of the Soviets to furnish certain guarantees.'[45]

Nevertheless, by 1930 technical-assistance agreements had been made to cover most aspects of aluminum manufacture. An agreement in 1930 with Compagnie de Produits Chimiques et Electrométallurgiques S.A. (France) covered the reduction of aluminum; and another contract, with Dr. Ing Straube of Karlsruhe, covered the manufacture of aluminum hydroxide, synthetic cryolite, and aluminum electrodes. A third agreement, with the Société du Duralumin S.A. (France), covered the manufacture of duralumin.[46] A fourth agreement with Frank E. Dickie, an independent American engineer, provided technical assistance to Aluminstroi, the Construction Bureau for Aluminum Plants.[47]

MICA MINING AND THE
INTERNATIONAL MICA COMPANY, INC.

The largest mica deposits in the U.S.S.R. were included in a Type I concession agreement in 1924 with the Russian-American Mining and Engineering Corporation, a subsidiary of the International Mica Company, Inc., of the United States. The concessionaire agreed to produce 35 tons of mica in the first year, increasing quantities gradually to 175 tons in the fifth year. A 5-percent royalty was paid on all production, and export was allowed by the operator. Modern mining equipment was imported and installed by the company.

---

[44] U.S. State Dept. Decimal File, 316–136–363 and 1230; 316–131–388 and 316–108–2008. The analyses of Tikhvin ore are in Geologicheskii komitet, *Godovoi Obzor Mineral'nykh Resursov SSSR za 1925/6* (Leningrad: 1927), pp. 47–8.

[45] *Vossische Zeitung*, November 18, 1929.

[46] Vneshtorgizdat, *op. cit.*, pp. 228 and 230. By 1930 Soviet aluminum production was on a pilot basis. The problems of development and the partially successful transfer of Western technology will be covered in Vol. II.

[47] A. A. Santalov and L. Segal, *Soviet Union Yearbook, 1930* (London: Allen and and Unwin) p. 358.

ASBESTOS PRODUCTION IN THE URALS

The Urals' asbestos deposits have been mined since the 1880s. The most important group of mines was at Baskenovo, about 90 miles northeast of Sverdlovsk; this group produced 96 percent of the 24,000 metric tons asbestos produced in Russia in 1914. Just before the Revolution, mines at Alapaievsk and Iltchirsk (in Irkutsk Province) were equipped and brought into production. The Neviask and Ostanino deposits were known but not exploited. In 1912 Russia exported 13,260 metric tons of asbestos, but exports ceased completely during the Revolution.

The impact of the Revolution was significant. No maintenance was done for several years, many of the mine buildings fell into disrepair, and the open-cut workings became watered. The essential problem, however, between 1917 and 1920 was to organize production and transport the mined asbestos to foreign markets.

Table 6–3   ASBESTOS PRODUCTION IN RUSSIA,
1913 AND 1923

Mines	*1913*	*1923*
	All grades, in metric tons	
Baskenovo Group:		
Grasmuchka River	1,300	None
Korevo	11,500	
Reftinsk	8,000 } 22,350	7,850
Mukhanovsk	1,400	
Okunevsk	150	
Alapaievsk	N.A.	350
Neviask	1,000	None
Ostanino	170	None
Iltchirsk (Irkutsk Province)	N.A.	None

Source: L. Berlinraut, 'Russian Asbestos Mining Reviving,' *Engineering and Mining Journal-Press*, CXXI, No. 4 (January 23, 1926), 164.

In 1920 only 1,300 tons of asbestos were produced (all from the Baskenovo group of mines), and of this more than 75 percent was of inferior grades.

The Alapaievsky, Neviask, Ostanino, and Iltchirsk mines were closed because of the lack of engineering and managerial skills.

In November 1921 a Type I concession was granted to the Allied Chemical and Dye Corporation of the United States, whose subsidiary, the Allied American Corporation, owned by the Hammers, had been operating under license in the U.S.S.R. since 1918. The concession was to restore and operate the Alapaievsky asbestos mines. The concessionaire repaired the buildings and organized production, and by 1922 had more than 1,000 men employed, or 44 percent of all asbestos mine workers in the U.S.S.R., as shown in table 6–4.

The agreement was made with the Ural Industrial Bureau for twenty years, and Allied was required to start work within four months. A sliding scale of required output was established, progressing from 1,200 tons in the first year to 2,580 tons in the fifth and subsequent years. The government had the right to purchase the concession after five years, and was to receive 10 percent of all production.[48]

Table 6-4   WORKERS EMPLOYED BY URALASBEST AND
             HAMMER CONCESSION, 1921-4

Producer/Year	*1921-2*	*1922-3*	*1923-4*
Uralasbest	1,385	2,487	3,067
Hammer	1,100	1,617	1,227
Total	2,485	4,104	4,294
% Employed by Hammer	44.30	39.40	28.60

Source: *Annuaire Politique et Economique*, p. 161.

Hammer has described the pitiful conditions of the workings when operations began.[49]

Six months after the concession agreement was signed, the company received 'one very deteriorated asbestos mine.' Piles of asbestos blocked the passages; there was a heap of 1,200 cubic sazhens of waste ore. There were no communications and no housing for workers or management. The company built 4,800 feet of mine passages and repaired shafts, workers' barracks, houses and schools. Within a year 1,200 poods of high grade material had already been shipped, 20,000 poods of ore were ready for shipment, and 1,100 workers were employed during the summer mining season. To achieve this, the concession imported modern mining and transportation equipment and built a sawmill and a 2½ verst narrow-gauge railroad.[50]

By 1925 the concession began to show a profit.

Uralasbest was created in 1921 to operate the Baskenovo group of mines, but it took many years and many major setbacks before Ruykeyser, an American asbestos mining engineer and consultant to Uralasbest, was able to perform his 'brilliant construction feat . . . in creating the Ural Asbestos Works.'[51] All the problems of Soviet development during the 1920s seem to be found in this trust: lack of working capital, personal jealousies, sabotage, inefficient foreign contracts, fire—but through sheer persistence, and at tremendous cost, a workable enterprise was finally built up.

[48] *Krasnaya Gazeta*, January 4, 1922.
[49] Armand Hammer, *The Quest of the Romanoff Treasure* (New York: Payson, 1932).
[50] *Ekonomicheskaya Zhizn*, No. 280, December 10, 1922.
[51] Shimkin, *op. cit.*, p. 226.

The Baskenovo open-pit mines are by far the most important asbestos deposits in Russia. In the early 1920s, production was primitive and without facilities for upgrading.[52] However, some asbestos was produced, despite the shortage of working capital, under the technical direction of Svedberg, who had been the prewar director and was retained by the Soviets as consulting director. The limitations on output were the extremely primitive mining methods and the absence of a mill to upgrade the mined chrysotile asbestos ore.

The first major step was taken by Uralasbest in 1928, when it concluded a Type III concession agreement with the Humboldt Company (Germany) to build a mill for upgrading the asbestos fiber and to reorganize mining methods.[53] Ruykeyser's description of the circumstances surrounding the mill contract is quoted in full:

> In 1928 I had fulfilled a contract with Amtorg in New York to lay out the preliminary designs, along generalized lines, for the proposed asbestos mill. The plans were accompanied by an extensive report covering all phases of the processes involved. I had pointed out wherein my ideas, based on actual experience with the subject, were at variance with the technical norms sent me as a basis for the drawing, ideas from which I could not depart. But disregarding such advice, without heed of consequence, a contract had been given a large German firm to build the plant. The flowsheet, or schematic arrangement of machines and processes, had been made by the engineers of the Trust under the direct supervision and approval of the technical director. This flowsheet was also contributed to by the Germans, a paltry five-ton sample of the ore being worked on laboratory scale in the preliminary testing. I was told that none of the Russian or German personnel had ever seen a chrysotile asbestos mill in operation; and yet, they had attempted to build what was to be one of the largest mills of its kind in the world.[54]

Not surprisingly, this mill failed to produce the desired results, although there is some evidence that sabotage was at least partly responsible for its failure. There are reports, for example, that wood chips, fatal to asbestos quality, were found along the production line. The mill was destroyed by fire in May 1929, and, as a result of the subsequent investigation, three Russian civil engineers were shot by the GPU and two sentenced to twenty years' hard labor. Svedberg, the technical director, was arrested for negligence.[55] The Soviet response was to order another mill—a copy of the first; this also failed

[52]   Photographs in W. A. Ruykeyser, *Working for the Soviets* (New York: Covici-Friede, 1932) indicate quite clearly the hand methods in use before Ruykeyser reorganized production in 1929.

[53]   U.S. State Dept. Dispatch No. 1528, Finland, Dec. 7, 1929. (Decimal File, 361.60d21/1.)

[54]   Ruykeyser, *op. cit.*, p. 60.

[55]   U.S. State Dept. Dispatch No. 1528, Finland, December 7, 1929. (Decimal File, 361.60d21/1.)

Table 6-5   ACQUISITION OF ASBESTOS MINING AND MILLING TECHNOLOGY BY URALASBEST, 1921 TO 1930

Year	*Mines* Technology	*Mines* Railroad	Design	Mill Construction (Stroiuralasbest)	Power Station	Final Products (Spinning and Manufacture)
1917	Hand methods	Prewar equipment	—	—	—	Exported only
1926	Hand methods			—	—	Hammer* Moscow plant concession with Czechoslovak management[1][2]
1928	Ruykeyser Reorganization and mechanization.[1]	Purchased from Austria (1927)	I—Humboldt*** Svedberg[1] II—Humboldt[1]***	Humboldt[1]*** Krupp**	Swedish General Electric	Multibestos Company (United States)[1] and equipment purchased in United States[3]
1930			III—Smith** Ruykeyser[1]	Smith** (Canada)[2]		

Sources: [1] Ruykeyser, *op. cit.*
[2] Berlinraut, *op. cit.*
[3] U.S. State Dept. Decimal File.

Notes: *   Type I pure concession.
  **   Type III technical assistance agreement.
  ***   Maschinenbau-Anstalt Humboldt of Cologne.

to perform. The consequence was the contract with Ruykeyser, and later with the C. V. Smith Company, of Thetford, Canada, to design a mill suitable for milling chrysotile asbestos fiber using Canadian experience. This was done, and finally, on the third attempt, the Soviets acquired a mill which would perform adequately. As late as 1939, this third mill was producing 95 percent of Russian asbestos fiber.

ASBESTOS ROOF SHINGLES MANUFACTURE

Asbestos products were manufactured in prewar Russia at the Red Triangle Works in Moscow. This works continued producing at about 25 percent of capacity (see table 6-6) for a few years after the Revolution, and closed in 1923.[56] In 1926, Hammer (Allied American) started to build a factory in Moscow, under a concessionary agreement, to manufacture asbestos roof shingles utilizing raw material from the Alapaievsky asbestos deposits, which had been operated by Allied since 1921. The plant utilized imported modern equipment and was managed by Dr. G. L. Rosenbaum, formerly head of a similar plant in Czechoslovakia.[57]

Table 6-6   MANUFACTURE OF ASBESTOS SHINGLES BY
FOREIGN COMPANIES

Year	Output (Millions of Shingles)
1921–2	2.17
1922–3	2.75
1923–4	3.92
1924–5	11.9
1925–6	16.6
1926–7	21.6
1927–8	38.5
1928–9	51.3
1929–30	65.9

Source: G. Warren Nutter, *The Growth of Industrial Production in the Soviet Union* (Princeton, N.J.: Princeton University Press, 1962), p. 429.

Production of shingles accordingly doubled in a brief period; but this was apparently insufficient, as a Type III technical-assistance agreement was signed in 1928 with the Multibestos Company of the United States for the construction and equipping of another asbestos products plant.[58]

[56] *Ekonomicheskaya Zhizn,* No. 14, October 17, 1923.

[57] *Ekonomicheskaya Zhizn,* No. 124, June 1, 1926.

[58] Another technical-assistance agreement between E. Waite and the Rubber Trust, is listed for asbestos products in American-Russian Chamber of Commerce, *op. cit.,* p. 101. E. Waite however, probably represented Multibestos Company in the U.S.S.R., so that this may not have been a separate contract.

CHAPTER SEVEN

The Industrialization of Agriculture

THE transfer of Western technology and labor skills in agriculture was attempted along five channels. Each was part of a complex set of aims; enlarging the scale of farming, substituting machinery for labor, converting the farming sector into an industry, and removing the class enemy—the *kulak*. The five transfer channels were: the large farming concessions, communes manned by foreign sympathizers, model seed and breeding farms, the modernization of the agricultural implement industry (particularly the tractor, which had a place of honor equivalent to electrification in the industrial sector), and the technical-assistance programs.

Bolshevik interest in large-scale agriculture began in 1924 and has been viewed as an anti-*kulak* measure, but it was equally a method of industrializing the farm sector. The *kulak* was the ideological enemy, but his ability to outproduce the *bedniak* and the *seredniak* made him, at least up to 1928–9, indispensable. There was a basic, naïve assumption (which saturated the thinking of the planners) that a large scale of operations would effect infinite economies in agriculture.[1] The large farms of the American and Canadian prairies attracted the attention of Gosplan and the Commissariat of Agriculture, not because their yields were significantly greater than those in the U.S.S.R., but because the sheer scale of operations and the massive substitution of capital for labor promised a simultaneous solution for two basic problems in the Russian economy: the technical backwardness and hostility of the peasant, the latter stemming from the policy of *prodrazverstka* (forced requisition of grain) and the growing demand for agricultural products from cities and planned industrial complexes. Perhaps a more obvious pressure was Russia's complete failure to regain her prewar position as a major grain exporter or even to reduce the grain imports necessary in 1928–9. The grave decline

[1] The Gigant, largest of the State farms (500,000 acres), had higher costs than less favored and smaller state farms, however.

in Soviet grain procurements in 1929 (down 23 percent from the previous year) was an immediate incentive to action.[2]

In 1928 the People's Commissariat for Agriculture drafted a proposal for the establishment of very large grain farms, and thirty experts were sent to the United States, Canada, and Australia to study large-scale foreign agriculture.[3] Zernotrust (the grain trust), which had been organized to develop large-scale farms, sent two further groups.[4] The Zernotrust program for 1928–9 provided for establishment of fifteen large grain farms with a total area of 150,000 hectares in the Northern Caucasus and Volga regions, to be cultivated by 635 tractors.[5]

THE KRUPP AGRICULTURAL CONCESSIONS

The first attempt to introduce large-scale farming was made with the aid of Krupp in 1924, after an announcement by the Commissariat of Agriculture that it considered agricultural concessions necessary to the development of livestock breeding, sugar beets, and silk worms. Processing and equipment enterprises were thought to be in particular need of foreign help.[6] However, the Krupp agreement, after two major changes, ended in failure. The new Zernotrust farms were consequently modeled on American and Canadian practice.[7]

The Krupp agricultural concessions were an ambitious attempt on the part of the Soviets to introduce modern agricultural large-scale methods into the U.S.S.R., but for Krupp the objective was to develop a market for German agricultural implements and equipment. The concession was also designed to revive Russian agriculture, eliminate the possibility of famine, and turn the U.S.S.R. once again into a grain-exporting country. Krupp'sche Land-concession Manytsch G.m.B.H. was partly financed by a United Kingdom company, Russian Land Concession Manytsch, Ltd., registered in London. The function of the latter was to finance the German company to the extent of 75 percent of the funds required for exploitation of the concession. The United Kingdom company had a basic capital of £40,000, of which £30,000

---

[2]   *Ekonomicheskaya Zhizn*, No. 187, August 16, 1929. See map of crop conditions on p. 2.

[3]   *Izvestia*, No. 114, May 18, 1928.

[4]   *Izvestia*, No. 92, April 21, 1929.

[5]   *Pravda* (Moscow), No. 168, July 21, 1928.

[6]   *Ekonomicheskaya Zhizn*, No. 331, November 11, 1924.

[7]   M. Farbman comments, 'The big American and Canadian farms served as a model for the new experiment and American agronomical engineers and experts were engaged to start it, while the great virgin plains in the southeast of Russia, where the meteorological and soil conditions resembled those of the wheat belt in America, were chosen as the scene of operations.' [*Piatiletka: Russia's Five Year Plan* (New York: New Republic, 1931), p. 130.]

was subscribed by the English group and £10,000 by Krupp. There was an obligation to raise a further £80,000 if required.

A model farm was established in the Don district of the Ukraine, equipped with the most modern equipment and operated according to the latest methods. The final agreement, signed on April 3, 1922, covered an area of 162,000 acres. In a further agreement later in the same year, this area was reduced to 67,500 acres in the Saal section of the Don district. The concession company was obligated to place 3,780 acres under cultivation annually until a total of 63,450 acres was under cultivation at the end of the sixth year.

The Soviet government had an option to buy the whole output at world market prices. At the end of the twelve years the Soviets might purchase the entire concession settlement, and either party would have the absolute right to cancel the agreement in any sixth year. The period of the concession was set at thirty-six years, at the end of which time the concession, with all its equipment, would revert to the U.S.S.R. in good condition; the government would reimburse Krupp for all improvements that had not been amortized.

A special tax was imposed, equal to 17.5 percent of the total annual crop yields, calculated at world market prices on the basis of Rotterdam Grain Exchange quotations; this was in addition to the usual taxes. Krupp was authorized to employ foreign labor to 50 percent of the total labor force and foreign administrative workers to 75 percent. There was a board of arbitration; books and administrative procedures by the company were under the supervision of a government inspection board. Workshops were established to repair, assemble, and improve agricultural machinery.[8]

A new concession agreement for farming in the North Caucasus area was signed by Krupp with the Concessions Committee in 1927. The purpose was changed from grain-growing to sheep-raising. Apparently substantial quantities of the land originally granted in 1923 could grow grain only at a considerable loss.[9] Liquidation was first considered but then replaced by the new agreement. Under the new agreement, 12,000 acres were to be used for grain and the balance of 66,000 acres for sheep-raising. Two thousand sheep were to be imported immediately, and 36,000 to be grazed within eight years.[10] Ten percent of gross receipts were paid to the U.S.S.R., which also had the right to buy the wool at world prices. The wages paid by the concessionaire were 30–40 percent higher than average Russian wages.[11]

[8] U.S. Consulate in Konigsberg (Germany) Report No. 2110, February 17, 1923, and *Ekonomicheskaya Zhizn*, No. 13, January 19, 1923.
[9] U.S. Embassy in Berlin, Report 2561, August 9, 1927. (316–133–626.)
[10] Amtorg, *op. cit.*, II, No. 18 (September 15, 1927), 2.
[11] U.S. Embassy in Berlin, Report 2561, August 9, 1927. (316–133–626.)

A significant change was that the Soviets now agreed to participate in losses (previously they had only participated in profits) and in the burden of financing and management on an equal basis. A mixed enterprise (Type II), the German-Russian Krupp Manushka Company was formed. Krupp's share of the capital was 3 million rubles and the Soviets' 1.5 million rubles. The capital invested by the Krupp concern was 'guaranteed,' and in the event that the undertaking was not successful, it was repayable in 1937.[12]

The soil was too salt, and tractors were more expensive to use than animals. Buildings were built and experiments conducted, but when things went wrong the bureaucratic process was slow and corrections could not readily be made. Grain raising failed, so cattle raising was substituted, and, when this failed, sheep raising—but too long a period elapsed between the substitutions.[13]

OTHER 'PURE' FARMING CONCESSIONS

An agreement between the U.S.S.R., the Volga-Deutsch Bank in the Volga region, and the Berlin firm Deutsch-Russische Agrar A-G (Druag) in late 1923 covered an agricultural concession on 67,000 acres of land in the Volga region. The land was to be used for any purpose seen fit by the German concessionaires. The Soviet government had an option on any products, although any portion not so taken might be exported. A tax equal to 14.5 percent of the total output was paid during the first two years of the life of the concession, but increased to 17.5 percent during the next two years and to 19.5 percent during the remaining years. Rent was equal to 10 percent of gross revenue and additional taxes equalled a further 10 percent.[14]

An extensive agricultural concession was also granted to the German Volga Bank, a Soviet joint-stock company, despite its name. This concession covered 270,000 acres in the German Volga and in the cantons of Federov, Krasnokutsk, and Palassov near the German Autonomous Commune. The concession was then broken up and sublet to German sub-concessionaires in areas of about 50,000 acres each. One such sub-concession was made to the German-Russian Agrarian Association. The company was required to cultivate the land according to an approved plan: 10 percent in the first year, 30 percent in the second, 80 percent in the third, and 100 percent in the fourth. The concession was set up to last for thirty-six years. The company paid to the bank a percentage of total production: 14.5 percent in the first year, 17.5 percent in the next two years, and 19.5 percent thereafter—an arrangement somewhat more liberal than in the Krupp concession. All state and local taxes had to be paid,

[12]   U.S. Embassy in Berlin, Report 3923, September 18, 1928. (316–133–823.)
[13]   *Berliner Tageblatt*, October 6, 1928.
[14]   U.S. Embassy in Berlin, Report No. 2110, November 19, 1923. (316–131–140.)

and upkeep of the roads in the area was a concession responsibility. The bank had the right to buy out the concession after twenty-five years.[15]

An Italian-Russian concession for agricultural and mineral development in the Kuban district was ratified in September 1922. One of the signatories, Commendatore Ferdianando Bussetti, discussed the matter with the U.S. Embassy in Rome shortly after signing the agreement. He indicated that the operation of the 100,000-hectare concession would be under the supervision of the Italian Agricultural Confederation, and that the objective was to grow wheat for export to Italy. Under the contract, 15 percent of production was to be paid to the Soviet government, a further 35 percent was to be sold locally, and the balance was to be exported. It was suggested that 30,000 Italians were to be transported to work the concession, and that they were to be free from Soviet law and under Italian jurisdiction.[16]

An agricultural concession was granted to Harold M. Ware of the United States in 1924. Ware formed the Prikumskaya Russo-American Association and established farms on several thousand acres near Piatigorsk, in the North Caucasus. His main objectives were to train Russian agriculturists in American methods and organize model agricultural enterprises in the U.S.S.R.[17] Ware brought a number of tractors and fifteen American specialists with him.[18]

Another concession agreement signed in 1923 transferred 15,000 dessiatins to the Nansen Mission for the organization of model and demonstration farms. The objective of the concession was to produce high-quality seeds and high-grade animals, together with the organization of model seed-cleaning stations and cooperative butter and cheese factories.[19] A much larger seed-growing concession, however, was Deutsche-Russische Saatbau A-G (Drusag).

---

[15] *Pravda* (Moscow), No. 244, October 27, 1923.

[16] U.S. Embassy in Rome, Report No. 456, October 2, 1922 (316–130–1242). This is a little far-fetched. There is no evidence that such a large number of Italians ever went to work in the U.S.S.R.

[17] U.S. State Dept. Decimal File, 316–136–1241.

[18] *Pravda* (Moscow), No. 198, September 2, 1924. Previously Ware had organized the export of tractors to the U.S.S.R. through the Society of Friends of Russia. The Ford Delegation of 1926 met Ware on several occasions and made unfavorable comments on his personal operations and ethics. For example, 'He intimated that provided we could arrange to give him a complete repair outfit (practically everything on his farm had been a gift) much good would result on both sides. . . .' (Presumably Ware was going to use his 'influence' with the Soviets on behalf of Ford.) Later, with reference to some tractors which Sherwood Eddy had prevailed upon the Ford Motor Co. to give to Ware, he commented to the Delegation that the tractors did good work, 'but that the Company failed to send along the tractors equipped with fenders, pulleys and assorted spares. We thought this a somewhat curious statement from one who had received the tractors as a gift.' [*Report of the Ford Delegation to Russia and the U.S.S.R. April-August 1926* (Detroit: 1926), Ford Motor Company Archives Accession No. 49, p. 145–6.]

[19] *Izvestia*, No. 166, July 26, 1923.

GERMAN-RUSSIAN SEED CULTIVATION COMPANY[20]

Drusag was founded in 1923 by Stinnes, the City of Königsberg, and a group of German agricultural implement firms including Sack, Kemna, and Lanz, together with the Soviet Commissariat of Agriculture. The concession was granted two properties: one in the Kuban area, suitable for seed growing, and the other near Rostov, used as a cattle-breeding station. Substantial investments were made in buildings and machinery, and within two years a greater area was under cultivation than that called for under the agreement.

In 1925 a new agreement replaced the old contract. The main alteration was that the rental fee, based on gross profits, was decreased. Further relaxations were granted in order to allow the concession to export from the Soviet Union so as to purchase foreign machinery and to pay interest on loans raised in Germany. The concession apparently operated well for a year after the reorganization, and in 1926–7 a profit of 450,000 rubles was reported. Then difficulties developed, so that further German and Russian investment was required. By 1927 a debt of more than 300,000 rubles was owed to Gostorg, in addition to the unamortized part of the original German loan. A further 600,000 rubles was borrowed: 450,000 from the German government and the balance from the City of Königsberg and German implement-manufacturing companies. Of this sum, 150,000 rubles was used to repay the balance of the German debt, 300,000 rubles was used to settle various Russian claims, and the balance was used as working capital to carry the enterprise over until the 1927 harvest. However, in 1927 the German obligation had grown to some one million marks, and the Soviets began to move the enterprise toward compulsory liquidation. Further negotiation kept the enterprise alive until 1932.

The existence of the Drusag concession from 1923 to 1932 enables us to make a brief comparison between 'tractorization' undertaken in the late 1920s and the experience of the concession—an island of private enterprise in a sea of collectivization.

The mass introduction of the tractor, the high cost of depreciation, the cost of fuel, the almost total lack of repair facilities, and the rough treatment the machine received in the hands of the peasant made it an extremely wasteful method of farming. The Drusag concession, farming land of good quality in a large plot of 27,000 acres, found animal power was often more economical than mechanical power. Animals, especially oxen, were cheap: a unit consisting of eight yoke oxen, a four furrow plow, and two men did the job as efficiently as, and at less cost than, a tractor. The tractor only came into its own when speed was a factor.

[20]   The information in this section is based on the German Foreign Ministry Archives.

The Russian however is inclined to think that, because the tractor turns over the soil at a prodigious rate and with lots of cheerful noise and bustle it is doing it more economically and efficiently than any other method.[21]

The contribution of Drusag was not, therefore, to a more efficient allocation of agricultural resources. For a period of ten years the enterprise contributed seed and pedigreed cattle to the state and collective farms, and although Gostorg made sizable investments from time to time, these were repaid, while the innovations developed by the concessions were contributed free of charge.

TECHNICAL ASSISTANCE IN AGRICULTURE

An early form of technical assistance was given by the International Agrarian Institute, established in 1923 by the International Peasant Soviet.[22] The institute consisted of five departments, for the study of peasant agriculture, agrarian legislation, agricultural practices and methods of work, the attitude of local Communist parties to this work, and the contribution made by peasant economies in the world toward the achievement of a higher standard of living. The institute established a library and published a monthly, *The Agrarian Question.*

The main objective of the institute was the world-wide collection of information concerning the peasant and his relation to agricultural technique and economics.[23] In 1924 the institute established an agricultural bureau in New York to study the theory and practice of agriculture in the United States, Canada, and the Latin American countries.[24] In the same year an American citizen, Coleman, founded an agricultural school in the U.S.S.R. with an American staff.[25]

The acquisition of agricultural technology increased as delegations went from and visited the U.S.S.R. A Soviet Agricultural Commission of twelve experts, headed by P. B. Asaultschenko, visited Denmark in June 1926 to study Danish agricultural methods. The commission purchased some animals for breeding purposes, although fewer than had been expected in Danish trade circles.[26] A Swedish model farm was established and stocked with

[21] L. E. Hubbard, *Economics of Soviet Agriculture* (London: Macmillan, 1939), pp. 260–1. Hubbard points out that the consumption of fuel alone by a tractor would in 1935 be 63 litres, or the equivalent of 630 kilos of grain—very nearly the whole yield.

[22] Charles H. Smith, of the American-Russian Chamber of Commerce, formerly with the U.S. State Dept., was also a member of the International Peasant Soviet.

[23] *Izvestia*, No. 3, January 4, 1924.

[24] *Pravda* (Moscow), No. 116, May 24, 1924.

[25] *Pravda* (Moscow), No. 198, September 2, 1924.

[26] U.S. Legation in Copenhagen, Report 216, July 25, 1927. (316–133–622.)

Swedish pedigreed animals. Nineteen Ardenne horses were delivered personally by the Director of Sweden's General Agricultural Service, who commented on the model farm being established:

> The Swedish model farm will be of a very great service for the demonstration of Swedish products and the use of Swedish agricultural machinery as well as for instruction in Swedish agricultural methods.[27]

A group of American specialists was induced to go to the U.S.S.R. One of them, Professor A. A. Johnson, was 'unduly enthusiastic' and voiced his 'unstinted praise' of Soviet development to the U.S. Consul at Berlin in September 1928 after a three-month visit to the U.S.S.R., where he had received an offer to act as agricultural adviser.[28]

This search for specialists extended throughout the range of agriculture. The grain elevators at Vladivostok and at Harbin, first operated by the Chinese Eastern Railway, were later operated on a concession basis when the area came under the control of the Soviet authorities. A group of Russian businessmen in the Far East joined with the railway administration and formed a joint-stock company to operate existing elevators and construct new ones. Such a move suggests the inability of the Soviet authorities to either operate or construct such units. As the elevators were handling nearly 100 million poods of grain a year, this was no small operation.[29] Attempts to make a similar agreement with a group of Italian grain importers for operation of Black Sea elevators was not successful; after extensive negotiations, the Italian group refused to participate without a Soviet guarantee of investment protection.[30]

Thomas Campbell,[31] according to *Izvestia* 'the biggest American farmer and one of the most prominent experts on the organization of grain production,' was invited to the U.S.S.R. by Zernotrust in 1929. The organization of Campbell's Montana farm had been noted by Soviet experts and the processes 'reproduced on a film 2,000 feet long which he has brought to the U.S.S.R. with him.' Campbell farmed 95,000 acres in Montana with 109 tractors and only 200 workers. The object of his visit was to advise in development of ten million acres for wheat growing. The scheme envisaged expenditure of $100 million on agricultural machinery and another $50 million on trucks and road-making equipment. Campbell was reported to have been interviewed

---

[27] U.S. State Dept. Decimal File, 316–133–631.

[28] U.S. Embassy in Berlin, Report No. 3924, September 18, 1928. (316–134–255.)

[29] A translation of the extensive agreement is in U.S. State Dept. Decimal File, 316–134–860 to 891.

[30] Several detailed reports on the negotiations are in U.S. State Dept. Decimal File, 316–134–782 and 316–134–791.

[31] Thomas D. Campbell, *Russia: Market or Menace?* (New York: Longmans Green, 1932). Campbell's book is of the 'I'm not a Communist but. . .' genre and contains nothing specific concerning his work in the U.S.S.R.

and approved by both President Coolidge and Mr. Herbert Hoover before his 1929 visit.[32]

While these ingredients for agricultural improvements became part of Soviet agriculture, the *kolkhoz* yield was less at the end of the decade than the yield on private estates had been during the first ten years of the century, although it represented a marginal improvement over the yield of prewar peasant farms.[33] The uneconomic replacement of the horse by the tractor and the persecution of the more effective peasants were disastrous to Soviet agriculture, and incipient transfer of advanced Western agricultural techniques was drowned by an intemperate ideology.

COTTON IRRIGATION

In July 1923 it was reported by the American consul in Riga that a group of German financiers, including Krupp and Stinnes, had formed an organization with the objective of reviving and enlarging the cotton industry of Turkestan. The Turkestan cotton crop had received numerous setbacks from drought, hot winds and marauding bands of *basmachi* who had succeeded in extensively damaging the Fergana irrigation system, essentially devoted to cotton. The population had fled to the towns as a result of the disturbances, so that the cotton fields remained uncultivated. Production had consequently declined heavily. In Bokhara, 1921 production of cotton fiber was less than 100,000 poods compared with 2.5 million before 1917. Between 1909 and 1914, the total Russian production of cotton had averaged 13 million poods per year; this declined to less than 2 million by 1922.[34]

In 1911 a mixed group of American and Russian engineers had visited the Karakouma Steppe in Transcaucasia to determine its suitability for growing cotton. The expedition, financed by John Hays Hammond, confirmed the prevailing opinion in Moscow that the steppes were not suitable for irrigation or cotton growing.[35] The 1911 expedition was led by Arthur P. Davis, a well-known American irrigation engineer. In 1929 the Soviets invited Davis to undertake complete supervision of the operation and extension of the irrigation system of central Asia, Sredazvodkhoz.[36]

---

[32] *Bank for Russian Trade Review*, I, No. 2 (February 1929), p. 16. This claim was marked with a marginal question mark in Decimal File 316–133–1167.

[33] L. E. Hubbard, *op. cit.*, Chap. XXII, 'Effects of Mechanization on Production.'

[34] U.S. Consulate in Riga, Report No. 1337, October 6, 1923. (316–139–361.)

[35] U.S. State Dept. Decimal File, 316–134–410/429.

[36] *Ekonomicheskaya Zhizn*, No. 133, June 13, 1929. By extraordinary good fortune, extensive documentation exists for the work of one of the consulting engineers to *Sredazvodkhoz*. This collection, now at the Hoover Institution, Stanford University, forms the basis of a chapter in Vol. II.

One unusual—and successful—experiment was the establishment of a Russian experimental station for cotton growing *in Persia*. This was established in 1926 in Mazanderan Province, the country's largest cotton-growing district. The station consisted at 222 acres with a large Soviet and Persian staff. Experimental work was done with all varieties of cottonseed, including the American types Weber and Acala, which did well, and Pima, which did less well. By improving seed quality and making cash advances to the planters in the surrounding areas, the Soviets came to dominate the area. The cotton was exported to Russia. Records of the experiment were transferred to the cotton-growing areas of Turkestan.[37]

Later in the decade the Chief Cotton Committee sent a delegation to the United States to study latest American achievements in cotton growing and cotton ginning; the ten specialists remained in the United States about six months. Particular attention was given to organization and mechanization problems. An agreement was also negotiated with a 'large cotton growing firm' for the establishment of a seed farm in the U.S.S.R. and for the mechanization of Soviet cotton gins. The Committee argued that the contract would 'permit the Commission to successfully bring the experience of American cotton cultivation to the Soviet Union.'[38]

MERINO WOOLS AND AN AUSTRALIAN EMBARGO

A decline in the breeding of sheep had become catastrophic by 1923. Said the President of the Wool Syndicate, 'The breeding of Merino sheep must be considered as completely ruined.'[39] As a result of the Revolution only 98,000–110,000 head of Merinos were left, compared to the more than two million head in 1912. Commercial sheep farming had almost ceased, as sheep farmers had left Russia and their flocks had dispersed. In 1923, only

Table 7-1 PRODUCTION AND IMPORTS OF MERINO WOOL
IN U.S.S.R., 1923–6

Year	Clipped in U.S.S.R.	Imports
1923–4	20,000 poods	480,000 poods
1924–5	28,000 poods	350,000 poods
1925–6	30,000 poods	None

Source: Possibilities of British-Russian Trade (London: Anglo-Russian Parliamentary Committee, 1926), p. 50.

---

[37] U.S. Consulate in Teheran, Report, August 6, 1926. (316–135–275.)
[38] *Ekonomicheskaya Zhizn*, No. 171, July 28, 1929.
[39] *Ekonomicheskaya Zhizn*, December 9 and 12, 1922.

20,000 poods of Merino wool was clipped, and less than half of all available supplies was collected. There was a parallel decline in the wool manufacturing industry.[40]

The solution came in two stages. Large quantities of Merino wool were imported in 1923–5, followed by heavy imports of Merino and other stud sheep for breeding. The latter created sufficient concern in Australia to cause the imposition of a ban on the export of Merinos, still effective in 1962. Between 1919 and 1927, Soviet purchases of Merinos for breeding were not too great: about 2,000 head during the whole period. In 1928–9 the Soviets stepped up buying far beyond normal and on one order purchased 30,000 stud Merinos. The subsequent outcry led to the embargo on stud Merinos on November 28, 1929.[41]

Supplementing the import of sheep, a group of Australian sheep breeders with capital and a flock of 1,500 Merinos settled in the southeast portion of the R.S.F.S.R., under an agreement with the People's Commissariat of Agriculture.[42]

Large purchases of high-grade pedigreed sheep were also made in the United States to improve and build up Russian stocks. In 1924, 2,766 sheep were purchased; in 1925, 1,621; in 1926, 2,628; and in 1927, 8,414.[43] They were shipped in groups of 1,000 to 3,000. For example, in 1927 four Russian peasants arrived in the United States to escort 2,700 pedigreed animals purchased in Utah, Montana, Oregon, and Ohio. This group included 1,550 prize stock Rambouillets, 1,000 prize Hampshires, and 150 Shropshires, purchased for a total of $160,000.[44]

REPLENISHMENT OF LIVESTOCK HERDS

The 1922 famine left the Soviet Union, particularly the southeast, with a much-depleted livestock population; most of the animals had been killed and marketed. The restocking project was offered for concession. In the Volga A.S.S.R., it was indicated that there were forty-five large cattle ranches, each of which could be put in order for £50 sterling, although livestock and supplementary equipment would cost a total of more than £1 million. It was suggested that the enterprise would be profitable; but there were no takers.[45]

[40] U.S. Consulate in Helsingfors, Report No. R-2100, February 28, 1923.

[41] Commonwealth of Australia, *Parliamentary Debates*, '12th Parliament, 1st Session,' p. 358.

[42] *Izvestia*, No. 35, February 12, 1924.

[43] Amtorg, *op. cit.*, II, No. 24 (1927).

[44] Amtorg, *op. cit.*, II, No. 19 (1927).

[45] *Russian Information and Review*, I, No. 20 (July 15, 1922), 462.

Breeding herds, as well as herds for sale, had been reduced to minute proportions. In July 1921, just after the establishment of a commission to reorganize and improve the livestock-breeding industry, it was found that, although breeding establishments occupied more than 35,000 acres, they contained very few breeding stock. Only 1,000 pedigreed horses, 114 bulls, 1,700 cows, and a few pigs, sheep, and goats remained in the breeding farms. Some improvement was made the following year by purchasing small herds from peasant farmers, but a decline of this magnitude required replenishment from outside.[46]

The failure of tractor production, a 175,000-head shortage of horses, the lag in agriculture, and possibly a military demand produced an unusual transaction in halter-broken wild horses in 1927–8. Britain had broken with the U.S.S.R. over the Arcos affair and Canada had immediately followed suit, so that officially there were no diplomatic relations between Canada and the U.S.S.R. However, the Canadian Department of Agriculture made four shipments, totaling 8,000 horses, from the western Canadian ranges to Leningrad, under official auspices. Canadian officials rounded up the horses and made the purchases, and two Canadian officers escorted them to Leningrad. Further, the price was only $30 per head! The horses were taken to a military camp outside Leningrad, inspected by General Budenny and cavalry officers, and then shipped down to the Ukraine.[47]

LIVESTOCK AND DAIRY INDUSTRY CONCESSIONS; UNION COLD STORAGE, LTD.

The Union Cold Storage Company, of the United Kingdom, had several concessionary arrangements with the U.S.S.R. The first was signed in May 1923 with the North Western Trade Department. The Trade Department assembled animal products in the R.S.F.S.R., with the technical and financial assistance of Union Cold Storage, who then exported and sold them abroad guaranteeing a minimum profit of 10 percent. This profit was then split: 67 percent to the Department and 33 percent to Union Cold Storage.[48]

G. H. Truss and Company, also of the United Kingdom, had a similar agreement with Khelboprodukt, concerning bacon exports, and provided equipment and technical assistance to build two bacon factories to produce for export. These were supplied on a credit basis.[49]

---

46   *Ibid.*, pp. 461–2.
47   *Ekonomicheskaya Zhizn*, No. 193, May 27, 1924.
48   *Ekonomicheskaya Zhizn*, No. 102, May 11, 1923.
49   A. Troyanovsky, *Eksport, import i kontsessii soyuz S.S.S.R.* (Moscow: Dvigatel, 1926) Troyanovsky adds the comment that ' . . . the Soviet purchasing-export organizations have conducted their eggs-exporting business mainly with the use of foreign capital.' P. 145.

Khleboprodukt concluded two further concession agreements in 1924 with Union Cold Storage. The first was a concession for the export of woodcocks, hazen-cocks, and partridges. Combined with this was a technical-assistance agreement in poultry-farming development with a view to the subsequent export of poultry. Union Cold Storage advanced credit, and the initial agreement lasted until September 15, 1927. The second concession agreement covered pig breeding. In 1922 there were only twenty pig-breeding farms left in the Soviet Union, with a total of 843 pedigree animals, compared to a total pig population of over 21 million animals in 1916.[50] [51] Union Cold Storage agreed to facilitate the export of pork to England through company distribution channels on credit, and also to provide technical assistance in Soviet pork production until September 15, 1929.

The Gostorg butter-export office in Leningrad also concluded an agreement with Union Cold Storage, in August 1924 for export of butter to the United Kingdom, the latter granting financial and machinery credits to facilitate the contract.[52]

The 'Arcos break' interrupted Union Cold Storage concessions, but, upon resumption of trade relations in 1928, they were the first United Kingdom concessions to be renewed. Under the 1928 agreement, the Union Company agreed to advance a credit of $2.5 million in exchange for the right to handle all Soviet imports and dairy produce for United Kingdom market. The credits, utilized for the purchase of machinery in the United Kingdom for the Soviet dairy industry, were spread over three years and were granted in addition to a credit of 80 percent of the value of dairy goods shipped. The dairy produce was sold by Union Cold Storage on a commission basis and credit was made available upon receipt of the produce in London.[53]

Butter production and export in 1924 were also facilitated by a concession agreement forming the Danish-Siberian Company (Sibiko), under which a Danish company obtained for five years the right to produce and export butter from Siberia. First-year production was set at a minimum of 200,000 poods, with 300,000 poods as the minimum annual quantity thereafter. This con-

[50]   *Pravda* (Moscow), No. 182, August 13, 1924.

[51]   Henry Wallace noted that the Siberian pigs were Yorkshires descended from 800 imported from the United Kingdom in the early 1920s. [*Soviet Asia Mission* (New York: Regnal & Hitchcock, 1946), p. 222.]

[52]   *Izvestia* (Moscow), No. 189, August 21, 1924. Union Cold Storage was handling almost all Russian exports of butter and eggs in the middle of the decade (including exports to Latvia, reexported to the United Kingdom) except for a small quantity handled by Truss, another Type II United Kingdom concession, and IVA, a German concession. [L. Segal and A. A. Santalov, *Soviet Union Yearbook, 1925*, (London: Allen and Unwin, 1925), p. 243.]

[53]   *New York Times*, March 16, 1928, p. 5, col. 3. Sir Edmund Vestey, who controlled Union Cold Storage, was quoted: 'We have been doing business with Soviet Russia for some time, and have found it quite satisfactory.'

stituted a considerable portion of Russian butter production at the time. The Danish company received half the profits made by Sibiko.[54]

A report from the Danish Legation in Moscow to the Danish Foreign Office in early 1925 suggests that the Soviets had problems even in butter production. The butter trust, Maslocentr, operated some 5,820 dairies and 680 cheese factories (about 80 percent of the prewar total), but production was only about 31 percent of the 1913 total. There were problems with 'irregularities' in distribution; by keeping producer prices low, regional dairy associations were able to make substantial profits for their own organizations which were not passed on to producers. A certain amount of Danish capital was involved in the regional associations. It was indicated that future attention would be concentrated on product standardization, training, and improved techniques.

These butter and egg exports were of major importance as, together with lumber, they replaced the lost grain exports on which the Soviets had placed major reliance for foreign exchange.[55] Hens had been nationalized soon after the Revolution, and eggs were nationalized under a decree signed by Lenin on March 3, 1920. A quota was allotted each farm to be delivered to government collecting points.[56]

FOREIGN AGRICULTURAL COMMUNES IN RUSSIA

The Ira commune was established in April 1922 in Tambov Province, on the estate of Prince Obolensky. Another commune, the Seyatel, was established on an estate requiring considerable repair, by about 1924. Local peasants and the Communists were reportedly friendly, and the former were reportedly impressed by such novelties as the welding of broken farm implements and the artificial hatching of eggs.[57]

In 1923 some 200 returned emigrants arrived in the U.S.S.R. from the United States and were organized by the Society for Technical Aid to Russia (which had about thirty branches in the United States) into five communes: the New World, the John Reed, the Red Banner, the Labor Field, and the Estonian. They were settled in the Ukraine and the Don Basin with $130,000 worth of equipment brought from the United States. About 20 percent were party members and the rest were sympathizers.[58]

---

[54]   *Ekonomicheskaya Zhizn*, January 11, 1922.
[55]   U.S. State Dept. Report No. 3945, September 25, 1928.
[56]   U.S. Consulate in Vibourg, Finland, Report No. 69, April 8, 1920. (316–125–713.)
[57]   *Izvestia*, No. 124, January 7, 1923.
[58]   'Longing for Home' *Izvestia*, No. 82, April 15, 1923. The Society for Technical Aid to Russia, located in New York, was performing the functions of a consulate (supposedly denied to the U.S.S.R., as there was no diplomatic recognition at the

Another group of repatriated emigrants, mostly metal and textile workers, arrived later in the year and also settled in South Russia. Their communes were organized according to city of origin in the United States. The Trud Commune had members predominantly from Boston; Harold (a dairy farming commune), from Chicago; Proletarian Life, from Cleveland; Krasny Loutch, an agricultural commune in Nikolaev, from Chicago; and so on.[59]

At Perm a group of returned agricultural laborers was given 10,000 dessiatins (27,000 acres) to farm.[60]

The California commune was established by an agreement between the Soviet of People's Commissars and a group of American agricultural workers largely from the western United States. The commune was granted 2,700 acres in Don *oblast* to establish various agricultural enterprises on a lease basis for twenty-four years. A fee equal to 5 percent of all crops grown was to be paid the Soviet government, with the first payment falling due after the third harvest. On expiration of the contract, the commune was to hand over all equipment and livestock.[61]

This commune was not destined for success; it was near bankruptcy within nine months. The major blow was the loss of three railroad cars containing the equipment and possessions of the settlers. These cars wandered about Russia for six months despite '348 inquiries to the railroads.' Two were permanently lost, and the commune had to pay the freight charges for the wanderings of the third, placing an impossible burden on their finances.[62]

Lenin had the announced aim of settling one model American group in each *uyezd*, which would have required about 250–300 such groups, a long way from the 25–30 that actually were settled.[63]

The communes, particularly the American communes, appear to have been utilized in an attempt to transfer more advanced agricultural practices into the surrounding areas. For example in the village of Posovka, Americans founded a commune in 1920 which created for a period of at least three years a series of 'circles' devoted to various problems: seed selection, agricultural exhibition, horticulture, and similar activities.

---

time). See, for example, the document issued to L. F. Rautanen in New York which is, in essence, a visa. (316–110–719.)

The Society for Technical Help to Armenia was also organized in the United States to return qualified Armenian laborers from the United States, to establish trade schools in Canada and Armenia for training specialists, and to maintain relations. (*Pravda*, No. 210, September 18, 1923.)

[59] *Pravda* (Moscow), No. 232, October 13, 1923.

[60] *Pravda* (Moscow), No. 246, October 31, 1922.

[61] *Ekonomicheskaya Zhizn*, No. 19, January 28, 1923.

[62] 'Now the Agricultural Communes Are Perishing,' *Pravda*, No. 260, November 16, 1923.

[63] *Pravda* No. 246, October 31, 1922.

The young Americans are continuing their efforts quietly, without noise. Their example was not fruitless. In various neighboring villages similar circles with agricultural purposes have been formed.[64]

The Finnish commune comprised a group of Finns and a few Americans on about 100 dessiatins of land fifteen miles from Leningrad, farmed on a cooperative basis. The commune failed because local peasants stole the equipment, there was lack of harmony in the group itself, and finally, taxes, at 5,000 rubles per year, proved to be too much of a burden.[65]

Another Finnish settlement was the Seattle Commune, started by Finns deported from the United States in 1921. This was more successful. The commune was visited in 1930 by M. Farbman, who reported that its wheat fetched higher prices than neighboring state farms.[66]

Gigant State Farm	...	...	...	...	128 kopecks/pood	
State Farm No. 2	...	...	...	...	175	,, ,,
Seattle Commune	...	...	...	...	193	,, ,,
Average all peasants	...	...	...	...	120	,, ,,

An agricultural union of Dutch descendants in the Ukraine concluded a foreign loan of $1 million for purchase of foreign equipment.[67]

Communes were supported by the Czechoslovakian government to the extent of fifteen million crowns in agricultural equipment, but, as this was distributed to all communes regardless of nationality, it is impossible to assess how much of this sum went directly to the aid of Czechoslovakian communes. The Czech Mission in the U.S.S.R. was also (in 1923) given the right to rent and organize shops for the assembly and repair of agricultural machinery.[68]

An Australian commune was established with help from the Society for Technical Help to the U.S.S.R. in Australia. Mainly from North Queensland, the group settled in 1921 in the Ukraine (with equipment brought from home) as the Australian Commune.[69]

There was a Canadian Dukhorbor commune with some 2,500 members— but this sect and the Mennonites tended to leave Russia, near the end of the decade when anti-religious pressures were applied.[70] There was also a

---

[64]   *Pravda* (Moscow), No. 276 (December 5, 1923).

[65]   U.S. Consulate in Helsingfors, Report, October 8, 1928 (316–133–843). This report is based on the experience of Lauri Rautanen, a United States citizen of Finnish descent; it is useful as being among the most balanced and objective of the excommunard reports. Although he had lost $1,500 and wanted to return to the United States, Rautanen did not regret his experience; ' . . . he wanted to see how it worked in Russia. He would not advise nobody to go to Russia.'

[66]   Farbman, *op. cit.*, p. 148.

[67]   *Izvestia*, No. 246, October 27, 1923.

[68]   *Pravda* (Moscow), No. 279, December 8, 1923.

[69]   *Pravda* (Moscow), No. 247, October 31, 1923.

[70]   U.S. State Dept. Decimal File, 316–135–251.

'Canadian commune' near Odessa formed by the Canadian Society for Technical Aid to Soviet Russia. They were allotted 1,500 dessiatins and employed several hundred Canadians and a few Russians. They brought equipment for their workshops from the United States.[71]

The Austrian commune, Imkommune Uhlfeld, was supported by both the Austrian government and the City of Vienna. The former contributed 800 schillings ($125) for each immigrant (the investment required by the U.S.S.R.). The City of Vienna gave a similar amount to commune members from Vienna. There were about 600 members in the commune, which settled in the Kirghiz Republic with the intent of founding an Austrian city based on regional agricultural development.[72]

JEWISH LAND SETTLEMENT PROGRAMS

With financial support from the Jewish community in the United States, Jewish settlers were encouraged to settle on various parts of the U.S.S.R. and particularly to undertake farming.[73] The act organizing the Committee for Settling Jewish Toilers on the Land was published in *Izvestia* on October 13, 1926, which outlines the land distribution and budgetary considerations in the program. Quite unknowingly, this organization aided the Bolshevik drive on private trade, renewed in 1924.

American assistance was organized under the Jewish Joint Distribution Committee, which had cooperated with American Relief in Russia and maintained a representative in the U.S.S.R. In 1925 land was set aside for these settlers, and the Joint Committee supplied tractors and other equipment, dug wells, provided cattle, gave loans for housing and farm building, and gave instruction in farming. By October 1925, the committee had settled 6,000 families on 500,000 acres in the Ukraine and Crimea.

Apparently the land settled could be used only with foreign assistance, as it was arid and water wells had to be drilled to a depth of 300–400 feet: hence the comment that 'this is why the country can be settled only by Jews who receive money from abroad'.[74]

[71] *Pravda* (Moscow), No. 47, March 2, 1923.

[72] The commune had a 12-page agreement with the Soviets. A translation is in the U.S. State Dept. Archives at 316–131–343.

[73] It should be noted that Jewish leaders in the United States, unlike many business men, took precise care to discuss their plans and actions with the State Department and ascertain the government viewpoint on such financial support, in order to avoid any possible misunderstanding. (See U.S. State Dept. Archives, 316–127–304.) There were similar organizations in other countries, but little is known of their activities. For example, Verein ORT, Gesellschaft zur Forderung des Handwerke und der Landwirtschaft unter den Juden, a German organization, registered to undertake operations in the U.S.S.R. *Ekonomicheskaya Zhizn*, No. 248, October 25, 1928.

[74] *Izvestia*, No. 157, July 11, 1926.

The Joint Committee also provided American plants and administrators for distribution and cultivation.[75]

Another 4,000 Jews settled by mid-1926. This number was held to be 'more than in the preceding 100 years, from the foundation of Jewish colonies during the reign of Nicholas I.'[76] Early in 1928, the Soviet government set aside for colonization by Agro-Joint some ten million acres in Eastern Siberia, between the Ussuri Railway on the north and the Amur River on the south. The administrative office was established in the spring at Khabarovsk and soon after, tractors, buses, automobiles, and settlers began to arrive. Adverse conditions forced half the settlers back to their homes in the first year, but very gradually a settlement was carved out of this previously unsettled land.[77]

Ikor, another United States Jewish organization interested in colonization, sent Dr. Charles Kanz to Siberia in 1928 to investigate conditions at first hand. Some 32,000 people, including the 1,000 immigrants who had arrived the previous year, lived in a total area of 42,000 square kilometers. Through Ikor and Ozet (a Soviet organization for establishing Jewish workers' settlements), quantities of equipment were shipped to the settlers during the 1929–30 season. A commission sent by Ikor to render technical assistance to the colony arrived in the U.S.S.R. in July 1929.[78]

The Joint Tractor Commission (1924) was an American-Jewish organization with the objective of generally developing Russian agriculture. At this time the commission had 135 tractors, which it rented out to peasants on condition that they create artels in groups farming not less than 20 dessiatins of adjoining land. Payment ranged from one to five poods of wheat per dessiatin.[79]

In 1923 the Jewish-American Committee imported 200 tractors, of which 75 were Waterloo Boy (make unknown) and the rest were Fordson. These were put to work in the Ukraine, generally at the disposal of collectives lacking horses.[80]

A joint-stock company, Akotprom, was formed in June 1923 to undertake commercial and industrial business in order to aid the Jewish Committee for Relief.[81] French Jewish circles also aided agricultural colonization. In 1923

---

[75] *Izvestia*, No. 64, March 10, 1923.

[76] *Izvestia*, No. 140, June 20, 1926.

[77] U.S. Consulate in Harbin, Report January 22, 1929. However, there are two sides to this story. Reports indicate that the Soviets had great difficulty after the first year in getting anyone to go to Biro-Bidjan, in Siberia, and gave each village and town a quota to fill for settlers to populate this 'God forsaken [sic] country.' [Report May 26, 1929, (316–108–529).]

[78] *Pravda* (Moscow), July 6, 1929.

[79] *Izvestia*, No. 140, June 20, 1926.

[80] *Pravda*, No. 166, July 26, 1923.

[81] *Ekonomicheskaya Zhizn*, No. 142, June 26, 1923.

some three million French francs were sent under an agreement, renewable annually, to Jewish families settling on the land.[82] In retrospect, one can only conclude that these settlements were little more than attempts on the part of the Soviet Union to extract foreign Jewish assistance. None of the settlements have survived.

THE FATE OF THE AGRICULTURAL COMMUNES

In early 1923 reports began to filter out of the U.S.S.R. concerning the desperate state of foreign communes. Many settlers were left without land allotments; others were in need of assistance, and some were caught in the squeeze between rising costs and low prices for grain and dairy produce.[83]

The commune was a failure, and its fate is well described in a *Pravda* article of late 1923. The author pointed out that incoming communes should have had every chance to become models of efficient agronomy. They brought in modern equipment, totaling to that time some $600,000 in value, and the membership, skilled and efficient, contained a large percentage of Party members. 'In general they are energetic, businesslike, Americanized people.'[84]

It was pointed out that in areas where land was lying idle, the commune Echo was given 'wild prairie' without a single building, with two of the sections connected by a narrow corridor 1 kilometer wide and 15 kilometers long. The Canadian commune in Odessa lost five baggage cars for six months; finally only three of the cars arrived.[85] The John Reed Commune in Podol Province did not obtain land for nine months, and then received a ruined estate. The Red Banner Commune waited seven months for land, and after working it for a while was expelled and force to sell its equipment to pay moving costs. The Novy Mir Commune received buildings infected with foot and mouth disease. The communes, it was stated, were breaking up. Some members were going back to the United States, and some were wandering all over Russia. Said the Soviets, ' . . . we are losing very precious and important breeding stations of agricultural knowledge; we are killing the cause with our own hands.'[86]

On the other hand, some communes must have survived for several years, as they were still importing American equipment in 1926. The Ira imported $35,000 worth of agricultural equipment in early 1926, the Agro-Joint

---

[82] *Ekonomicheskaya Zhizn*, No. 18, January 27, 1923.
[83] IS Report, December 8, 1923. (316–133–339.)
[84] *Pravda* (Moscow), No. 260, November 16, 1923.
[85] *Pravda* (Moscow), No. 260, November 16, 1923. Elsewhere it is stated that two cars out of three were lost.
[86] *Ibid.*

commune just over $39,000 worth of equipment, and AIK, in the Kuzbas, $4,345.[87]

In the end, however, they all perished.

THE AGRICULTURAL EQUIPMENT MANUFACTURING INDUSTRY

Toward the end of the nineteenth century, Russian farming, as a result of the introduction of modern agricultural machinery and implements, underwent extensive technical improvement. Peasant credit associations, funded by government banks and the zemstvos (district councils) encouraged this trend. Spurred by these changes, the manufacture of agricultural implements expanded rapidly; by 1908 there were over 500 plants, not including peasant industries, also of considerable importance. In 1908 the plants produced more than 390,000 ploughs, 8,800 seeders, 61,000 reapers and mowers, 22,000 threshers, and 31,000 winnowers.[88] By 1913 the number of establishments increased to more than 800, employing 39,000 workers and including very large plants funded with Western capital. By far the largest was the International Harvester plant, covering sixty-two acres at Lyubertsy, near Moscow. This plant, opened in 1911, provided employment for 2,000. The company had an extensive and well organized service network in Russia; the Omsk (Siberia) branch of International Harvester was the largest overseas branch operated by the company.[89]

Agricultural exhibitions, credit associations, and other forms of government aid enabled Russia to develop a relatively advanced agricultural economy before World War I. Agricultural products were exported on a large scale; at the turn of the century Russia had become the world's largest exporter of wheat.

The equipment plants survived the Revolution; exactly the same number (825) were reported available for use in 1923 as in 1913, but their output had declined catastrophically. In 1923, the Soviets produced only 12 percent of the ploughs, 70 percent of the scythes, 26 percent of the sickles, and between 1 and 8 percent of other implements which had been produced in 1913.[90]

The early 1920s were characterized by continuing crises in the industry. The 1921–2 plan for agricultural machinery was less than 50-percent fulfilled,

[87]   *Amerikanskiai torgovlia i promyshlennost'* (New York: Amtorg Trading Company, June 1926), p. 40.
[88]   *Russian Yearbook: 1912* (New York: Macmillan, 1912), pp. 157–61. This evidence appears to refute the numerous statements that agricultural machinery output in prewar Russia was negligible. For an example, see Friedman, *op. cit.*, p. 81.
[89]   *World Harvester*, November–December 1953.
[90]   *Biednota*, No. 1427, January 26, 1923.

and productivity per worker only 43 percent of prewar.[91] *Kooperativnoe Delo* for June 1922 describes the chaos into which the industry had descended. Of the 825 enterprises working in 1913, only 73, or 9 percent, were working at all, and most of these in a half-hearted manner.

To overcome production difficulties, the industry was consolidated. Prerevolutionary works in the Ukraine were now grouped into two trusts: Ukrselmashtrest and Zaporozhtrest. In October 1923, eleven of the twenty-one plants in these two trusts were combined in the Vseukrainsky Selmashintrest, and the remaining ten were closed down. Specialization of output was increased. Drill seeders were now produced at Elvorty, Helferlich-Sade (in Kharkhov), and Kiranon-Fuks. Reapers were produced by the Donsky (Nikolaev) and Kopp (Zaporozhia) works. Threshing machines were produced at Elvorty, Helferlich-Sade, and Lepp-Valman. However, major deficiencies reported for 1925–6 suggest that concentration did not get to the root of the problem.[92]

Selmashstroi reported in 1923 that the decline was due to the high cost of production and inadequate financing. The deficiencies had now become monumental. Production and imports together failed even to offset normal wear and tear, and peasants were reverting to the use of primitive, hand-made wooden equipment.

ATTEMPTS TO DEVELOP A SOVIET TRACTOR, 1922 TO 1926

The Soviets made numerous unsuccessful attempts to produce a workable tractor in the early years of the 1920s. These ended in failure, and the Soviet Union then turned to the United States for assistance in constructing the massive tractor plants of the Five-Year Plan.

Two designs were completed in the Soviet Union about 1923, both by I. B. Mamin. The 'Gnom' design was selected as being suitable for Russian agricultural conditions, and Mamin was sent to Germany (with 130,000 rubles) to purchase the necessary production equipment. The Balakov factory in Samara was turned over to 'Gnom' mass production. It was anticipated that 150 of these small, 16-horsepower, oil-driven tractors would be built in the first year and 250 to 300 per year thereafter. No complete units were produced, although some engines were used for a while as stationary power units.

The other Mamin design was the crude oil tractor, 'Karlick,' with a one-cylinder 12-horsepower engine. This was built at the Old Neurepublik works at Marmstadt on the Volga. Some were produced, but, like the 'Gnom', they

---

[91]   *Pravda* (Moscow), No. 279, December 8, 1923.
[92]   U.S. State Dept. Decimal File, 316–129–969.

were too heavy, too clumsy, and insufficiently powered for field use, and were used only as stationary power units.[93] Another tractor, the 'Bolshevik', a 4-cylinder, 20-horsepower machine was also attempted at the Bolshevik Works in Leningrad. Only a small number were produced, in 1923–4, and production ceased entirely before 1926. The Ford Delegation suspected it was for military transport work, as it was too large and clumsy to perform as a tractor.[94]

The 'K.P.Z.' tractor was a 4-cylinder, 50-horsepower machine built at the Kharkov Locomotive Works. This was a copy of the German tractor, 'W.D.' It was expensive (15,000 rubles) and much too clumsy for field use. Production stopped before 1926.[95]

Several hundred of the 'Zaporojetz' were built at the Ukraine Agricultural Machinery Trust. This was a 3-wheeled, 1-cylinder, 12-horsepower machine, very heavy (2 ton) and useful only as a stationary power unit. It was priced at 5,000 rubles, expensive when compared to the imported Fordson (1,800 rubles).[96]

Two additional tractor models were attempted at the Kolomensky Machine Works at Golutviko near Moscow. One was the 'Mogul', a 4-cylinder, 12–25-horsepower machine: an 'exact copy of an American tractor by the same name.'[97] The other was a 2-cylinder, crude-oil copy of the Swedish tractor, 'Avance,' but with transmission and gears as in the 'Mogul', built in the same plant. Production of both was very small and ceased by 1925–6.[98]

Work was also started on an experimental electric plow: an example of Lenin's preoccupation with electrification. A contract was issued in 1923 to plow 16,000 dessiatins with 16 electric plows. When the season was over, only one had worked any length of time, and only 477 dessiatins had been plowed. In the following year, 5 plows undertook 4,000 dessiatins, but actually plowed only 300. The trailer was found to be 'extremely heavy and constantly buried in the ground.'[99] It was expensive and impractical; the experiment was discontinued in 1926, although it has been revived at intervals since that time.

Work also started on several models of oil-fueled tractors. 'An exact copy of an American tractor built in 1922'[100] (100 'Holt') was placed in production at the Bolshevik plant, near Leningrad. The carburetors, ignition system, and other parts were imported from the United States. Work continued for one

---

[93] *Report of the Ford Delegation to Russia and the U.S.S.R. April–August 1926* (Detroit: 1926), Ford Motor Company Archives Accession No. 49, p. 42.
[94] *Ibid.*, p. 41, The report has photographs of these Russian models.
[95] *Ibid.*
[96] *Ibid.*
[97] *Ibid.*, p. 40.
[98] *Ibid.*, p. 46.
[99] *Ibid.*, p. 102.
[100] *Ibid.*, p. 103.

year. Between 1924 and 1926 the plant only made spare parts, but this also ceased in 1926. The Ford Delegation (1926) reported the 'Russian Holt' to be a product of extremely high cost and poor quality.

INTERNATIONAL HARVESTER COMPANY AND NATIONALIZATION

According to Keeley,[101] the International Harvester plant at Lyubertsy, just outside Moscow, continued operation through both revolutions and the winter of 1919–20 with only a single three-day strike. Cromming, the German manager, produced equipment for the Bolsheviks on a cost-plus-10-percent basis, the percentage to cover the living expenses of the chief executives and himself. Cromming agreed with the Workmen's Committee to supply food (no small promise), in return for complete authority over technical operations of the plant. Cromming apparently acted on his own initiative; he was reported as not knowing whether the parent United States company had even wanted to continue operations after the Revolution.

In 1921 the Soviets offered an agricultural equipment manufacturing concession to an unknown United Kingdom tractor manufacturer. The offer was passed along to International Harvester, who in turn passed it on to the State Department with a notation that the company was cool to the proposition but worried lest British and German interests accept a concession to manufacture tractors and freeze out International.[102]

It is clear that, although Cromming operated the Moscow plant and International Harvester was concerned for the welfare of employees inside the U.S.S.R., including several engineers sent in 1921, the company did not press for modification of United States policy. Mr. Legge of International is quoted as saying, 'Nothing has occurred up to the present which would justify considerations of change in policy of this Government.'[103] In 1924 rumors circulated about an impending takeover of the Moscow plant[104] which was, in part, accomplished before the end of 1924. The enterprise immediately slumped into substantial deficit, a subsidy of 1.8 million rubles and a credit of 466,000 rubles being required on expenses of 3.49 million rubles. Even more catastrophic was the effect of the August decree of the Council of Labor and Defense equalizing prices for domestic and imported tractors. In February 1925,

[101] U.S. State Dept. Decimal File, 316–107–97.
[102] A copy of the proposed concession agreement is in U.S. State Dept. Decimal File, 316–130–1162. There is a marginal notation, marked HH (Herbert Hoover), that great importance was attached to this offer—presumably on the part of the Administration.
[103] U.S. State Dept. Decimal File, 316–108–23.
[104] Rumors noted in 361.115 of the Decimal File, 316–108–1279.

Glavmetal confirmed the first year's program of 1,000 hay harvesters and 600 reapers planned for Lyubertsy. The hay harvesters were estimated to cost 130 rubles apiece, against 190 rubles for imported harvesters. Glavmetal then reversed itself and requested Vesenkha to dismiss the 'acceptance committee' which had been taking over the factory from the International Harvester Company.[105]

A rapprochement took place in 1925. In August, International Harvester was granted permission to conduct trading operations within the U.S.S.R. and supply spare parts for agricultural machinery.[106] The company then began to advance substantial credits for the purchase of American-made equipment.[107] At the end of 1925, all International plants were denationalized; according to the German Embassy, they were found too complex to operate and International Harvester temporarily re-entered its own factories.[108]

The Bolsheviks had the last word. The Selmash trust was liquidated November 16, 1926 and a committee established to wind up business, including the claims of the Lyubertsy works of International. On March 7, 1927, the trust was placed under moratorium, and all claims against it suspended. The United States Riga consul comments:

> Thus the legal guarantees which existed at the time when the creditors entered into business with the syndicate [i.e., trust] were suddenly withdrawn, leaving the creditors of a Government organization at the mercy of a Government commission and depriving them of a part of the lawful interest on their money. It will be noted that the moratorium is entirely one sided and does not suspend the obligations of the syndicates debtors . . .[109]

As late as 1929, International was still trying. It negotiated a contract for the sale of 5,900 International tractors on three-year credit terms, including clauses which allowed the U.S.S.R. to send technicians to the United States for training and required International engineers to give consulting services on the establishment of a network of tractor-repair shops.[110]

The contribution of Lyubertsy and the International Harvester Company to Soviet industrialization is best summed by a Soviet publication:

> The Lyubertsy enterprise is a shining example of the good sense of 'Nep.' The Harvester Company rendered the hated Bolsheviks the same service that Harriman performed in Chiatury and Krupp in the Ukraine.

[105] *Ekonomicheskaya Zhizn*, No. 29, February 5, 1925.
[106] *Torgovo-Promyshlennaya Gazeta*, No. 185, August 15, 1925.
[107] German Foreign Ministry Archives, T120–3033–H10945. The company advanced $2.5 million on 18-month terms.
[108] *Ibid.*
[109] U.S. Consulate at Riga, Report 4449, April 12, 1927. (316–111–924.)
[110] *Izvestia*, No. 149, July 3, 1929.

These firms helped them to train a nucleus of skilled workers in these enterprises and to learn the process of production which soon enabled them to continue production without the capitalists. Today there are few concessions left in Soviet Russia and not even the Vorwaerts dares to assert any longer that the Bolsheviks have introduced capitalism. . . .[111]

At the same time, 1,300 60-horsepower Caterpillar tractors were purchased for delivery in November–December 1929, with similar clauses for technical assistance. Caterpillar sent engineers and technicians to the U.S.S.R. to instruct in the operation of tractors, and Russian engineers went to Caterpillar plants in the United States for further instruction on maintenance. The company opened a permanent office in Moscow to solve problems arising in the utilization of their tractors.[112]

POSITION AT MID-DECADE

The 1924–5 plan for tractor manufacture concentrated production in larger prewar plants taken over by Glavmetal; Krasnyi Putilovets was planned to produce 500 tractors, Gomza 500, and the Kharkhov plant 120.

These targets were not achieved, and attempts to create a tractor industry were described by Dr. G. Schlesinger, a German tractor expert, as 'creating a laughable impression and extremely amateurish.' In an effort to induce the peasant to buy the miserable product of the Soviet tractor factories, a decree was published in August 1925 equalizing prices for Soviet-made and the much cheaper and better-quality imported tractors. In effect, the prices for imported tractors were raised.

Table 7–2   PRICE SCHEDULE FOR SOVIET AND FOREIGN
TRACTORS (DECREE OF AUGUST 1925)

Russian		*Rubles*
Krasnyi Putilovets (copy of Fordson)	(with plow and spares)	1,800 (cost 4,000 rubles)
Kolomenets	(with plow and spares)	2,500
H.P.Z.	(without plow)	8,000
Zaporozhets	(with plow and spares)	2,000
Karlik	(with plow and spares)	2,000
Bolshevik (planned)	(with plow and spares)	8,000
American		
Fordson	(with plow and spares)	1,800 ⎫ (now including 165 rubles
International (30 h.p.)	(with plow and spares)	4,000 ⎭ tractor subsidy tax)

Source: Ekonomicheskaya Zhizn, August 18, 1925.

An implementing decree of the Council of Labor and Defense had the stated objective of providing the largest possible distribution of tractor power

[111]   Theodor Neubauer, *Lyubertsy; a Cross Section of the Five Year Plan* (Moscow: Co-operative Publishing Society of Foreign Workers in the U.S.S.R., 1932), p. 17.
[112]   *Ekonomicheskaya Zhizn*, No. 160, July 16, 1929.

for the improvement of land cultivation.[113] Imported Fordsons and Internationals normally sold well below the prices of the few domestic tractors; after the 1925 decree the imported Fordson and the Krasnyi Putilovets copy of the Fordson both sold at 1,800 rubles, as indicated in table 7–2. The stated objective, of course, was not fulfilled: the domestic product was far below the imported quality. The peasant preferred the imported tractor, but surplus accruing from taxation of the imported tractor was used to offset the deficit in domestic production, and in effect subsidize domestic tractors.[114] Agricultural productivity suffered while industry tried to overcome production problems.

Russian tractor works in this period were chronically inefficient. The Putilovets required 350 man-days per tractor produced, and at the Kharkov Works the assembly of a tractor motor required eight man-months.[115] In 1926 an inspection of the agricultural machinery factories of Riazan, Tula, Orel, and Belokhuminsky revealed that the raw-material supply, particularly that of iron and steel, was hopelessly deficient. Tula, for example, received only 8 percent of its iron and steel requirements in 1925–6. In addition, equipment was out of repair and in need of replacement.[116]

The dismal plight of the tractor-building industry was investigated in June 1925 by the above-mentioned Dr. Schlesinger, at the invitation of Orgametal. Conditions must have been pretty miserable; *Ekonomicheskaya Zhizn* made the point that 'one must not become downhearted.'[117]

Schlesinger's specific recommendation was a plant to built 10,000 tractors a year 'with the special machine tools that are being built by American factories for Ford,' to replace the outmoded tractor works.

The 1925–6 plan for domestic tractor-building allowed for only 1,800 tractors:[118]

Type 'FP' (Fordson-Putilovets)	900 tractors
'Kolomenets'	250 tractors
'Zaporozhets'	300 tractors
'Karlik'	100 tractors
'Bolshevik'	100 tractors
'Comintern'	150 tractors
	1,800 tractors

[113] Decree is reprinted in *Ekonomicheskaya Zhizn*, No. 186, August 18, 1925.
[114] This was almost the supreme insult so far as the Ford Motor Company is concerned: the unauthorized Soviet copy of the Fordson was subsidized at the expense of the imported Fordson. The 'subsidy tax for Russian tractor industry' was 165 rubles on a Fordson—about 8 percent of cost.
[115] U.S. Consulate at Riga, Report No. 3237, September 28, 1924. (316–133–516.)
[116] *Ekonomicheskaya Zhizn*, No. 87, April 16, 1926.
[117] *Ekonomicheskaya Zhizn*, No. 130, June 11, 1925.
[118] *Ekonomicheskaya Zhizn*, No. 290, December 19, 1925.

The intent in 1925-6 had been to supply 16,750 tractors, of which 1,800 were to have been made in the U.S.S.R. The balance of 14,950 tractors (89.2 percent) were planned as imports.[119] Actually, less than 900 tractors were produced, and most fell to pieces after a few weeks or months in operation; in effect, almost all usable tractors were imported.

KRASNYI PUTILOVETS AND THE FORD MOTOR COMPANY

Although the International Harvester plant had been the largest in tsarist Russia, the oldest and most famous undoubtedly was the Putilovets in St. Petersburg, which was founded in 1801, and 100 years later was claimed as the largest manufacturing plant in Russia and also the largest in Europe, apart from Krupp in Germany and Armstrong in the United Kingdom.[120] The firm had licensing agreements with Western companies; one with the Bucyrus Company (United States) dated from the early 1900s and covered the manufacture of placer dredges and steam shovels.[121] The Revolution dispersed its skilled workers and managers, and it was not until January 1922 that some sections began operating again, with German engineering assistance. We do know something of the mechanical condition of the plant during the period 1917 to 1922 (the five years of 'technical preservation'). A report exists which indicates that equipment was intact, although '60 percent worn out'; blame for non-operation was placed on the enemies of the people:

> It was at that moment impossible without any prepared plan to put all in order, because of the opposition (not shown openly) of the different specialists towards the Working Peasant Power.[122]

Later some émigrés from Detroit were sent to Putilovets, and the 1926 Ford Delegation reported that the works was well equipped with United Kingdom, German, and American machine tools, and that it was

> . . . not at all badly arranged, with machines in progressive order, and it was the only shop visited that was provided with special tools and fixtures to any extent. The manufacturing methods, jigs and fixtures strongly reflected Ford practice at the old Dearborn plant.[123]

The plant had then been reopened about a year before, and employed some 800 workers. The delegation estimated production at three tractors per month.

[119] U.S. Consulate at Riga, Report 3529, January 18, 1926. (316–133–559.)
[120] *The Works 'Red Putilovez': A Short Historical Description.* Typewritten ms, undated, origin unknown. Hoover Institution, Stanford University.
[121] *Designed for Digging: The First 75 years of Bucyrus-Erie Company* (Evanston: Northwestern; 1955), p. 85.
[122] *The Works 'Red Putilovez': A Short Historical Description*, p. 15.
[123] *Ford Delegation Report (1926)*, pp. 48–9.

There was a sprinkling of ex-Ford Motor Company employees throughout the plant, including the final inspection area.

Ford, the arch-capitalist, then attracted the envious attention of the Communists. *Fordismus* and *Fordizatsia* as work methods became bywords; if Ford methods would work in a capitalist country then they must surely work in a socialist country.[124] The initial relationship between the Ford Motor Company and the Soviets was purely one of trade. Between 1922 and 1926, Ford sold 20,000 tractors to the U.S.S.R., each with its own set of replacement parts. By 1927, more than 85 percent of all trucks and tractors used in the U.S.S.R. were Ford-built from Detroit. The balance was a mixture of imported Fiats, Case, Internationals, and some United Kingdom models, together with the scrambled output of the A.M.O. plant in Moscow (attempting to reproduce Fiat trucks and repair White trucks), the ex-International Harvester plant, and the decrepit prerevolutionary tractor plants in Moscow and Kharkov.

The 1926 Ford Delegation to the U.S.S.R. found Ford products everywhere. The Ukrainian government owned 5,700 tractors, of which 5,520 were genuine Fordsons. Azneft had 700 automobiles, of which 420 were Fords. The major problem facing Soviet organizations was servicing, and this was also the primary interest of the five-man Ford team. The delegation traveled throughout the U.S.S.R. giving lectures and lessons on servicing and cost reduction, and setting up training schools and service organizations along Ford lines elsewhere in the world. The existing servicing was found to be 'wretched.' Charts and diagrams produced in abundance on request meant nothing: in practice, little in the way of either maintenance or repair was being done:

> Our surprise can be imagined when we arrived in the Ukraine, the richest tractor district in Russia, and were unable to find a single Fordson repair shop worthy of the name. No special repair equipment existed anywhere, although fourteen full sets of Fordson (repair) equipment had lately been received for Ukraine alone. . . .[125]

In 1923 the State Trade Commission had been given the responsibility of developing a network of sale and repair shops to be tied in with the major repair points established by the Fordson sales organization in the U.S.S.R. Apparently the trade commission had not established its repair shops, and the Fordson shops had been neglected.[126]

The 1928 Sorensen mission to Russia inspected the Krasnyi Putilovets plant, and, as Sorensen relates it:

---

[124]   'Fordismus,' *Bolshaya Sovetskaya Entsiklopediya* (1933).
[125]   *Ford Delegation Report (1926)*, p. 49.
[126]   *Ekonomicheskaya Zhizn*, No. 48, March 3, 1923.

We came into . . . the assembly room and I stopped in astonishment. There on the floor lines they were building the Fordson tractor. . . . What the Russians had done was to dismantle one of our tractors in the Putilov Works, and their own people made drawings of all the disassembled parts.[127]

However, as Sorensen pointed out, it was a long way from pulling a machine to pieces to building workable copies, and the Russians had neither the specifications nor the skills to turn out good copies. The Fordson-Putilovets tractor experiment provided little more than technical education.

In brief, at the mid-point of the 1920s, the Soviets had five prewar agricultural machinery plants, suitable for small-scale tractor construction. However these plants were costly to operate and technically backward. They made a hopelessly insufficient and inefficient contribution to agricultural development.

The solution was to turn to American technology. The poor Krasnyi Putilovets works was therefore completely re-equipped with American equipment[128] and, by technical-assistance arrangement, placed under the management of the engineering consultants Frank Smith, Inc.[129] A series of large-scale tractor building plants was then envisaged, utilizing the latest American mass production methods. The first of these was the Stalingrad (followed by the Chelyabinsk and Kharkov), designed by Albert Kahn, a United States construction design firm, and built by McClintock and Marshall, also of the United States.[130]

Albert Kahn had been the builder of the large mass-production plants of the American automobile manufacturers, and he incorporated the skills and ideas of American experience in mass production. The Stalingrad tractor plant was designed to produce 40,000 tractors a year in two shifts. With United States assistance, the Soviets produced similar tractor and automobile plants in the 1930s.

The Soviets had a clear concept of the advantages to be gained from importing this technology *in toto*, and the contribution it would make to the achievement of the first Five Year Plan:

> The utilization of its [i.e., Kahn's] technical assistance assures the execution of the construction work of the Traktorstroi within the specified time and guarantees the employment of all the achievements of modern American technique.[131]

---

[127] Charles E. Sorensen, *My Forty Years with Ford* (New York: Norton, 1956), p. 202. The plant certainly did not impress Sorensen, who suggested they take some sticks of dynamite and 'blow it out of its misery.'

[128] Friedman, *op. cit.*, p. 238.

[129] U.S. State Dept. Decimal File, 316-131-654.

[130] *Ibid.*

[131] The agreement between Albert Kahn and Glavmashinostroi is reported in *Torgovo-Promyshlennaya Gazeta*, No. 109, May 16, 1929.

The Kahn company prepared construction plans in the United States while at the same time instructing a group of engineers from Traktorstroi. The company then hired American engineers to handle the erection of the buildings, worth about 8 million rubles ($3 million). The production equipment was purchased in the United States.[132]

Table 7–3 TECHNICAL-ASSISTANCE AGREEMENTS (TYPE III)
WITH THE POST-REVOLUTIONARY TRACTOR
CONSTRUCTION INDUSTRY TO 1930

Technical Process	*Western Partner*
Preliminary consulting	Dr. Ing. G. Schlesinger (Germany)
Gear-cutting technology	Brown Lipe Gear Co. (Syracuse)
Electrical-equipment manufacturing	The Electric Auto-Lite Co. (Toledo)
Axle-manufacturing	Timken-Detroit Axle Company (Detroit)
Engine technology	Deutz A-G, Hercules Motor Company (U.S.)
Plant design	Albert Kahn, Inc. (Detroit)
Plant steel structure erection (Stalingrad)	McClintock and Marshall (U.S.)

Source: American-Russian Chamber of Commerce, *Economic Handbook of the Soviet Union*, pp. 97–101.

Although the tractor industry, heralded as the basis for socialist agriculture in the same manner that electrification had been associated with industrialization, was a major problem for much of the decade, the gravest shortages occurred in production of the simpler kind of equipment. Scythes, sickles, pitchforks, plows, harrows, and winnows were prohibited from import, as it was planned to supply all internal demand from Russian factories. The simpler kinds of agricultural equipment were subject to a heavy duty of 4.5 rubles per 100 kilograms, whereas the more complicated mechanical equipment was allowed in duty-free; reapers, binders, disc harrows, and all newly invented or improved equipment required by model farms were allowed in without duty. However, the massive shortages of simple equipment reduced the ability of the peasant to work his land, and in some areas the peasant actually returned to the use of wooden implements.[133]

We may conclude therefore, that in agriculture the transfer of Western technology was not notably successful. The hostility of the peasant, the collectivization of agriculture, the undue attachment to imaginary massive

---

[132] *Bank for Russian Trade Review*, II, No. 7 (July 1929), 4; and U.S. State Dept. Decimal File, 316–132–28/44.

[133] U.S. Consulate at Riga, Report 3481, December 5, 1925. (316–133–540.) The deficiency in 1925 amounted to 140,000 plows, 614,000 harrows, and 17,000 winnows.

economies of scale, and the misunderstanding of the factors making for success in Western large-scale agriculture made for ineffective transfer.

Kuibyshev's lengthy report of April 1927 suggests the great gap between the Soviets' achievement and their fantastic claims. While Krasnyi Putilovets was struggling to make a few ersatz copies of the Fordson tractor, the effort was thus described by Kuibyshev:

> . . . a mass of difficulties has been solved brilliantly, the production of tractors is getting cheaper and cheaper and the quantities produced by the Red Putilovets are ever increasing. . . .[134]

In the agricultural equipment industry, nothing of substance was achieved in tractor production until the very end of the decade, and implement manufacture was unfortunately ignored in favor of the tractor—the favored Bolshevik symbol of industrialization. The failure of adapted prerevolutionary plants to make tractors, whether of native design (the Gnom) or stolen design (the Fordson) forced the Soviets to arrange for Western tractor manufacturers to install packaged 'knocked-down' plants in the U.S.S.R.[135]

CREDITS GRANTED BY AGRICULTURAL MACHINERY PRODUCERS TO THE SOVIET UNION, 1925

The Soviet Union had no trouble purchasing agricultural machinery on credit terms. The *Ford Delegation Report (1926)*, for example, notes:

> International Harvester, which lost huge sums of money in Russia through nationalization of its property and equipment, are now extending two years credit to the Soviet Government.

An International Harvester invoice dated August 18, 1925, indicates that the cost of the International 15–30 tractor to the Soviet government was $1,150 and the 10–20 tractor $775 (both f.o.b. New York). Terms were as follows:

> 50 percent three months after purchase
> 16.6 percent August 15, 1926
> 16.6 percent November 15, 1926
> 16.6 percent May 15, 1927

Interest was charged at 8 percent in the first year and 6 percent in the second.

Case Machinery was granting about the same terms. Advance-Rumley, which had about 600 to 800 of its 'Old Pull' tractors in the Soviet Union, was offering less favorable terms, and this limited its sales. An invoice dated August 12, 1925, places cost to the Soviet government at $1,000, and offers terms at 10 percent with order, 40 percent against documents in New York, and 25 percent in each of two payments, to be made November 1, 1926, and November

---

[134] *Izvestia*, No. 94, April 27, 1927.
[135] Construction of the Stalingrad and other tractor plants is covered in Vol. II.

1, 1927. Dodge Brothers was offering nine-month terms with only 6-percent interest for lots of more than 50 tractors, but required 50-percent payment against documents for any size of purchase. Massey-Harris, in Canada, sold 300 binders in August 1926 on terms of 10 percent with order, 20 percent against documents, 10 percent three months from date of delivery, and the balance in August 1927. Fordson, who sold the bulk of the tractors in the U.S.S.R., required 25 percent down and the balance over nine months or one year. These terms were not, however, as favorable as those obtained by the Soviets for automobiles and trucks. Steyer in Austria and Mercedes in Germany both gave three-year credits, and Renault in France two years.

Of a total 24,000 tractors in Russia in August 1926, 20,000 were Fordsons, 2,400 were International Harvesters, 700 were Advance-Rumley, and 900 were miscellaneous (including Soviet makes).

In the light of these statistics, statements that the Soviet Union developed without foreign financial assistance are seen to be manifestly untrue.

CHAPTER EIGHT

Fishing, Hunting, and Canning Concessions

THE small group of fishing, hunting, and canning concessions was more important as a contributor to foreign exchange earnings than as a channel for the direct transfer of technology. Furs, for example, were the second most important Soviet export and indirectly, by generating foreign exchange, aided the technological transfer process.

NORWEGIAN FISHING CONCESSIONS

In early 1923, an agreement was made between the Norwegian firm Vinge and Company and the People's Commissariat of Supplies, under which the Norwegians were given the privilege of hunting 'sea animals' within the territorial waters of North Russia. The company equipped fifty-six ships for this purpose. Vinge and Company paid 200,000 Norwegian crowns for this right.[1]

For the second year of operations the Soviets demanded negotiation with the ships' owners who had been organized with Vinge as their bargaining agent in the first year. In the second year, rental was set at $10 per ton for ships employed hunting seals, with a minimum payment of $40,000. Provision was also made for Russian scientists to study fishing methods and fishing locations, on board the 'best' of the ships in the fleet.[2]

An additional contract was also concluded for the 1924 season, under which Vinge was granted the right to fish for white sturgeon along the Russian Arctic coast.[3]

A concession was granted to the Norwegian citizen Christensen in May 1923 to hunt whales and reduce these to food products within a zone extending along the Arctic coast of Russia. It was granted for a period of fifteen years, and the

---

[1]   *Russian Economic Review*, III, No. 8 (June 10, 1923), 12.
[2]   *Ekonomicheskaya Zhizn*, No. 71, December 23, 1923.
[3]   *Ekonomicheskaya Zhizn*, No. 303, October 7, 1924.

Soviet government received a portion of the profits unstated but not less than £2,000 sterling per year. Each ship manned by Christensen was required to have at least six Russian seamen, and shore enterprises operated by the concession were required to employ not less than 25 percent Russian workmen.[4]

A group of German fishing firms working in the Murmansk area was granted a concession in 1924 to fish in certain northern waters disputed by the U.S.S.R. and Germany. The group holding the concession was known as Wirtschafteliche Verband der Deutschen Hochseefischerein and was based in Bremen.[5]

FUR AND SKIN CONCESSIONS

The Hudson's Bay Company of the United Kingdom and Canada concluded a concessions agreement with Vneshtorg in April 1923, under which the company agreed to export to Kamchatka, in the Far East, goods to the value of $350,000, at prices not exceeding the London market price plus 20 percent. The company could also purchase furs on the peninsula in cooperation with Vneshtorg. The furs were to be exported to London, where 10 percent of the value was payable to Vneshtorg, and any profit resulting from the ultimate sale of the furs was to be divided equally between Hudson's Bay and Vneshtorg. A similar agreement was reported with Glavconcern for smoked fish and furs.[6] The company was required to pay all state and local taxes, license fees, and export and import taxes.

The winter buying season did not go untroubled for Hudson's Bay. There were petitions from Kamchatka in which hunters requested the government

> . . . to free them from the criminal activities of the Hudson's Bay firm . . . agents of the firm deliberately value furs at 50 percent below last year, and sables of the highest quality are valued at the same price as skins of the lowest quality. . . . The firm has double income whereas the population suffers treble losses.[7]

The Persian lamb fur market in the United States was dominated by Brenner Brothers, of New York. In the fall of 1922, Kalman and Feival Brenner made a buying trip into Russia and purchased 'a considerable quantity of furs,' for delivery to Paris and New York. They considered uncertainty too great to warrant more extensive dealing, although they were offered an 'attractive proposition.'[8]

[4] *Izvestia*, No. 113, May 24, 1923.
[5] U.S. State Dept. Decimal File, 340–5–806.
[6] *Rigasche Nachrichten* (Riga, Latvia), April 14, 1923.
[7] *Pravda* (Moscow), No. 40, February 19, 1924.
[8] U.S. Consulate at Riga, Report 2729, September 25, 1922. (316–107–1034). This deal apparently went through because Brenner's Siberian representative had a brother who was a 'high government official in Moscow.'

Karl Brenner, a partner of the firm, was approached by Arcos agents in 1924 with another $1 million proposal. In return for the exclusive right to purchase furs within the U.S.S.R., they could buy at 15 percent under the market price or be repaid at an interest rate of 10 percent. Brenner pointed out that Arcos had overheads of 35 percent in handling furs while Brenner had a 50 percent markup. They considered the U.S.S.R. had reached the end of its financial resources and refused to deal.[9] The company registered for business and purchased 500,000 rubles of furs in the 1924–5 season.[10]

In the same season, J. Wiener, of New York, was registered for operations in the U.S.S.R. and purchased 400,000 rubles worth of furs.[11]

Probably the largest of the fur concessions was that of Eitingon-Schild, which in 1924–5 handled 4 percent of the total trade turnover between the United States and the U.S.S.R.[12]

A dispute between the Eitingon-Schild concession partners in United States courts revealed the substantial profits made by a few successful concessions. Representing Eitingon-Schild, Otto B. Shulhof, of New York City, went to London and then to Moscow in 1922 to negotiate a contract for the marketing of Russian skins and furs. Eitingon himself was a Russian émigré and had considered himself persona non grata so far as the Soviets were concerned. Shulhof held that when the concession was about to be signed (he had all required signatures except those of Krassin and Bogdanov) he found that Eitingon had signed a fur concession directly with Arcos, Soviet trade representatives in London. Shulhof sued for $1 million damages for breach of contract, in lieu of the 10-percent commission. Just before going into court, he raised the damage claim to $2 million. Examination of Eitingon-Schild accounting records indicated that the concession profits for two years were over $1.5 million. Net sales of the concession had been $7,340,178, which after deduction of cost and 7 percent royalty, left a net profit of $1,846,759.[13] The contract had run initially for one year, during which Eitingon-Schild advanced the Soviets 50 percent of the value of the skins and furs and split profits equally with them. During the second year, the concessionaire was required to make more substantial advances, and his profit was limited to 15 percent of the selling price of the furs.[14] Apart from the Hammer operations, no other case is known where large profits were made from concessions.

9   U.S. Consulate at Riga, Report 2550, December 8, 1924. (316–108–1277.)
10 U.S. Consulate at Riga, Report 927, January 17, 1925. (316–111–915.)
11 *Ekonomicheskaya Zhizn*, No. 192, August 25, 1925.
12 U.S. State Dept. Decimal File, 316–108–1543.
13 An independent accountant in later evidence held that profits were only $1,079,973 over two years.
14 *New York Times*, various issues, November 1927.

SIBERIAN FISH CANNERIES

In the Soviet Union the only variety of fish canned in 1923 was salmon, of which about 30 million pounds were canned annually and almost all exported. Of the twenty canneries in Siberian waters, fifteen were owned and operated by Japanese, two by Russians, two by Americans, and one by the British. There were also eighteen crab canneries, of which fifteen were Japanese-owned and operated and three were Russian. The entire Siberian fishing industry in 1923 employed about 34,000 persons, of whom 29,000 were Japanese. The Japanese also leased 62 percent of the fishing stations.[15]

AMERICAN CONSTRUCTION OF SALMON CANNERIES IN KAMCHATKA

In 1927–8, two large salmon canneries, one with five canning lines and one with three canning lines, were built to can salmon for export. The construction of these new canneries indicates a complete dependence on the most advanced Western engineering achievements. Nearly all the firms involved in construction came from the Pacific coast of the United States.

Table 8–1   CONSTRUCTION AND EQUIPMENT OF
KAMCHATKA SALMON CANNERIES, 1928

Structural Equipment Supplied	*Company*
Coolers	Isaacson Iron Works, Seattle
Steam engines	Nagle Engine and Boiler Works
Steel barges	Wallace Bridge and Structural Co.
Conveyers	International B.F. Goodrich Co.
Boilers	Pennsylvania Boiler Works
Diesel engines	Fairbanks Morse
Transmission equipment	Link Belt
Canning Equipment Supplied	
Electric strapping equipment	EBY Co.
Lift trucks	Parker
Cannery equipment	Seattle-Astoria Iron Works
Canning equipment	Smith Canning Machine Co.
Pumps	Worthington Pump Co.
Tinplate	Bethlehem Steel and United States Steel
Fish cutters	Wright and Smith
Fillers, retorts	Troyer-Fox
Lacquering machines	Seeley
Nailing machines	Morgan

Source: Amtorg, *op. cit.*, III, No. 7 (1928).

---

[15]   U.S. Embassy at Tokyo, Report 13, January 29, 1925. (316–108–1310.)

A floating crab cannery with a capacity of 500 48-pound cases a day was manufactured for the U.S.S.R. by the International Packing Company in Seattle, in 1928.[16]

After a Russian fishing industry delegation had visited the United States, the equipping of nearly all Siberian and Far Eastern canneries was given over to American firms.[17] Similarly, an Odessa fish cannery with a capacity of 10 million cans of fish a year was equipped with Western canning machinery.[18]

In brief, fur concessions enabled the Soviets to enter the foreign market and, with the help of Western partners, build this into their second largest generator of foreign exchange. The canneries, also a significant exchange generator, were equipped completely by Western manufacturers, primarily from the United States.

[16] Amtorg, *op. cit.*, III, No. 7 (1928).
[17] Amtorg, *op. cit.*, III, No. 2 (1928).
[18] Amtorg, *op. cit.*, III, No. 12 (1928).

CHAPTER NINE

Restoration of the Russian Lumber Industry
1921-30

SEVEROLES TRUST AND FOREIGN LUMBER COMPANIES

RUSSIA has extensive forestry resources—probably the finest in the world. Under the tsars, lumber trade possibilities were not fully recognized and the industry developed slowly in the years immediately preceding World War I. In 1913 Russia had exported 10 million cubic meters of sawed timber; by 1929 this volume of exports had been almost regained.

There were no Soviet exports of lumber in 1919–20. In 1921 the industry recovered slightly and exported 35,000 standards, or about 3 percent of the average yearly prewar shipment. Reorganization in 1922–3 created four trusts: Severoles in the northern forest area, Sapodles in the western forest area, Dvinoles in the Dvina forest area, and Exploles in the Far East.

The trusts, however, were incapable of increasing production. Penetration of prewar markets was impossible, owing to their inability to organize production; shortages of equipment, tools, provisions, and labor made sizable production impossible.

Negotiations for assistance were opened with foreign lumber companies in 1921 and resulted in the formation of four mixed companies (Type II concession agreements, with some elements of the Type I and Type III), which took over the operation of the greater part of the northern forests in the Severoles trust. The foreign companies were predominantly British and German and held 49 percent of the shares, 51 percent being held by the Soviet government. The Soviets also had the right to grant further concessions to build sawmills and woodworking mills in the trust areas. The foreign companies were entrusted with entire management of forests and mills and had the obligation to supply machinery, tools, housing, and food for those workmen supplied by the Soviet government. The poor state of the railroad system meant that only areas close to rivers and ports could be exploited.

For timber in the Luga and Pliussa forests, near the Estonian border, the Soviets made an agreement with the Estonian companies Arbor and Narova. These companies were entrusted with the operation of the sawmills, but export arrangements were left in the hands of the Soviet government.

In the Dvina forests, the Dvinoles trust owned shares in a mixed Russo-Latvian company organized along lines similar to those of the Severoles agreement.

Sapodoles was dependent on Polish and Lithuanian technical assistance.[1]

Table 9-1   THE SOVIET LUMBER TRUSTS AND
FOREIGN CONCESSIONS

Trust	*Foreign Operator of the Trust Area*
Severoles	Russangloles, Ltd. (United Kingdom)
Onega	Russnorvegloles, Ltd. (Norway, United Kingdom)
North Dvina-Vichegoda	Russhollandoles, Ltd. (Holland, United Kingdom)
Sapodoles	Polish and Lithuanian lumber companies
Dvinoles	Russo-Latvian Company (Latvia)
Exploles	Rorio Rengio Rumian (Japan)
	Raby-Khiki Kansha (Japan)
	Rorio Rengio Kumai (Japan)
Non-Trust Area	
Mga-Rybinsk	Holz Industrie Aktien Gesellschaft Mologa (Germany)

Sources: 1. U.S. State Dept. Decimal File, 316-135-479.
        2. Troyanovsky, *Eksport, import i kontsessii soyuz S.S.S.R.*, p. 16.

RUSSANGLOLES, LTD.

Russangloles, Ltd. was a stock company organized under British law, and the most important of the lumber joint-stock or mixed companies. It was registered on February 7, 1922 with a nominal capital of £150,000. Its objective, noted in a Memorandum of Association, was to develop timber properties, sawmills, and transportation (including docks, railroads, roads, etc.) in order to merchandise timber products. The company could borrow money to achieve this objective.[2] Of the six company directors, three were Russian, two were British, and one was Latvian. The foreigners had all been in the lumber business.

Russangloles was the operating arm of an earlier concession agreement made between Severoles and the London and Northern Trading Company, Ltd., on December 31, 1921. This company had been organized in the United Kingdom

---

[1] *Timber News and Sawmill Worker* (London), June 10, 1922.
[2] The complete Memorandum of Association is available in a dispatch, dated February 16, 1922, from the American Vice Consul in London (316-135-479).

on September 20, 1919 with a nominal capital of £1 million to operate sawmills in the Archangel area and merchandise substantial quantities of lumber already stored there. Four of the directors of the London and Northern Trading Company were British and one Russian—Morduch Schalit, earlier a timber merchant in Archangel and the former owner of the property taken over by the company.

It was not unusual for concessions to be in operation before official announcement, and this was the case with Russangloles. There is in the State Department files an agent's report, dated August 1921, describing a stormy meeting held at the town of Petrozavodsk, in Olonetz Province, concerning 'the question of handing over to the English the working of woodlands and forests in the province.' This concession was submitted to the regional committees and commissariats to enlist local support, as local peasants objected to losing their timberlands.[3]

Russangloles was given the right to exploit timber lots in the Pomozdinsky and Kontzegorsky areas for a term of twelve years. The rental consisted of a gross income percentage, a stumpage fee, and a separate fee for sawmills and

Chart 9-1 ACQUISITION OF FOREIGN LUMBER MARKETS: PHASE I (1922-4)

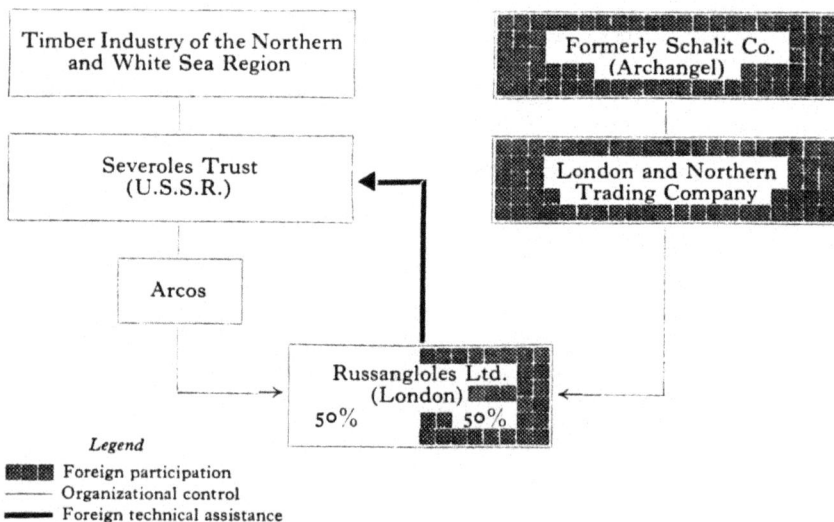

---

[3]   The agent reported that the 'meeting was so stormy . . . it was almost necessary to have recourse to troops but they also voted for a second discussion refusing to attack the people.' (316–135–477.) It has been noted elsewhere that concession operations often caused local trouble (apart from the Party-inspired 'strikes'), and a case could be made that the concessions were seen locally as a means of perpetuating an unwanted Bolshevik rule.

building and transportation facilities. In addition, taxes were levied by the central and local governments. Export duty was payable, and the Soviet government reserved the right to purchase any timber prepared for export.[4]

Severoles was the largest of the Soviet timber trusts, covering the whole of the gigantic white wood resources of the Russian northland. It was this enormous area that was taken over, developed, and operated by Russangloles. The other two trusts in the western area, Sapadoles and Dvinoles, were considerably smaller and were operated by Estonian and Latvian companies in mixed company arrangements with the U.S.S.R.

Severoles was also the principal shareholder, along with British lumber companies, in the White Sea Timber Trust, Ltd. (organized in the United Kingdom to sell sawed lumber on the European market), and its auxiliary concerns: the Russian Wood Agency, Ltd. (a timber brokerage firm), the Russ-Norwegian Navigation Company, Ltd., and the Norway-Russian Navigation Company, Ltd., which used leased Norwegian ships to transport timber materials and products to foreign markets.[5]

In each of these trusts, and in the Far East trust discussed later, timber development, construction of sawmills, transportation, and ancillary operations were undertaken by foreign companies. In effect they transferred their skills to Russian operations, and in each area created extensive and successful timber operations.

Chart 9-2 ACQUISITION OF FOREIGN LUMBER MARKETS: PHASE II (AFTER 1924)

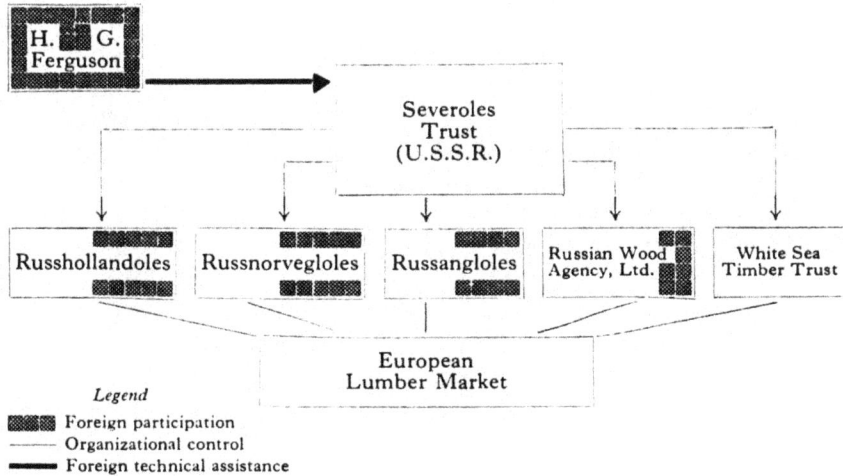

---

[4] *Ekonomicheskaya Zhizn*, No. 60, March 17, 1923.
[5] Troyanovsky, *op. cit.*, p. 16.

Sales were made through a wholly Russian-owned trust. As the original agreement has never been published, it is impossible to determine precisely the part played by Western firms. Severoles acted as a broker, obtaining sawed lumber from concessions and selling it to Western timber merchants for advance royalties. This operation generated scarce foreign exchange.

Lumber sales to Germany, however, did not go through the trusts. The German Mologa concession output was substantial and financed on credit by Deruwa (the German-Russian Merchandise Exchange Society) and the Berlin branch of the Russian Bank of Commerce (the Aschberg concession). Advance payments were made through Deruwa beginning in 1923 for all lumber sold through the organization in Germany.[6]

RUSSHOLLANDOLES, LTD.
(RUSSIAN-DUTCH TIMBER COMPANY)

Russhollandoles, Ltd. was a mixed company similar to Russangloles formed in the spring of 1922 by Severoles and a Dutch timber firm, Altius and Company, with some British financial participation. The objective was to develop for a period of twenty years the forest resources of the North Dvina and Vichegoda River area in the Archangel region. The area covered over 400,000 dessiatins and included property formerly belonging to the Altius company. Half the shares were owned by the Soviets and the other half by the Dutch and United Kingdom concessionaires. Operations began in August 1922, and in the first three months a quarter million railroad sleepers and the stock of 2,500 standards of lumber had been exported to the United Kingdom and Holland.[7]

Another very large timber concession, Russnorvegloles, was concluded in July 1923 with a group of Norwegian firms and a Dutch company (Backe and Wigg, of Dramman; Backe and Wagner, Prytz and Company, and Altius and Company). The capital stock was set at £300,000 divided equally. The Soviets were granted the right to contribute their share in timber instead of cash. The company was registered in the United Kingdom. The area covered was about 2.9 million dessiatins, of which about two million was forest land in the Onega River area. The term of agreement was twenty years, after which all equipment and buildings became the property of the U.S.S.R.[8] The capital stock was divided proportionately between Severoles and the Dutch and Norwegian companies.

---

[6] U.S. Consulate in Königsberg, Report, March 6, 1923. (316–135–501.)

[7] *Ekonomicheskaya Zhizn*, No. 53, March 9, 1923.

[8] *Ekonomicheskaya Zhizn*, July 6, 1923; and U.S. Consulate in Christiania, Norway, Report, July 19, 1923. (316–135–531.)

The three mixed companies—Russangloles, Norvegloles, and Hollandoles —organized by Severoles advanced 15 million rubles credit in the first year of operation, as well as providing necessary working capital and technical assistance to get the northern timber areas back into operation.

British lumber companies also had an arrangement with Dvinoles known as Dvinoles Export, Ltd. There was in addition an agreement between Finnish companies and Dvinoles called Repola Wood, Ltd. Both companies exported unsawed timber. The cutting operations were financed by the foreign partners; the wood was exported and cut by foreign mills.[9]

In brief, to restore timber cutting operations and renew contact with Western markets, the Soviets used the good offices of the former owners, although a superficial examination of the organizational structure of the Soviet trusts and the mixed companies does not indicate the full extent of these arrangements.

EX-CHANCELLOR WIRTH AND THE MOLOGA CONCESSION

An important Type I concession was the 'Society for Economic Relations with the East' (Gesellschaft fur Wirtschaftliche Beziehungen mit den Osten), headed by ex-Chancellor Wirth and ex-Reichstag Deputy Haas, and including the German firms Himmelsbach, Dortmund Association, Bop und Reiter, Schuckart und Schuette, Voegele, and others—and signed in October 1923. It included timber production and export, and the construction of a railroad in Northwest Russia. By the end of 1923, the Mga-Rybinsk railroad alone had received an investment of almost 25 million rubles.

Under the agreement, which created an operating company, Holz Industrie A-G Mologa, one million dessiatins of forest land was granted to the concession and 5,000 dessiatins was required to be cut annually. In addition, the concessionaire built a wood sleeper-treating plant for 1,000,000 sleepers annually, together with a pulp and chemical works, including ten plants for the chemical treatment of tree stumps. The Soviets received a royalty which varied between 2.5 and 22 rubles per cubic sazhen marketed by the Mologa concession. The railroad construction had to be completed within three years. The life of the concession was twenty-five years, with provision for an extension to thirty-five years upon mutual agreement. At this time properties would revert to the Soviet state.[10]

The concession got under way in 1924; seven ships of timber were loaded in the first nine months, and the Mga-Rybinsk Railroad was started. There was a report of a labor disagreement on the railroad construction in September

---

[9]   Troyanovsky, *loc. cit.*
[10]   U.S. Embassy in Berlin, Report 135, October 12, 1923. (316–135–545).

1924, but this was settled and the threatened strike collapsed when Mologa submitted to the demands of the workers.

By 1926 Mologa work was not going well, and Dr. Wirth visited Leningrad in April to renegotiate the concession. The proposals made by Wirth were briefly as follows:

1. That the royalty payable to the Soviet government be reduced by 30 percent. (A 15 percent reduction was granted.)
2. That machinery for use in the concession enter the Soviet Union duty-free instead of at the previously agreed preferential tariff. (This was granted.)
3. That railroad freight charges be reduced to 50 percent of those normally paid. (This was not granted.)
4. That permission be granted to bring in timber specialists from Germany. (This was granted.)
5. That labor hours be increased by 20 percent. (This was not granted by the Soviets, but it was agreed that overtime be paid at 40 percent above the regular wage rates.)

In addition, Dr. Wirth agreed to build a cellulose factory, two additional sawmills, and an electric power station on the Mologa River to serve the concession area. At this time, between 25,000 and 32,000 men were employed by the concession in cutting and shipping lumber to Germany.[11]

In early 1927, the Mologa representatives in Moscow (Levin and Berdichevsky) were alleged to have bribed Soviet officials, specifically those employed by Mostroi (the Moscow Construction Trust), the Lyubertsy Agricultural Machinery Works (formerly the International Harvester Plant in Moscow), and officials of Grozneft. The trial opened in 1927. The Soviet officials were sentenced to death and Levin, the Mologa representative, to five years' imprisonment.

By mid-1927 Mologa was again in a very precarious position, and the Germans decided to withdraw and allow the Soviets to take over.

Mologa was exceptional in that it received preferential treatment. The renegotiation of 1926, for example, was clearly favorable to German interests. The accusation of bribery was a characteristic move to force expulsion of the concession as soon as production was organized and sufficient equipment introduced into the concession areas.[12]

---

[11]　U.S. State Dept. Decimal File, 316-135-595.

[12]　Coleman, U.S. Consulate at Riga, Report 4516, May 19, 1927. (316-135-615.) Coleman's conclusion reads: 'Ksandrov's assurances of friendliness to the Molo-goles merely confirms the long known fact that this concession has been particularly favored by the Soviet Government who saw in it one of the concrete manifestations of a Soviet-German rapprochement. But incidentally they also reveal that in spite of

In an interview published in *Ekonomicheskaya Zhizn*, No. 85, March 22, 1927, Ksandrov, deputy chairman of the Chief Concessions Committee, argued that the real reasons for the Mologa financial difficulties lay outside both the concession agreement and the attitude of the U.S.S.R. toward the agreement. He stated that the Society for Trade with the East had been formed in Berlin in 1923 and this company formed also the Holz Industrie Aktien Gesellschaft Mologa with an initial capital of 300,000 marks, increased in 1926 to 3 million marks. During the first year, the company erected ten frame saws instead of the stipulated six, and a major part of the investment—about 2.35 million rubles—was made in the first year, resulting in an operating loss of 576,000 rubles. This induced Mologa to request changes in the agreement. Ksandrov pointed out that the changes were made; consequently the 1925–6 production was 1 million rubles, compared to 4.5 million rubles in 1924–5. Also the concession was granted a two-year extension on the railroad construction program, a postponement of stumpage payments, and a grant of Soviet financial support. Up to March 4, 1927, credits from Gosbank amounted to 4.5 million rubles, in addition to 420,000 rubles loaned by the Bank of Trade and Industry, a revolving credit of 3 million rubles, and a government subsidy of 2.2 million rubles granted in January 1926 and repayable in March 1927. Ksandrov then concluded that 'the main reason for the financial difficulties of the Mologoles is a lack of a solid financial basis.' The initial capital of 300,000 marks was used during the initial organizing period; the concessions then had to borrow capital at high interest rates (15 to 16 percent in the first year, 13 percent interest in the second year, and 7 to 8 percent in the third year), and Anglo-American capital, which was anticipated at lower rates of interest, was not forthcoming.

Therefore, Ksandrov said:

> In view of the economic and political importance of this concession, the Soviet Government granted considerable privileges already at the conclusion of the agreement, that assured large profits from the concession to German capitalists.

A rather different explanation of the decline and liquidation of the Mologa concession is given by M. Klemmer in his 1927 report to Western Electric Co. and is the basis for his advice that pure concessions, as distinct from technical-assistance agreements, were not suitable objects for investment. Klemmer reported that the Mologa concession developed normally in its first years, but

---

the exceptionally friendly attention shown to Herr Wirth's concession, the prominent German interests backing the latter proved unable to overcome the reluctance of the international money market to make investments in the Soviet Union. . . . It is a striking coincidence, characteristic of the Soviet regime, that the failure of the concessionaires *(sic)* to obtain new investments was immediately followed by sentences in a Soviet criminal court of several officers of the Mologoles to prison for alleged bribing of employees of Soviet commercial institutions. . . .'

then 'the cost of labor and all the prices went so high up' that export did not pay; the concession then acquired permission to sell on the internal Soviet market. This appeared profitable, as lumber prices were two to three times higher than in the previous years. However, Soviet organizations paid only after long delays, and, coupled with rising prices for materials and labor, this put Mologa in another difficult financial position. Klemmer points out that Gosbank loans were insufficient to meet commitments, and Mologa was forced to go abroad for financial assistance.[13]

It would appear, then, that credits were advanced by the U.S.S.R. to Mologa, but that these were insufficient to offset the disadvantages of selling on the internal market. Any foreign enterprise operating within the U.S.S.R. and this certainly applied also to Harriman and Lena—faced insurmountable difficulties in an environment where normal business facilities, such as credit and terms of trade, were controlled by an arbitrary organization whose interests were not coincident with those of the Western organization.

In conclusion, the Mologa 1925–6 balance sheet indicated a profit. This profit did not satisfy the Concessions Committee, and in February 1927 Ksandrov proposed reorganization of the concession:

> It is obvious . . . that the fate of the concession enterprise depends entirely on a thorough solution of the financial problem, and that the failure of the concessionaire to solve this problem in a satisfactory manner will make the liquidation of the concession inevitable.[14]

Two months later, according to *Ekonomicheskaya Zhizn*, the Soviets liquidated Mologa.

The German government, it was argued, had refused to continue financing Mologa; therefore the concession was unable to establish a stable financial basis and 'a friendly agreement was reached by both parties to liquidate the concession.'[15] It was also stated that Mologa would be reimbursed the fair value of the concession property and a committee was appointed to appraise its value. Operations were then transferred to the Northwestern Lumber Trust (Severoles).

The only reimbursement was a payment for raw materials taken over. In the final analysis, the reimbursement for the 20 million marks invested by German firms was about 5.7 million marks, or 25 percent of the investment. Nevertheless, this was a considerably more favorable settlement than any other concession received. The creditors received 27 percent of their debts; the stockholders lost their investment.[16]

[13]　Klemmer Report (1927), pp. 22–3 (316–60–95).
[14]　*Ekonomicheskaya Zhizn*, No. 85, March 22, 1927.
[15]　*Ekonomicheskaya Zhizn*, No. 120, May 29, 1927.
[16]　*New York Times*, September 29, 1928, p. 21, col. 2.

THE EXPLOLES TRUST IN THE FAR EAST

In early 1923, the Soviet government completely reorganized the timber industry in the Far East. All timber resources east of Lake Baikal, except those areas under concession or reserved for concessions, were grouped into the Exploles trust. This included timber lands and wood product factories, including sawmills and veneer plants. Plants within the trust were not immediately nationalized; there were eight private sawmills and six nationalized mills. The veneer factory was privately owned—an essential feature, as the trust was in its early years financed by private capital from émigré Russians in Harbin. The trust then negotiated concessions with foreign capital.[17] An agreement was concluded in early 1923 between the Far Eastern Revolutionary Committee, the forerunner of the Far Eastern Soviet Government, and the Japanese syndicate, Ookura Gumei.[18] The grant was six million acres covering seven forest districts in Maritime Province, six for a period of twenty-four years and one for one year.[19]

The 1925 Treaty of Friendship and Recognition between Japan and the U.S.S.R. contained several protocols concerning concessions. Protocol 'B' led the way to more timber concessions in the Far East. The Far Eastern Timber Industry syndicate and Rorio Rengio Rumian were later relinquished because of difficulties imposed by the Soviets concerning the erection of sawmill and paper factories and the application of labor regulations.[20]

In 1927 a third timber concession was granted to a group of Japanese lumber companies in the Primorsky District.[21] The Raby-Khiki-Kansha concession was formed to exploit some 5,400,000 acres of forest and to ship the timber to Japan. The period of the concession was six years (until 1933), and renewal could be discussed during the sixth year. At least 7.5 million board feet of lumber had to be removed annually. Twenty-three dwellings were erected for Soviet lumber inspectors; and 350,000 rubles (a special fee), a royalty, and stumpage fees were paid after sale on the Japanese market. Sawmills and pulp mills were erected. Foreigners were employed but could not comprise more than 25 percent of total employment except in sawmills. There was a requirement to employ Soviet technical students in all operations.[22]

Another agreement was signed in April 1927. The Rorio Rengio Kumai, which employed 2,000 men, consisted of 2.7 million acres near the Tartar Straits, with an annual output of 7.5 million cubic feet.[23]

[17] U.S. Consulate in Vladivostok, Report, March 1, 1923. (316-135-502.)
[18] U.S. Embassy in Tokyo, Report 579, April 30, 1923. (316-108-455.)
[19] *Russian Daily News* (Harbin), May 13, 1923.
[20] C. Conolly, *op. cit.*, p. 45.
[21] Amtorg, *op. cit.*, II, No. 7 (April 1, 1927), 1.
[22] U.S. Embassy in Tokyo, Report 399, January 11, 1927. (316-135-435.)
[23] Amtorg, *op. cit.*, IV, No. 8 (April 15, 1929).

Later in 1927 an effort was made to attract foreign timber concessionaires on a much larger scale. It was announced, for example, that large unexploited timber regions of the Far East, extending for some 62,000,000 acres, had been divided into fifty-one blocks and that concessions could be obtained for these regions.[24]

ACTIVITIES AFTER THE DEPARTURE OF THE CONCESSIONS

Exit of Western companies and their concession operations was followed by the operation of the same northern lumber areas by prison labor: specifically political prisoners and *kulaki* under the management control of the OGPU. Although this proposition will not be examined in depth, there is considerable evidence that those lumber stands developed by the concessions (Dvina, Onega, and Komi in the northern forest areas) were precisely those areas turned over to OGPU prison camp operations. The loading of foreign ships with the sawed lumber was also undertaken by forced labor.[25]

New sawmills constructed were, however, still built by Western companies and with Western equipment after the departure of the concessionaires. The Dubrovsk sawmill, with a capacity of 5 million cubic feet of lumber a year, was built by the Bolinder Company in 1928 and 'largely' utilized Swedish equipment.[26] Another large sawmill, built in 1928 at Volinkinsky, near Leningrad, with a capacity of 2.5 million cubic feet per year, utilized equipment from both the United States and Sweden.[27]

The technical backwardness of the Russian lumber-processing industry, even as late as 1929, is suggested by the admission by Lobov that only 1 percent of Russian lumber was kiln-dried, compared to more than 60 percent in the United States.[28]

PULP AND PAPER MILLS

All pulp and paper mill technology was imported from Western countries. The Kondopozh (Lake Onega) paper mill, built in 1928, with an annual capacity of 25,000 tons of newsprint, had two turbo-generators built in Sweden and a 3,000 kilowatt steam plant and paper-making machine from

[24]   Amtorg, *op. cit.*, II, No. 20–1 (November 1, 1927), 10.
[25]   A. Pim and E. Bateson, *Report on Russian Timber Camps* (London: Benn, 1931). Swianiewicz, who had personal experience of the Soviet prison system, makes the point that lumber had to take the place of grain in generation of foreign exchange. In 1920–30 an acute manpower shortage developed; this led to OGPU operation of the northern forest areas. (S. Swianiewicz, *Forced Labour and Economic Development*, London: Oxford University Press, 1965, pp. 113–4.)
[26]   Amtorg, *op. cit.*, III, No. 2 (1928), 23.
[27]   Amtorg, *op. cit.*, III, No. 3 (1928), 41.
[28]   Amtorg, *op. cit.*, IV, No. 4 (1929), 77.

Germany. Nine Soviet paper technicians studied paper-making in Canada before returning to operate the plant.[29]

In 1926-7 the total Russian output of paper was 267,000 tons. A single plant, the Balakhna paper mill on the Volga River in Nijnhi-Novgorod Province, with a capacity of 105,000 tons, raised this overall capacity in 1928-31 by just under 50 percent. The Balakhna mill had three paper-making units: one bought in Germany and two in the United States. The larger of the two United States units had a bed width of 234 inches and, at the time of installation, was the fastest American sectional-drive paper machine in the world. Its finishing delivery speed was 1,200 feet per minute. The complete electrical installation for the mill was supplied by General Electric, whose engineers supervised installation and initial mill operations. The final unit was not completed before 1931.[30]

TECHNICAL ASSISTANCE IN THE LUMBER INDUSTRY

The mixed trading company agreements of 1923-4 contained technical-assistance clauses. The British, Norwegian, German, and Dutch lumber companies were required to cut and transport the lumber. In undertaking these operations, they entered the timber areas of the U.S.S.R. to organize production and shipping. There is little doubt that these concessions granted in the timber and sawmill industry between 1922-27 worked closely with the Soviet government on the technical sphere and furnished considerable capital for lumber operations.[31]

In every case, operations ultimately proved unprofitable, and by 1928 the last foreign operations in the lumber industry had closed, except for the Japanese concessions in the Far East. The technical-assistance components, however, persisted. Harry Ferguson, Ltd., provided technical assistance under the Russangloles, Ltd. agreement, and his contract for assistance was still in operation in 1929, several years after the ejection of the British concession-aires.[32]

After closing the concessions, the Soviets purchased technical assistance in the form of Type III agreements. For example, in September 1928 the Stebbins Engineering and Manufacturing Company, a firm of architects and engineers of Watertown, New York, was approached by Amtorg with a request for a consultant to make a report on Soviet pulp operations.[33]

---

[29] Amtorg, *op. cit.*, III, No. 8 (1928), 195.

[30] *Monogram*, November 1943.

[31] See, for example, the United States Consulate Report from Helsingfors dated December 24, 1929. (316-135-663.)

[32] U.S. State Dept. Decimal File, 316-131-642.

[33] The Amtorg letter reads in part, 'We wish your representative to come to the U.S.S.R. in a consultant capacity on organization and production problems.'

In 1929 the British-European Timber Company, a United Kingdom firm, sent a group of engineers to forested areas in Mezen, Pechora, and Siberia.[34]

SOVIET LUMBER TRADE FROM 1921 TO 1928

As a result of these transfers of foreign skills and technology, Soviet exports of sawed lumber grew from a mere 48,000 standards in 1921 to 569,000 standards in 1928—an increase greater than tenfold. However, 569,000 standards was still less than one-half of 1913 Russian export of sawed lumber.

The destination of these exports was significantly oriented to the operation of the mixed trading companies. In 1913 about half of sawed lumber exports went to the United Kingdom. The most important of the Type II agreements (made in the 1920s) was made with United Kingdom lumber merchants and lumber importers. In 1928 some 389,000 standards went to the United Kingdom—about 60 percent of the amount exported to Britain in 1913. However, the total 1928 Soviet lumber exports were only 46.7 percent of those in 1913. In other words, the relative proportion of lumber going to the United Kingdom was considerably greater in 1928. Holland and Germany, who possessed concession arrangements in lumber, show a similar increased importance as importers of Soviet lumber, whereas France and Belgium, with no concession arrangements, took an insignificant proportion of their 1913 imports of Russian lumber (13.9 and 20.1 percent, respectively).

Table 9–2 EXPORTS OF SAWED LUMBER FROM THE U.S.S.R., 1913–28, BY DESTINATION

Destination	1913	1926	1927	1928	1928 as percent of 1913 exports
		(Export in Standards)			
United Kingdom	642,800	217,542	332,597	389,610	60.0%
Germany	194,100	15,634	41,607	48,318	24.9
France	83,700	16,406	2,116	11,666	13.9
Holland	161,200	41,720	40,334	66,292	41.1
Belgium	70,000	6,114	6,099	14,095	20.1
Others	65,800	15,908	14,799	39,257	49.5
Total	1,217,600	313,324	437,552	569,238	46.7%

Source: U.S. Consulate at Helsingfors, Dispatch Number 1370, July 10, 1929.

An examination of lumber exports by type of lumber suggests a similar orientation toward countries with concessionary arrangements. Almost all sawed lumber (87 percent) was marketed by means of the United Kingdom

[34]   Amtorg, *op. cit.*, IV, No. 6 (1929), 117.

Type II concessions, using the market knowledge and skills of the private concessionaires. Part of the balance was shipped through the German Mologa concession. Beams, alder veneer, and pit props also show a strong orientation toward the United Kingdom market.

Companies underwriting timber contracts with the U.S.S.R. had complaints about Soviet trading practices, as the Soviets entered the market on their own account after 1924-5. The Soviets had a practice of appearing in the lumber market at the last minute and underselling not only Swedish and Finnish timber but also their own earlier contracts, and thus 'disturbing' the market, from the veiwpoint of the British trade. Twenty leading United Kingdom timber merchants formed a coalition on 1929 and made arrangements to purchase all Russian timber in specific grades forthcoming in a particular year at agreed prices.[35]

More than 90 percent of all Soviet timber exports during the 1920s was going to countries with mixed company arrangements. In brief, all Soviet timber was produced and most marketed with foreign capital and technical assistance.

[35]   U.S. Embassy in London, Report 3342, February 7, 1929. (316-135-647.)

CHAPTER TEN

'Sovietization' of the Tsarist Machine-Building Industry[1]

THE LENINGRAD MACHINE-BUILDING TRUST (LENMASHSTROI)

THERE was a well-established general and precision machine-building industry in Russia before the Revolution. This was located primarily in Petrograd and Moscow and included the locomotive construction plants in the Ukraine. After the Revolution, the industry went through a chaotic transformation.

Table 10-1   PLANTS COMPRISING THE LENINGRAD MACHINE-BUILDING TRUST IN 1923

Prerevolutionary Name	Soviet Name	Position in 1923
Putilovets	Krasnyi Putilovets	Open, under War Commissariat
Aivaz	Engels	Working intermittently
Atlas	Economizer	Under War Commissariat
Pneumatic	Pneumatic	Under War Commissariat
Truba	Krasnaya Truba	Not known
Metal Petrograds	Metallic (Stalin)	Under War Commissariat
Nobel	Russky Diesel	Under War Commissariat
Lessner	Karl Marx	Closed
Arthur Koppel	International	Closed
Struk-Ekval	Ilytch	Closed
Phoenix	Sverdlov	Closed
Tilimans	Northern Mechanical and Boiler Works	Closed
Vulcan Pipe Works	Vulcan	Closed

Sources: 1. *Ekonomicheskaya Zhizn*, No. 10, October 12, 1923.
2. *Spravochnyi katalog rossiskoi promyshlennosti* (VSNKh, Moscow: 1923).
3. U.S. State Dept. Archives.

[1] Agricultural machinery is covered in chap. 7 and transportation equipment in chap. 14, except for aircraft manufacture, which is covered in chap. 15.

In Petrograd, half the machine-building plants were closed in 1923, and those open were working on an intermittent part-time basis and were later trustified.[2]

The Putilovets in Petrograd employed more than 6,000 before the Revolution. In 1920, renamed the Krasnyi Putilovets, the works employed 1,000 but produced almost nothing. Continual strife between the technical executive staff and the workmen's committee was aggravated by the fact that unskilled workers received higher pay and more food than skilled technicians and managers. The plant remained more or less in this condition through the early 1920s. In 1929 the Putilovets arranged a technical-assistance contract with Frank Smith Co., Inc., of the United States.[3] The Ford production chief, Sorensen, also visited the plant in 1929 and, when asked by a Soviet official what he thought of it, suggested they put a few sticks of dynamite in the middle of the shop floor and blow it out of its misery.[4]

Other operating plants were in little better condition. The Nobel Gas Engine Works (renamed Russky Diesel) was well equipped in 1921, but produced only a few repair jobs. The Arthur Koppel works, formerly a producer of fire escapes and light structural steel work for the city of Petrograd, was completely at a standstill. Keeley reported that they were trying to build a couple of peat excavators.[5] The Lessner, renamed the Karl Marx, reopened with 100 skilled workers imported from Finland in late 1921 or early 1922.[6]

Lenmashstroi concluded a technical-assistance agreement with the Metropolitan Vickers Company of the United Kingdom in March 1927. For a period of five years the trust used the patents and manufacturing rights for Vickers turbines, paying to the company a royalty dependent on the number of turbines produced. Russian engineers were sent to the Vickers' plants in England for study, and a large crew of English engineers went to the trust's plants in the Soviet Union.[7] Vickers' assistance was concentrated in the old Petrograd Metal Works, renamed the Stalin. The assistance concerned turbine design and construction problems. The Stalin plant was the only producer of turbines until 1930; they were all produced with Vickers' assistance and

---

[2] This information is based on report by Royal Keeley in U.S. State Dept. Decimal File, 316–107–99/100. Keeley, an American, was in Russia from September 1919 to August 1921. He investigated, at the invitation of Lomonosov, industrial and economic conditions in various plants in Moscow and Petrograd. These visits received support from Lenin and Rykov. Keeley reported personally to Lenin on several occasions. He was imprisoned from May 1920 to August 1921 'because he knew too much about Russian conditions.' (U.S. State Dept., Division of Russian Affairs, memorandum to Secretary of State, October 18, 1921. 316–107–106/12.)

[3] U.S. State Dept. Decimal File, 316–131–642.

[4] Sorensen, *op. cit.*, p. 202.

[5] Keeley, *op. cit.*

[6] *Makhovik* (Petrograd), December 13, 1921.

[7] *Torgovo-Promyshlennaya Gazeta*, No. 60, March 15, 1927; and Allan Monkhouse, *Moscow 1911–1933* (Boston: Little Brown, 1934), pp. 185–6.

comprised the total Soviet output. Other plants in the trust were reestablished with German technical assistance.

MOSMASH AND GERMAN TECHNICAL ASSISTANCE

The tsarist-era machine-building plants in Moscow were grouped after the Revolution into Mosmash. Their names were changed and most were restarted with German technical assistance.

Table 10–2   PLANTS COMPRISING MOSMASH IN 1923

Prerevolutionary Name	Soviet Name
Bary Engineers	Parostroi
Bromley Brothers	Krasnyi Proletariat
Gratcheff	Krasnya Presnia
Singer Goujon	Serp i molot
Danhauer and Kaiser	Kotloapparat
Dobroff and Nabholz	Melnitchno-Tkatskoie Oborudovanie
Jaquot	Press
List-Butirsky	Boretz
List-Sofisky	Hydrophil
Kramer	Krasnyi Stampovstchik

Source: Annuaire, op. cit., p. 84 rear.

The Bromley Brothers Works in Moscow kept running throughout the Revolution under its English manager and was nationalized in 1918. This was one of the better-organized plants in the Soviet Union, but it ran into the same difficulties as others, and by 1921 its production was negligible.[8] It was renamed the Red Proletariat and brought into the trust. Moscow's oldest and largest semi-fabricated metal materials plant was the Singer Goujon. It produced structural shapes, steel sheet and plate, wire, rope, and similar products. The plant was nationalized in 1918 and a former English foreman made manager. In 1920 the plant was at a complete standstill; official records indicated an output of only 2 percent of 1913. After being renamed the Serp i molot and absorbed into the trust, the works made a good recovery with German technical assistance. By 1923 the plant was producing 80 percent (by weight) of the Mosmash output.[9] The trust was also interested in producing steam and diesel engines, turbines, and pumps, as well as fabricated metal-work.[10] A technical-assistance agreement was made in 1926 with Gasmotoren-Fabrik Deutz A-G, of Germany, which gave the trust the right to construct

[8]   Keeley, *op. cit.,*
[9]   *Ibid.*
[10]   *Annuaire,* rear p. 84.

and assemble all types of Deutz motors (with and without compressors), stationary engines, and main and secondary engines for river and marine craft. All patents, designs, experimental data, and other information generated in the German plants passed from Deutz A-G to Mosmash. There was the usual exchange of engineers, Deutz engineers going to the plants of the trust and trust engineers going to Deutz plants in Germany for training. Royalties were paid on all production.[11] Further, there was probably an implied reciprocity clause of some type in the agreement. In mid-1927, the Soviets ordered two freight-passenger ships from the Janssen and Schnilinsky A-G shipyards of Hamburg and specified Deutz diesel engines.[12]

GOMZA AND THE WESTINGHOUSE BRAKE WORKS

Gomza was the largest of the machine-building trusts, and in 1924 consisted of eighteen units, including iron ore mines, smelting plants, and works producing machinery, tools, locomotives, wagons, and agricultural machinery. In 1925, the Westinghouse Air Brake Works was nationalized and added to this trust. Of the eighteen units, only fourteen were operating. Of the remaining units, two were in a state of 'technical preservation' and two in liquidation. The trust was notoriously inefficient, accumulating a loss of 3.7 million rubles in 1922-3, 7 million rubles in 1923-4 and over 4 million rubles in 1924-5 and in 1925-6.

The Westinghouse Air Brake plant in Moscow (moved by the company to Yaroslavl in the early 1920s) was not nationalized until after the Soviets had assured themselves of its facilities and were confident of having enough skilled engineers and workers available. It is noteworthy that any activities connected with transportation—and particularly railroads—were handled with great care by the Soviets.

There is little question that Westinghouse also played a cautious game in an attempt to evade the nationalization decree. The manager of the Yaroslavl plant, when interviewed in 1922 by officials of the U.S. State Department, reported that relations between management and labor were excellent, that the company did not import raw materials, that the Soviet government owed the company half a million rubles, and that he felt the time was ripe for a further investment by the parent company. He claimed that profits could be transferred out of the Soviet Union with only a 3-percent penalty, while the fee for imported funds was only 10 percent. Westinghouse did not bite.[13]

---

[1]   *Torgovo-Promyshlennaya Gazeta*, No. 279, December 3, 1926.
[2]   U.S. State Dept. Decimal File, 316-130-605.
[3]   U.S. State Dept. Decimal File, 316-139-31.

During the Civil War and famine, the company supplied its Russian workers with flour and clothing. Consequently, the Party had trouble stirring up Westinghouse workers when the time came to demand nationalization. The end was foreshadowed in a *Pravda* article on January 18, 1924, under the title, 'With the Lackeys of American Capital.' The article complained about conditions in the Westinghouse plant. The company was accused of using the Taylor system to carry out twelve months' work in six months and bribing the factory committee by supplying food and clothing. The essence of the complaint was:

> . . . at the present time they are paying only 25 percent more than other factories. The cells have now opened the eyes of the workmen. At present the workers not only distrust but even hate the administration.

This was followed by a demand that the secretary of the cell should be present at collective bargaining meetings—presumably to 'protect' the interests of the workers.[14] The company was nationalized in 1925 and the works absorbed into Gomza.[15]

GOMZA AND THE GERMAN AND SWEDISH LOCOMOTIVE PROGRAM

In August 1920, Professor Lomonosov, formerly director of traffic on the tsarist railroads and in 1920 director of all railways in the Soviet Union, went to Germany and later to Sweden to negotiate for railway supplies, the Soviets' most urgent requirement.[16]

The locomotive stock at this time was about 16,000 of which only about 6,000 were able to operate at all. The position was so critical that workers were released from the Red Army transportation corps to help repair locomotives.[17] The Sormovo locomotive works was able to make capital repairs to thirty-six locomotives in the last half of 1920 but only to nine in the first half of 1921. Sormovo repaired 246 cars in the second half of 1920 but only 31 in the first half of 1921.[18] The Tver wagon construction works made 100 new freight trucks and repaired 603 in the last half of 1920, and then closed down. At this time more than 10,000 locomotives and many more wagons were awaiting or undergoing repair.[19] In August 1921, of a listed rolling stock of 437,152 cars, only 20,000 were in first-class condition, and fewer than 200,000 were able to run

---

14   The complaint was phrased, 'The Americans have played a dirty game with us but they are called a cultured and liberal nation.' (*Trud*, No. 42, February 24, 1923.)

15   *Pravda* (Moscow), No. 15, January 18, 1924.

16   U.S. State Dept. Decimal File, 316–163–721.

17   U.S. State Dept. Decimal File, 316–163–724.

18   In 1890 the Sormovo Works was making complex rolling-mill equipment and was able to machine one-piece 20-ton forgings. See Foss Special Collection, Hoover Institution Library.

19   U.S. State Dept. Decimal File, 316–163–849.

at all.[20] The equipment and locomotive problem was solved by purchasing European and American locomotives; sending defective locomotives to Latvia, Estonia, and Berlin for repair; and importing German technicians and railway materials for wagon repair.

In July 1920 the U.S.S.R. made an agreement with the Nyquist and Holm A/B locomotive construction company at Trollhatten in Southern Sweden. The agreement has been variously described. The Stockholm Consulate, in an interview with C. W. Beckmann, chief engineer at the plant, reported that Gunnar W. Andersson had purchased controlling interest for Kr 7 million. In addition, he had a contract from the Soviets for 1,000 locomotives. Andersson, who knew nothing about locomotives, became president and director general; Lomonosov assumed technical direction.[21]

The Berlin Embassy reported the Soviets had advanced a loan of $1.5 million to the company to extend the locomotive construction plant at Trollhatten.[22] The Soviets themselves stated the arrangement was no more than a credit. In view of the special 'arm's length' relationship with Andersson, the latter explanation is unlikely.[23] What is quite clear is that the Soviets financed locomotive construction in Sweden at a time *when they had five locomotive construction plants in 'technical preservation,' one with completely new equipment*,[24] and notwithstanding a precarious financial and foreign exchange position. Later the following month about 1,500 'high-grade' locomotives were purchased from Germany, delivery beginning early 1922.[25] These were of basic American decapod design adapted to Russian conditions.[26]

The imported Swedish and German locomotives were sent to the Putilovets in Petrograd for assembly under the supervision of Waldemar Sommermeyer, representing the German builders, and Karl Kainer, representing Nyquist and Holm. The status of locomotives in January 25, 1922 was as follows:

Locomotives	On Order	Delivered	Assembled
From Germany	1,350	220	
From Sweden	600	12	53
From United States	250	24*	
Total	2,200	256	53

Source: U.S. State Dept. Decimal File, 316–163–890.
* These were probably Baldwin Locomotive units. The Russian Ambassador in Washington reported on September 1920 that Baldwin Locomotive had sold 50 locomotives 'indirectly' to the Soviet Union with payment through a Spanish account (316–163–836).

[20] *Ekonomicheskaya Zhizn*, No. 210, September 21, 1921.
[21] U.S. State Dept. Decimal File, 316–163–731.
[22] U.S. Embassy in Berlin, Report 53, December 8, 1921. (316–130–1174.)
[23] See page 269.
[24] See page 269.
[25] U.S. State Dept. Decimal File, 316–163–739.
[26] *Trud*, No. 104, May 14, 1922.

Locomotives were assembled at Putilovets as a temporary measure, and some 2,000 extra workers were engaged under supervision of Swedish and German engineers. Between November 1921 and January 1922 about 53 locomotives were assembled and sent to Nikolaev and Northern Railways. During January, twelve were returned as defective due to 'systematic damage' by railway workers. As the locomotives were driven under the supervision of German instructors, 160 of whom had been sent from Germany, this was presumably sabotage.[27]

In addition to outright purchase of locomotives in Sweden, Germany, and the United States, the Soviet Union contracted for large-scale repairs in Estonia and Germany. The first Estonian contract was with locomotive-building plants in Reval for repair of 2,000 'sick' locomotives. Payment under this and similar contracts was in damaged locomotives; i.e., a percentage of the delivered units was retained by the Estonian firms as payment in kind.[28] The second Estonian contract, valued at over $2 million, was signed on December 21, 1921 with the Dvigatel plant (representing a group of Estonian and English builders), the Russo-Baltic works, the Peter shipyard, the Fr. Krull, and the Ilmarine, all in Reval. This contract covered an initial 200 freight units of the 0-8-0 type and extended later to 1,000. The repairs were classified into three categories, and a fixed price was paid for each class of repairs with additions for missing parts according to a fixed scale. Cash advances were made and 40 percent paid on delivery of the repaired locomotives at the Russian-Estonian frontier. Payment was in American dollars. All steel and parts, except copper fire-boxes, were the subject of a separate agreement between the Estonian companies and Krupp of Germany. The latter also arranged financing of the program with the Deutsche Bank. The British Vickers-Armstrong Company participated in the repair contract by leasing the Russo-Baltic works through a specially formed subsidiary, the Anglo-Baltic Shipbuilding and Engineering Company. The major portion of the order was divided between Anglo-Baltic, the Dvigatel, and the Peter shipyard. The plants were kept busy for about one-and-a-half to two years.[29]

The Soviet Union made numerous attempts to acquire American locomotives. On April 22, 1919, Martens, operating as the 'representative of the U.S.S.R. in the United States,' claimed 200 locomotives ordered by the Kerensky government as the property of the Soviet Union. His letter was left unanswered.[30] The next recorded attempt was in February 1920, when Mayor

[27]   U.S. State Dept. Decimal File, 316–163–836.
[28]   U.S. State Dept. Decimal File, 316–163–856.
[29]   U.S. State Dept. Decimal File, 316–163–881 *et. seq.*
[30]   U.S. State Dept. Decimal File, 316–163–453.

Friedenberg (of Riga), who had just returned from Moscow, announced that he had been commissioned to enter into negotiations for purchase of 600 American locomotives and 'large quantities' of machines, tools, and rails. Payment was proposed in gold and platinum.[31] Ten days later the Riga Consulate reported that Friedenberg was going to attempt to order directly from Baldwin Locomotive or American Locomotive for delivery to Latvia, and then turn the locomotives over to the U.S.S.R.[32] It was reported via Finland two months later that representatives of 'American firms' had accepted a Soviet order for 400 locomotives at Reval, Estonia.[33] Purchase of American locomotives was also attempted through Latvia.[34]

In the main, however, the bulk of the locomotives purchased were either Swedish or German and were classified 'Eg' (German-built) or 'Esh' (Swedish-built). The basic design was the Vladikavkaz Railroad 0-10-0, introduced in 1912 and built after 1926 at all five Russian locomotive construction works. The only difference was a larger superheater in front of the engine. More powerful variants were introduced in the 1930s, but this basic type was still being produced after World War II and is still the basic steam freight-hauler in use on Soviet railroads today. For passenger locomotives the Soviets inherited a mixed group of pre-revolutionary makes and selected the Vladikavkaz Railroad type S 2-6-2, known as the 'Sv', built originally for use on

Table 10–3 LOCOMOTIVE CONSTRUCTION BY GOMZA
           WORKS, 1921–3

Prerevolutionary Name	*Soviet Name*	*Position, 1921–3*
Sormovo	Krasnoye Sormovo	Closed, then opened with German technical assistance
Kolomna	Kolomna	Partly open, for wagon repair
Bryansk	Profintern	Closed 1922–3
Hartmann (Lugansk)	Lugansk	Closed 1922–3
Kharkov	Kharkov Locomotive	Closed 1922–3

Source: German Foreign Ministry Archives, T120–4249–L092272.

[31] U.S. State Dept. Decimal File, 316–163–678.
[32] U.S. State Dept. Decimal File, 316–163–680. The State Dept. reply (marked 'not sent') suggested that the Friedenberg matter be allowed to develop along these lines. It was drafted by Poole of Russian Affairs but killed by the Second Assistant Secretary.
[33] U.S. State Dept. Decimal File, 316–163–703. An intercepted radio message to Martens in the U.S. directed him to purchase 100 locomotives directly from Baldwin Locomotive.
[34] U.S. State Dept. Decimal File, 316–163–705.

the Warsaw-Vienna railroad. This locomotive was redesigned to carry a larger firebox and superheater and was put into production after 1925 with the designation 'Su'. Several hundred were built in this basic design.[35]

The decline in repairs continued throughout 1921 and 1922, and the position was stabilized only by this flow of new locomotives from abroad.

This decline continued; Russian locomotive shops were idle although in good mechanical condition. They had lost many skilled workers but had enough to turn out some new locomotives. The orders, however, were going abroad, not even the newly equipped Murom plant outside Moscow could get locomotive orders. Pressure built up to halt the export of 'sick' locomotives to Estonia for repairs and place orders in the idle Russian plants. In June 1922, Glavmetal refused to sanction a shipment of 200 'sick' locomotives to Estonia. The trade union organizations added to the pressure by accusing Lomonosov of selling out the proletariat to Estonian capitalists.[36] As a result of this pressure, deliveries under both the Estonian and German contracts slowed after 1922, and the idle Russian plants were restarted, with German assistance, by about 1924–5.

Table 10–4   CONSTRUCTION OF STEAM LOCOMOTIVES
IN RUSSIA AND THE U.S.S.R., 1906 TO 1929

Year	No. Built	Year	No. Built	Technical Assistance
1906	1,270	1921–2	115*	
1913	609	1922–3	96*	
1914	762	1923–4	169*	
1915	883	1924–5	148*	
1916	616	1925–6	302	German post-Rapallo technical assistance
1917	410	1926–7	359	
1918	200	1927–8	479	
1919	74*	1928–9	575	Baldwin Locomotive technical agreement
1920	90*	1929–30	625	

Sources: 1. U.S. State Dept. Archives.
2. German Foreign Ministry Archives.
3. G. W. Nutter, *op. cit.*, p. 432.

* These figures, from Nutter and originating in Soviet sources, are doubtful. They are probably major or capital repairs counted as new locomotives; the Archival sources support this argument.

Productivity in the Gomza trust was about 20 percent of that of 1913. The State Railroad system—the major customer—calculated it was paying

[35] J. N. Westwood, *A History of Russian Railways* (London: George Allen & Unwin, 1964), pp. 86–93.
[36] U.S. State Dept. Decimal File, 316–163–913.

prices six times greater than prewar for Gomza products, and smaller articles made by the trust were being sold on the open market at half price in order to sell at all. Consequently, it is not surprizing that the trust was covering only 7 percent of *direct* costs (i.e., it was making no contribution to fixed costs). The statement was made that, ' . . . we cannot close down as this would throw 80,000 men out of employment and the railways would suffer.'[37] The problem, of course, was lack of orders. While German, Swedish, and American locomotives were being imported in quantity, Gomza was largely idle. On the other hand, there was ample evidence that the skills to manufacture locomotives were lacking. The engineers had fled, and those locomotives that were being repaired broke down after a few days back in service.[38]

THE BALDWIN LOCOMOTIVE TECHNICAL-ASSISTANCE AGREEMENT OF 1929[39]

The Baldwin Locomotive Works Company, with a group of fifteen manufacturers of input parts and supplies for locomotives, made a sales-cum-technical agreement with the Soviet Union on April 12, 1929. Baldwin agreed to sell its products and those of the allied companies to Amtorg on a revolving credit basis. A total of $5 million was made available ($2 million within eighteen months of date of signature). Separate technical-assistance agreements (not available from the State Department files) were also signed to assist Gomza in the development of locomotive production. The credit terms were:

> 20 percent payable 24 months from date of dock receipt
> 20 percent payable 36 months from date of dock receipt
> 20 percent payable 48 months from date of dock receipt
> 20 percent payable 60 months from date of dock receipt.[40]

These advances carried a 6-percent interest rate. Baldwin and the associated companies agreed to send their engineers into the Soviet Union for locomotive erection and engineering work, and, as the contract reads:

> . . . agrees to receive at its works and assist in placing at the works of such firms whose products will be supplied under this agreement, and will also assist in placing in shops and on railroads in the United States a reasonable number of workers, foremen and engineers sent from the U.S.S.R. for a period of time provided in each case separately, so as to enable these workers, foremen and engineers to get fully acquainted with American practice.[41]

[37] U.S. State Dept. Decimal File, 316–107–1044.
[38] U.S. State Dept. Decimal File, 316–163.
[39] A copy of the agreement is in the U.S. State Dept. Decimal File, 316–163–1301.
[40] Clause 9 of the agreement.
[41] Associated companies were American Steel Foundries, Athey Truss Wheel, Brill Car Company, Electric Controller and Manufacturing, Fairmont Railway Motors,

The agreement was signed by A. A. Zakoshansky for the Soviet Union and Charles M. Muchnic, Vice President for the Baldwin Locomotive Works Company.

GENERAL ELECTRIC DIESEL-ELECTRIC 'SURAM' LOCOMOTIVE

Russia had been a pioneer in diesel traction. Prerevolutionary shipbuilding yards and locomotive construction plants in Petrograd and Kharkov had undertaken a great deal of innovatory work in the direction of diesel-electric and diesel-mechanical propulsion. There were diesel electric ships in tsarist times built in Russian shipyards. The Tashkent railroad had been an early innovator in diesel traction and had actually built a gas turbine locomotive.[42] This promising start came to a complete halt in the 1920s. Efforts to continue diesel locomotive construction were halting and unsuccessful. They culminated in the import of the General-Electric-designed 'Suram' locomotive, named after the mountain pass in the Caucasus, in 1932.

In 1922 an experimental power plant was built, using the Tashkent railway turbine and a compressor system designed and built by Armstrong-Whitworth in the United Kingdom. The claims were great but nothing more was heard of it.[43] Two years later a locomotive design competition was announced for a 16-ton, 930-mile-radius locomotive with a tractive effort of 26,000 pounds at 9 m.p.h. The sole entrant was a design by Professor Gakkel, which was subsequently built at the Putilovets and Baltic plants under German supervision. The locomotive was powered by a Vickers 1,030 h.p. diesel engine reclaimed from a submarine, coupled with some Italian generators. This was the Lenin Memorial Locomotive, presently preserved in Moscow. Westwood says it was withdrawn from service in 1927 after running only 25,000 miles and spending much of its active life out of service. It spent many years as a mobile generator.[44]

Russian designs were not forthcoming; it was obvious that the designers had fled with the Revolution. Prototype locomotives were then ordered in Western countries. These used both diesel-electric and diesel-mechanical systems. The most successful under Russian conditions was a Krupp 1-E-1 diesel electric, and in 1927 a trial order was placed with Krupp for an improved

Locomotive Terminal Improvement, Southwark Foundry and Machine, Standard Steel Car, Superheater Company, Sunbeam Electric, Westinghouse Air Brake (expropriated without compensation in 1925), Wilson Welder, G. D. Whitcomb, Locomotive Firebox, and Nathan Manufacturing.

[42]   Westwood, *op. cit.*, p. 67.
[43]   *Ibid.*
[44]   *Ibid.*

version of this prototype with a Mann-type four-stroke six-cylinder engine which enabled the Soviets to make use of their technical-assistance agreement with the Mann company. Brown-Boveri traction engines of 140-kw hourly rating were also ordered. These prototypes were not built in the Soviet Union, however, until 1932, when production started at Kolomna. The design produced was identical to the German E-e 15. This decision ended an unsuccessful prototype development program which had been continued for some years at the Kolomensky works. It had produced some prototypes for secondary lines in the late 1920s, but Westwood indicates these had not been successful, owing to frequent burnouts.[45] Future locomotive construction was based on foreign design and particularly on the General Electric design for the 'Suram' model; indeed some elements of the current (1966) VL 23 design are the same as those in the original 'Suram' delivered about thirty-four years ago. Diesel-electric traction is an area where the Soviets have shown neither innovatory nor construction ability.[46]

Apart from purchasing prototypes, the Soviets induced Western companies to undertake the solution of specific mechanical problems. In the development of industrial locomotives using gasoline engines, the technical problems were solved by an American company hoping to sell such locomotives to the U.S.S.R. In 1926–7 the Koehring Company sold several four-cylinder industrial locomotives to the Soviet Union and in the following year received an inquiry about six-cylinder units. The company pointed out that ordinary Russian grade kerosene would not be sufficiently volatile, although the 'export' grade produced by the Standard Oil refinery at Batum would be suitable. With the assistance of the Department of Commerce, which canvassed American oil companies for Koehring, data was developed on the characteristics of Russian kerosenes, and engineers from 'one of Koehring subsidiary companies' developed an engine suitable for efficient operation on this grade of fuel.[47]

TECHNICAL ASSISTANCE TO GOMZA REFRIGERATION EQUIPMENT PLANTS

Gomza's efforts in refrigerator and cold-storage plant construction received technical assistance from German and United Kingdom firms from about 1926 until well into the 1930s. In late 1926 an agreement was signed between Gomza and A. Borsig G.m.b.H., of Berlin, for assistance in construction of refrigerators utilizing the Borsig system. The German firm prepared construc-

---

[45] *Ibid.*, pp. 67–9.
[46] *Ibid.*
[47] Records of the U.S. Bureau of Foreign and Domestic Commerce, File 312 (1927).

tion designs and working plans for the trust, utilizing its own patents and experience. There was an exchange of refrigeration engineers between Gomza and Borsig plants. Further such technical-assistance contracts were signed with Maschinenfabrik Augsburg-Nurnburg A-G and L. A. Reidinger A-G, also of Augsburg, for construction of cold-storage facilities.[48]

Dairy produce agreements with the Union Cold Storage Company, Ltd. (of the United Kingdom), allowed the company to establish cold-storage facilities in the U.S.S.R. to handle food products being exported under the trading agreement.[49]

GENERAL TECHNICAL ASSISTANCE FOR ORGAMETAL

The first *overall* technical guidance for the reconstruction of the heavy-machine industry came under a three-year agreement signed in later 1926 between Orgametal (the heavy industry syndicate) and the German company, Verein Deutscher Werkzeugmaschinen Fabriken Ausfuhr Gemeinschaft (known as Faudewag). This company set up a joint technical bureau in Berlin to design new plants and re-equip the tsarist heavy-machine industry. The company supplied engineers, technicians, and skilled workers; superintended construction and reconstruction; and supplied machinery, raw materials, working supplies, and design services.[50] The agreement was renewed in 1929, and Faudewag added more functions. It was still in force in the early 1930s.[51]

The Faudewag project, which supervised all Orgametal work, was followed by an extensive technical-assistance agreement with the Frank Chase Company, of the United States.[52] The most significant agreement was made at the end of the decade, in connection with the large-scale construction projected under the first Five-Year Plan. Almost all major projects under the Plan were designed by American companies.[53] Albert Kahn Company of Detroit had the basic task of supplying technical advice to the Building Committee of Vesenkha, in addition to contracts with Glavmashstroi for construction of new machine-building plants and with Traktorstroi in Stalingrad for construction of tractor

[48]   Vneshtorgizdat, *op. cit.*, p. 227.
[49]   See chap. 7.
[50]   *Torgovo-Promyshlennaya Gazeta*, No. 279, December 3, 1926.
[51]   Vneshtorgizdat, *op. cit.*, p. 228. This expanded Faudewag agreement supervised all Orgametal projects. The company office in Berlin replaced the Russian-operated and staffed Buiro Inostrannoi Nauki i Tekhniki (BINT), organized in Berlin in 1920 to collect foreign technical data. BINT employed 100 Russians in 1921 but the staff was reduced to 5 by Ipatieff, who considered the cost too great in light of the returns. (Ipatieff, *op. cit.*, p. 330.)
[52]   U.S. State Dept. Decimal File, 316–131–642.
[53]   This is covered in detail in Vol. II.

plants.[54] The Five-Year Plan as a concept is almost completely a myth of the propaganda mills. First, there were no hard and fast dates for beginning and ending specific projects in sequence. Each contract had its own time sequence and was not always well integrated with other construction projects. A set of dates was necessary, however, for the propaganda image of 'scientific socialism at work.' Second, the complete design work, supervision of construction, provision of equipment, and, in many cases, actual factory construction were done by Western companies under contract. They were kept to the all-important dates by heavy penalty-bonus clauses. The fact that some large plants were finished ahead of the planned date had nothing to do with 'socialist construction.' It was quite simply that the Western firms responded to the substantial bonuses payable for completion ahead of the contracted date. When the Soviets attempted to repeat the feat of Western private enterprise later in the 1930s, they were totally unsuccessful and became very secretive about new projects.[55]

SKF (SWEDEN) AND THE MANUFACTURE OF BALL BEARINGS[56]

Prior to the Great War in 1915, the Swedish company Aktiebolaget Svenska Kullagerfabriken (SKF), an internationally known manufacturer of ball bearings and transmissions, established an extensive and well equipped plant in Moscow. This plant was nationalized in 1918 but continued to work at full speed under its Swedish engineers through the Revolution. Sometime in 1920, negotiations started between SKF and the Soviets for a concession arrangement. Agreement was reported by the *Chicago Tribune* in October 1921, but not by the Soviets for another eighteen months. The details are fairly clear, but the exact date of signature remains unknown.

The SKF company was given the right to produce balls, bearings, and transmissions and to export up to 15 percent of these products. Complete supply to Soviet industry was anticipated. The company was guaranteed a 15-percent profit. In return, the company was allowed to purchase its own prewar property (two plants and the remaining stock of raw materials) for a payment of 200,000 gold rubles. The plants were then re-equipped by SKF,

[54] *Torgovo-promyshlennaya Gazeta*, May 16, 1929; and U.S. State Dept. Decimal File, 316–131–674.
[55] Vol. II uses data from the German Archives and suggests that the construction under the second and third Five-Year Plans, in which the Soviets relied much more on their own resources, was almost catastrophically below projected targets. At least part of this problem was caused by diversion of the finest of available skills and equipment into military production.
[56] Sources for this section are the *Chicago Tribune* (Paris edition), October 3, 1921; *Izvestia*, No. 63, March 22, 1923; and the U.S. Consulate in Stockholm, Report, April 4, 1923.

who supplied all patents and management, the Soviets supplied raw materials. Some 400 workers were employed, with Swedish engineer Wilhelm Adrian as manager. Three-quarters of the workers were Russian and the balance Swedish ' . . . paid in Swedish money and fed on imported Swedish food.' The intent, according to Adrian, was to raise the standard of Russian labor by mixing skilled Swedish workers with the Russians.

A completely new SKF plant was built under the agreement and produced, with the re-equipped tsarist-era plants, about 2-3 million rubles' worth of bearings per year, and the company paid a rental based on this annual volume at a progressive rate. Previous to the Revolution, only bearings had been produced in Russia; the steel balls were imported from Sweden. The Soviets required the steel balls to be manufactured in the U.S.S.R., and up to that time the company was required to keep on hand in its Moscow warehouses a stock of balls equal to three times the quantity of bearings.

The Soviets were represented by two members on the Board of Directors, although nominally and probably in practice the plant was run by a Swedish management. Provision for arbitration was made with a board comprising two members from each side and a president appointed by the Moscow High Technical School; i.e., the Soviets had a say in management and a majority in arbitration. All former SKF claims were cancelled by the concession. The agreement was viewed by the United States consul at Riga with some distaste:

> The Soviets having forced the owners to pay for the use of their own property over a long period of years, will probably hold the transaction out to the world as evidence that property once nationalized by them has actually been bought back by the original owners.[57]

The company was required to buy back its own plant and also required to amortize its new equipment over twenty-five years, a lengthy period when compared to a more normal requirement of five years. As the hidden intent of the Soviets was to nationalize once again after the new plant and techniques had been assimilated, the 'guaranteed 15-percent profit' was meaningless. The concession was expropriated long before the expiration of the amortization period. One has to examine Soviet attitudes to Western business to appreciate the overriding importance of good faith in enterprise societies. Company after company went into the U.S.S.R. with an agreement based on good faith, and all eventually learned the meaning of the 'dictatorship of the proletariat.' SKF had to buy back its own property for cash, make a second investment from its own capital stock, and amortize that for the purpose of estimating its 'guaranteed profit' on the basis of a twenty-five year stay. Finally, however, the whole investment was re-expropriated under conditions which effectively

[57]   U.S. State Dept. Decimal File, 316-131-721.

precluded anything but a purely arbitrary Soviet settlement. One can understand why details of these investments are difficult to come by. The picture of the capitalist entrepreneur as a hardnosed calculating machine is shattered by the story of his dealings with the Soviets.

One by-product of the SKF agreement was technical assistance in the production of high-quality steel. Under the SKF concession, the Soviets were required to supply steel for the bearings. This posed a problem, as all high-grade steel had previously been imported and there were no facilities for production of this type of steel. The problem was solved in a characteristic manner: the Soviets asked for technical assistance and the SKF Company installed Swedish steel men in the Zlatoust steel plant in the Urals.

The transfer of Western ball-bearing technology was not completed by the time of the second expropriation of SKF. Two further agreements were made in 1930: one with Vereinigte Kugellager Fabriken A-G, of Berlin, and the other with S. A. Officine Villar Perosa (RIV), of Turin, Italy.[58]

STEAM BOILERS AND MECHANICAL STOKERS

Steam boilers are essential for industrial production operations where coal is a useful fuel. The relative decline of the economy under the Soviets may be well illustrated by the increasing age of steam boilers between 1914 and 1924.

Table 10–5   AGE OF STEAM BOILERS IN RUSSIAN
PLANTS, 1914 AND 1924

Age	1914	1924
Under 10 years	35.5 percent	4.8 percent
Under 25 years	49.0 percent	53.0 percent
Under 35 years	11.5 percent	31.0 percent
Over 35 years	4.0 percent	11.2 percent
	100.0 percent	100.0 percent

Source: Troyanovsky, *op. cit.*, p. 383.

In 1914, 35 percent of boilers were less than ten years old but in 1924 less than 5 percent fell into this category. This suggests negligible replacement. Even more important, in 1914 only 15 percent of boilers were more than twenty-five years old; by 1924 the figure had increased to 42 percent. There were 138 boilers in Briansk and Dnieper factories in 1923; of these, 111 had been built before 1900.[59] Imports of boilers immediately after the Revolution

---

[58]   Vneshtorgizdat, *op. cit.*, pp. 228–9. Barmine, *op. cit.*, p. 210, testifies to the low quality of Russian ball bearings in this period. See Vol. II for further information.

[59]   *Izvestia*, No. 278, December 5, 1923.

sank to zero. Importation began again in 1921, rose to almost one-third of the prewar level, and then declined after 1924. Steam boiler accessories followed a similar pattern. The decline after 1924 was due to local production by a concession.

In 1922 a concession was granted to Richard Kablitz, a Latvian firm, which took back its old prewar Petrograd factory and started again to produce steam boilers, mechanical stokers, fuel economizers, and similar equipment. This was by far the largest such plant in the U.S.S.R. Production expanded rapidly, and by the end of the decade Kablitz had equipped over 400 Russian factories with boilers and stoking equipment.[60] In the last two years of the decade, Kablitz turnover was substantial: more than 900,000 rubles in 1925–6, 1.4 million in 1926–7 and more than 1.6 million in 1927–8.

In brief, the Kablitz concession, operating from 1922 to 1930, enabled the Soviets to eliminate importation of boilers almost completely since the firm organized production and trained Russian workers in boiler production. It made a very significant contribution to the re-equipment of Soviet industry. The success may be established by the decline of boiler imports in the face of increasing boiler age. By 1929, Kablitz had served its purpose. Taxation was increased to the point where production was no longer profitable, and the Soviets took over the Kablitz operation.[61]

PRECISION ENGINEERING TECHNOLOGY AND ITS ACQUISITION

Many skilled instrument-makers fled Russia during the Revolution, but in 1918 a group of these returned from the United States with a group of American deportees and formed the Russian-American Instrument Company in Moscow. They brought their own machinery from the United States, employed about 300 unskilled Russian workmen, and ran what was considered to be 'one of the best factories in Russia. Members of the Third International were taken to see it as an example of the finest conditions.' As the government was unable to supply food, the enterprise broke up.[62]

In 1921, the pre-Revolutionary plants producing instruments, watches, and precision equipment were grouped into *Techmekh* (the Precision Engineer-

---

[60]   *Bank for Russian Trade Review*, II, No. 2 (February 1929), 10; and *Izvestia*, No. 223, October 2, 1923.

[61]   U.S. Consulate in Riga, Report 5997, March 25, 1929 (316–110–1014). In the view of the Latvian Foreign Office, it was impossible to establish Latvian firms in the U.S.S.R., as the Soviets 'would force them out of business either through taxation, labor legislation, charges of economic espionage or some other method of persecution if the enterprise should become too prosperous or compete with a Soviet industry.'

[62]   Keeley, *op. cit.* The trade unions also protested this plant.

ing Trust). These comprised the former Duber plant (renamed the Geophy-
sika), the former Tryndin (renamed the Metron), and the Unified Watch
Works, formed from smaller pre-Revolution plants.[63] The process of trustification did not appear to achieve very much, and the next few years saw a
succession of concession agreements with foreign companies. These were of
all three types and were allocated one to each branch of precision engineering.
Calculating machines, typewriters, sewing machines, clocks and watches,
razor blades, drawing instruments, and similar items were all subject to
agreements. The Soviet Union took the opportunity to change over to the
metric system. This problem was tackled by yet another concession, the
Franco-Russian Association for the Study of the Metric System (SOVMETR)
a French-Soviet mixed Type II company which undertook the changeover
and the production of the necessary weights and measures. The difficulties of
changeover varied by industry and were dependent to a great extent on
conditions during the prerevolutionary period. In the electrical industry,
there was no difficulty, as the industry had been developed on the basis of the
metric system; but textiles, equipped extensively with British equipment,
posed considerable difficulties which Gosmetr (State Office for Metric Weights
and Measures) was unable to solve for some years.

The Singer Sewing Machine Company operated numerous plants, warehouses, and retail units in prerevolutionary Russia, including manufacturing
units in Moscow, Leningrad, and Vladivostok. These plants, producing one
quarter of a million household sewing machines, were valued by Singer at
$75 million.[64] In addition, the wholesale and retail Singer network in tsarist
Russia included 50 central agencies and warehouses and more than 3,000
individual outlets for the sale and servicing of sewing machines. The Singer
sales force alone employed 27,500 in 1914.

Nationalization of the Moscow and Petrograd Singer plants in 1917 and
the Vladivostok plant in 1923 was completely unsuccessful. The equipment
was found to be much too complex to operate on the basis of shock tactics
and revolutionary slogans. The factories were denationalized and returned to
the Singer Sewing Machine Company in 1925.[65] This company, like many
others, assumed incorrectly that this admission of inability implied that the
Soviets did not wish to renationalize. No sewing machine output figures have
been recorded for the period 1917 to 1926–7; technical problems probably

---

[63]   *Annuaire*, p. 29; and Troyanovsky, *op. cit.*, p. 385.
[64]   Based on claims filed with the U.S. State Dept. in 1922 (Decimal File, 316–109–
1330). Including Russian government treasury bills and accounts in Russian banks,
the Singer claim was over $100 million. (Foreign Claims Settlement Commission
of the United States, Claim No. SOV-40,920.)
[65]   Denationalization, and the reasons for it, are noted in the German Foreign Ministry
Archives, T120–3033–H109454.

inhibited production.[66] In 1926–7, the first full year after denationalization and restoration of operations to the Singer Sewing Machine Company, the plants produced 200,000 machines, a figure which rose to 500,000 by the end of the decade.

In the early years of the New Economic Policy the Miemza concession was granted for the operation of a clock manufacturing plant in Moscow. After expropriation this became the Second State Clock Factory and was supplied with additional equipment from the Ansonia Clock Company in New York.[67]

The clock and watch industry production problems were overcome in a manner more suggestive of the massive 'turn-key' acquisitions of the 1950s. In June 1929 Techmekh negotiated a contract with two United States firms when Swiss firms refused to sell equipment necessary for watch plants. This contract called for establishment of two complete watch and clock factories. The first contract, with Dubert, was for a plant to produce 200,000 pocket and wrist watches a year to sell at retail prices between 20 and 40 rubles. The Soviets obtained five-year credit terms, and the plant was built in the early 1930s. This became the First State Watch Factory. The other plant was supplied by Ansonia for the production of one million alarm clocks and 500,000 large clocks for public squares, railroad stations, and public institutions. This plant was also supplied on five-year credit terms and was named the Second State Watch Factory. In both contracts, provision was made for the supply of manufactured and semi-manufactured parts until such time as the plants were able to develop their own input from internal Russian sources. About twenty-five specialists were sent from the United States to establish the plants and supervise production for the breaking-in period.[68]

Typewriters were not produced in the Soviet Union until after 1930. In 1929, the Moscow Soviet decided to build a typewriter factory and instructed Techmekh to negotiate with foreign firms for construction. An agreement was made with the Underwood Company for technical assistance to manufacture typewriters and calculating machines and for the intermediate-term sale of machine parts for assembly in Russian plants. During the first two years, the new factory only assembled machines. In the first year, 5,000 machines were planned for production, and in the second, 10,000. This figure was scheduled to rise to 218,000 annually after ten years. Typewriter

[66]   The U.S. State Dept. has a report (origin unknown) to the IX Congress of Soviets noting that the figure for sewing-machine production was 318 in the first half of 1920 and 187 in the first half of 1921. Even this miserable contribution has the air of 'something is better than nothing' and is dubious.

[67]   S. Weinberg, *An American Worker in a Moscow Factory* (Moscow: 1933), p. 18–19.

[68]   *Torgovo-Promyshlennaya Gazeta*, No. 147, June 30, 1929; and *Ekonomicheskaya Zhizn*, No. 191, August 21, 1929.

ribbons and supplies were produced by the Alftan concession after about 1924.[69] Pencils and stationery items were made by the Hammer (American Industrial) concession. These companies were the only producers of these items in the Soviet Union.

In the case of precision equipment, we can trace the start of a process of acquisition which was to be developed more extensively from the late 1930s to the 1950s. This was the purchase of single items or prototypes which were examined, broken down, and then used as the basis for Soviet production. The Fordson (Putilovets) tractor was probably the first effort in this direction. Purchases of small lots of Western machines began about 1927. For example, in September of that year, a number of calculating machines were bought in the United States, but only one or two each of a large number of makes and models.[70] Burroughs, Monroe, Marchant, and Hollerith were represented in the purchase. In more difficult areas, such as marine instruments, technical-assistance agreements were made: in the case of marine instruments, with Sperry Gyroscope Company of the United States.[71]

CONCLUSIONS

The process by which the tsarist machine-building industry was restarted and modernized is quite obvious. A great number of the plants were physically intact after the Revolution; skilled labor and engineering personnel were missing. Both had been dispersed by the political upheaval.[72]

---

[69] *Ekonomicheskaya Zhizn*, No. 346, November 28, 1924.

[70] Amtorg, *op. cit.*, II, No. 18, September 15, 1927, 5.

[71] A. A. Santalov and Louis Segal (eds.), *Soviet Union Year Book, 1930* (London: George Allen & Unwin, n.d.), p. 359.

[72] The Foss Special Collection at the Hoover Institution illustrates the comparatively advanced technology of tsarist industry. Foss, graduate of the St. Petersburg School of Mines, was variously builder and manager of the Briansky Works, the Kolomna Locomotive Works, the Sormovo Works, and the Alexandrovsky plant between 1890 and 1917. The collection comprises eighteen large folders of high-quality photographs stressing the technical side of these plants.
  The photographs emphasize particularly the size of these prerevolutionary enterprises; some shops at the Alexandrovsky and Sormovo were very large by contemporary world standards. General neatness and order, uncharacteristic of post-revolutionary plants, is very noticeable (see the 'General view of blast furnaces and coke ovens' in the Alexandrovsky folder). A high degree of Russian craftsmanship is demonstrated in photographs of the erection of the manual training school at the Kolomna Locomotive Plant, particularly in the stone and brick work. This craftsmanship is conspicuously missing in post-revolutionary buildings.
  Complex machinery was made in these plants. The Briansky Works folder has photographs of intricate steel castings, stampings, bevel gears, helical screws, locomotive parts, small tools, and armaments, as well as complete locomotives and wagons. Kolomna Service Locomotive No. T1027 (dated 1897) is an impressive piece of equipment. Of particular interest (in the Sormovo Works folder) is a photograph of a large planer under construction (dated 1887) and an almost complete 3-high plate-rolling mill. The latter is complete with run-out tables, cast rolls, and screw-down mechanism. The rolls are about 84 or 96 inches wide and of great

Several of the more complex machine-building plants were allowed to continue unmolested (e.g., Westinghouse Air Brake and Citroen). The alternative was to see the plants at a complete standstill. The foreign owner viewed the situation with a measure of hope. In some cases (Singer and International Harvester) the plants were nationalized and then denationalized. This was also seen as a sign of a genuine return to capitalism. Others were restarted with German technical assistance forthcoming under the Rapallo economic protocols. At the end of the decade, after a decision had been made to orient to American technology, a series of agreements were made with American companies: Baldwin Locomotive, Frank Chase, Albert Kahn, Sperry Gyroscope, and Underwood, for example. In diesel and engine building, the decision was to continue with German (Deutz and Faudewag) technical assistance.

In sum, the restored tsarist machine-building industry was on the way to modernization at the end of the decade. Construction of new plants was on the drawing boards of top American and German companies.

---

interest in the light of Soviet assertions that this equipment was not built in Russia until after 1930. In the Alexandrovsky folder there are photographs illustrating forging and machining a one-piece 20-ton steel ingot into a connecting rod for the cruiser *Bogatyr* (about 1890). Other features are the racks in Pickling Shop No. 1 at the Kolomna Works. These are the same model in use in Welsh tinplate mills in the early 1950s. The worker's dress is decidedly better than that of the post-revolutionary period.

The reader who is interested in pursuing this comparison further should compare the complete Foss collection with examples of the *same* plants in the Soviet period. One source for Soviet data is the booklets published by the Chief Concessions Committee describing plants offered as concessions to foreign entrepreneurs. For example, see I. N. Kostrow, *The Nadedjinsky and Taganrog Metallurgical Works* (Moscow: 1929). The plants were in a pitiful state, having been allowed to run down during twelve years of Bolshevik rule. There is a photograph of the open-hearth shop of the Nadedjinsky Works, which indicates that the shut-down plants only needed *work* to get them into operation. Nadedjinsky appears partially in operation, but one furnace is obviously 'cold,' with debris and trash heaped around the furnace doors.

CHAPTER ELEVEN

Electrical Equipment Manufacturing Industry and Goelro[1]

THE FORMATION OF TRUSTS

A RUSSIAN electrical equipment industry was established in the decade before the Revolution. In 1917 the industry was concentrated in Petrograd (about 75 percent) and Moscow, and employed some 60,000 workers. The Soviets nationalized the industry, which came through the Revolution with its equipment substantially intact.

From 1921 onward, the government invited a series of foreign experts and companies into the U.S.S.R. to make recommendations for modernization. The first known report by a Western engineer painted a chaotic picture. Some plants were closed; in those that remained open, employment was 5 to 10 percent of the prewar level (about 4,000 in 1920) and production even less. Many skilled Soviet workers had entered military service to get food and shelter; the more skilled foreign workers had returned home; and those domestic workers that remained were largely inefficient. Wages did not correspond to ability. Bench workers often earned more than skilled technicians. Communists possessing little or no technical ability served as technical directors, and 'white' skilled engineers were serving in minor posts. Stocks of raw materials ran out; no means existed for importation or domestic supply.

On the other hand, the industry was in relatively good shape technically; only a few plants required re-equipment.[2]

---

[1] This chapter is based on Soviet sources published inside and outside the U.S.S.R., on reports submitted to the U.S. State Dept. by representatives of American companies invited to examine the condition of the electrical industry, and on material on Allgemeine Elektrizitäts Gesellschaft (A.E.G.) from the German Foreign Ministry Archives.

[2] See the Report by B. W. Bary, electrical engineer, to the U.S. Consulate at Vibourg, October 1921. The covering letter describes the report as 'competent,' 'comprehensive,' and 'a measure of the true conditions.' (316–139–11.)

Confirmation of the excellent technical state of the industry comes from a surprising source—Charles P. Steinmetz, the inventive genius of General Electric Company, who was certainly not unsympathetic to the Bolshevik Revolution:

> It is interesting to note that Russia had a considerable electrical industry before the war, so that in 1913 more than half the electrical machinery used in Russia was built in Russia . . . (but) in 1920 the output of the electric factories in Russia was very low. It is stated however that their equipment including tools, etc., was perfectly intact and ready to resume large scale operation.[3]

The first step in reconstruction was to organize the industry into four trusts. The total industry contained thirty-two plants, of which twenty-six were in operating condition and six completely idle, or, as the Soviets expressed it, 'in a state of technical preservation': i.e., in working condition but not operating. The twenty-six were working very intermittently. The four trusts formed were: (1) the Electro-Technical Trust for the Central District (or GET), to manufacture high tension equipment, (2) a trust for manufacture of electrical high-tension equipment (Elmashstroi), (3) the low-tension equipment trust, for telephones and radio apparatus, and (4) the accumulator-manufacturing trust.

The formation of the trusts brought prerevolutionary managers back to positions of authority; although usually these were technical men, one at least had been a company director. Lew Zausmer, a former officer of the Russian General Electric Company, became one of the trio of directors controlling the Electro-Technical Trust.

Concurrently with this reorganization and the return of former managerial and technical personnel, invitations were sent to foreign electrical equipment manufacturers to participate in the development of the industry. On March 29, 1922, Maurice A. Oudin, President of the General Electric Company, informed the U.S. State Department that 'his company feels that the time is possibly approaching to begin conversations with Krassin relative to the resumption of business in Russia.' The State Department told Oudin that this was a question of 'business judgment.' Oudin then added that negotiations

---

[3] Charles P. Steinmetz, 'The Electrification of Russia,' p. 3 of typescript supplied to the writer by the Schenectady Historical Society, New York.

The reports of Western company representatives are of particular interest and agree with Steinmetz on this point. These engineering reports were to form the basis of managerial decisions to enter or not to enter into agreements with the U.S.S.R. As the reports were made by engineers, they are important for their estimates of the technical state of the electrical plants. These engineers had unrestricted access granted by the Soviet authorities and collected detailed data. The writer gives this data greater weight than that from any other source, including the intelligence reports found scattered throughout the U.S. State Dept. Archives. These engineers (Bary, Reinke, Keeley, Klemmer, and others) were skilled observers, knew the Russian language and also many of the engineers in the plants they visited.

were currently under way between General Electric and A.E.G. (German General Electric):

> . . . for resumption of the working agreement which they had before the War. He expects that the agreement to be made will include a provision for cooperation of Russia.[4]

Within four weeks an offer was made to International General Electric Company to participate in a joint mixed-capital company:

> We believe that the low rate of wages as well as the excellent conditions of the outfit (equipment) of the works will give you sufficient economic grounds for taking part in our business, either in the way of supplying us with certain materials, or by a partial finance in exchange for the products worked out by our factories.[5]

Table 11-1 AGREEMENTS BETWEEN FOREIGN COMPANIES AND THE ELECTRICAL EQUIPMENT TRUSTS, 1922-30

Trusts formed from prerevolutionary plants	Affiliated foreign firm	Type of concession*
Electro-Technical Trust (GET)	International General Electric	III
	Allmanna Svenska Elektriska A/B (A.S.E.A.)	I and III
	Allgemeine Elektrizitäts A-G (German General Electric)	III
	Metropolitan-Vickers, Ltd.	III
	Radio Corporation of America	III
Elmashstroi	Allgemeine Elektrizitäts A-G	III
	Metropolitan-Vickers, Ltd.	III
	John J. Higgins (U.S.)	III
Low-Tension Trust	Ericsson (Sweden)	I
	Radio Corporation of America	III
	Compagnie Générale de TSF (France)	III
Accumulator Trust	Gaso-Accumulator A/B (AGA) (Sweden)	I and III
New Soviet undertakings		
Electroselstroi	Allmanna Svenska Elektriska A/B	II and III
Electroexploatsia	International General Electric Co.	II and III

Sources: 1. U.S. and German Archives.
2. *Annuaire, 1925–26.*
3. Troyanovsk, *op. cit.*
4. Klemmer Reports to Western Electric Co., 1926 (U.S. State Dept. Decimal File, 316–141–630) and 1927 (U.S. State Dept. Decimal File, 316–60–95).

* See chap. 1 for definition of concession types.

[4] U.S. State Dept. Decimal File, 661.1115/402. Memorandum from D. C. Poole to Secretary of State, March 29, 1922.
[5] U.S. State Dept. Decimal File, 316–139–58. Letter from the Electro-Technical Trust to the International General Electric Company, Schenectady, May 2, 1922.

Two points are notable: first, the statement that the equipment in the plants was in good working order, and second, the timing of the letter from the Electro-Technical Trust to General Electric. It arrived just four weeks after the State Department conversation.[6]

After 1922 a series of similar invitations was sent, and agreements were concluded between all four trusts, individual plants within each trust, and most major Western electrical equipment manufacturers, including International General Electric, A.E.G., A.S.E.A. (Sweden), Westinghouse (through its U.K. subsidiary, Metropolitan-Vickers), Ericsson of Sweden, Brown-Boveri (Switzerland), Western Electric, and Siemens, as well as numerous smaller companies.

These agreements were made at two organizational levels: the trust and the individual plant. At the trust level they provided technical assistance, patents, drawings, and exchange of personnel (Type III agreement). At the plant level the contracts provided for technical assistance and also, in some cases for plant operation as a pure Type I concession by the Western entrepreneur. Table 11-1 lists the four trusts formed by the Soviets from prerevolutionary factories together with the affiliated foreign partner, and the Soviet enterprises Electroselstroi and Electroexploatsia which were developed by the Soviets and did not incorporate prerevolutionary plants. They had affiliated foreign partners and operated in the form of 'mixed' companies, or Type II concessions with technical assistance features.[7] One Western company managed to evade nationalization after the Revolution. A.S.E.A. (Swedish General Electric) operated its Leningrad plant from the time of the Revolution throughout the 1920s and even managed to get its Yaroslavl plant, built in 1916, denationalized and converted into a Type I pure concession in 1924. There was also an independent factory, the Carbolite, operating outside the control of the trusts and coming directly under Glavelectro until it was abolished.[8]

The four trusts will now be considered in more detail.

THE ELECTRO-TECHNICAL TRUST (GET)

GET was responsible for manufacture of high-tension equipment and was formed by grouping together the major prerevolutionary dynamo and electric motor works located in Moscow and the Ukraine, including the

---

[6] It may be that Zausmer, the ex-officer of General Electric and a director of the Electro-Technical Trust, had some influence on this decision. He is quoted by a Berlin newspaper as follows: ' . . . the Russian electrical industry cannot develop without the support of the highly developed electrical industries of Germany and America.' (*Boerson Courier*, September 25, 1922.)

[7] *Annuaire, op. cit.* (rear page 24).

[8] The German Foreign Ministry Archives refer to a 'Carbo project'; otherwise nothing is known of this operation. (T120–4247.)

Kharkov works of the General Electric Company and its twelve assembly divisions in major industrial centers throughout the Soviet Union. All types of heavy electrical machinery, including generators, motors, transformers and turbines, were produced.

Table 11–2   PLANTS COMPRISING THE ELECTRO-
TECHNICAL TRUST

Prerevolutionary Name	Soviet Name	Production
Russian General Electric	Dynamo A-G (Moscow and Petrograd)	Electric motors
Allgemeine Elektrizitäts A-G	Electrosila (Kharkov)	Electrical equipment
Allmanna Svenska Elektriska A/B	(A.S.E.A. concession)	A.C. electric motors

A.S.E.A. obtained its prerevolutionary plant as a Type I concession and in 1927 received another Type I concession to build and operate a plant at Yaroslavl for production of alternating current electric motors.[9] By 1928 the company was producing 500 motors a month at Yaroslavl, 'the output sold on partial credit terms mainly to state-owned enterprises.'[10] The construction involved an outlay on buildings and equipment of between 15 and 18 million rubles. The new plant had 28,000 square meters of floor space and 1,500 employees, and in 1929 produced at the rate of 30,000 electric motors per year. In weight this was 48,000 tons of equipment, valued at 14 million rubles. Production included alternating current motors ranging from 1/4 to 700 h.p. Equipment for the Yaroslavl factory came from the Swedish General Electric factory at Stockholm. A royalty was payable by the Soviets on all production during the life of the concession, agreed upon at thirty-five years but expropriated long before the final date.

The widest impact of G.E. technology came, however, from agreements made after the Swedish General Electric concessions. There had been negotiations between A.E.G. in 1922 and 1923 following the letter sent by GET to International General Electric. These negotiations were not immediately successful. Their failure probably placed G.E. at a competitive disadvantage; Siemens-Schukert Werke A-G, for example, had granted credits as early as 1922. Metropolitan-Vickers (the Westinghouse subsidiary) had been in the U.S.S.R. from about 1922 onwards. The G.E. company therefore continued negotiations through its German subsidiary.[11]

The first technical-assistance agreement was concluded between Uchanov, Chairman of the Electro-Technical Trust, and A.E.G. in October 1925. This

9   Amtorg, *op. cit.*, III, 374.
10   *Ibid.*, E. P. Lindgren, Director of A.S.E.A. (Swedish General Electric).
11   U.S. State Dept. Decimal File, 316–139–41.

agreement included the manufacture of General Electric generators, electric motors, and transformers of high-voltage types. The trust was given the right to produce A.E.G. products and use 'all patents, protective certificates, inventions, construction and experiments belonging to A.E.G. in the field of high-voltage currents.'[12] General Electric was required to furnish data on request and to accept and train Russian engineers in German plants for a period of five years. The agreement was supplemented and continued by other agreements which continued the technical-assistance program until 1938. A royalty was payable on all production of high-voltage electrical products for which A.E.G. held manufacturing rights from the parent company in the United States.[13] As a *quid pro quo* for technical assistance, substantial quantities of equipment were purchased on credit terms for the plants comprising the trust.

Table 11–3   PRODUCTION OF HEAVY ELECTRICAL
EQUIPMENT IN RUSSIA AND THE U.S.S.R., 1913 TO 1929–30

Year	Power transformers (thousand kva)	Electric motors (A.C.) (thousand kw)	Turbo-generators (thousand kw)
1913	96.3	N.A.	N.A.
1918 to 1922–3	None	N.A.	N.A.
1923–4	76.5	N.A.	N.A.
1924–5	196.0	104.4	10.3
1925–6	127.4	N.A.	16.3
1926–7	291.7	N.A.	51.8
1927–8	403.2	258.6	75.0
1928–9	791.1	321.7	136.5
1929–30	1525.0	632.6	186.0

Source: Nutter, *op. cit.*, p. 441.

Table 11–3 indicates production of transformers, electric motors, and turbo-generators from 1913 to 1929/30. There was no Soviet production of these items in the years before 1924. Their production coincided with the technical-assistance agreements and the operation of the A.S.E.A. Type I concession. The recovery and development of the Soviet electrical equipment industry in these fields was almost entirely dependent on General Electric technology transferred to the Soviet Union through A.E.G.

In addition to the agreements outlined in this chapter, there was a technical-assistance agreement between the United States firm of John J. Higgins and GET in 1929 and an important Radio Corporation of America agreement,

---

[12] U.S. Consulate in Hamburg, Reports No. 149, December 13, 1925 (316–108–1543); and No. 360, October 12, 1925 (316–130–552).
[13] *Ibid.* See also International General Electric section, p. 198.

which included General Electric and Westinghouse patents in the field of communications, concluded in 1929 and discussed at length in chapter 14.

Even while this technical transfusion was in progress, the Party propagandists were unable to restrain themselves from 'agitprop.' A challenge was issued 'from the workers' of the ex-A.E.G. plant in Kharkov to the A.E.G. plant in Berlin to engage in 'revolutionary emulation,' and a delegation of working men from Berlin was invited to the Kharkov plant 'all expenses paid.' The benefits of 'revolutionary emulation' to the General Electric Company were not spelled out.[14]

THE ELECTRICAL MACHINE TRUST (ELMASHSTROI)

This trust grouped high-tension equipment plants in Petrograd, including the Siemens A-G plant (renamed the Electrosila), with the Volta factories in the Urals. Elmashstroi negotiated an agreement with A.E.G. in late 1923 for technical assistance. A.E.G. was required to supply drawings, machines, and apparatus for the production of high-tension equipment, together with aid in construction of electrical manufacturing plants within the U.S.S.R. Russian engineers were sent to Germany for training and German engineers were sent to the trust offices and plants in Leningrad. The agreement ran initially for five years, and a percentage of all production was paid to A.E.G. as a royalty.[15]

The most important plant in the trust was the Electrosila, originally built in 1893. This trust had a chaotic history of technical assistance under the Soviets. In tsarist times the plant had produced steam turbines and generator equipment. In 1923 Electrosila adopted the designs forthcoming under the A.E.G. agreement. Then came four management changes in rapid succession,

Table 11–4   THE ELECTRICAL MACHINE TRUST (ELMASHSTROI)

Prerevolutionary Name	Soviet Name	Production
Siemens-Schukert A-G	Electrosila	Electrical machinery
Nordische Kabel Werke A-G	Sovkabel	Electric wire and cable
Koltschugin	Sovkabel	Electric wire and cable
Svetlana Gluklampenfabrik	Svetlana	Electric light bulbs
Druzniai Gorka*	—	Porcelain insulators
Kernilov*	Proletarii	Porcelain insulators
Petrograd Armaturfabrik A-G	—	Armatures

Source: U.S. State Dept. Archives.

* Transferred in 1923 from the Glass and Porcelain Trust, and later transferred back to the same trust. (U.S. State Dept. Decimal File, 316–111–957.)

[14] 'Challenge to the Proletarians of Berlin from the Workers of the Electro-Technical Factory of Kharkov,' *Trud*, No. 244, October 23, 1929.
[15] *Izvestia*, No. 7, January 9, 1924.

and by 1925–6, turbines were being built under a ten-year agreement with Metropolitan-Vickers. This was apparently not too successful, because one year later a further change occurred. As A. Monkhouse, the Metropolitan-Vickers chief engineer in the Soviet Union, puts it, 'a great American company contracted to render technical assistance to this and other factories and thus American designs were introduced.'[16]

The 'great American company' was International General Electric. Russian engineers were then sent to the United States for training, whereas previously they had gone to the United Kingdom. In 1931 the Metropolitan-Vickers company again obtained the technical-assistance contract, and this heralded yet another series of management changes.

In the tsarist era, electric light bulb production was concentrated at Svetlana Gluklampenfabrik in Petrograd. In 1913 the plant produced 2.85 million electric light bulbs, and in 1916 over 4.58 million (a good example, incidentally, to show the fallacy of using 1913 as a comparative base). Production in 1920 fell to about one-quarter million, but later recovered (with the use of imported wire), reaching a level between the 1913 and 1916 outputs (3.82 million in 1922–3).[17] In May 1923, *Ekonomicheskaya Zhizn* published an interview with the chief of Glavelectro, A. G. Holtzman, who had just returned from negotiating with Osram in Germany, Phillips in Holland, and General Electric in the United States for the introduction of the latest in Western techniques in the manufacture of electric light bulbs. A joint-stock company was proposed, in which the Soviets would provide the plant (the tsarist Svetlana plant) and the foreign partners would introduce modern equipment.

The objective was as follows:

> . . . Russia would develop within two years to the same extent as now exists in Western Europe and America. The Russian bulbs must not be worse nor more expensive than those produced by the aforementioned firms.[18]

In the following months, agreement was also reached with the International Electric Light Cartel. With the aid of Western technical experience, production was increased from 1,500 to 7,500 bulbs per day. At first, tungsten wire was purchased abroad, and later Russian tungsten wire was used. From an output just under four million in 1922–3, there was a significant increase to thirty-three million bulbs in 1929–30.[19]

---

[16] A. Monkhouse, *Moscow 1911–1933* (Boston: Little, Brown and Co., 1934), pp. 194–5.

[17] Nutter, *op. cit.*, p. 458.

[18] *Ekonomicheskaya Zhizn*, No. 96, May 3, 1923.

[19] Nutter, *loc. cit.* It is known that a Polish Type I concession, Yan Serkovsky, operated an electric lamp plant in Moscow. As the Svetlana was the only plant able to produce electric light bulbs the plant was possibly leased to this group. (U.S. State Dept. Decimal File, 861.602/211.)

THE LOW-TENSION TRUST

The Low-Tension Trust was comprised of the tsarist-era plants in Leningrad, Moscow, and Nizhni-Novgorod which had made telephone and telegraph apparatus. In 1923 this was probably the most efficiently operated Soviet trust. The trust president, Joukoff, was a party member but, unlike most of his confrères, who were long on talk and short on management ability, Joukoff had excellent management abilities, was entirely responsible for financial matters, and was directly supported by a team of 'white' technical experts who managed internal operations of the plants.

The 'white' technical directors were hold-overs (former engineers, not former directors) from the prerevolutionary electrical industry. They included Mochkovitch, formerly chief engineer of the Heisler Company (owned by Western Electric) and Kolotchevsky, formerly of the B.T.M. company. These technical directors functioned alongside 'red' directors. The latter were party members who nominally directed the plant but in practice left the 'white' technical men to operate independently in the technical sphere. The equipment in all the plants in the trust was intact and maintained in good order. Each plant operated as an independent profit-making unit.

The ex-Western Electric Heisler plant employed some 850 men: slightly less than its 1917 employment level of 1,100. In mid-1923, the plant was busy on an order for 900 train-dispatching sets for the Railway Administration, its only major customer.

Table 11–5 PLANTS COMPRISING THE LOW-TENSION TRUST

Tsarist name	Number of workers 1913[1]	1916[1]	1923[2]	1926[1]	Production
Ericsson (Red Dawn)	1275	2700	900	2800	Automatic telephone equipment and switchboards
Heisler A-G	845	900	850	1200	Telegraph equipment and loudspeakers
Siemens Halske A-G	750	2200	600	1300	Radios, R.R.-signaling meters
Electro-vacuum plant (new)	—	—	—	250	Radio and roentgen tubes
Marconi plant	—	—	—	250	Military radios
Telephone plant	—	1200	—	1000	Radio receiving equipment
Siemens	—	1200	—	700	Telephone sets

Sources: [1] Klemmer report to Western Electric Company, 1927 (U.S. State Dept. Decimal File, 316–141–630).
[2] Reinke report (U.S. State Dept. Decimal File, 316–108–672).

The Ericsson plant employed 900 (considerably fewer than the 3,500 employed just before the Revolution) and was making Ericsson-type telephones—the only producer of telephones in the U.S.S.R. It was operated as a concession and was able to produce all types of telephone equipment except lamps (which were imported from Germany or Sweden), and cords and cables, (which were bought from the Cable Trust). Troubles were reported in 1923; Soviet raw materials were of poor quality, and some items, such as enameled wire and magnet steel, were either in short supply or unobtainable. Production, therefore, averaged only about 7,000 sets per year, although capacity was 12,000 telephone sets annually. Nutter[20] gives the telephone output as rising from 13,300 in 1923/4 to 117,000 in 1929/30. As Ericsson was still the sole producer, this was also the measure of Ericsson's ability to increase production during the decade.

The Siemens Halske works in Petrograd, previously a manufacturer of telephone equipment, employed some 600 and was preparing to change over to the manufacture of radio equipment under technical direction of Compagnie Générale de TSF (which Reinke erroneously calls French General Electric).[21] Since the Revolution, this plant had been at a standstill except for a little repair work.[22] Reinke, the Western Electric engineer who visited the plant, concluded that the chance of a mixed company or pure concession for Western Electric, the previous owner, was remote. Reinke concluded that the U.S.S.R. was 'encouraging only badly run factory trusts to get into mixed companies.' However, he did comment that the trust was anxious to associate itself with a large foreign firm. He explained this on the basis that although the plants were operating efficiently, they lacked the ability to progress.[23] This observation is confirmed by the subsequent agreement between the Low-Tension Trust and Compagnie Générale in June 1923 and Ericsson in 1924. Even a well-run trust required foreign technology to make technical progress. In the 1920s this could be explained on the basis of a negligible research and development investment. More recently the notable absence of Soviet innovation which can compete in the Western marketplace has had to be explained on quite different grounds.[24]

---

[20]   *Ibid.*, p. 448.

[21]   Based on the Reinke Report (mid-1923) (State Dept. Decimal File, 316-108-672). This was supplemented by two later reports in 1926 and 1927.

[22]   Keeley Report (316-107-100).

[23]   'The present technical men are those formerly in control, and they are doing practically as good a job as in 1917. They can get on very comfortably without us. But what they lack is the ability to go ahead. The same difficulty existed in 1917 when the factories depended on the foreign mother companies to lead the way.' (Reinke, *op. cit.*)

[24]   Klemmer lists electrical products not produced in the Soviet Union in 1927, four years after the Reinke Report. These were: generators above 5,000 kw, all types of high-tension equipment and transformers, fine insulated wires, special lamps (including all over 200w), high-tension insulators, carbon brushes and carbon materials (including telephone carbons), heating appliances, nickel steel accumulators, measuring instruments, automatic telephone equipment (including pneumatic tubes), condensers, all types of electrical consumer equipment (including vacuum

TECHNICAL ASSISTANCE TO THE LOW-TENSION TRUST

In June 1923 the Compagnie Générale de TSF of France signed a technical-assistance agreement with the Low-Tension Trust to re-equip its plants with modern machinery and processes, to supply technical assistance, and to build electrical substations in the Moscow area. A new electro-vacuum plant was established by the Compagnie Générale, using French methods of producing cathode ray tubes and radio tubes. The old Petrograd plant of Siemens was equipped to manufacture radio transmission equipment for radio stations. Other plants of the trust were similarly modernized, 'after which Russian radio technique (will be) on the same level as the French,' as Klemmer says in his report. The trust sent its engineers to France for training, and French engineers went to the trust plants to provide the engineering and operational assistance required. Equipment was supplied on five-year credit terms.[25] Patents were transferred from France and, unlike other contractors, the French were able to negotiate a payment (the amount unknown) for the technical-assistance features. The very extensive nature of the Compagnie Générale agreement is suggested by the transfer of over 38,000 drawings and 3,000 technical specifications in the first two years of the cooperation.[26]

The Compagnie Générale agreement was followed by another with Ericsson of Sweden, which took over its old plant in Petrograd for the manufacture of telephones. This was, in effect, a formality, as Ericsson engineers had been working in Petrograd almost continuously since the Revolution. Modern machinery, imported from Germany and Sweden, included automatic screw machines and automatic punching, milling, and tooth-cutting equipment from the United Kingdom and the United States. Inspection and test equipment was installed. This re-equipped plant started production in 1926, at first with Swedish raw materials and later with Soviet-produced raw materials. Ericsson had four engineers in the plant with complete authority to control and approve every step of the production of automatic telephone equipment. All drawings

cleaners), electrical medical apparatus (including roentgen tubes), and special electrical apparatus. (Klemmer, *op. cit.*, p. 42.)

Some of these items were the subject of technical-assistance agreements apparently not known to Klemmer (for instance, medical apparatus, nickel accumulators, high-tension equipment, high-tension insulators, and transformers). Most came within the scope of technical-assistance agreements by 1930.

25 The Soviets erected 43 internal radio stations between January 1923 and January 1927; all except the experimental models were with French technical assistance. Klemmer states the manufacturer in 22 cases; 16 were built by the Low-Tension Trust-Compagnie Générale operation, 4 were built by local laboratories on an experimental basis, and 2 radio stations were imported. Later, more powerful stations were built either in the U.S. by RCA or in the Soviet Union with RCA technical assistance after assurances by the State Dept. to RCA that they would not be used for propaganda (see chaps. 14 and 18). (316–141–712 *et seq.*)

26 *Izvestia*, No. 15, January 18, 1924; and No. 35, February 12, 1924. See also *Soviet Union Yearbook 1927*, p. 169.

and technical information were supplied by Ericsson. Locally made Russian drawings and technical instructions had to receive approval of an Ericsson engineer before use. Between ten and twelve Russian engineers were trained in the Ericsson Stockholm plant for periods ranging from three to six months and then returned to Leningrad, ultimately to take over production control.[27] Credit for the arrangement was supplied by a consortium of Swedish banks.

The technical contribution of the foreign electrical companies enabled the trust to increase its output from two million rubles in 1922 to more than thirteen million rubles in the year 1924–5. According to Klemmer, this increase was mainly due to the work of Ericsson.

The 1927 Klemmer Report[28] indicated that 1926 output in the electrical equipment industry was 20 percent greater than the previous year, with Ericsson showing the most progress. Several new shops had been opened and about one-third of the plant had received new equipment. At this point about one-third of the employees of the Low-Tension Trust were working for the Ericsson Company.

There was a less significant agreement for the manufacture of long-distance receiving sets, including the transfer of patents, with the German company Telefunken Gesellschaft für Drahtlose Telegraphie.[29]

In 1926–7 all Low-Tension Trust products were copies of Western equipment. Klemmer noted that the trust microphones were an 'exact copy' of the Western Electric Model 373-W, the loudspeakers were the balanced armature accord type (Western Electric Model 4002) and the amplifiers and public address systems had been copied from Western Electric systems. The Russians had produced domestically designed radio valves, but according to Klemmer these would not work. In 1926 they were producing, and attempting to export to Latvia, the Western Electric Models 216-D, 102-D, 205-B, and 211-D.[30] Klemmer should have known; he was an engineer with Western Electric.

The trust teletype machines were allegedly designed by A. F. Shorin, but Klemmer points out that the design was no more than a Morcum printer combined with the Murrey keyboard. Further, although the Kaupush distributor (of which the trust manufactured about 20 in 1926–7) was claimed as a Soviet design, it was actually based on the Baudot repeater. Quite clearly these manufacturing efforts were part of a learning process, although the products manufactured were in many cases useless.

The electrical industry was the advanced sector of the economy, and the Low-Tension Trust just described was the most advanced trust within the

[27] Klemmer, *op. cit.*, p. 27.
[28] U.S. State Dept. Decimal File, 316–60–124.
[29] Vneshtorgizdat, *op. cit.*, p. 228.
[30] Klemmer, *op. cit.*, p. 28.

electrical industry. Other branches were using 40–50 percent imported materials and more extensive foreign technical assistance.[31]

THE ACCUMULATOR TRUST

The Accumulator Trust employed about 250 in 1923. Combined within it were the prerevolutionary accumulator, lighting, and illuminating fixture firms in Moscow and Petrograd. In 1912 the value of product for this sector was 2.4 million rubles; in 1922/3, the value was only 0.6 million rubles. In December 1924 an agreement was made by the trust with the Swedish company Gaso-Accumulator A/B (AGA) whereby the Moscow Lukes (or Lux) plant was leased under a concession agreement. The company was required to produce equipment valued at 210,000 rubles in the first year (one-third of the current Soviet output), rising to 470,000 rubles in 1926–7. AGA paid 75,000 rubles to the trust for the stock of raw materials and unfinished work in the plant. The company was required to re-equip the plant and after twenty-five years turn the plant over to the government. A royalty of 3 percent was paid on gross turnover.[32]

Insulating materials were the subject of an agreement between Centroprobizol and the Swedish Company Vakander in 1927. This was a Type III agreement which ran for five years and included supply of the complete equipment for a plant to produce all types of insulating materials. The agreement included construction, start-up assistance, training of engineers, and the supply of production and technical data. Russian engineers were allowed to make 'a thorough study of the Swedish production methods.'[33] This agreement was followed by a General Electric technical agreement with the Izolit insulation materials plant in 1930.[34]

The Soviets formed two trusts which did not include major prerevolutionary institutions and indeed had had no exact equivalent in tsarist times. One was Electroselstroi, a joint-stock company founded in June 1924 with the same objective as the United States Rural Electrification Authority: to expand the use of electricity in rural areas. Electroselstroi undertook construction of district electric generating stations of a standard type and sold electric motors, generators, and allied equipment to state farms and collectives. The Swedish General Electric Company was a shareholder (with a participation of 250,000 rubles purchased for cash) along with the People's Commissariat for Agriculture, Gosstrakh, Gosspirt, and Sakharotrust. The Swedish company

---

[31]   Klemmer, *loc. cit.*
[32]   U.S. State Dept. Decimal File, 316–139–554.
[33]   Amtorg, *op. cit.*, II, 14.
[34]   *Ibid.*

had the function of organizing and supplying equipment for sale by the trust and no doubt its share subscription was 'a fee' for this privilege.[35] The General Electric Company was also one of the 'main shareholders' in Electroexploatsia, the second of these trusts, specifically designed to promote the use of electrical systems, in accordance with Lenin's dictum that 'socialism is electrification.'[36]

THE INTERNATIONAL GENERAL ELECTRIC COMPANY
CONTRACTS OF 1928 AND 1930

A contract of fundamental importance was signed in 1928 by the Soviet Union and the International General Electric Company. Under this contract the company supplied to the Soviet Union $26 million worth of electrical equipment on six-year credit terms. The Soviets claim that G.E. agreed to consider all prewar claims against the U.S.S.R. as settled.[37] Technical assistance was an integral part of the agreement. This began what General Electric has described as 'a continuous uninterrupted record of close technical collaboration and harmonious commercial association.'[38]

The 1928 agreement was followed by a long-term technical-assistance agreement signed in 1930, under which 'vast amounts' of technical, design, and manufacturing information flowed from General Electric in Schenectady to the Soviet Union. The Soviet Union established an office at Schenectady and G.E. a parallel office in Moscow.

There was the usual exchange of personnel, training of Soviet engineers in the U.S., and dispatch of American engineers to the U.S.S.R. to implement the agreement. The Electrozavod transformer plants, the Izolit insulation material plant, the Dynamo locomotive plants, the Electrosila plants, Electroapparat and Electric works in Leningrad, and the turbine plant in Kharkov received groups of G.E. engineers. In general, however, the great impact of *direct* General Electric technological assistance was not in the period 1917 to 1930. Development before 1930 was dependent on Metropolitan-Vickers and A.E.G. (i.e., *indirect* G.E. technical assistance). The General Electric era was after 1930.[39]

[35]   U.S. State Dept. Decimal File, 316–139–56. *Annuaire, op. cit.,* rear p. 24.
[36]   Troyanovsky, *op. cit.,* p. 791.
[37]   *Izvestia,* No. 247, October 23, 1928.
[38]   *Monogram,* November 1943.
[39]   The 1928 General Electric contract was closely examined in Germany. The Rapallo Treaty contained a clause that compensation would be relinquished only for German claims against the U.S.S.R. so long as the Soviets did not make payments to any other power. The Soviets argued that G.E. was a private company, not a power, and that therefore the Rapallo clause did not apply. The Germans considered the G.E. agreement a violation of the Rapallo Treaty, as the company received a payment of

THE METROPOLITAN-VICKERS ELECTRICAL COMPANY— MASHINOSTROI TECHNICAL ASSISTANCE AGREEMENT

In addition to German assistance in the electrical industry, two other European manufacturers rendered substantial assistance and equipment. In 1927 the Brown-Boveri Company of Switzerland opened an office in Moscow to implement the installation and erection of equipment supplied under a number of contracts with the U.S.S.R. Little is known of the content of these agreements.[40]

Far more important was Metropolitan-Vickers, a United Kingdom subsidiary of Westinghouse. The company has operated in Russia since the turn of the century, installing several large electricity-generating plants and the electrification of the Moscow tramway system in 1906. Just before World War I, the company became associated with Russian General Electric (the Dynamo works) which then took over the Metropolitan-Vickers plants in Moscow.[41]

After the Bolshevik Revolution, Metropolitan-Vickers returned to Russia and by 1924 had several large contracts in progress. Each major technical advance made by the company in its U.K. plants was transferred to the Soviet Union. In the early 1920s significant advances were made in the operating speed of generators. A world record was set by a Metropolitan-Vickers generator of 38,500 Kva (3,000 rpm.) installed in a Soviet power station in 1926. Similarly, in the same period there was an increase in transmission voltages; Metropolitan-Vickers manufactured transformers for Soviet 110-kV and 115-kV systems were installed in 1923, some five years before the start of the British grid system utilizing similar transmission voltages. In 1922 the company developed outdoor switchgear for 132-kV systems. Several 1500-MVA 132-kV circuit breakers were installed in the U.S.S.R. within two years of initial development. These sales of the latest products of the Metropolitan-Vickers laboratories were followed in 1927 and 1931 by long-term technical-assistance agreements. The 1927 agreement was initially signed with Mashinostroi for six years at £30,000 ($150,000) per year and covered that turbine construction which formed the basis of the Soviet turbine industry.[42] The company maintained extensive erection and technical facilities in the Soviet

---

$575,202 as compensation for its claims on the U.S.S.R. G.E. claims this was only a partial settlement. The Foreign Claims Settlement Commission (Decision No. SOV-3119) made an award of $1,157,407.26 plus interest to G.E. This dispute, of course, has not been settled. (340-6-517.)

[40] U.S. State Dept. Decimal File, 316-131-1010.

[41] Westinghouse left Russia in 1913 except for a bank account. This was expropriated, and Westinghouse has received $5,703.44 from a claim amounting to $49,400 plus interest. Letter from Westinghouse to writer, March 4, 1966.

[42] J. Dummerlow, *1899–1949* (Metropolitan-Vickers Electrical Company, 1949).

Union, an office at Electroimport, a company office at Leningrad and a 'compound' with several buildings at Perlovka, just outside Moscow.[43] Company engineers established the manufacture of turbines according to company plans on 'a large scale' under R. Cox, its chief mechanical engineer, in the U.S.S.R. Soviet engineers and foremen were sent to the United Kingdom for training. In 1931 another agreement with GET expanded the scope of the transfer of turbine technology. These agreements endured both the Arcos break of 1927 and the notoriety surrounding the arrest and expulsion of six Metropolitan-Vickers engineers in 1933 on grounds of economic espionage and sabotage.

Steam turbines had been made in the Petrograd Metal Plant (later renamed the Stalin) early in 1906. By 1914 there were seven plants in Russia manufacturing naval turbines and one manufacturing stationary steam turbines; after 1917 the Petrograd plant alone continued working, but only on repairs to existing turbines and the manufacture of spare parts. Neither this nor any other Soviet plant had experience with high-power hydraulic turbines.

To summarize, by the end of the decade the Soviet electrical industry had undergone a complete overhauling in methods of production, variety of goods produced, and quantity produced. This had been achieved in the face of disaster by restoring the prerevolutionary technical personnel, injecting foreign managerial and engineering personnel and foreign-developed technology into the most important of the prerevolutionary plants. Whereas in 1913 the industry value of output was 45 million rubles, in 1924–5, one year after the introduction of foreign technology, it was 75 million (1913) rubles, and by the end of the decade more than 200 million (1913) rubles. Imports of electrical equipment increased from 7,592 tons (valued at 14 million rubles) in 1925–6 to 26,465 tons (valued at 45 million rubles) in 1927–8. Eighty percent of these imports were electrical machinery and high-tension apparatus (i.e., capital goods).

The variety of goods also expanded under foreign guidance. Steam turbine generators of up to 10,000 kw, hydro-turbine generators of up to 8,750 kw, transformers of up to 38,000 volts, high-voltage armatures, oil switches, and mercury rectifiers were being produced by the Electro-Technical Trust and Elmashstroi by the end of the decade. Production of electric light bulbs was modernized and arrangements had been made with foreign firms to introduce the manufacture of mercury lamps, automatic car headlights, and pocket lights. The Low-Tension Trust was now producing radio transmitters and receivers, although large stations for international communications and

---

[43]   *Correspondence Relating to the Arrest of Employees of the Metropolitan-Vickers Company at Moscow*, Command Paper 4286 (London: H.M.S.O., 1933) pp. 2–3.

propaganda were built by RCA in the United States.[44] Watt meters, X-ray apparatus, automatic telephones, and exchanges were being built in the U.S.S.R.

Research establishments, including the State Electrical Engineering Experimental Institute, were also established, complete with 'unique' equipment manufactured by the General Electric company.[45]

All trusts and plants within the trusts received foreign technical assistance. All technological progress resulted from a transfer from West to East. Further, rather than just restoring and modernizing the prerevolutionary plants, the foreign associates introduced the latest innovations from Western laboratories —sometimes before they had been utilized in the Western country of origin.

SOCIALISM IS ELECTRIFICATION; THE GOELRO PROGRAM

The most important customers for electrical machinery are power stations, utilizing hydro, peat, and coal fuel methods of energy conversion.

The original Goelro program outlined by Lenin demanded 100 power stations as the basis for a socialist economy. This was revised downwards in the Zinoviev speech of January 1921 to 27 stations, and followed by ample discussion but little concrete action.[46] Two years later only three projects were receiving any attention, and that was rather desultory. Studies inherited from the tsarist period included one which had been expanded into the Dniepr project, but a few scattered site borings comprised the total achievement. The general feeling was that Dniepr should be offered as a concession. Volkhov, Svir, and Nizhni-Novgorod were at various points of early construction, but three years after the announcement of Goelro, the program had hardly moved.

The Svir hydroelectric project, north of Leningrad, ran into almost innumerable difficulties, which stretched its construction period from 1920 well into the 1930s. The fifteen-month preliminary investigations of the project were handled by an American engineer, Emegess, employed by the

---

[44] It should be clearly noted that RCA pointed out the propaganda possibilities to the State Dept. The latter described these warnings as 'theoretical' (316–141–714 *et seq.*). See also chap. 18.

[45] *Monogram*, November 9, 1943; and *Bank for Russian Trade Review* (January 1929), pp. 8–9.

[46] Telegram Quarton, Vibourg to U.S. State Dept., April 11, 1921: 'Confidential. Although Soviet papers contain little on electrification accomplishments and only reiterate bombastic plans the truth is that slight progress has been made due to the lack of electrical goods, technical supplies and skilled labor. To date most energy has been devoted to collecting material and making paper plans. The colossal Svir electric station has not materialized, and is no further advanced than six months ago except that a small and inadequate quantity of building materials has been collected. . . .'

Cooper Company, also working on the Dniepr project.[47] Various other American (J. G. White Company) and Swedish (Karlsrads Mechaniska A/B and Vattenbyggnadsbyran A/B) construction companies were involved in various aspects of the Svir dam and site construction. The generators were supplied by Metropolitan-Vickers and the turbines by Werkstaden Kristinegamm A/B of Sweden. The project was finally completed in 1933 at an estimated cost of $500 per horsepower compared to an average cost of approximately $100 per horsepower in the United States.[48]

At Volkhov the construction process was also extremely slow. Graftio, the engineer in charge, used Swedish engineers to implement Swedish construction methods.[49] The 10,000 h.p. turbines from Sweden arrived at the end of 1923, and date of completion was set at 1926. By April 1927, despite extensive foreign assistance from A.S.E.A. and Metropolitan-Vickers, the Volkhov station was still not fulfilling expectations. It was described as 'irregular, capricious and unreliable.'[50] The problem was in the use of generators from two sources: four from A.S.E.A. and made in Stockholm, and four made at the Electrosila works in Leningrad with its mixed history of technical assistance. The Electrosila generators contained materials of different specification from those in the Swedish generators, and problems arose when the eight generators were operated simultaneously.[51]

The high-tension insulators (Hewlitt type) for the 130 kilometers of transmission lines to Leningrad were manufactured by the General Electric Company and the Thomas Company in the United States. The total cost of the project was estimated by Klemmer at 90 million rubles, of which 6 million was spent on imported equipment and technical assistance. In return for this substantial investment, the plant did not generate more than 20,000 kw in 1927[52] or about seven times the cost per kilowatt of capacity constructed at the Zages project.[53]

The world-famous 650,000 h.p. Dniepr project, supervised by Col. Cooper, builder of Muscle Shoals in the United States, used four 80,000 h.p. turbines manufactured by the Newport News Shipbuilding and Drydock Company, linked with vertical 77,500 kw. General Electric design generators. The total

[47] Emegess made a report to the U.S. State Dept. concerning the methods used by the Soviets to keep Col. Cooper in ignorance of the true conditions in Soviet Russia. (316–139–131.)
[48] Emegess Report. (316–139–128.)
[49] *Ibid.*
[50] *Ekonomicheskaya Zhizn*, No. 85, April 1927.
[51] *Ibid.*
[52] Klemmer, *op. cit.*, pp. 16–7.
[53] See table, p. 205.

value of $2.5 million was granted by G.E. on five-year credit terms. Cooper Company engineers were sent to Russia in the summer of 1926 to make a feasibility study for this project. They examined the prerevolutionary construction plans and the structural and geological problems of the site. In particular, they raised questions concerning labor supply, raw materials and transportation, all of which were considered inadequate for the size of the proposed project.[54]

The initial study was followed in October 1927 by the visit of Professor E. G. Alexandrov, Chairman of the Technical Council and Vice-President of Dnieprstroi, to the United States, where he visited construction machinery plants and raw material supply and water power projects. He especially noted operating principles and types of materials used. Alexandrov expressed the hope that the 'best methods' could be applied at Dnieprstroi. By this time some $1.5 million in equipment orders had been placed in the United States for Dniepr. This equipment included dump trucks, steam shovels, pneumatic drills, forges, and similar construction items. Credit terms obtained varied between one to one and a half years.[55]

A construction agreement was then made with both the Cooper Company and Siemens A-G of Germany to undertake supervision of the dam construction. Cooper reported on the project to the American section of the All Union Western Chamber of Commerce which was a Soviet institution with functions rather different from those of Western chambers of commerce. The dam was to be considerably larger than any existing dam in the world, exceeding in volume the Nile Dam by 18 percent and the Wilson (Hoover) Dam by 10 percent. The electric power station was designed to yield 2.5 billion kwh at a cost equivalent to this supply of electrical energy in the United States. As *Ekonomicheskaya Zhizn* phrased the goal, 'The United States is a country in which electrical energy is used wherever possible. The U.S.S.R. must also become such a country.'[56] The ultimate capacity was designed to be 650,000 h.p. The dam itself was 51 meters high and 720 meters across. The first five generating sets, each with Francis-type turbines and 77,500 kw. generators as well as the outdoor equipment (transformers, oil circuit breakers, switchboards, etc.) were manufactured and installed by General Electric. Equipment used in construction was imported from the United States and Germany. Two massive stonecrushers were specially made in Germany. Even the equipment for the dining halls, to seat 2,000 workers at one time, was imported. The only purely Soviet work traced was the longer of the two bridges which were built

[54] *Pravda* (Moscow), No. 171, July 28, 1926.
[55] *Ekonomicheskaya Zhizn*, No. 237, October 16, 1927.
[56] *Ekonomicheskaya Zhizn*, No. 215, September 15, 1928.

Table 11–6 TECHNICAL ASSISTANCE AND EQUIPMENT
SUPPLY IN THE GOELRO PROGRAM, 1920–30

Project	Consultants/Supervisors on Dam/Plant Construction	Equipment Supply Generators and Transformers	Turbines/Boilers
Svir	J.G. White Engineering Co. J. Cooper Inc. Karlsrads Mechaniska A/B Vattenbyggnadsbyran A/B	Metropolitan-Vickers Electrosila (with General Electric assistance)	Werkstaden-Kristinegamm A/B
Volkhov	A.S.E.A.	4 A.S.E.A. 4 Electrosila	A.S.E.A. Metropolitan-Vickers
Nizhni-Novgorod	Thomson-Houston (U.K.)	Metropolitan-Vickers	*
Dniepr	H. Cooper Company Siemens A-G	5 General Electric 4 Electrosila (General Electric assistance)	9 Newport News
Shatura	Metropolitan-Vickers	Brown-Boveri Erste Brun. Maschinen Fabrik (Czechoslovakia)	Brown-Boveri
Shterovka	(under construction 1930)	Metropolitan-Vickers	Metropolitan-Vickers
Zages	**	Electrosila (General Electric assistance)	—
Ivanovo-Voznessensk (Ivgres)	Krupp	Metropolitan-Vickers	Metropolitan-Vickers
Moges		Metropolitan-Vickers, General Electric	Metropolitan-Vickers
Chelyabinsk		Metropolitan-Vickers, General Electric	Metropolitan-Vickers
Zuevka	(under construction 1930)	Metropolitan-Vickers	Metropolitan-Vickers
Zlatoust		Metropolitan-Vickers, Westinghouse, General Electric	Metropolitan-Vickers
Nigres (Gorki)		Metropolitan-Vickers, General Electric	Metropolitan-Vickers
Baku (Krassnya Zveska)		Metropolitan-Vickers	Metropolitan-Vickers
Belovo		Unknown	Metropolitan-Vickers
Orekhovo		Metropolitan-Vickers	Metropolitan-Vickers
Saratov		Unknown	Rateau(France)

Sources: 1. 'A Portfolio of Russian Progress,' *Monogram*, November 1943.
2. INRA, *op. cit.*
3. A. Monkhouse, *Moscow 1911–1933* (Boston: Little, Brown and Co. 1934).
4. J. Dummerlee, *op. cit.*
5. *Wrecking Activities at Power Stations in the Soviet Union* (Moscow: State Law Publishing House, 1933).
6. Klemmer Reports, U.S. State Dept., Archives.

* A German firm, name unknown.
** 'Foreign consultants,' INRA, *op. cit.*, p. 276.

over the Dniepr; this was of short-span construction and, according to Scheffer, 'entirely Russian work.'[57]

The Zemo-Avtchalin hydroelectric development (Zages) at Tiflis, in the Caucasus, was begun in 1922 and completed in 1927. The project engineer was Russian (Melik-Pashaev) and the supervising engineer Armenian (Chichinadze), but 'foreign consultants' were used in some stages.[58] The station developed a useful capacity of 40,000 kw, compared to 60,000 kw at Volkhov, and an annual output of 150 million kw hours, compared to 225 million kw hours at Volkhov.[59] Four turbo-generators were manufactured at the Stalin plant (formerly Petrograd Metal) with German assistance and by Electrosila with assistance from A.S.E.A. Cost of construction was 21 million rubles: well in excess of the original estimate of 6.9 million rubles but substantially cheaper than Volkhov both in terms of cost of construction per kw of capacity and per kw hour of electricity produced. (See table 11–7.)

Table 11–7   COMPARATIVE CONSTRUCTION COST AND
ENERGY COST AT THE VOLKHOV AND ZAGES PROJECTS, 1927

	Volkhov	*Zages*
Comparative cost per kw of capacity	1,250 rubles*	500 rubles
Cost per kw hour	3.5 kopecks	1.3 kopecks

Source: Ekonomicheskaya Zhizn, No. 143, July 1927.
* Klemmer put the Volkhov capacity at 20,000 kw (useful) in 1927; on this assumption construction cost would be 3,750 rubles per kw capacity.

The textile complex at Ivanovo-Voznessensk, claimed as the largest in the world, had a peat-burning power station erected by Krupp.[60] The status of the other projects is listed in table 11–6.

A few large foreign companies undertook the greater part of the construction, installation, and equipment of these power stations. Metropolitan-Vickers obtained the lion's share of the work. A list of the most important orders received by the company in this period includes three turbo-alternator sets for Krasny Oktiabr (Leningrad), two of which were 45,000 kw units; all the switchgear and transformers for Shatura and Nizhni-Novgorod; large-capacity

---

[57]   P. Scheffer, *op. cit.,* p. 99. Foreign assistance and equipment were so commonplace that any purely Russian project at this time was usually noted as being exceptional and therefore worthy of recording.

[58]   *INRA,* p. 276.

[59]   *Ekonomicheskaya Zhizn,* No. 143, July 1927. Another Soviet source suggests this station had a smaller capacity and was started before the Soviet occupation of the Caucasus and completed in 1925. (*Annuaire,* p. 255.)

[60]   P. Scheffer, 'Aus dem Textilbezirk von Ivanovo-Voznessensk,' *Berliner Tageblatt,* June 22, 1929.

turbo-generators for Moges (Moscow), Baku, Chelyabinsk, and Ivanovo-Voznessensk; medium-capacity generators for Shterovka and the Third Cotton Trust; smaller-capacity turbo-generators for Irkutsk, Novo-Sibirsk, and others; and all the switchgear equipment for Volkhov, the oil-well electrification program for the Baku area, and the Moscow-Mytishe electric railway.[61] To give a comparative estimate of the importance of the Metropolitan-Vickers contribution, the turbo-generators supplied for the Krasny Oktiabr plant, in themselves only part of the generating equipment, equaled the total generator capacity already produced in the U.S.S.R. at the time (90,000 kw versus 92,600 kw); and Metropolitan-Vickers was only one of a number of foreign firms supplying similar equipment. Further the existing generator capacity of the U.S.S.R. was all being produced with foreign technical assistance.

In brief, all electric energy stations built in this period, whether coal, peat or hydroelectric, were based on Western technology. Station equipment was either supplied directly from abroad or, if of Soviet construction, was built in a plant with Type III technical assistance. The Svir, Shatora, Shterovka, and Ivanovo plants, for example, utilized generators built abroad and installed by Western engineers in the Soviet Union. Volkhov and Dniepr used generators made abroad and in the U.S.S.R. Similarly, turbines were either manufactured abroad or in Soviet plants with Type III technical-assistance agreements. A larger selection of foreign companies was utilized in this area of technology: Werkstaden-Kristinegamm and A.S.E.A. of Sweden, Newport News and General Electric of the United States, Krupp of Germany, Metropolitan-Vickers of the United Kingdom and Brown-Boveri Company of Switzerland.

THE PROCESS OF HYDROELECTRIC TECHNOLOGY ACQUISITION

In 1925 the Leningrad Metal Plant manufactured a 4,500 h.p. hydraulic turbine for the Zages project. This was the first turbine produced after the Bolshevik Revolution, and a copy of three turbines imported for the purpose from Germany.[62] In the following year the plant produced a second turbine: a 1,500 h.p. unit for the Leninaken hydro project in Armenia. These were produced with A.E.G. technical assistance. In 1927 an agreement was made to construct Metropolitan-Vickers turbines under license and with United Kingdom technical assistance; thus 'the manufacture of big Francis turbines (for the Dzoraget and Rion stations) was mastered in the course of 1927–30.'[63]

---

[61] *Bank for Russian Trade Review*, March 1929, p. 15.
[62] *INRA*, p. 276.
[63] *Ibid.*

In 1927 the Electrosila plant in Leningrad (formerly Siemens A-G) manufactured four vertical generators for the Zages project: the first ever produced in the Soviet Union. This was followed by an order for four generators for the Volkhov project. These to be coupled with four Swedish made A.S.E.A. generators. There was a further order for four generators for the Dniepr project, to be coupled with five General Electric generators. Electrosila had assistance agreements with A.S.E.A. and the International General Electric.

The acquisition process is now clear. There was a primary stage when generators and turbines were both imported and installed by foreign engineers. This was succeeded by the acquisition of foreign technical assistance and by the use of plants inherited from the tsarist era. A specific technology was established with imported equipment and technical designing, supervisory, and engineering skills. Orders for capital equipment to modernize the plants of the electrical trusts were dependent upon the granting of technical-assistance contracts. Normally the Western company was glad to donate the technical-assistance aspects to acquire the order for the major installation.

Substitution of domestically produced machinery for imported machinery then followed. In hydroelectric projects, several installations utilized both equipment manufactured abroad and equipment domestically produced with foreign assistance. The technical advantages were dubious, but the educational aspects were undeniable. Comparative data on operating performance was generated and found useful as a check on the efficiency of domestic production. The final stage was reached when only domestically produced equipment was used, with or without foreign assistance. In hydroelectric projects this did not occur in the 1920s.

Concurrent with the progress of import substitution, there was increasing technical sophistication. Manufacture shifted from the small and simple to the complex and large. The 'gigantomania' of the 1930s was an uncontrolled technical escalation of this nature. There is nothing in Marxist theory, in the absence of the discipline of the market place or a theory of production and diminishing returns, which dictates a cut-off point for either complexity or size. By definition, the largest and the most complex is always the most efficient, and only in the last few years has the assumption been challenged in Soviet technico-economic literature. By the same measure we would expect to see a degree of over-engineering in Soviet design. In the 1920s it was much too early to see the flowering of this phenomenon, but the politico-economic structure established in this period was destined to move Soviet industry along this road. Volumes II and III will pick up and trace the threads from this inauspicious starting point.

It is also interesting to note that many of the associations described here for the 1920s have continued uninterrupted to the present date. Karlsrads Mechaniska Werkstad A/B had a contract for the Svir project in 1923. In 1963 the same company completed a paper mill, and in 1964 a pulp mill. This long-term association is not at all uncommon. The transfer process is still underway.

CHAPTER TWELVE

The Chemical, Compressed Gas, and Dye Industries

NITROGEN FIXATION: BASIS OF A CHEMICAL INDUSTRY

THE immediate chemical industry problem in 1921 was synthesis of ammonia from the elements: i.e., nitrogen fixation. This would eliminate use of Chilean saltpeter and facilitate production of calcium cyanamide needed for the manufacture of ammonia and cyano compounds.[1]

In 1921 V. I. Ipatieff, Chairman of the Chemical Committee of Vesenkha, made an extended trip through Europe to investigate purchase of these processes for use in the U.S.S.R. He found the best available process was owned by I. G. Farben of Germany, who would not sell or grant a license to manufacture in the Soviet Union. The remaining alternative was to install plants for production of calcium cyanamide to produce fertilizer in peacetime and ammonia and nitric acid in wartime. Ipatieff investigated several processes, including those of Bayerische Stickstoff Werke in Germany, but was denied access to the best-known plant, the nitrogen fixation plant at Oslo, Norway.[2]

A Commission on Fixation of Nitrogen was then organized and all available foreign literature acquired. Research was started, not to develop a nitrogen fixation process, but to determine which of the foreign processes was the best. Domestic production of ammonia was recognized as the key problem, with special significance for military purposes, and this was taken up by both the War Technical Administration of Vesenkha and the Chemical Branch of Gosplan.

The manufacture of nitric acid, also dependent on ammonia technology, had also been ignored. This was a major gap in Soviet industry—particularly

---

[1] V. I. Ipatieff, *Life of a Chemist* (Stanford: Stanford University Press, 1946), pp. 327–8. Ipatieff fled Soviet Russia and left us a first-hand account of the chemical industry in tsarist and Soviet Russia. The Gumberg Papers at the State Historical Society in Madison, Wisconsin, also contain data on Chemstroi.

[2] *Ibid.*, p. 379.

Chart 12–1   THE TRANSFER OF NITROGEN INDUSTRY
TECHNOLOGY TO THE U.S.S.R.

PROCESSES

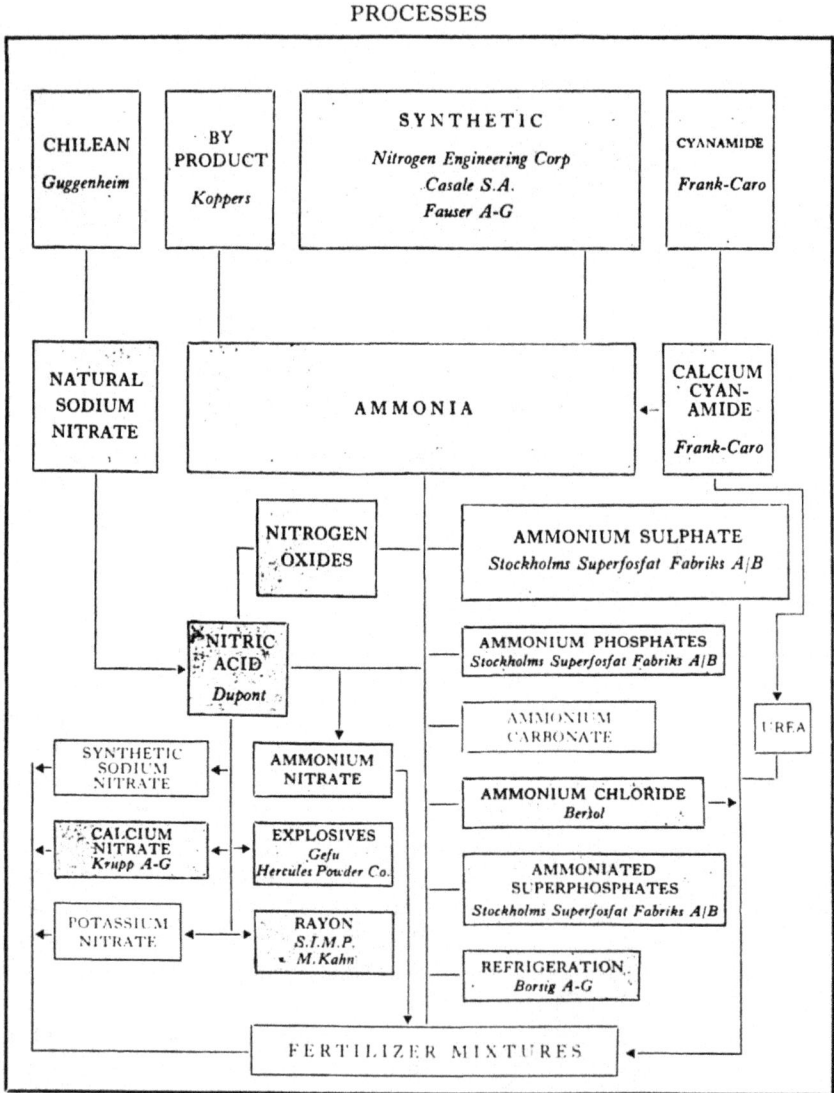

Technology transferred from the West between 1917 and 1930.

Source: Based on United States Tariff Commission, Report No. 114, Second Series.
Chemical Nitrogen (Washington D.C. 1937). With data from text of chapter
added.

in the military sector (nitric acid is an essential ingredient in explosives manufacture). The three available synthetic ammonia processes available were the Cloudt in France and the Casale and Fauser in Italy. Ipatieff selected the Casale process as the most suitable; it was not too expensive and a small plant (20,000 tons per year) could be readily installed. A Soviet commission was dispatched to Italy; the final arrangement was for a 16,000-ton-capacity plant built by the Italian company at Dzerdjinsky in 1927. Russian engineers were trained at Casale Ammonia S-A in Italy, and Italian engineers built and initially operated the Dzerdjinsky plant. Essentially the only differences from the I. G. Farben process, which had been refused, were in the type of catalyst and the operating pressures used.

For a solution to the calcium cyanamide problem, Ipatieff visited Bayerische Stickstoff Werke and Borsig A-G in Germany and the Superfosfat A/B in Sweden. The Swedish method, obtainable on more advantageous terms, was adopted, and several plants were ordered from Sweden. This was the basis of the Soviet superphosphate industry.[3]

SYNTHETIC PRODUCTION OF AMMONIA IN THE UNITED STATES[4]

The technical revolution brought about by synthetic ammonia was felt throughout the heavy chemical and allied industries, from agriculture to explosives. The opening of a single synthetic ammonia plant in Niagara Falls utilizing an atmospheric nitrogen process cut the price of ammonia by 50 percent in one week. Cheaper ammonia stimulated development of refrigeration, established effective competition against the Chilean saltpeter monopoly, replaced sodium nitrate in the chamber process for the manufacture of sulphuric acid, and introduced an entirely new method of nitric acid production.

Several synthetic ammonia processes were developed simultaneously in Europe and the United States. General Chemical, a subsidiary of Allied Chemical and Dye, spent between $4.5 and $5 million on research and development of the Haber process, followed by an investment of $125 million in the Hopewell plant, opened in 1928. The Mathieson plant, using the Nitrogen Engineering process, was built in 1921 and followed by another in Niagara Falls using the Casale process, built by Ammonia Corporation of New York. In 1924 Dupont acquired American rights to the Claude process and in 1927 acquired American rights to the Casale process and then proceeded to improve both processes. At the end of the decade the effectively competing

[3]   *Ibid.*, p. 426–8.
[4]   Based on W. Haynes, *American Chemical Industry* (New York: Van Nostrand, 1948), IV, 85.

processes in the United States were those of the Dupont Company (Claude-Casale) and the Nitrogen Engineering Corporation (Haber-Bosch). It was not until 1936, after the expenditure of more than $24 million on development of synthetic ammonia, that net operating results began to show a profit.

It was American technical ingenuity and originality in developing techniques for handling very great pressures and temperatures which enabled successful replacement of early methods of ammonia manufacture and introduction of a much cheaper method. Research was partly financed by the Army Ordnance Department, the Department of Agriculture, and a special Congressional appropriation of $185,000.[5] The value of the developed technology is suggested by the payment of $1.25 million for Japanese and Chinese rights to the Claude process. The reader may compare this figure to the $150,000 received from the Soviet Union for similar rights.[6]

MANUFACTURE OF NITRIC ACID AND THE DUPONT COMPANY

There was a small production of nitric acid in tsarist Russia. In 1920 eight small plants produced 360 tons per year. During the 1920s major technical advances were made in the West, and by the end of the decade three companies were offering nitrogen fixation processes for the manufacture of nitric acid.

The Soviets found themselves in an excellent bargaining position. Dupont, Nitrogen Engineering, and the Casale Company were competing suppliers with more or less equivalent processes. The Soviets used their monopsonistic power to drive prices down from opportunity costs (probably well in excess of $100 million when one considers the absence of input suppliers in the U.S.S.R.) to a mere $150,000—the price ultimately paid to the Dupont Company after a number of such plants had been erected. Only if the three Western owners of fixation processes had merged into a joint bargaining unit could the price extracted from the U.S.S.R. have approached Soviet opportunity costs. It appears that from the strictly technical viewpoint the Dupont process had a slight competitive product edge by virtue of the 120 lb.-per-square-inch pressure used, but this was insufficient to offset Soviet buying power.[7]

In early 1929, negotiations began between Chemstroi and Dupont concerning the sale of their ammonia oxidation process and nitric acid technology. Dupont had expended over $27 million developing the process.[8] This was in addition to the substantial investment made by the earlier French and Italian

[5]   *Ibid.*, p. 90.
[6]   See page 213.
[7]   F. D. Miles, *Nitric Acid; Manufacture and Uses* (London: Oxford University Press, 1961), p. 34.
[8]   *Dupont: The Autobiography of an American Enterprise* (Wilmington: Dupont, 1952), p. 95.

owners of the process. To attempt to recoup anything like this amount from the Soviets would have been naïve; there were other processes available and the alternative always existed that the Soviets could develop the process themselves. For Dupont, any return over marginal cost of supplying the process was advantageous. However, marginal costs were zero as, according to the agreement, the U.S.S.R. paid the expenses of both the Soviet and the Dupont engineers. Consequently the $150,000 fee to Dupont was a return on research and development investment and a 'windfall' gain to the Dupont Company.

In requesting advice from the State Department, the Dupont concern argued that the process was neither secret nor covered by patents, that the end use of nitric acid is the manufacture of fertilizer, although it is the basic fundamental raw material for dyes, celluloid, photographic materials, medicine and artificial silk.[9] Dupont argued that if they did not supply the process it could be bought elsewhere, and that several plants had already been erected in the U.S.S.R. by Casale and Nitrogen Engineering of New York. Further, the company argued that there was nothing exclusive about the Dupont process: 'Our superiority . . . is based entirely upon the economic advantages of our engineering design.'[10]

The copy of the agreement from the State Department files indicates that Chemstroi

> . . . (wishes) to use in Russia the Dupont process for the oxidation of ammonia and to place at its disposal sufficient data with respect to the design, construction and general information as to permit the satisfactory operation of such plants . . . the Company shall serve the Russian Corporation in an advisory capacity and furnish upon request services of engineers and chemists so as to accomplish the purpose of the contract.

The agreement further stipulated that Chemstroi might use the Dupont processes for the oxidation of ammonia to manufacture 50–65 percent nitric acid and that Dupont agrees

> . . . to place at the disposal of Chemstroi sufficient data, information and facts with respect to the design, construction and operation of such plants as will enable Chemstroi to design, construct and operate ammonia oxidation plants. . . .

---

[9]   In 1927 more than two-thirds of U.S. nitric acid was being used for explosives. Dupont said the acid was 'too weak' for explosives manufacture. However, the State Dept. appears to have accepted this rather surprising statement.

[10]   Letter from Dupont to U.S. State Dept. (316–139–572). The Dupont-Chemstroi agreement is in the U.S. State Dept. Decimal File, 316–139–570. This agreement is well worth reading from one viewpoint alone: the remarkable two-facedness of the Soviets. They can call themselves a 'Russian Corporation,' etc., to give the Western company the impression it is dealing with fellow businessmen, and then present the Dupont work as a 'feat of socialist construction.'

Dupont was therefore to act in an advisory capacity in the construction and initial operation of all such plants. The fee for the use of the process was $10 per metric ton of yearly rated capacity for the first plant and $10 per ton on subsequent plants, until the total fee was $50,000. In addition, a flat fee of $25,000 per plant was payable until the total fees paid amounted to $150,000. As has been pointed out, this was rational profit-maximizing action for Dupont, but hardly for the Western world.

Chemstroi was allowed to request reasonable services of Dupont engineers and chemists, their salaries and expenses to be paid by Chemstroi. In the case of the first plant Dupont provided construction engineers and chemical engineers to build and start up the plant and train sufficient local personnel to continue operations. In all, five such plants were built. Permission was granted by Dupont to enable Chemstroi to pass on the technical information to other state organizations (a similar request caused R.C.A. some amusement; their patents and processes were being sequestered either way).[11] In addition, Dupont agreed to accept Chemstroi engineers and technicians in their United States plants for training.

Table 12-1   SOVIET ACQUISITION OF BASIC CHEMICAL
TECHNOLOGIES, 1925–30

Technology	*Western Process*	*Soviet Plant*
Nitrogen fixation	Nitrogen Engineering Corp (modified Haber-Bosch)	Berezniki (1929–1932)
	Nitrogen Engineering Corp (modified Haber-Bosch)	Bobriki (1929–1932)
	Casale Ammonia S-A. (Italy)	Dzerdjinski (1927)
	Fauser (Italy)	Gorlovka (1930)
Calcium cynamide	Stockholms Superfosfat Fabriks A/B (Sweden)	Karakliss
Nitric acid	Dupont Company	Five plants (one erected before 1930)
Sulphuric acid	Bersol (Russo-German Company)	Samara
	Hugo Petersen (Berlin)	N.A.
	Lurgie Gesellschaft fur Chemie und Hüttenwesen m.b.H.	Technical assistance

Sources: 1. V. I. Ipatieff, *op. cit.*
2. U.S. State Dept. Archives.
3. German Foreign Ministry Archives.

The first Dupont plant for nitric acid was built at Chernorechenski, near Gorky. The capacity of the combine was 115,000 tons of superphosphates a year and included plants for the manufacture of ammono-phosphates, calcium carbide, cynamide, and nitric and sulphuric acids. Alcan Hirsch, a New York

[11] See below, page 300, n. 18.

consultant, was chief engineer for Chemstroi and supervised construction of the combine by Western companies. Hirsch comments that the nitric acid plant was built according to the Dupont specifications and 'incorporates apparatus made of nickel-chromium steel and all the equipment is of American manufacture throughout.'[12]

As has been pointed out, 'turn-key' purchases were also made from Dupont's competitors, so that the Soviets ended up in a better position-than any of their suppliers independently. They had the sum of Western technical experience within two to three years of perfection of that process. In other words, the Soviet Union was able to acquire a greater knowledge of the processes involved in nitrogen fixation, nitric acid production, and other areas by expending a microscopic amount of money. An agreement covering the production of ammonia from coke was made with Nitrogen Engineering of New York, and another contract with the same company covered construction of a $10 million synthetic ammonia plant. Yet another contract with NEC established a ten-year technical-assistance agreement for all NEC-Haber-Bosch technology.[13]

SOLIKAMSK POTASH DEPOSITS

Phosphatic fertilizers, either from bones or from phosphate rock, were not produced in any quantity in prerevolutionary Russia. Nutter gives a total of only 55,000 tons for 1913. Toward the end of the 1920s, production of both natural and rock phosphate fertilizer jumped substantially to a total of 484,000 tons.

The substantial increase in natural phosphate output in 1929–30 may well be associated with the kulak extermination program and massive slaughter of cattle. Natural phosphate is bone meal.

Increase in rock phosphate output stems partly from development of the Khibini apatite deposits on the Kola peninsula. These deposits of apatite-nepheline contain about 28–32 percent phosphoric acid. One of the major

12 Alcan Hirsch, *Industrialized Russia* (New York: Chemical Catalog Company 1934), p. 83. This phrase has a much deeper implication than first reading might convey. Let the reader ask the question, which plants in the U.S.S.R. were able to produce stainless (i.e., nickel-chrome) steels in 1927? There was one, and that used the old hand-mill process and was unable to turn out the larger sheets of very different quality used in chemical engineering. In other words, if the apparatus had been denied, the Soviets would first have had to acquire a stainless steel production unit.
Alcan Hirsch was a most effective agent for the transfer of chemical engineering technology. He was quite sympathetic to the aims of the Bolshevik Revolution. After the extermination of the kulaks, the show trials, and the forced labor construction of industry (all of which he witnessed) he could still write in 1934: 'Soviet Russia has not as yet reached unprecedented eminence in the arts, science or industry although I believe that sociologically it is far ahead of the rest of the world.' (P. 273.)
13 Vneshtorgizdat, *op. cit.*, p. 226; and Hirsch, *op. cit.*, p. 78.

technical difficulties in initial development was presence of nepheline, which had to be separated out. A concentrating and refining plant was built, with a capacity of 250,000 tons of apatite concentrates per year (more than the increase in output from 1928–9 to 1929–30). The presence of nepheline was overcome by a flotation process, utilized by the first such nepheline treatment plant in the world, designed and built by General Engineering Company of Denver and utilizing all United States equipment. The by-product nepheline was used in the manufacture of glass, ceramic wares, pottery, porcelain, and electrical insulators. In brief, the by-product became useful in many other industries, all with their own technical-assistance agreements with foreign firms.[14]

In 1924 there was a production crisis in the largest potash production operation, Kubtrestpotash, which badly missed its production targets although the 'mixed' trading company Wostwag had an agreement to take its complete output for export.[15] Two years later, prospectors found extensive deposits of potash (sylvanite and carnallite) in the Solikamsk district while drilling for oil.[16] It was decided by Vesenkha to favor development of Solikamsk over Kuban. The report of the prospecting expedition found its way from the Geological Committee of Vesenkha to the State Department in Washington, D.C.[17] The deposit was offered as a concession to Lyman Brown, previously American Relief Administrator in Russia. He operated on the fringes of concession-promotion of Soviet opportunities. By August 1927, Dillon, Read and Company was in process of raising $30 million to finance the development of Solikamsk and an associated chemical combine and oil pipe line. The fund-raising was killed by unilateral action on the part of the State Department; the Soviets then decided to start development with their own resources, utilizing Western skills under Type III assistance agreements.

A potash trust was formed and an agreement concluded with the German company, Deilmann Bergbau und Tiefbau Gesellschaft, of Dortmund, to design the mine and plant at Solikamsk.[18] The resultant Berezniki-Solikamsk complex included a salt refinery to produce 160,000 tons of stone salt annually,

[14] Amtorg, *op. cit.*, IV, No. 6, p. 110.

[15] *Ekonomicheskaya Zhizn*, No. 115, February 19, 1924.

[16] Much was made in the Soviet press about this oil-potash discovery (see *Torgovo-Promyshlennaya Gazeta*, No. 99, pp. 107–9 and 118, for 1929). This was, however, an extension of a field developed before 1917 (See A. A. Trofimuk, *Uralo-Povolzhe-novaya neftiania baza S.S.S.R.* (Moscow: Gostoptekhizdat, 1957), pp. 144–5.

[17] The 31-page Provisional Report includes the drill core logs. These suggest a very substantial deposit of potash salt (316–138–352). The Soviets must have needed Western technology badly in this area, to allow out the drill logs. At about the same time they sentenced the representatives of a Swedish company to eight years in jail just for making a market survey of dairy equipment requirements.

[18] Vneshtorgizdat, *op. cit.*, p. 22.

a plant to procure 1.2 million tons of potash, chemical plants to utilize the potash, a brick plant, and other industries. Two shafts were planned for the mine: one was sunk by the trust to a shaft depth of 35 meters, and the main shaft was sunk to 260 meters by the German company, Gefrierschachbau, using freezing methods of sinking. The nature of the overburden required use of methods beyond Soviet capabilities at the time.[19] The degree of technical uncertainty felt by the Soviets is probably indicated by the fact that one year after development was started the project was still being offered as a concession. The program finally involved some thirty German engineers. The first mine, with a capacity of 1.5 million tons of ore, and the first concentrator, with a capacity of 1.2 million tons, were completed in 1933.

MANUFACTURE OF SULPHURIC ACID

Sulphuric acid capacity was modernized with the help of German firms. Lurgie Gesellschaft für Chemie und Hüttenwersen m.b., of Frankfurt, provided assistance for construction of a sulphuric acid plant with a daily capacity of 80 tons of monohydrate. The company also provided equipment and started operations for the Soviets. General technical assistance for sulphuric acid production was provided under another agreement, with Hugo Petersen, of Berlin.[20]

Bersol (the Russo-German company) was primarily interested in development of poison gas facilities, but was also instrumental in establishing factories for production of potassium chloride, sulphuric acid, superphosphates, and other chemicals.[21]

Development of an acids capacity is an essential prerequisite to plastics production. While nitric and sulphuric acid production was under development, moves were being made to acquire a plastics base. *Ekonomicheskaya Zhizn* of November 30, 1926, reported that a concession agreement had been signed with Société Industrielle de Matières Plastiques (S.I.M.P.) for production of cinema and photographic film and articles made from celluloid. S.I.M.P. was granted a factory at Podmoskovnia, just outside Moscow. The French company repaired this facility and started production in 1927. This was followed by a joint American-German concession in early 1928, under which a plant was built to produce noninflammable film, artificial silk, and also paper, utilizing a patented process based on the use of corn stalks. The German participant was Deutsche-Russische Film Allianz A-G (Derufa), and the American was the Euroamerican Cellulose Products Corporation of New

[19] *Ekonomicheskaya Zhizn*, No. 86, April 11, 1928; and A. Hirsch, *op. cit.*, p. 64.
[20] Vneshtorgizdat, *op. cit.*, p. 228.
[21] Troyanovsky, *op. cit.*, p. 836.

York, represented by Montifiore Kahn (not the Albert Kahn firm with Vesenkha agreements).[22] The patents were held by the New York firm which 'thought it best' not to enter directly, but through German intermediaries. Investment amounted to $1.5 million, but little is known of the process itself.[23]

COKE OVEN BY-PRODUCTS

The Russian chemical industry was not insignificant in size before the Revolution. The production of coke oven by-products, an important source of chemicals, was well developed in tsarist times. Table 12–2 compares 1914 production of by-products with 1915 and 1926.

Table 12-2   COKE OVEN BY-PRODUCTS, 1914, 1915, AND 1926

	1914	*1915* (*Metric tons*)	*1926*
Tar	486,700	529,000	645
Ammonia water	197,300	209,800	0
Ammonium sulphate	169,000	117,230	0
Sal ammonia	64	196	0
Benzol	767	49,230	145
Oils	145,640	200,300	0
Goudron	201,700	248,300	0

Source: Quoted by J. Douillet, *Moscow Unmasked* (London: Pilot, 1930), pp. 47–8. Douillet had been Belgian Consul in Moscow and obtained the data from a Belgian engineer with personal working knowledge of the Russian coke by-product industry before and after the Revolution.

In 1914 production was substantial in both tar and ammonium sulphate. The war affected different branches of the industry differently. Tar output increased, while that of fertilizers decreased. The industry completely collapsed in the early 1920s and the Soviets were unable to restore production even by 1926. The only plant operating in the first few years of the decade was the Enakievo Coke Benzol Works, formerly owned by the Russo-Belgian Company. In 1921 John Reed, the noted American Communist, organized 300 unskilled American workers, to whom Lenin donated a coke benzene plant to operate:

> A year afterward the Chemical Administration sent a Commission of engineers to report on the coke-benzene plant. Atrocious conditions were uncovered, and the ovens were found to be badly damaged. The workers were soon returned to the United States. . . .[24]

[22]   U.S. State Dept. Decimal File, 316–139–562.
[23]   *Berliner Tageblatt*, April 28, 1928. It may be noted that the use of German intermediaries was a common practice among American firms at this time, no doubt to avoid adverse publicity in the United States.
[24]   V. N. Ipatieff, *op. cit.*, p. 322.

Then for a period of some years no attempt was made to utilize coke by-products, officially because Koksobenzol and Ukrchim questioned the right of the Central Coal Industry management to concern itself with these products. Nothing was done while the dispute was in progress.[25] The coke-benzol industry was finally grouped under Koksobenzol. Of the twenty-two by-products plants incorporated into the trust, fifteen were fully equipped and had an annual aggregate capacity of 16,000 tons of benzol. Output in 1926 was a mere 145 metric tons. Before the Revolution, Russian coking had been dependent on foreign coke-oven technology. The Donbas ovens installed before World War I consisted only of Coppe and Piette systems.[26] Although about 800 ovens were available, output of coke was only 9,800 metric tons for 1920, compared to 4.3 million metric tons in 1913. By 1922 output recovered slightly to 110,000 and in 1923 to 130,000 metric tons. This enabled some attention to be placed on by-product recovery.[27] This recovery was brought about as coal supplies found their way once again to the ovens, but still only 4 percent of ovens were in production.[28]

THE RUSSIAN-AMERICAN COMPRESSED GAS COMPANY (RAGAZ)

Ragaz was a joint-stock company organized in January 1926 by the International Oxygen Company of New Jersey and the Soviet Metalosindikat for development of industrial gases in the U.S.S.R. Both parties held an equal share, and it was agreed that the concession would last until 1941. It was taken over by the Soviets in 1932.

Seven plants were established by Ragaz for manufacture of oxygen and acetylene for industrial uses. This included locations in Moscow (Rostokin), Sverdlovsk, Rostov on Don, and Baku. In addition, some seventeen welding plants, three acetylene gas generating plants, and two special schools for training welders were established at various points throughout the U.S.S.R.

The Moscow plant was opened in April 1927 and combined a special school with facilities for production of oxygen and acetylene. The second plant, which manufactured oxygen only, opened at Rostov in April 1928. The others followed. The Ragaz company also held the contract for the welding the Baku-Batoum and Grozny-Tuapse pipelines built between 1926 and 1929—the only pipelines built in the U.S.S.R. in this period.

---

[25]   *Ibid.*, p. 288.
[26]   Coppe ovens were at Petrovsky, Mariupol, Donetz-Urevsky, Taganrog, and Stalino. Piette ovens were at the Providence works. (316-131-949.)
[27]   *Coal Age,* January 8, 1925, p. 47.
[28]   Polish Foreign Ministry Report. (316-107-1262.)

In 1928 Ragaz produced 345,000 cubic meters of oxygen and 66,500 cubic meters of acetylene, and one year later 500,000 cubic meters of oxygen and 77,000 cubic meters of acetylene—the total Russian production. After the manufacture of industrial gases and the establishment of welding schools, the next problem was manufacture of welding equipment to replace imports. This was done under a technical-assistance agreement in 1929 with a German company, Messer A-G, of Frankfurt, specialists in the development of automatic welding equipment.[29] and later with technical assistance from General Electric for more advanced forms of welding equipment.[30]

BASIC AND INTERMEDIATE DYES

Imported dyes came exclusively from I. G. Farben, under an arrangement made in 1922 by a joint German-Russian commission containing I. G. Farben representatives. The latter agreed to maintain a warehouse in the U.S.S.R. and to import dyestuffs through Russgertorg (the mixed trading company). The commission also undertook to arrange for production of dyes through a jointly owned subsidiary—Igerussko. In return, the Soviets agreed to buy I. G. Farben products up to 70 percent of requirements of all coal tar dyes and medicines. The arrangement lasted until 1929. It was hardly profitable for the Soviets—only four intermediate dyes were manufactured by Igerussko, and the impression is gained that I. G. Farben was rather uncooperative. In return for a guarantee of gross sales, I. G. Farben was supposed to provide technical assistance also to the chemical and pharmaceutical industries. The agreement was not renewed. The Soviets complained they had not received any technical assistance, and the Farben company charged it had not received the agreed share of the Russian market.[31] There is a distinct possibility that I. G. Farben was shortchanged, as the Soviets made another dye agreement in 1924, a couple of years after the I. G. Farben agreement.

Before the Revolution, the German firm of Berger and Wirth A-G operated a large dye, ink, and paint manufacturing plant in Petrograd. This plant remained closed until 1924, although it was largely undamaged and nominally part of the Chemical Trust.[32] In February 1924, Berger and Wirth received a Type I concession agreement to reopen and modernize its old plant. The company was required to install new equipment. During the second year, a production level of 390 tons of dyestuffs was required, and in the third year 30,000 poods of printing inks, dyes, varnish, and paint. All technical advances

---

[29]   Vneshtorgizdat, *op. cit.*, p. 228.
[30]   *Monogram*, November 1943, p. 18.
[31]   *Bank for Russian Trade Review*, II, No. 1 (January 1929); and U.S. State Dept. Decimal File, 316–136–1421.
[32]   Report, April 13, 1923, U.S. State Dept. Decimal File, 316–108–362.

made by the company in Germany were required to be incorporated into the Russian plant. The agreement was to last for twenty-four years, at which time the plant was to revert to the Soviets in good condition. A royalty of 15,000 rubles per year plus 10 percent of sales was paid to the Soviets. Foreign workers were not allowed to exceed 20 percent of the labor force. In 1929 the company employed about 120 with an annual output of two million rubles in a new and completely mechanized plant.[33]

In 1924, when Berger and Wirth started work, the State Aniline Trust, which grouped together the prewar dye industry plants, was not in good shape. Of eight plants forming the trust, two (the Derbenevsky in Moscow and the Vladimirsky) were closed, two (the Butinsky and the Kinkshensky) were about to be closed, and four others (the Experimentaly, the Trigor, the Krasny Lutch, and the Central Laboratory) were on a heavily reduced schedule and working for the Military Trust. In 1923, just before the Berger and Wirth agreement, the trust sustained an overall loss of 876,451 rubles on a minute output. In 1913 the industry had produced 4,000 metric tons of synthetic dyes; in 1920-1 no output has been reported. There was then pressure on the Soviets to conclude a concession agreement in this sector. The opening of the Berger and Wirth plant and the implementation of the I. G. Farben technical agreement through Igerussko had an immediate impact on production.

Table 12-3   DYE PRODUCTION IN THE SOVIET UNION

Year	Production (metric tons)
1913	4,290
1920	170
1921	none
1922	none
1923/4	1,800
1924/5	n.a.
1925/6	8,290
1926/7	7,370
1927/8	10,250
1928/9	13,300
1929/30	16,790

Source: Nutter, *op. cit.*, p. 425.

By the end of the decade, the Soviets were able, with the help of I. G. Farben and Berger and Wirth, to claim legitimately a production of dyestuffs four times greater than prewar—wholly due to foreign efforts.

[33] U.S. State Dept. Decimal File, 316-139-549; and Haynes, *op. cit.*, p. 59.

Smaller concessions in this and allied fields were negotiated with the Leo Brand Company for production of cosmetics and with H. Brock for production of laboratory drying and desiccating equipment.

GLASS MANUFACTURING INDUSTRY

The earliest technical assistance in glass-making came under the Rapallo Treaty protocols involving a German group in the Kuban for production of Glauber's salts, and the processing of these sulphates for use in glass manufacture. Arsky said, ' . . . we must admit that we are quite incapable of doing this ourselves just now or even in the next ten-fifteen years,' and then realistically he added that, ' . . . the concessionaires will profit but it will bring wealth to us and we must pay for that.'[31]

The only completely modern glass-making plant built in the decade of the 1920s was the Bely Bychok plate glass works, built in 1927 and equipped with two ovens and twenty imported Fourcault-type furnaces and glass machines; the complete plant cost $3.6 million.[35] Later, in 1927, four American glass-machinery operators were hired and spent between one and two years in the U.S.S.R. They toured Soviet glass-making plants and introduced Russian workers to new American equipment as it was imported to replace the pre-revolutionary machinery.[36]

Simultaneously, a Ukrainian delegation arrived in the United States to study American glass factories. The delegation was sent by the Porcelain and Glass Trust of the Ukraine to study the application of American glass-making machines and methods to the Ukrainian industry. The delegation visited Pittsburgh, the Ohio River glass plants, Detroit, Buffalo, and Trenton, New Jersey. The delegation then announced that a large-scale plan of expansion had been worked out which involved purchase of 'considerable machinery abroad.'[37]

RESINOTREST

There was a rubber goods manufacturing industry in tsarist Russia. The important components were the Treugolnik (Triangle) plants in Moscow and Petrograd, combined by the Soviets into Resinotrest. Progress at these works and the tsarist Bogatyr, Caoutchouc, and Provodnik factories (also incorporated into Resinotrest as Rubber Manufacturing Plants Number 1, 2, and 3) went very slowly. The latter three plants employed about 10,000 in 1923,

[34] *Krasnya Gazeta*, September 3, 1921.
[35] Amtorg, *op. cit.*, II, No. 14, 5.
[36] *Ibid.*, No. 15, 5.
[37] Amtorg, *op. cit.*, II, No. 8, 2.

but were only partly in operation, producing rubber galoshes and tire canvas. The Petrograd Treugolnik plant employed about 10,000 and also produced galoshes. The essential problems were those of raw materials, skilled labor, and equipment.[38]

The Petrograd Treugolnik plant was selected for improvement and completely modernized in the mid-1920s. New activities were added, including asbestos spinning and manufacture of brake linings, yarns, packings and similar products. Its employment was boosted to 22,000 by 1928, and the company was placed under management supervision of two American consultants.[39]

The establishment of a rubber-reclaiming industry was initiated by a technical-assistance agreement between Resinotrest and the Akron Rubber Reclaiming Company in 1930.[40] The manufacture of rubber tires was initiated with the aid of the Seiberling Rubber Company, which completely outfitted a tire manufacturing plant at Yaroslavl and provided technical assistance in operations.[41]

CONCLUSIONS ON THE CHEMICAL INDUSTRY

During the decade the tsarist plants were restored and modernized and the Soviets added a new dye-manufacturing plant (built by Berger and Wirth under their concession agreement) and glass-manufacturing plant (from the United States), expanded a Treugolnik rubber plant (with American assistance), and obtained, through concession agreements, two foreign plastics operations.

The most significant items were the transfer of technology for the manufacture of synthetic ammonia, and nitric and sulphuric acids, and the creation of a compressed gas industry. The Dupont, Casale, and Nitrogen Engineering processes were transferred to the Soviet Union and formed the basis for development of chemical complexes under the so-called Five-Year Plan. These complexes were the Berezniki-Solikamsk, where the NEC synthetic ammonia plant was backed up by a Westvaco chlorine plant, and the Chernorechensky complex designed on the basis of the Dupont synthetic ammonia and nitric acid plants. A third complex was started at Bobriki (later Stalinogorsk) based on a second NEC synthetic ammonia plant.[42] Modernization of the basic chemical

---

[38] IS reported that Treugolnik 'refused' to join Resinotrest and had 'suffered accordingly' but gave no details. (316–108–408.)

[39] Ruykeyser, *op. cit.*, pp. 209–10. The engineering section was run by a German engineer, Hertwig. (316–108–415.)

[40] A. A. Santalov and L. Segal, *Soviet Union Year Book, 1930* (London: Allen and Unwin, 1930), p. 357.

[41] *Ibid.*, p. 359.

[42] Hirsch, *op. cit.*, pp. 73–85.

capacity, vital for industrialization, was essentially an achievement of foreign enterprise; once again, indigenous Soviet technology is notable for its absence. There is no trace in the engineering literature, Western or Soviet, or in archival material, of any Soviet contribution, unless the 35-meter Solikamsk shaft (which *may* have been a Soviet project) is counted as a technological contribution.

CHAPTER THIRTEEN

Clothing, Housing, and Food Concessions

THE FORMATION OF TRUSTS IN THE TEXTILE INDUSTRY

ALL large textile firms were nationalized by the decree of 1918 and management placed in the hands of a Chief Committee of the Textile Industry. The home textile industry, based on hand work but without hired labor, remained in private hands.

Available cotton spindles in 1920 totaled about seven million, but only a little more than ten percent of these were working. In the flax industry, only one quarter of 400,000 available spindles were working. Thus, although spindle capacity was about the same in 1920 as in 1912, output was very much less. This decline was the result of poor administration. Substitution of 'ignorant, sometimes unscrupulous Soviet officials' for the former owners, a labor and fuel shortage, and inability to provide food for the workers were the main causes. Rations were small and in irregular supply, and output was largely restricted by time wasted in foraging expeditions.[1]

In late 1921, the textile industry was organized in a number of trusts. These were the Tambov, comprising five factories producing coarse cloth; the Simbirsk, comprising six factories producing coarse cloth; the Moscow Trust, combining thirty-two plants in the Moscow industrial district and called also the Worsted and Finishing Trust; the Silk Knitting Trust, comprising fifteen factories; the Bogorodsk-Glukov Trust, with ten factories; the Orechovo, with ten factories; the Ivanovo-Voznessensk, with twenty-seven factories, and the Vladimir with ten cotton-spinning plants. Later the Petrograd district was organized as was the Linen Administration, comprising seven factories in the Vladimir-Kostroma provinces. Altogether, the Linen Trust comprised seventeen factories, including the large Kostroma plant.[2]

---

[1] *Wool and Textile World*, July 7, 1921.

[2] *Krasnya Gazeta*, August 24, 1921. These figures are somewhat different from those

Trustification was accompanied by the return of emigrants from the United States: usually deportees with ideological sympathies with the Revolution. In the summer of 1922, Petrograd *Pravda* reported that an 'American Department' had been organized in the Thirteenth State Clothing Factory by a group of deportees led by Comrade Summer and using methods described as the last word in efficiency, in an effort to create 'a genuinely American attitude to work.'[3] Another group of thirty-six American tailors joined the Moscow Tailoring Combine. It is interesting to note how a comparatively small group can affect a major organization:

> [they] have raised its work to such a level of efficiency that the Combine has become a model establishment . . . there are now six cutters to 150 machines, whereas formerly there were fifty cutters when hand machines were used.[4]

Demand for textiles was intensified by good harvests in the middle 1920s, but the cotton crop was insufficient to meet the demand, so that imports were necessary. In 1923–4, some 10 million poods of cotton was produced and another 8–9 million, valued at $75 million, was imported from the United States. The Chase National Bank advanced credits to the Textile Syndicate for the purchase of this cotton, payment being collected against documents in Moscow. In 1925, negotiations between Chase and Prombank extended beyond the finance of raw materials and mapped out a complete program for financing Soviet raw material exports to the U.S. and imports of U.S. cotton and machinery.

Imports were still insufficient to meet demand, and in March 1926 most cotton mills suspended work during Easter for an extended summer vacation. Wool factories closed for most of the summer discharging half of their workers and paying the rest at half rates.[5] The crisis recurred in 1927. Again numerous factories were closed. These supply problems were compounded by technical problems. In the Kostroma plant, some 45,000 spindles were crowded into a space designed for 20,000. These were of widely varying types, and about three quarters were from thirty-five to sixty years old. Few repairs had been undertaken since the Revolution, and spare parts were removed from machines already in operation. The steam engines providing power dated back to 1880.

---

given by M. Dobb. In particular, Dobb places only 7 plants in the Moscow Trust instead of 32, and quotes his source as Y. S. Rozenfeld, *Promishlennaia Politika S.S.S.R.* (1926). (Dobb, *op. cit.*, p. 134.) The propaganda image of a 'destroyed industrial structure' is hardly consistent with this comparatively large number of plants ready for trustification.

[3]   *Pravda* (Petrograd), No. 175, August 6, 1922.

[4]   'Emigrants Returning from North America,' *Pravda* (Moscow), No. 246, October 31, 1922.

[5]   *Izvestia*, No. 191, August 23, 1925.

As a result of this technical backwardness, substantial orders were placed abroad for textile machinery, particularly in the United Kingdom and Germany. In 1927–8, the U.S.S.R. purchased 11,471 tons of 'machines for spinning and twisting cotton, wool, flax, silk and bast fibres' from the United Kingdom alone. This may be compared with purchases of only 3,896 tons of cars, trucks, and fire engines from the same source. Textile machinery was the largest single category of exports from the U.K. to the Soviet Union in the years 1926 to 1928.[6]

THE RUSSIAN-AMERICAN INDUSTRIAL CORPORATION (RAIC) AND SIDNEY HILLMAN[7]

Several small groups of American emigrants arrived in the early 1920s. One, as already mentioned, joined the Moscow Tailoring Combine. Another, comprising 120 deportees with 200 sewing machines and other equipment, arrived a few months later. They took over an old sewing factory and established the Third International Clothing Works.[8]

In 1922 a much more ambitious project, of major significance in modernizing the textile and clothing industries, was begun. The project was initiated by Sidney Hillman and the Amalgamated Clothing Workers of America, whose official position was as follows:

> Russia has been pleading in vain with the rulers of the world for industrial credit. It is the duty of labor to give Russia the credit denied her by the ruling class. The Amalgamated has made the beginning with the clothing industry. Let us be big enough to perform our duty fully and quickly.[9]

In an *Izvestia* article, Hillman pointed out that the aim of the union was not solely to establish a clothing industry in the Soviet Union: 'our aims are much higher, we will begin with this industry and then grant credits to the other clothing trusts.'[10]

---

[6]   A. A. Santalov and L. Segal, *Soviet Union Year Book, 1930* (London: Allen and Unwin, 1930), p. 331.

[7]   Board of Amalgamated Clothing Workers of America, *Bibliography of the Amalgamated Clothing Workers of America* (New York, 1939). Section IV is a list of references to the Russian-American Industrial Corp.

[8]   *Pravda*, No. 225, October 6, 1922.

[9]   Amalgamated Clothing Workers of America, Sixth Bienniel Convention, *Report of the General Executive Board* (Philadelphia, May 1924), p. 90. Hillman was not typical of American unionists. Samuel Gompers thundered long and loud against Soviet treachery and brutality. He was wholly opposed to any form of economic or trade links with the Soviet Union. [See S. Gompers and W. E. Walling, *Out of Their Own Mouths: A Revelation and Indictment of Sovietism* (New York, 1921).] Most present-day American unionists follow in the Gompers tradition. (See the speeches of Meany, *et al.*) Comparison with the record of American businessmen (both then and now) is revealing: see chaps. 17 and 18.

[10]   *Izvestia*, No. 252, November 10, 1921.

An agreement was drawn up between Vesenkha and a company formed by Hillman and Amalgamated Workers called American-Russian Industrial Workers Association (Artina) later changed to Russian-American Industrial Corporation (known as RAIC or RAIK). The full text of the agreement was given in the *Nation* and was intended to act as a model agreement for a series of such worker enterprises, which were conceived as the equivalent of the foreign commune in agriculture.[11] RAIC made three contracts with the Soviet Union. The first was a general contract (November 1921) authorizing the company to do business and to underwrite contracts made by the union treasury. The underwriting included a minimum dividend and repayment of principal if the corporation should be liquidated. The second agreement was with Vesenkha and similar to the first. The third and most important was with the All-Russian Clothing Syndicate and covered the first project: that of operating the prerevolutionary clothing and textile plants.

RAIC was capitalized at $1 million, and stock was sold to union members at $10 per share. The union appropriated $10,000 from the union treasury to defray initial organization expenses and also bought $50,000 worth of stock. RAIC was linked also to the all-Russian syndicate of the Sewing Industry, which was founded in 1923 with a capital of 900,000 rubles. Sixty percent of the syndicate was owned by various Soviet state institutions (Vesenkha held eighty shares; Moscow Sewing Industry, twenty shares; Petrograd Sewing Industry, 600 shares; Tartar Clothing Industry, twenty-five shares; Nijhny-Novgorod Sewing Trust, five shares; Experimental Factory twenty shares; and the Kharkow Sewing Trust, twelve shares). *The balance of 40 percent was owned by RAIC.* This was an arrangement similar to the General Electric ownership of shares in Electroexploatsia and Electroselstroi. The syndicate opened fifteen branches across Russia. This provided a channel for the transfer of capital, equipment, management techniques, and skilled labor from RAIC to the textile and clothing industries.[12]

In June 1922, six clothing factories in Petrograd and three in Moscow were turned over to the control of the joint board. It was then announced that the new capital would go mainly for new and improved equipment, and in August RAIC announced that the first shipment of spares for American machines currently in use in the U.S.S.R. had been made. By late 1923 RAIC was

[11] 'Contract with Soviets', *Nation*, CXIV (June 1922), p. 728. The *Nation* was a very useful vehicle for spreading news of the aims and work of these enterprises and communes and in denying rumors (true *or* false). For example, when Americans were trying to leave the Kuzbas Commune (American Industrial Corp.), the *Nation* vehemently denied any such pressure existed or that any exodus was under way.

[12] *Izvestia*, No. 207, September 14, 1923. It is likely, although no evidence can be presented, that the syndicate utilized the 3,000 outlets, 50 agencies, and 50 warehouses and manufacturing plants built by the Singer Sewing Machine Co. (Foreign Claims Settlement Commission of the United States, Claim No. SOV-40, 920.)

operating nine clothing plants in Moscow as well as plants in seven other Russian cities. This was independent of the arrangement to aid, technically and financially, the clothing syndicate.[13] By late 1923 RAIC was operating twenty-five clothing plants in Moscow alone and employed 15,000 workers.[14] The union also supplied skilled personnel to aid plants operating outside the syndicate, and provided specialized personnel for research and other operations. (For example, the Moscow experimental factory had a manager supplied by the union in the United States.)[15]

The capital and technical skills were supplied by the union, and the workers and raw materials were provided by the U.S.S.R. Both sides were equally represented on the board of control, and the enterprise run on a cooperative basis.

The books had opened for subscription in June 1922; by August more than $100,000 had been subscribed, and by September more than $300,000. It was announced on September 15, just three months after formation of the company, that a dividend of 8 percent would be paid. There were immediate protests in the current news media that this was a payment from capital and not earnings. Hillman denied this claim:

> So far as our information goes we expect the dividend to come out of the earnings of the Syndicate. Under our contract with the Soviet government, if these earnings are insufficient the Soviet makes the dividend good on our filing a claim. We have filed no claim, and reports that the Soviet has sent money here for this specific purpose are incorrect.[16]

In April 1924 the Amalgamated Clothing Workers of America opened two banks: the Amalgamated Bank of New York and the Amalgamated Trust and Savings Bank of Chicago. These banks called their 'most important function' the transmission of dollars to Russia. By 1927 some $20 million had been sent, in addition to $200,000 in food gifts and another $300,000 in cash gifts. The money was 'largely used for the purchase of machinery and raw materials for the clothing trusts of Russia.'[17] RAIC also interested itself in Syndchveiprom, the syndicate for the united confectionery trusts, but, apart from a financial investment, the degree of participation is not known.[18]

---

[13] *New York Times*, October 31, 1923, p. 17, col. 6.
[14] *Nation*, January 19, 1924, letter from S. H. Walker.
[15] *Nation*, November 7, 1923, p. 524.
[16] *New York Times*, September 2, 1923, Sec. II, p. 11, col. 1. Payment out of capital would, of course, be an offense against the 'blue sky' laws.
[17] *Nation*, May 25, 1927, pp. 569–70.
[18] *Annuaire*, p. 133.

THE TRILLING, NOVIK, AND ALTMAN
CLOTHING CONCESSIONS

In September 1926, a Type I concession agreement was concluded with O. Trilling, of Poland—the former owner of the Spartak factory in Moscow. The concession produced woolen goods, including blankets, thread, and carpets. The plant had been part of the Mossukno and was in a very run-down condition, producing only 2 percent of the trust's output, although reportedly working at capacity. Trilling was required to re-equip the plant completely so that by the second year of operations it would produce not less than 200,000 meters of cloth, and by the end of the third year 300,000 meters. In addition, Trilling was required to produce 150,000 meters of blanket cloth a year. The necessary equipment was to cost not less than $80,000 and had to be imported.

Trilling was employing 230 workers by 1929 and had introduced

> considerable alterations and improvements in the factory, which was obsolete. . . . the whole plant was electrified and much new equipment introduced. The daily output of the spinning department was increased from 400 to 2,500 kilograms of wool yarn. In the weaving department twenty-seven new looms were installed and automatic drying machines were purchased for the washing department. . . . Additional equipment will be imported to produce Jacquard blankets, an article which is not manufactured at the present time in the Soviet Union.[19]

Upon expiration of the concession, the enterprise was to be turned over to the Soviets without compensation, free from debt, and in a technical condition not less favorable than that for the final two years of operations. In the meantime a yearly payment was to be made to the Soviet government. This was to be not less than 40,000 rubles per year and equal to 6 percent of the sales volume of the factory. The concessionaire was given the right to establish a share company either abroad or in the U.S.S.R., with a capital of not less than 400,000 rubles, and with all members to be approved by the Soviet government. The term of the concession was to be fifteen years, although the concession was actually expropriated long before this date.[20]

The second clothing concession was granted to Novik and Sons to operate the Baranov factory for manufacture of caps and hats. They were required to equip the plant and start operations within nine months of date of signature. Production was to be not less than 20,000 dozen caps and hats per year, in addition to 13,000 dozen felt snow shoes and 20,000 meters of felt cloth per year. Novik paid an annual rent of 32,000 rubles and from the end of the second year onward an additional annual royalty of 50,000 rubles per year. At the end of the agreed term of twelve years, the factory was to be turned over to the Soviet government in good condition and without charge.

[19] *Bank for Russian Trade Review*, II, No. 2 (February 1929), 10.
[20] *Ekonomicheskaya Zhizn*, No. 237, October 14, 1926.

A third concession was granted to the Austrian citizen, Altman, who took over the former Gorbachev plant to produce knitted goods. The concession was required, within fourteen months from date of signature, to produce annually 25,000 kilograms of cotton and 50,000 kilograms of woolen yarn, of which not less than 30 percent was to be used for the manufacture of stockings and gloves. Altman was required to import equipment for production of knitted goods. The equipment was to be valued at not less than 120,000 rubles, in addition to equipment for wool-spinning valued at not less than 60,000 rubles. A royalty of 8 percent was payable on knitted goods turnover and 5 percent on woolen goods turnover.

Turnover was required to be not less than 400,000 rubles in the first, 800,000 rubles in the second, and one million rubles in the third year. Annual rent was set at 8,000 rubles. The factory was to revert to the state at the end of eighteen years with complete equipment and in good working order.[21] The concession was later taken over by Tiefenbacher and expropriated before the eighteen years had expired.

There had been numerous small shoe-manufacturing concerns in tsarist Russia. Aktieselskabet United Shoe Machinery Company of Copenhagen (the Danish subsidiary of United Shoe Machinery Corporation of the United States) had leased shoe machinery to over sixty-two plants before 1914. This equipment was valued at five million rubles. In addition equipment was stored in Petrograd warehouses. These factories and their equipment were confiscated in 1918.[22] In the 1920s a concession was negotiated with the Union Shoe Company of Vienna for technical assistance and the use of imported Austrian equipment.[23]

TECHNICAL ASSISTANCE TO THE TEXTILE INDUSTRIES

In July 1929 an agreement was concluded with the U.S. firm, Lockwood, Green and Company, under which four American textile machine-building specialists were sent to the Soviet Union 'for technical aid in the reorganization of Soviet textile mills as well as drafting projects for new textile mills.' The agreement included 'material responsibility' by the American company for the rationalization proposals of its engineers and was coincident with an increase in the purchase of American textile machinery.[24] Another contract aimed at rationalizing the accounting system in Russian textile mills; this contract was made with the New York firm of management consultants, Eugin

[21] *Ibid.*
[22] Foreign Claims Settlement Commission of the United States, Claim No. SOV 4-353.
[23] U.S. State Dept. Decimal File 316-131-344.
[24] *Ekonomicheskaya Zhizn*, No. 153, July 7, 1929, and No. 159, July 14, 1929.

Szepisi.[25] The design of plants for specialized textile products intended for the export market was represented by the agreement with C. T. Steinert, of Frankfurt, for the design and construction of a plant for manufacture of kid leather.[26]

There is little question that these design contracts stemmed directly from 'uneconomic conditions' prevailing in the textile and allied industries. Textilstroi (trust for building textile plants) was organized in 1926 with the aim of reducing construction costs of textile plants. Investigation in 1928 showed that the trust had been undertaking construction without definite plans or sufficient materials and labor. This had resulted in heavy over-expenditures and slow construction. Administrative costs were out of line with results achieved; in 1927–8 over 500,000 rubles had been spent without producing any 'concrete results' whatsoever.[27]

FRENCH TECHNICAL ASSISTANCE TO THE SILK INDUSTRY

The silk trust (Shelkotrust) was formed in 1921. It consisted of thirty-eight prerevolutionary factories in the Moscow and Vladimir districts, including some plants with a large prewar output. The planned output for the first year of production was 1.9 million arshines (compared to 60 million for the same plants in 1913). This target was not achieved. The largest plant in Shelkotrust was the Moscow plant of the Société Anonyme Franco-Suedoise pour la Fabrication de Soie en Russie, built in 1889 and considerably enlarged in 1911. Before the Revolution the plant had employed over 2,000, but, even by 1930, with extensive foreign assistance, employment was still in the region of 350–400.[28]

In 1923 negotiations were begun with the former French owners concerning further investment. These resulted in several agreements after some four or five years of discussion. In February 1928 a contract was made between Iskustvennoie Volokno (a Soviet company), the French firm Soieries de Strasbourg S-A, and Professor E. Bronart for production of artificial silk by the viscose process. The agreement was for ten years and the French parties undertook to give technical assistance in the construction and operation of a new plant in Leningrad utilizing the patents and processes of the French firm.[29] By 1930 the firm had built two plants, one in Leningrad and another in Moscow. This was followed by an agreement to build a third plant at Mohilev

---

[25]   Vneshtorgizdat, *op. cit.*, p. 227.

[26]   *Ibid.*, p. 229.

[27]   *Ekonomicheskaya Zhizn*, No. 223, September 25, 1928.

[28]   J. Douillet, *op. cit.*, p. 48; and *Ekonomicheskaya Zhizn*, No. 277, December 9, 1921.

[29]   *Ekonomicheskaya Zhizn*, No. 46, February 23, 1928; and Vneshtorgizdat, *op. cit.*, p. 230.

using equipment supplied by a German firm, Oskar Kohorn A-G, of Chemitz. The Kohorn company also had a direct technical-assistance contract with Shelkotrust for the supply of data and assistance in the manufacture of artificial silk by the viscose process. Combined output of the German-assisted plants was 20,000 kilograms per day of artificial silk, but nothing is known of the exact number and location of these plants.[30]

EUROPEAN BUTTON CONCESSIONS

Even the lowly button had a number of manufacturing concessions. Tiefenbacher Knopfabrik A-G, button manufacturers of Vienna, signed a concession agreement in July 1926 and was still manufacturing buttons under this agreement at the end of the decade. The company sent equipment from its Vienna plant to Moscow and took over the factory previously occupied by the Altman company.[31]

Skou-Keldsen also had a button concession at Poltava in the Ukraine and another in Leningrad. At one time the company applied for further works in Kiev and Odessa, but there is no record that the application was successful.[32] Two other manufacturers of buttons were Stock A-G and Block and Ginsberg, both German companies.

TECHNICAL ASSISTANCE TO THE FOOD INDUSTRY

Technical assistance in the food industries consisted of equipping plants in key processing industries and designing of plants for the Five-Year Plan.[33]

A concession agreement between Okman (an Estonian) and the Kharkov Provincial Council of People's Economy created a joint company to run beer and malt breweries in the Ukraine. This was a Type II concession, and both parties deposited 85,000 rubles capital. The company had three directors: Okman, and two others appointed by the Provincial Council, which received 60 percent of the profits.[34] H. Langmann and Sons, of the United Kingdom, had a concession for growing hops for the brewing industry.

[30] U.S. Embassy in Warsaw, Report No. 294, October 7, 1930.

[31] U.S. State Dept. Decimal File, 316–131–345 and 316–111–916.

[32] U.S. State Dept. Decimal File, 316–131–668.

[33] A number of concessions were rumored to be in this field but concrete evidence for them does not exist. For example, in 1922 the Bolshevik Southwestern Economic Conference opened negotiations with the Chicago meat-packing firm, Morris and Company, with a view to granting a concession to operate the slaughterhouses and meat-packing factories at Alavir. At the same time, the Conference bought 100 refrigerator cars in the United States. At about the same time, the American Association of Manufacturers was negotiating with the Ukraine Bank to equip sugar mills in the Ukraine; two of its members were in Kiev to conduct the negotiations. Both these are mentioned in IS Report at 316–139–522 but there is no confirmation elsewhere.

[34] U.S. State Dept. Decimal File 316–131–119.

Gaier, a French firm, equipped a plant in the Ukraine to produce oil from various seeds.[35] In 1930 a technical-assistance contract was concluded with Harburger Eisen und Bronzwerke A-G for design, construction, and supply of equipment for oil-crushing mills. A similar agreement was made in the same year with the Dutch firm, N.V. Maatschappij Tot Exploitatie von Veredelinsprocedes, for technical assistance in the saccharification of wood pulp to produce cattle fodder and glucose.[36]

Design of meat-packing plants was the subject of a contract between H. G. Henshien of Chicago and the food industry.[37] The German firm, Hect-Feifer, enlarged the Odessa meat-packing plants and arranged for the export of preserved meat to Germany.[38] The Mechanical Manufacturing Company, of the United States, provided technical assistance to the meat-packing industry.[39]

The design of condensed-milk plants was the subject of a contract with the McCormick Company, of Pittsburgh.[40] Another design-assistance contract was with Penick and Ford, Inc., of Cedar Rapids, Iowa, to plan factories for production of corn products.[41] General technical assistance to the food industry was the subject of an agreement with Webber and Wells, Inc., of Chicago.[42] The Romanoff Caviar Company had its nationalized plants returned, and, as the company had German and American owners, it must be concluded that the Soviets were interested in developing the foreign exchange potential of caviar.[43]

Three large bakeries were constructed by the McCormick Company. These were not only the largest in the Soviet Union but among the largest anywhere in the world, with a daily capacity of 200 metric tons, produced during three shifts. Operations were completely mechanized, so the workers numbered only seventy per shift. McCormick engineers designed the plants and supervised construction, installation, and initial operation of American equipment.[44] The output of bread in Moscow in 1927–8 was 175,000 tons and in Leningrad 278,000 tons. These were significant increases from 1925–6, when the Moscow output had been 74,000 tons and the Leningrad output 147,000 tons. Each of

[35]   *Izvestia*, No. 7, January 9, 1924.
[36]   Vneshtorgizdat, *op. cit.*, p. 228.
[37]   American Russian Handbook, p. 99.
[38]   Polish Foreign Office Report, October 7, 1929.
[39]   A. A. Santalov and L. Segal, *Soviet Union Year Book, 1930*, (London: Allen and Unwin, 1930), p. 358.
[40]   *Ibid.*
[41]   *Ibid.*, p. 100.
[42]   *Ibid.*, p. 101.
[43]   Report 93130, April 12, 1930 (316–130–1293).
[44]   *Bank for Russian Trade Review* II, No. 7 (July 1929), 16.

the new plants built by McCormick was able to produce 74,000 tons per year on two shifts. There is little doubt that the whole increment in bread output came from these mechanized American bakeries.[45]

Most of the sugar refineries in the Ukraine were put back into operation by German technical assistance forthcoming under the Rapallo Treaty. In 1929, however, there were, still ten refineries in a state of 'technical preservation,' and three new refineries were planned to replace these.[46]

Concessions were rare in the tobacco field. There was one in 1924 with A. Lopato and Sons, of Harbin, China, for the operation of the latter's prerevolutionary plant in Chita, Siberia. A fifteen-year lease was granted the company, which paid the Soviets 5 percent of gross output, and a tax equal to $3\frac{1}{2}$ percent of the market price of tobacco.[47]

TECHNICAL ASSISTANCE IN HOUSING AND PLANT CONSTRUCTION

The American-Russian Constructor Company (ARK) made a private Type I concession agreement for house repair with the Moscow Soviet. Practically all the stock was held in the United States. Houses in need of repair were allotted to the company by the Moscow Soviet for terms of 8, 18, or 36 years, according to the amount of capital required to place them in habitable condition. The company was to furnish all materials and labor, repair the houses, and keep them in good repair for the stipulated period. During this term the company was to have renting privileges. Of the rent collected, 80 percent accrued to the company and 20 percent to the Moscow Soviet. Taxes were paid by the tenants. About 24 Americans (mostly of Russian origin) were employed by the company.[48] Little is known about the specific operations of ARK, but it probably expired in the early 1930s when the Soviet ran out of houses in need of repair. In 1923 the functions of the concession were extended to 'construction and repair work, organization, leasing and operating plants producing construction materials in the RSFSR and allied republics. . . .'[49]

In late 1923, following a decree of the Soviet of People's Commissars which removed a number of institutions and organizations from Moscow to relieve the housing shortage, an agreement was made with Geoffrey and Curting, Ltd. (United Kingdom), to undertake capital repairs on these buildings.

---

[45]   Calculated from data in *Bank for Russian Trade Review* II, No. 7 (July 1929), 16.
[46]   *Pravda* (Moscow), No. 98, April 28, 1929.
[47]   U.S. Consulate at Harbin, China, Report No. 2824, September 20, 1924.
[48]   U.S. Consulate at Riga, Report 212, December 23, 1922.
[49]   *Ekonomicheskaya Zhizn*, No. 105, May 13, 1923.

A large company was formed for this work, but nothing has been reported about specific operations.[50]

By 1925 the housing situation had become desperate. Resultant fatigue was blamed for many industrial accidents. One article warned against placing too much reliance for construction on cooperatives and suggested that the greater part of the needed house building should be done by 'commercial organizations.'[51] This was followed by an agreement in March 1929 with the Longacre Construction Company, of the United States, to build according to the 'latest technical methods' some four million rubles' worth of workers' housing in Moscow.[52]

Another concession in housing, between Tsentrozhilsoyuz (the Central Union of Dwelling Cooperatives) and the German firm, P. Kossel A-G in 1926, provided for the establishment of a Type II joint-stock company to build houses, hotels, and apartments. Rusgerstroi had a share capital of six million rubles equally subscribed by each party. Kossel received 1.9 million rubles for patents turned over to the joint company. The Soviets received the same amount free. The concession was stipulated to last twenty-five years, but Kossel was ejected in 1928. In the meantime, the company established cement, glass, and woodworking plants.[53]

A series of articles in *Ekonomicheskaya Zhizn* suggests why concessions were attempted in the field of housing and why the plants of the Five-Year Plan were designed and built by foreign companies. Several meetings of the Soviet of Labor and Defense were devoted to the question of the extremely poor results of industrial and domestic building programs. There was no responsible supervising organ; each production unit had tried to become self-supporting. This resulted in poorly designed projects whose costs had usually been underestimated. There were gross technical inefficiency and poor technical training. The input industries—especially the glass, paper and chemical industries—were inefficient, and supplies of these products were irregular and of poor quality.[54]

SMALL HOUSEHOLD ITEMS

The Alftan pure concession granted in 1924 produced typewriter ribbons and carbon, waxed, colored, and parchment paper.[55] Elia Shulmann took over

---

[50]   *Pravda* (Moscow), No. 224, October 4, 1923.

[51]   *Torgovo-Promishlennaya Gazeta*, No. 268, November 24, 1925.

[52]   *Izvestia*, No. 51, March 2, 1929.

[53]   *Ekonomicheskaya Zhizn*, No. 180, August 8, 1926.

[54]   *Ekonomicheskaya Zhizn*, various issues for April 1928, December 1928, and January to June 1929. Negotiations were reported in the Soviet press with the American companies Van Soon and McDonald for construction of large cement plants (*Izvestia*, No. 248, October 26, 1929).

[55]   *Ekonomicheskaya Zhizn*, No. 346, November 28, 1924.

his prerevolutionary factory in Moscow for a concession to manufacture typewriter ribbons, carbon paper, indigo, copying paper, stencils, and inks. The factory employed 150 and was the largest in the U.S.S.R. making these articles. In 1926 Shulmann, a Latvian citizen, concluded another agreement for the manufacture of steel pens, penholders, drawing pins, paper clips, pencil sharpeners, and fountain pens.[56] A Finnish firm, Raabe, was granted a concession to operate the nail factory at Nerecht, in Kostroma Province.[57]

After the demise of the Harriman manganese concession, United States manufacturers were decidedly cool to further concessionary ventures. One, however, was concluded in the record time of three weeks between the Gillette Safety Razor Company and the U.S.S.R. Gillette was obligated to build a plant in the Soviet Union—the first time an American company decided to build on Soviet territory.[58]

THE HAMMER CONCESSIONS

The first Hammer concession was granted to Allied Chemical and Dye for operation of the Urals asbestos deposits, discussed in chapter 6. The best-known of the Hammer concessions was one granted in 1925 for production of pencils, pens, celluloid drawing instruments, and similar items. The cedar, graphite, and colors were imported. Machinery and skilled labor were brought from Germany. Four factories, located in Moscow, employed at their peak about 1,000 persons.[59] The pencil concession was, in effect, a monopoly, and, at the end of the first year's business, a turnover of $2.5 million, with net profits of $600,000, was reported. Some $450,000 of the profits was reported as having been exported. The second year's turnover was $3.5 million, on which profits were $550,000. A turnover tax of between 6 and 10 percent was payable, together with an income tax of 10 percent on gross income and a tax of 50 percent of all profits in excess of the first 20 percent of profits based on invested capital.[60] It was reported in 1927 that Dr. Hammer was seeking a $500,000 loan in New York for further expansion of the pencil factory. Obligations by Centrosoyuz were offered as security. Further security was offered in

[56]   Troyanovsky, *op. cit.*, p. 861.

[57]   *Pravda* (Moscow), No. 250, November 3, 1923.

[58]   *New York Times*, December 10, 1929, p. 8, col. 4. Nothing more was reported; it is presumed the agreement was not implemented.

[59]   U.S. State Dept. Decimal File, 316-136-1240. Hammer's monopoly resulted from product superiority rather than agreement. Alexander Barmine, *One Who Survived* (New York: G. P. Putnam, 1945), p. 157, says, 'The State Mospolygraph Trust undertook to make cheap pencils, but the quality was so bad they could not compete with Dr. Hammer's more expensive goods.' High import tariffs were placed on pencils to protect the State Pencil Trust (Karl Liebnecht factory). (*Ekonomicheskaya Zhizn*, August 11, 1923.)

[60]   U.S. Embassy in Berlin, Report 4457, April 11, 1929.

the form of Russian government loan bonds.[61] This appears as a pre-Harriman attempt to break United States policy against long-term loans to the Soviet Union. The concession was turned over to the Soviets on December 20, 1929, in accordance with a clause in the contract which enabled the Soviets to buy out at any time at an agreed valuation.[62] There are unique features about the Hammer concessions. The pencil concession had a smooth and profitable history, quite unlike most other concession agreements. The purchase clause was invoked and accepted without the usual protest.

[61]   *New York Times*, November 22, 1927, p. 40, col. 2.
[62]   *New York Times*, December 22, 1929, p. 31, col. 2.

CHAPTER FOURTEEN

Transportation and the Transportation Equipment Industries[1]

RECONSTRUCTION OF THE RAILROADS

THE heart of Russian transport is the railroad. Development in tsarist times was limited by weak track, which in turn limited size of locomotives employed. The tsarist Ministry of Transport had a rather limited view of locomotive construction, and its was not until 1912 that the Vladikavkaz Railroad in the North Caucasus introduced a ten-coupled freight steam engine. This was the finest engine available in the 1920s and became the standard Soviet type. However, the comparative backwardness of the Russian railroad system was not due to lack of experimentation or innovative ability. Westwood points out the long Russian history in *steam* traction, from tsarist times to the Soviet research.[2]

Restoration of railroads and ports, both heavily damaged in the Civil War, were the essential prerequisites to economic development.[3] This reconstruction was begun in the immediate post-Rapallo period, with extensive German

---

[1] Locomotive construction is covered under Gomza (chap. 10).

[2] Westwood, *op. cit.*, p. 93.

[3] Just how badly the railroads were damaged is controversial. The American Relief Administration (in a telegram to the Dept. of Commerce, U.S. State Dept. Decimal File, 316–107–853) argued, 'Railroads functioning with old employees who apparently take pride in their accomplishment. Main yards on the whole clean. . . . We have traveled entirely on regularly scheduled trains and on time in every instance except once when two hours late due to wreck on main line . . . however barring ARA supplies no freight moving and passenger traffic limited foreign relief agents, government officials, repatriated refugees and occasional troop movements.' On the other hand, Hilger (then German Relief representative) states, 'The transport system was in complete ruins and what railroad travel still continued was disturbed by repeated attacks on moving trains.' (Hilger, *op. cit.*, p. 45.)

The most probable view is that little freight was moving, many bridges were out (especially in the Don), and main lines in the north were clear because of large numbers of workers rather than 'old employees.'

technical assistance, and completed between 1922 and 1924. German trade figures for exports to Russia in 1921-2 (table 14-1) suggest how much importance was attached to this phase of Russo-German cooperation.

Table 14-1   GERMAN EXPORTS TO THE U.S.S.R. AND
PROPORTION OF RAILROAD MATERIALS
(IN CURRENT PAPER MARKS)

1		2	3	4	5
Year	Month	Total Exports (in millions of marks)	Locomotives (in millions of marks)	Other RR Material (in millions of marks)	Proportion of RR Materials (percentage)
1921	June	18,166 million	—	3,422	18.8
	July	64,261	—	17,390	27.1
	August	130,248	—	88,944	68.3
	September	128,704	17,255	84,607	79.1
	October	54,771	—	21,417	39.1
	November	112,678	36,667	31,743	60.1
	December	136,255	—	8,628	6.3
1922	January	43,272*	42,554*	7,797*	—
	February	6,278	—	6,278	100.0

Source: U.S. State Dept. Archives, 340–650. Column 5 calculated.
* Figures as given in source.

UNITED STATES TECHNICAL ASSISTANCE TO
THE RAILROADS

Two groups of American railroad engineers investigated conditions of railroads in European Russia in the middle and end of the decade. The first group, under H. G. Kelley, former President of the Grand Trunk Railroad, made an inspection of the Ekaterina Railroad and the Donetz Railroad on behalf of Percival Farquhar, who was negotiating a large concession to run both railroads and related iron and steel plants.[4] The second investigation was made in 1930 under the supervision of Ralph Budd, of the Baltimore and Ohio Railroad. The recommendations of the Budd Report were implemented by 150 engineers from the B&O after 1930.[5]

The impulse to grant major railroads as concessions resulted from their declining ability to handle traffic, although the honeyed phrases of the Kelley

[4]   H. G. Kelley, *General Report on Ekaterina Railway, Donetz Railway* (New York, 1926). A copy is at U.S. State Dept. Decimal File 316-131-744, with supplement at 316-131-872.

[5]   The B&O work will be covered in Vol. II. The Russian Railway Service Corps, an American organization, and the Inter-Allied Railway Commission in Siberia did major reconstruction work between 1918 and 1922. There is extensive material on this in the U.S. State Dept. Archives. The 1,100-mile Turkman-Siberia railroad was built under the direction of an American deportee, Shatof.

report slur over the operating and physical deficiences of the systems examined. Advance data supplied by Amtorg to Farquhar gives the daily average number of loaded cars handled by the Ekaterina Railroad. Traffic declined from 3,351 cars daily in October 1925 to 3,066 in February 1926, and on the Donetz system from 4,011 daily in October 1925 to 3,911 in February 1926.[6]

Both railroads had been built well before the Revolution. In the case of Ekaterina, the report indicates date of construction of the twenty-one divisions; fifteen sections were opened for traffic before 1900, and all divisions (except the Apostolovo via Snigirevka) were open for traffic before 1910. These were well-established railroads, built to provide transportation for the tsarist-developed iron and steel plants and coal mines of the Donetz. The Ekaterina comprised over 1,600 miles of first main track, and the Donetz, 1,459. Both railroads serviced coal fields, iron ore mines, manganese mines, iron and steel works, and the Ukrainian agricultural region. They constituted the most important combined system in the U.S.S.R.

They were built according to European standards with light equipment but had always been substantial net earners. The aim of the Kelley study was to determine the cost of modernization according to American standards. The first recommendations were that train weight should be increased from 1,100 net revenue tons to 3,500 net revenue tons and that suitable locomotives and capacity should be provided for the expansion. It was pointed out by Kelley that to move the anticipated 1927–8 traffic with existing equipment would require thirty-eight trains daily, while with the proposed greater train weight only twelve daily trains would be required, 'reducing the train density . . . and making room for the steadily increasing traffic of the railway in products of agriculture, manufacturing and miscellaneous commodities.' The equipment and physical resources required to support such a system were then given in detail.

The basic objective of the report was clearly to determine the requirements for expansion. Indeed, it is clear from the report that the roads were handling far less than their prewar volume. The total train mileage operated by the Ekaterina in 1913 was more than 15 million train miles, whereas in 1924–5 (latest year given) the mileage was a little over 4.5 million, or about one quarter of the 1913 volume.

In terms of car miles or locomotive miles, the proportion was about the same.[7] Total tonnage of all classes of freight carried in 1913 on the Ekaterina was 40 million, compared to 13.5 million in 1924–5. Figures for the Donetz system are not given. It may be presumed they were less, as the physical

---

[6]   U.S. State Dept. Decimal File, 316–131–745/6.
[7]   Kelley, *op. cit.*, p. 125. Again, use of 1913 as a base is misleading. Traffic increased substantially between 1913 and 1917.

operating conditions were not as good as those for the Ekaterina. The poor condition of the bridges on both lines may well have been a contributory factor to limited operations. The Ekaterina line had 1,774 bridges less than 70 feet in length and 81 bridges greater than 70 feet in length; 245 of the former and 37 of the latter had been destroyed or damaged by the Civil War and Intervention. Considering that railroad destruction was the focal point of military activity, the damage perhaps is not as great as one might have expected. Of the smaller activity, bridges, some 206 had been rebuilt and the balance of 39 put into temporary working order. Only 23 of the 81 major bridges had been rebuilt, leaving 14 operating under temporary operating conditions. These limitations were compounded by the poor condition of the roadbed and generally inadequate maintenance.

The appendix to the Kelley report includes an estimate of the amount of repair work required to restore the bridges on both systems. This estimate, when coupled with the equipment repair backlog, suggests that a massive job would have had to be accomplished before the railroads could be put into prewar operating condition.[8]

THE BEGINNING OF RAILROAD ELECTRIFICATION

Two Soviet railroads were electrified before 1930. This was recognized as an alternative which enabled increased capacity without new line construction. The first line to be electrified was a 13-mile suburban line in Baku in 1926. It was installed under German supervision. The overhead system and rolling stock were similar to that of the Berlin high-speed, multiple-unit, side-door trains. The rolling stock was made in the Soviet Union using German patterns and models and under German supervision.[9]

The second line to be electrified was the Moscow-Mytishchi line, an eleven-mile commuter line completed in 1929. This was also of German construction and utilized imported German equipment.[10]

Complete railroad electrification came under serious consideration about 1928-9, and several engineering delegations visited Western Europe, the United States, and Mexico to study various types of electrification systems. In 1929 the People's Commissariat of Transportation selected the Suram Pass section of the Trans-Caucasian railroad as a trial section for electrification.

---

[8] There are numerous omissions in the Kelley report which give rise to the thought that the report, as donated to the U.S. State Dept., had been considerably doctored or censored to disguise the true state of affairs. There is, for example, an inconsistency between the buoyant, flowery accolades to Russian maintenance skill and the statistical information given in support.

[9] Ruykeyser, *op. cit.*, p. 80.

[10] Westwood, *op. cit.*, p. 41.

This was a strategic section carrying oil to Batum for export, and the system decided upon there was to be used as basis for future electrification. General Electric was chosen to develop a suitable locomotive design and to provide the first eight main line units. There had been no construction of electric locomotives in the Soviet Union up to this time, so the G.E. prototype, the 'Suram', was transferred to the Dynamo works and construction of diesel electrics based upon it.[11] The system was a 3,000-volt direct-current one with 120 metric tons locomotive weight, using a 6-axle, articulated, 2-truck design. This was 'in accordance with the exhaustive studies and recommendations of General Electric.'[12] J. N. Westwood points out that current Soviet diesel-electrics stem directly from the initial G.E. design.[13]

DEVELOPMENT OF THE RUSSIAN AUTOMOBILE INDUSTRY

Russia took an early interest in the automobile; there were more than 500 automobile taxis in Moscow before 1910. Many of the vehicles were imported; nevertheless, tsarist Russia could claim the distinction of having produced automobiles without foreign technical assistance, while the Soviets, after spending a decade, finally gave up and handed the problem over to foreign companies.[14]

The Baltic Engineering Works in Moscow was producing 250–300 automobiles annually as early as 1912 and expanded its production during the war. Mechanically the Baltic was a good automobile although more expensive than its European and American competitors.[15] The Baltic plant was completely re-equipped with American machinery early in 1917, but this effort was not completed by the time of the Bolshevik Revolution. The Soviet administration put 1,000 men to work to complete the plant. This was achieved in 1920, but the plant was abandoned later the same year.[16] Next year the Baltic was placed under Red Army management and with German assistance turned its attention to heavy military vehicles. Production in late 1922 was about two

11 *Monogram*, November 1943.
12 *Ibid.*
13 Westwood, *loc. cit.*
14 The following Russian automobiles were produced before the Bolshevik Revolution: the Leutner (1911–1915), Marck (1906–1910), Russo-Baltic (1909–1913), Sevronsky (1901–1905 and 1911–1915), and the Tansky (1901–1905). [G. R. Doyle, *The World's Automobiles, 1880–1955* (London: Temple, 1957).] The Soviets have not (in 1966) produced a completely indigenous automobile design; see Vols. II and III.
15 U.S. State Dept. Decimal File, 316–164–402.
16 Keeley, *op. cit.* Compare this to the claim that there were no automobile-manufacturing plants in prerevolutionary Russia, as stated in *Ekonomicheskaya Zhizn*, No. 46, February 25, 1925.

units per month.[17] A few years later attention was turned to buses, of which there were none in Russia. By a heroic effort *one* was manufactured, 'consisting of parts nearly all made in Soviet Russia, except the frame and axle.'[18] Later in 1928–9 the Italian Fiat truck was produced at the Baltic under an agreement with the Fiat company[19] and also a few British Mark IV tanks were copied from a prototype.[20]

The new AMO automobile factory was also completed in 1917 just before the Revolution. It was located in a modern building with the latest in American equipment and was designed to employ 6,000 workers. Between 1919 and 1921 the only output was repair work on a few White trucks. For this AMO employed about 1,200, under supervision of Adams, an American deportee.[21]

The Soviets have claimed there was no automobile manufacturing in Russia before 1930, although actually they had two large, well-equipped plants intact after the Revolution. As with the Westinghouse, Citroen, Singer, and other operations, Soviet skills were not available to operate the inheritance.

The Citroen plant offers an interesting example of the dilemma in which the Communist Party found itself. The plant was allowed to operate unnationalized for some years. In 1921 the firm formally applied for release from the nationalization decree, and the response was immediate enforcement of nationalization.[22] The highest levels of the Party had been well aware of the vacuum created by the Communist takeover of industry. They allowed larger plants to operate in 'capitalist hands' until solutions presented themselves. On the other hand the workers in these plants were forced to do more work under capitalist discipline and naturally pressured for nationalization. Where this pressure was taken up by the lower ranks, implementation of the nationalization decree was forced upon the Party.

The solution to the automobile-manufacturing problem was formulated slowly. The AMO plant continued miniscule production of trucks (much less than the planned 2,000 per year). The AMO truck was unsatisfactory in quality and very expensive to produce.[23] Until the 1930s, however, it was the only one in production. Beginning in 1929, production was reorganized and upgraded as the result of a technical-assistance agreement with the A. J. Brandt Company, of the United States.

[17] *Pravda*, No. 188, August 23, 1922. Probably armored cars.
[18] Heroic, as it was reported under the title, 'Our achievement—the first Soviet bus' almost as a military victory. Which parts, if any, were actually made within the USSR. is difficult to determine.
[19] U.S. State Dept. Decimal File, 316–131–417.
[20] See chap. 15.
[21] The Keeley report *op. cit.* states that the AMO output in 1921 could have been handled by any American garage with less than 20 men.
[22] Swedish Export Association, Report, 1922. (316–107–782/3.)
[23] *Ekonomicheskaya Zhizn*, No. 134, June 1, 1925.

The first tentative steps in the direction of a mass production automobile industry had been taken in 1925. A large-scale motor-vehicle driving contest was instituted to 'ascertain the types of automobiles, motor trucks, and motorcycles best suited to Russian conditions.'[24] The total stock of automobiles in the U.S.S.R. at this time was less than 16,000, of which only 10,000 were running,[25] so it is not surprising that endurance, mileage, and acceleration were tested, among other characteristics. Participants were 169 vehicles, one of each current make, including 82 passenger cars, 48 trucks, 21 special vehicles (fire engines, etc.) and 18 motorcycles. Among the entrants were all European and American models of note; if the manufacturer did not enter voluntarily (which was the case with most American producers), a vehicle was purchased by Amtorg and entered involuntarily.[26] AMO entered a truck, but this was assembled from imported parts not of Russian manufacture. The record does not show whether it completed any of the tests.[27]

The Contest Committee evaluated the results and published a report of its findings. *Ekonomicheskaya Zhizn* reported these and carried an interview with Z. T. Litvin-Sedoy, Chairman of the Committee.[28] He pointed out that both American and European manufacturing had undergone fundamental changes since the war, in both methods of construction and techniques. (He was referring to mass-production techniques, substitution of metal for wood in automobile coachwork, and the use of improved alloy steels.) It was pointed out that prewar reputations did not necessarily apply in 1925, except in the case of Mercedes, which maintained its 'excellent' reputation. The report was critical of American automobiles, but less critical of American trucks. It feared the latter could dominate the market because of their low cost, but the high fuel consumption, unknown composition of materials used, and the difficulty of acquiring spare parts were held to be serious objections. It is interesting to note, in the light of subsequent agreements, that the Ford entry failed and that, despite its low price, it was held to be very expensive in operation.[29]

Negotiations with the Ford Motor Company began in January 1926, and one immediate result was that International General Motors sent its Baltic representative, T. E. Eybye, to explore possibilities for General Motors business. Eybye was decidedly negative; he reported that he felt prospects

[24] *Ekonomicheskaya Zhizn*, No. 46, February 25, 1925.
[25] *Ibid.*
[26] U.S. Consulate in Riga, Report 3254, October 2, 1925.
[27] *Ekonomicheskaya Zhizn*, various issues for early 1925.
[28] *Ekonomicheskaya Zhizn*, No. 216, September 22, 1925.
[29] U.S. Consulate in Riga, Dispatch 3516, January 12, 1926 and Dispatch 3851, June 16, 1926.

were slight and that it was inopportune for G.M. to establish itself in the Soviet Union.[30]

The first version of the Five-Year Plan, drawn up in 1927, made provision for production of only 3,500 autos per year. This small output was vigorously assailed by V. V. Ossinsky, Director of the Central Statistical Administration, on the grounds that the U.S.S.R. was 'catastrophically backward' in automobile production, and that on both economic and military grounds there were insurmountable arguments for the establishment of a plant capable of producing 100,000 automobiles per year.[31]

In the fall of 1928, the 'activization of concessions' policy failed to produce foreign bidders to erect an automobile plant in the Soviet Union. Subsequently the Soviets incorporated their plans into the Five-Year Plan. In 1928 Ossinsky was sent to the United States to negotiate with Ford, General Motors, Durand, and Studebaker. Ford was the most promising as a supplier of automotive experience and equipment required. Negotiations moved along three separate lines: (1) American ownership and operation on a concession basis, (2) a mixed company, and (3) Soviet ownership and operation with technical assistance and financial help from the United States.

Ossinsky was followed to the United States by Meshlauk, of Vesenkha, who conducted final negotiations with both General Motors and Ford. A psychological ploy was added in the Soviet press when the Soviets suddenly announced their intention to build an automobile plant 'with their own resources' capable of producing 100,000 cars per year. Gipromez and Glavmashstroi were directed to produce plans and work out a manufacturing schedule 'within two weeks'—an absurd proposal.[32]

THE SOVIET AUTOMOBILE INDUSTRY
AND HENRY FORD

On May 31, 1929, V. I. Meshlauk, a member of the Presidium of the Supreme Soviet, and Saul G. Bron, President of Amtorg, signed an agreement with the Ford Motor Company under which the Soviets contracted to purchase $30 million worth of automobiles and parts before 1933 and the Ford Motor Company agreed to furnish technical assistance until 1938 in the construction

[30]　*Ibid.*

[31]　V. V. Ossinsky, 'The American Automobile or the Russian Peasant Cart', *Pravda* (Moscow), Nos. 162, 163, and 194, of July 20, 21, and 22, 1927, states: 'If in a future war we use the Russian peasant cart against the American or European automobile, the result to say the least will be disproportionately heavy losses, the inevitable consequences of technical weakness. This is certainly not industrialized defense.'

[32]　'Towards New Victories on the Industrialization Front,' *Torgovo i promyshlennaya Gazeta*, No. 53, March 5, 1929.

of an automobile-manufacturing plant at Nizhni-Novgorod. The plant, to be completed by 1933, was to produce the Model A (called by the Soviets Gaz-A), the Ford light truck (Gaz-AA), and the heavy truck (AMO-3). All Ford patents were placed at the disposal of Gipromez, and Ford engineers rendered technical assistance in the introduction of Ford manufacturing methods. Soviet engineers were given facilities to study Ford methods at the River Rouge plant in Detroit.

The Ford plan adopted included a schedule which potentially gave the Soviets their 100,000 automobiles per year:

		Proposed total output	*Percent imported*
1st year	1929–30	6,000	100 percent
2nd year	1930–31	24,000	100
3rd year	1931–32	48,000	50
4th year	1932–33	96,000–100,000	25

The first year's schedule covered manufacture of bodies, fenders, hoods, and all sheet metal work in the new Austin-designed plant at Nizhni-Novgorod, while assembly of complete vehicles was located at the temporary plant. The second year's schedule extended this program to cover the manufacture of fittings. The third year added engine production, by which time it was planned that the technical-assistance contract with the Brown Lipe Gear Company would have developed gear-cutting technology. The fourth year phased in rear and front axles made in the Soviet Union with the assistance of the Timken-Detroit Axle Company. This last year phased in domestic production of all instruments, batteries, and electrical equipment imported up to that time from Detroit.[33] Raw materials and semi-manufactured inputs were concurrently developed to phase into the above schedule. The plan included, for example, the manufacture of automobile-quality steels at Prioksky, Sormovo, and Vyhksunsk, and at the Novosormovo foundry. Glass was to be developed at Sormovo.

The development and learning process noted previously in this study is repeated. The first stage involved assembling automobiles manufactured abroad and imported as parts. For this purpose Ford converted an unused railroad shop at Lublin. This had the capacity to assemble 10,000–12,000 vehicles per year and was, of course, a training ground while the main plant was under construction. Production was transferred in stages to the new plant and imported parts gradually cut off. By 1934 all parts were being supplied internally, although many were of indifferent quality. In the late 1930s, Ford

[33] *Pravda*, No. 128, June 7, 1929; and Sorenson, *op. cit.*, chap. 15.

obtained one of the Nizhni-Novogorod Model A (Gaz A) automobiles which had been exported by the Soviets to Turkey. It was shipped to Detroit and there pulled to pieces; Sorenson comments 'it was a pretty poor reproduction of Model A.'[34] The Ford was still in production in the late 1930s and by 1938 production was 84,000 units per year.[35]

The automobile industry is, then, an excellent example of a planned step-by-step transfer of Western technology at minimal cost. Ford was happy to sell $30 million worth of parts and throw in invaluable technical assistance for nothing. Technical assistance in production of axles, tires, bearings, and other items required payment but, as the marginal cost to American companies was slight, the Soviets reaped a gigantic harvest of technological knowhow for almost no outlay.

Table 14–2 TECHNICAL ASSISTANCE CONTRACTS (TYPE III)
IN THE SOVIET AUTOMOBILE CONSTRUCTION INDUSTRY TO 1930

Western company	*Soviet trust*	*Nature of technical assistance*
A. J. Brandt Company	Avtotrest	Reconstruction of AMO truck plant
Brown Lipe Gear Co.	Avtotrest	Geat-cutting technology
Ford Motor Co.	Avtotrest	Nizhni-Novgorod and Moscow plants
Hercules Motor Co.	Avtotrest	Truck engines for AMO plant
C. F. Seabrook Co.		Technical assistance on road building
Seiberling Rubber Co.	Resinotrest	Construction of tire plant
Timken-Detroit Axle Co.	Avtotrest	Axle and bearing technology
Austin & Co.	Glavmashstroi	Construction and design

Sources: Soviet Union Year Book, 1930, pp. 357–9.
U.S. State Dept. Archives.

As the Ford agreement was being signed in June 1929, another was being negotiated with Arthur J. Brandt for assistance in reorganizing the AMO truck plant. Preliminary technical work for the reorganization was undertaken in the Detroit office and works of Brandt, while American engineers were sent to the AMO works to investigate production conditions. Facilities were upgraded to produce 25,000 of the Ford 2½-ton truck (AMO-3), whereas previously only a few hundred a year had been produced.[36] In the following September, ten AMO engineers went to Detroit for training.[37]

One month after the signing of the Ford agreement, the Austin Company made a construction proposal to Glavmashstroi under which it guaranteed

34   Sorenson, *loc. cit.*
35   Report by Oberkommando der Wehrmacht, (OKW/Wi Rü Amt/Wi), March 1941. Miscellaneous German records, T 84–122.
36   *Torgovo-Promyshlennaya Gazeta,* No. 127, June 6, 1929.
37   *Ekonomicheskaya Zhizn,* No. 149, July 2, 1929.

to complete the Nizhni-Novgorod plant within fifteen months of conclusion of a definite contract. Austin had built the Ford and other automobile plants in the United States and had ample construction and engineering experience in this field.[38]

The contract was signed early in August; the Austin Company paid $250,000 for drafting the project and a special compensation for supervising construction and installation of equipment. Penalty clauses came into effect if costs were higher than estimated, and there was a bonus for completion at less than the estimated cost. Five engineers were delegated from Avtostroi to work with Austin in drafting the project. Austin was able to negotiate a 'cost plus' contract for supervisory operations, and compensation was calculated, as a percentage of the total cost of all building operations, including equipment, boiler room, foundry, and power station.[39]

Although these plants were built completely by Western enterprise and equipped and initially operated by Western firms, the myth has been perpetuated that these were designed, built, and run by the Soviets. Even large Western suppliers unwittingly reflect this belief. For example, the General Electric house organ, *The Monogram*, comments on the automobile-manufacturing units just described:

> When the Soviet Union built its mass production automobile and truck plants in Moscow and Gorki, where the *Ziz* and *Gaz* cars and trucks take shape on moving conveyors, General Electric, in addition to supplying hundreds of motors and controls for various high speed and special machine tools, also supplied especially designed electric apparatus to aid the mass production of vital parts. . . . For the mass production of drive shafts and rear axle housings for the *Gaz* cars and trucks General Electric designed and built special high speed arc welding machines to suit the exact requirements set down by the Soviet Engineering Commission.[40]

TELEGRAPH COMMUNICATIONS AND FOREIGN CONCESSIONS

In August 1921, a contract was signed with Det Store Nordiske Telgraselskab (the Great Northern Telegraph Association) of Denmark for the operation of telegraph lines between the Soviet Union and the Far East and all interconnections with foreign countries. A fee of 1 franc 20 centimes was payable to the Soviet Union for each word transmitted. The firm had to undertake repairs, keep the line in order, and install new apparatus capable of transmit-

---

[38] *Torgovo-Promyshlennaya Gazeta*, No. 169, July 26, 1929; and No. 253, November 1, 1929.
[39] *Ekonomicheskaya Zhizn*, No. 185, August 14, 1929.
[40] *Monogram*, November 1943.

ting 110 words per minute; the existing apparatus could transmit only 20 words per minute.[41]

Before the First World War the Indo-European Telegraph Company of London operated telephone and telegraph lines across central Europe, through Poland and Russia to Odessa, and through the Crimea to Persia, in addition to a cable line under the Black Sea from Odessa to Constantinople. Service was discontinued during the war. On April 12, 1922, the company signed a concession agreement with the Department of Posts and Telegraphs and again took over control of its lines through the Soviet Union. The lines appear to have been in a reasonably satisfactory condition, and workable for 200 miles northwest and 300 miles southeast of Odessa, into the Crimea. The underwater cable was also in good condition. Only a short section between Erevan and Tiflis required minor repairs.[42]

Three years later, in June 1926, a similar concession agreement was concluded between the Trans-Siberian Cables Company, a subsidiary of Great Northern, for the renewed operation of its overland cable to China. The company paid the Soviets one gold franc for each word transmitted along the line.[43]

The necessity for these concessions is rather obscure. The lines were operating when the concessions were granted. In 1913 the Indo-European cable to Persia carried one million words. This fell to 800,000 words in 1920 but was up to four million in 1923 and five million by 1926, when the concession was concluded.

It was reported in *Krasnya Gazeta* that the telegraph concessions would be of enormous advantage; without them Russia would be unable to connect to the European lines, and in any event the existant lines would be repaired and modernized. In addition to the word fee in gold the latest high-speed Western apparatus would be introduced. This would produce 'millions of francs in gold which will enable us to carry on trade with abroad.'[44] It appears in retrospect that existant traffic was straining the lines to capacity and that the concession was a device to get equipment modernization.

THE RADIO CORPORATION OF AMERICA
TECHNICAL ASSISTANCE AGREEMENT

In March 1926, General Harbord, president of RCA, requested advice from the State Department concerning a Soviet request to have RCA build a modern high-power radio station in Moscow capable of communication with

[41]   U.S. Consulate in Riga, Report 1199, September 3, 1921. (316–107–29.)
[42]   Minutes of proceedings of the 55th Ordinary General Meeting of the Indo-European Telegraph Company, Ltd., April 26, 1922, pp. 4–5.
[43]   U.S. Consulate in Riga Report 3820, June 5, 1926.
[44]   U.S. Consulate in Riga, September 5, 1921.

the United States. RCA was concerned, 'as it would . . . undoubtedly afford an opportunity for their peculiar governmental doctrines to get additional circulation in this country,' and consequently: 'a station built by us, and perhaps subsidized by credit facilities, enabling Russia freely to communicate with the United States, might be a liability to us with the American public.'

In later verbal discussions with the State Department, General Harbord appears to have been hesitant concerning the Russian proposition, as it would mean 'placing in the hands of Soviet Russia uncensored and untrammeled direct means of communication between Soviet Russia and the United States over which they could send messages of any kind, including propaganda.'[45]

It was then reported that the radio station in question would cost an estimated $2.5 million and that the Soviets did not have a powerful enough station for communication with the United States. A memorandum in the Far Eastern Division files argues that the question of utilizing the station for propaganda purposes or directing subversive activities in the United States was more theoretical than practical.[46] On April 9, 1926, the State Department sent a letter to RCA indicating that the Department did not desire to express any opinion concerning the proposed transaction.

The matter then lapsed until 1927. Another letter, dated May 25, 1927, from General Harbord to the State Department, indicates that RCA anticipated further negotiations for a 'modern, high powered radio station capable of communication with the United States.' Harbord requested an indication as to whether the letter of April 9, 1926 still held good in the light of Soviet propaganda 'being promulgated from Soviet offices in London directed against the United States and other countries and that evidence

[45]   Documents in this section are in the U.S. State Dept. Decimal File 316–141–714/78. The first part of Roll 141 contains material on Soviet propaganda and other communications with the Near and Far East. At this stage of the negotiations, the State Dept. view was that 'completion of the station in question would put into the hands of the Soviet regime a very powerful instrument which might be used to the detriment of the interest of the United States.' See Memorandum, Johnson, Far East Division, March 1, 1926 (316–141–714). This view was to change considerably over the next few years, for reasons which are not clear.

[46]   There are however, hundreds upon hundreds of documents in the State Dept. files alone indicating this was very much a practical matter. The exact wording of part of the memorandum is, 'I am inclined to the opinion that the theoretical possibilities are not of such cogency as to justify our according to them a decisive influence in this matter.'
The draft of the State Dept. letter to Harbord is also interesting. The draft prepared by R. F. Kelley makes reference to the possibility that the station might be used for subversive activities in the United States, but this was scratched out and does not appear in the letter that went to RCA. The erased paragraph reads 'With regard to the possibility of the utilization of the wireless station by the Soviet regime to facilitate the direction of communist subversive activities in the United States, I am not prepared at this time to make any comments. I note from your letter that you realize both the possibility and undesirability of such utilization.' The final letter went out over the signature of Kellogg, Secretary of State.

thereof had been furnished to our government.' The State Department reply of June 1 indicated that their position remained the same.

RCA made an agreement with the State Electro-technical Trust on June 30, 1927. This covered the transfer of patents and technical information. In addition, RCA furnished the delegation with tenders and quotations on a considerable quantity of radio apparatus, including a high-powered radio installation for Moscow. These amounts quoted were to be paid 70 percent cash, with the balance due over a period of five years at 6 percent. RCA agreed '. . . to grant exclusive licenses to the Trust to manufacture, use and sell all patents, applications for patents and inventions owned or controlled by the Radio Corporation of America and/or the General Electric Company and Westinghouse, to the extent that it has, or will have, the right to grant licenses in and for the territory for the Trust as hereinabove provided for. . . .'[47]

It was agreed that meetings of RCA engineers and those of the Soviet trusts would be held not less than once a year, and alternately in their respective territory, in order to exchange necessary technical information.

In addition, RCA agreed 'to furnish to the Trust complete manufacturing information in respect to terminal apparatus for use in radio picture transmission, including facsimile transmission, but not including television.' Manufacturing information was supplied for terminal apparatus, including 'complete specifications, working drawings, description of process of manufacturing, detailed basic calculations for construction of apparatus and the privilege of sending the representatives of the Trust to factories, laboratories and working stations of the Radio Corporation and General Electric Company or parts owned and controlled by them.'[48]

The agreement was made contingent on Amtorg placing a firm order with RCA within four months of the date of ratification for a minimum sum of $600,000.[49] In brief, in exchange for an order valued at $600,000, RCA transferred the sum of the technical knowledge accumulated by the leading firm in the industry.

GERMAN AID FOR RECONSTRUCTION
OF PETROGRAD HARBOR

This was the largest port in Russia. Its facilities were severely damaged in the Revolution—probably more so than any other sector of the economy. As late as December 1921, most of the port was still out of commission.

---

[47] *Ibid.*, Frame 749.

[48] *Ibid.*, Frame 760.

[49] There was also a traffic agreement covering the use of radio circuits between the U.S. and the U.S.S.R. and the supply of high-speed automatic and duplex com-

Of eight cranes, two were continually out of order, two intermittently out of order, and two unusable. The telephone system of the port could not be repaired, 'on account of lack of cable, wire, and commutators.'[50] The harbor itself, although it was the main base of the Red Navy, was not freed of mines until 1922. The harbor was not dredged from 1917 until 1923. German and British steamers calling at the port in 1921 were serviced by lighters when these were available. Although the port was a high-priority project for repair and a port telephone system was an essential part of that operation, *Krasnya Gazeta* admitted five years after the Revolution that nothing had been done.[51]

In 1922, tenders were received from German companies for repair of the port and the city facilities of Petrograd. Friedlam A-G handled the technical work of the restoration of harbor facilities, while the actual reconstruction was done by Julius Berger. Gas-works design was undertaken by Pintsch and construction also by Berger. Canals, general buildings, and cement works became the responsibility of Hecker, another German firm.[52] The city itself was the subject of another agreement 'to make the necessary repairs to all buildings that are now falling to pieces (and to) repair railways, the water and sewage systems, and other institutions belonging to the municipality.' German engineers and equipment were brought in as the navigation system opened in 1922. As payment, the Germans received the right to develop the clay industry, establish a brick plant, and export lumber to Germany.[53]

By late 1922, Petrograd Harbor was being cleared of debris and put back into operation. Groups of the unemployed were used for this job, together with Latvian Communist Party members.[54] Repairs to the ice breakers went more slowly. The only unit fit for service was named the Lenin; the Svyatogor and the Ermak required extensive work.

RECONSTRUCTION OF THE RUSSIAN SHIPBUILDING INDUSTRY

The shipbuilding yards at Petrograd and Nikolaev had been heavily damaged in the Revolution. Nearly all such facilities were in a chaotic condition; this

---

mercial radio communications apparatus. The agreement, together with letters from the International General Electric Co. and Westinghouse Electric International releasing patent rights in favor of the Soviet trusts, may be found in the U.S. State Dept. Decimal File 316–141–757/771.

[50]   *Krasnya Gazeta*, December 29, 1921.

[51]   U.S. Consulate in Helsingfors, Report 2110, May 15, 1922. (316–107–765.)

[52]   U.S. Consulate in Helsingfors, Report 135, August 21, 1922. (340–5–547/9.)

[53]   U.S. Consulate in Helsingfors, Report 2230, April 29, 1922 (316–107–752); *New York Times*, April 28, 1922, p. 2, col. 7.

[54]   IS Report, September 21, 1922. (316–10–1018.)

sector suffered more than most. The Petrograd yards, previously known as Nevsky (renamed the Lenin), Putilov (renamed Northern Shipbuilding), the Baltic, the Izhorsky, and the Ochtinsky (renamed the Government Works for River Ships), were grouped into the Sudotrust. In 1924, a technical commission was appointed to consider ways and estimate the costs of clearing the Petrograd yards. The commission had a number of German members, and the Krupp engineer Ledeke did the actual job of estimating costs of repairs. This was a military matter under the Northwestern Military Industry Committee and part of the post-Rapallo military cooperation agreement. The preliminary inspection of the Izhorsky yards, the largest, indicated that only nine of the seventeen workshops were in operable condition; the others needed complete rebuilding. Of four shipbuilding stocks, only the third could be used for ship construction and then only if the associated workshops were also put back into operation. Ledeke also estimated the cost of installing a submarine department in the yards. The Krasny Putilovets plant was inspected to estimate cost of installing turbine construction facilities for class 1 destroyers.[55]

Reconstruction of the Russian merchant fleet was slow. In 1925 the hulls of 11 vessels were laid, in 1926 a further four and in 1928 another 17. By May 1929 only 15 had been completed and 30 were still under construction.[56] No oceangoing ships were completed before 1930, except three 6,000-ton-gross motor ships with engines made with German technical assistance. At the same time two larger tankers, of 11,500 tons gross, were under construction in French shipyards with imported Sulzer engines. Somewhat larger vessels, of 9,000 to 11,000 tons gross, were undertaken at Soviet yards, at first with imported Sulzer engines and then with engines made with foreign technical assistance.[57] Again, the simple was built, while the complicated was purchased. Interestingly enough, the graduated process is still going on. In the 1960s Soviet yards were making all Soviet naval craft and tankers up to about 35,000 tons. Larger tankers were made to Soviet order in Italy and Japan and other special ships in British and Danish yards. Naval craft have always been constructed in Soviet yards, with the use of imported shipbuilding equipment, except for the World War II acquisitions noted in Volume II.

FOREIGN AID IN SHIPPING OPERATIONS

The first of a series of shipping agreements was made in January 1922 between the German Orient Line, the Soviet Volunteer Fleet, and Narkomvneshtorg (People's Commissariat of Foreign Trade). Under this agreement, the

---

[55]   U.S. Consulate at Hamburg, Report No. 417, December 12, 1925.

[56]   *Izvestia*, May 12, 1929.

[57]   Details from *Motor Ship Reference Book* (London, Temple Press) years 1925 to 1930.

tonnage of the Orient line was handed over to the Soviet Volunteer Fleet on preferential rate terms (20 percent lower that market rates). This enabled the fleet to establish a service between Hamburg and Odessa, Novorossisk, and Constantinople.[58]

Russtransit was a German-Russian joint-stock mixed company also organized in 1922, between the Commissariat of Foreign Trade, Ways, and Communications, and a group of five German firms, including the Orient Bank, Wenkhouse of Hamburg, and the Hamburg-Amerika line. The company established shipping routes between Germany and the Near East via the Baltic, the Marinsky canal system, the River Volga, and the Caspian Sea. This reduced the shipping time between Hamburg and Enzeli on the Caspian from a period of 4-6 months to only 3-4 weeks. Russtransit purchased several 10,000-ton vessels to operate on the river, canal, and lake routes.[59] In 1923 the turnover was 1.2 million rubles, on which the profit was 200,000 rubles.[60] The Hamburg-Amerika line put up 50 percent of the capital and received 50 percent of the profits.[61]

There were also some smaller shipping concessions. The Bergen Steamship Company was organized by the Soviets and the Russian-Norwegian Navigation Company in 1923 to provide shipping services for Arcos.[62] Another agreement was made with a German company, August Bolton, in 1924, and in April 1926 negotiations were concluded for a shipping concession on the River Volga to be operated by an Anglo-Dutch group headed by the Cunard line.[63] This was a mixed company, with the share capital split 50:50, to operate all passenger and freight services on the Volga. All boats, docks, workshops, and stores were transferred to the new company. Cunard was required to invest cash equal to the value of the boats and plant turned over to the company. The latter formed the Soviet contribution. The management was exclusively in the hands of Cunard, which had the right to hire and dismiss personnel. The Soviet government was not entitled by the terms of the agreement to interfere in the internal operations of the company.[64]

Shipping tonnage was almost completely destroyed by the Revolution, and even in 1930 only 4 percent of Soviet trade was being handled in Soviet flag vessels. The mercantile fleet was gradually built up by purchases abroad and not in the 1920s by domestic production of ships.

[58]   IS Report, January 19, 1922. (316–108–0006.)
[59]   *Ekonomicheskaya Zhizn*, No. 116, May 27, 1923.
[60]   *Ekonomicheskaya Zhizn*, No. 151, April 3, 1924.
[61]   Hilger, *op. cit.*, p. 178. Hamburg-Amerika Line also owned 50 percent of Derutra (German-Russian Transport Company), another mixed Type II operation.
[62]   *Ekonomicheskaya Zhizn*, No. 57, March 15, 1923.
[63]   *Pravda*, No. 175, August 3, 1924.
[64]   U.S. Consulate in Bremen, Report April 1, 1926. (316–108–1668.)

THE BEGINNINGS OF THE RUSSIAN AIR LINES

The first Russian air line was the Moscow-Konigsberg (Germany) route, started in August 1922 and, according to *Biednota*, 'created according to the plan of Red Pilot Grant and exploited exclusively by the RSFSR.'[65] In fact the line was installed and operated by the mixed company, Deruluft (German-Russian Aviation Company), and used German and Dutch (Fokker III) aircraft. Deruluft was formed specifically to conduct a regular air service for passengers, mail, and freight between Germany and Moscow. It had a stormy life and, as Hilger points out, the line survived only 'because of mutual necessity.'[66]

Dobrolet, an all-Russian company, was started one year later with German technical assistance. This company used Junkers aircraft, made in the U.S.S.R., throughout the 1920s. The third airline was Ukr-Vozdukh-Put, a private company formed in the 1920s and operated on Ukrainian routes up to 1929. The company used Dornier Comet II and III aircraft.[67]

Table 14–3   RUSSIAN SCHEDULED AIRLINES IN 1925

Route	Operating company	Equipment
Moscow-Konigsberg	Deruluft*	Fokker III
Moscow-Kharkov	Ukr-Vozdukh-Put**	Dornier Comet III
Kharkov-Rostow	Ukr-Vozdukh-Put**	Dornier Comet III
Kharkov-Odessa	Ukr-Vozdukh-Put**	Dornier Comet III
Kharkov-Kiev	Ukr-Vozdukh-Put**	Dornier Comet II
Kagan-Tazbaz	Dobrolet***	Junkers
Kagan-Dushambe	Dobrolet***	Junkers
Baku-Enzeli (Persia)	Junkers****	Junkers
Baku-Leningrad	Junkers****	Junkers

Source: U.S. State Dept. Decimal File, 316–164–244, 372.
Notes: *Type II concession.
    **Private company, expropriated in 1929.
    ***All-Russian company.
    ****German company.

In addition to the three regular airlines, the Junkers company operated some routes with its own equipment under a leasing arrangement. By the middle of the decade, the air fleet consisted of just under 100 passenger planes (Junkers, Dorniers, and Fokkers) together with another 50–80 light planes.[68] The first Soviet-built planes, copies of the British De Havilland observation

[65] *Biednota*, August 26, 1922.
[66] Hilger, *op. cit.*, p. 178
[67] U.S. State Dept. Decimal File, 316–164–205.
[68] U.S. State Dept. Decimal File, 316–164–225.

plane, were produced in 1925 and at once used on a Moscow-Peking propaganda air expedition. The expedition was billed as using all-Russian-built planes, whereas in fact it used modified Junkers and De Havilland copies with imported engines.[69]

[69]   U.S. State Dept. Decimal File, 316–164–391.

CHAPTER FIFTEEN

German-Russian Military Cooperation and Technology

THE Versailles Treaty forbade Germany, equipped with some of the most extensive and advanced munitions plants in Europe, the manufacture of any armaments. Soviet Russia was isolated and under attack from within and without. Her armaments plants operated only intermittently, and she had a pressing desire to expand military production for internal control and world revolution. The obvious came to pass. The German-Russian military cooperation of the 1920s and 1930s has been documented elsewhere.[1] One aspect of this transfer has, however, been missed. The military transfer was part of a much wider economic cooperation and included the reconstruction of Russian industry as well as purely military construction. It is the industrial aspects of the military cooperation which are of interest to this study.

In April 1921, Menshevik Victor Kopp reported to Trotsky concerning his trip to Germany. Kopp had visited the armaments plants of Krupp, Blohm und Voss, and Albatross Werke and found them ready to supply both equipment and technical assistance for the manufacture of war materials. Post-Rapallo negotiations widened this visit into full-blown cooperation on the economic aspects of military production.[2] Purely military production was placed under the control of Gesellschaft zur Förderung Gewerblicher Unternehmungen (or GEFU) with a capital of 75 million reichmarks.[3] This

---

[1]   The most detailed study is in C. F. Melville, *The Russian Face of Germany* (London: Wishart Co., 1932). A more recent book by J. W. Wheeler-Bennett, *The Nemesis of Power* (New York; St. Martin's Press, 1964), is a useful supplement. Gustav Hilger and Alfred G. Meyer, *The Incompatible Allies* (New York; Macmillan, 1953), is less than forthright. Hilger was German economic attaché in Moscow throughout this period but reduces the cooperation to 'scholars and journalists with axes to grind.' (Fn., p. 189.)

[2]   Trotsky Archives, Harvard University, Document T-666*.

[3]   Hilger, *op. cit.*, GEFU functions after 1925 were taken over by WIKO (Wirtschaftskontor).

production included reopening the Junkers aircraft plant at Fili, developing poison gas plants, establishing factories for production of artillery and shells, tanks, and submarines. Further, the Soviets themselves placed heavy emphasis on military production and grouped many of the best-equipped tsarist works as a part of RVS, including the Putilovets, Koppel, Lessner, Phoenix, Atlas, and Pneumatic plants.[4]

TSARIST AND JUNKERS AIRCRAFT TECHNOLOGY

Aircraft development and construction had made vigorous progress in tsarist Russia under such designers as Igor Sikorsky and V. Slessarev, but the industry collapsed completely after the Bolshevik Revolution. There was no indigenous Soviet aircraft technology in the 1920s and the ill-fated 'Maxim Gorki,' designed in 1934, was the first indication of a revival in a truly remarkable prerevolutionary activity.[5]

Igor Sikorsky (since the Revolution a resident in the United States) had been the nucleus of a promising aircraft technology. In 1913 he designed and built two planes of *four-engine design*. The first was the Russki Vityazyi, a five-ton aircraft with room for seven passengers, built in St Petersburg; the second Sikorsky design was the 'Ilya Mourometz', with four 100-h.p. engines, a payload capacity of 1,500 kilograms, and a maximum speed of 55 m.p.h. Lack of more powerful engines was the impetus behind the four-engine design; a similar restriction made the 'Maxim Gorki' an eight-engine (750 h.p. each) plane rather than the originally planned six-engine (1,000 h.p.) plane.

The four-engine Ilya Mourometz was built in Russia as a bomber, and about 75 went into service in World War I. Wing span was 102 feet: only 21 inches less than the Boeing B-17 of World War II. Engines were a restricting factor, and 11 different makes were used including the Russian-built Baltic. Production of these planes was in fact limited by engine production.[6]

This interest in aviation was adopted by the Soviets. After World War I the German aircraft manufacturers Junkers, Dornier, and Rohrbach were forced, under the 'London ultimatum' to move their plants and personnel abroad. Junkers-Werke went to the U.S.S.R. and, under the April 1922

---

[4] U.S. State Dept. Decimal File, 316–107–391.

[5] Interest in aviation developed early in Russia. Curtiss made a trip in 1912 and estimated over 100 aircraft in use by the Imperial Russian Army at a Sevastopol base. When the United States entered the war in 1917, its combined Army and Navy air forces consisted of little more than 100 planes. ['Aviation in South Russia, 1912'. (316–164–170).]

[6] *Ibid.*, and H. Hooftman, *Russian Aircraft* (Fallbrook: Aero, 1965), pp. 142–3.

military agreement reopened the prerevolutionary aircraft plant at Fili in mid-1923. Machinery was obtained from the evacuated section of the Russo-Baltic works in Riga and installed at Fili by Junkers engineers. In the tsarist era, the plant had made RB-150 h.p. motors for the Ilya Mourometz. Under Junkers management the plant built Mercedes-Benz motors under license and the all-metal Junkers-design aircraft.[7]

Thus the famous all-metal Junkers aircraft was under construction in the Soviet Union some ten years before Lockheed and Douglas brought out their first all-metal designs in 1933. The Soviets can legitimately claim that the first all-metal plane was produced in the U.S.S.R.

Even before Junkers had moved, the Soviets were buying aircraft engines, Deutz Type UMX and complete aircraft abroad. Some 280 Fokker D-7 fighter aircraft were ordered and delivered from Holland.[8] In July 1924, the Junkers Company opened up a second aircraft plant in Tver Province under a 49-year concession arrangement, with the right to export airplanes. All the test pilots and engineers were Junkers personnel from Germany.[9]

By 1924 the Soviets began to make their own wooden aircraft, one year before the first Russian bus was produced. At first they purchased Fokker drawings, the De Havilland prototype, and imported engines. They then used engines domestically manufactured with German (Deutz A-G) technical assistance. Machine tools for the aircraft plants were supplied by Nielsen and Winther in Denmark.[10] Spruce for building the wings and fuselage was imported from the state of Washington—which in itself created a small stir in Washington, D.C.[11] The most successful of these early afforts was the copy of the De Havilland Tiger Moth, still in use in 1966 and variously called the R-1, U-2, and today the PO-2. Up to 1948, when production ceased, several thousand had been produced in about 20 versions. It was first used as a military observation plane, then as a night bomber in World War II, and is presently used as an ambulance plane and crop duster. Production of simple planes such the Tiger Moth R-1 before automobiles is not illogical. Construction of such a plane is a very simple matter involving wood and canvas, and is much less complex than automobile production. Utilizing first imported engines and then engines made with German technical assistance, the Soviets trained their cadres of aircraft engineers and technicians.

---

[7]   IS Report, August 17, 1923. (316–108–641/2.)
[8]   U.S. State Dept. Decimal File, 316–164–193.
[9]   U.S. State Dept. Decimal File, 316–164–215.
[10]   U.S. State Dept. Decimal File, 316–164–208.
[11]   Telegram from Governor Hart of Washington to the President, January 24, 1923. (336–129–332.)

German technical assistance, supplemented by assistance from other countries, was quite extensive. Barmine recounts how, because of the large-scale purchases of aircraft equipment and components in Europe, the aircraft manufacturers signed technical-aid contracts, trained Russian engineers and sent their specialists and designers to the U.S.S.R. to build and equip aircraft plants. Barmine singles out the French aircraft industry to 'share with the American the credit of helping the U.S.S.R. to build its air power.'[12] Technical assistance in the manufacture of aircraft parachutes, and particularly the packing techniques, was provided by Irving Air Chute Co., Inc., of the United States.[13]

Numerous efforts, some successful, were made to obtain American aircraft engines and, especially, large quantities of the war surplus Liberties available in the domestic United States market at $1,000 each. The latest Curtiss engines were also secured.

In the early 1920s, the Hall Scott Motor Company sold a large lot of aeronautical equipment to the Vimalert Company of New Jersey; this found its way to the Soviet Union.[14] In late 1925 some thirty cases of aircraft engines were shipped by Amtorg to Autoimport in Moscow. These were assumed by the State Department to be Liberty engines, not automobile engines, as they were purchased by Zautinsky, the aviation purchasing agent for the Soviet Union and shipped from Little Rock, Arkansas, where the large quantities of surplus Liberty engines were stored and sold.[15] This shipment was followed by another thirty-three Liberty engines on May 6, 1926 via the Hamburg-Amerika Line to Leningrad. These had been purchased by Zautinsky in a very roundabout manner. They were originally sold to the Leoning Aircraft Company, resold to Ayers Airco, then to a dealer named Epstein and another dealer named Kelly.[16]

Table 15–1   SOVIET PURCHASES OF AMERICAN
AIRCRAFT ENGINES, 1926–9

Date	Number shipped	Type and make
Nov 8, 1925	30	Liberty 400 h.p.
May 6, 1926	33	Liberty 400 h.p.
Dec 27, 1929	10	Curtis Conqueror

Source: U.S. State Dept. Decimal File, 316–164–267, 164–289, 164–317.

---

12 Barmine, *op. cit.*, p. 179.
13 A. A. Santalov and L. Segal, *Soviet Union Year Book, 1930* (London: Allen and Unwin, 1930), p. 358.
14 U.S. State Dept. Decimal File, 316–164–250.
15 *Ibid.*
16 U.S. State Dept. Decimal File, 316–164–250.

These comparatively small purchases were followed by very intensive efforts to obtain a larger quantity of the Liberty motors, if possible at the low price of $1,000. However, it was reported that the Soviets were willing to pay up to $10,000 per motor and give a bonus to anyone able to acquire a substantial quantity at an export price of $2,000.[17] One effort to buy a batch of 200 was made by the Payne Export and Import Company of New York in August 1927. The State Department indicated it did not look with favor upon the transaction. Payne later tried to buy through the Vimalert Company. At the same time Fox and Company attempted to purchase 700 on behalf of the Soviets. The Chase National Bank of New York, in an aside from its banking business, was actively trying to arrange export of Liberty motors at $2,000 each to the U.S.S.R.[18] A few weeks later one Max Rabinoff, a dancing instructor in New York, tried to buy 488 Liberty motors, allegedly for use by Deruluft (the German-Russian mixed company) on its flights to the Soviet Union. However, Rabinoff wanted the motors shipped to the U.S.S.R. to 'avoid customs duties.'[19] None of these orders was filled; it would appear that the Department of Justice was one step ahead each time. However, in 1929 the Curtiss Company filled an order for ten Curtiss Conquerers with spare parts—a much more advanced engine than the Liberty.[20] Just two years previously, in June 1927, the State Department had indicated that it did not look with favor on the sale of 100 Curtiss type D-12 engines to the U.S.S.R.[21] This was a situation parallel to the shipment of a high-powered radio station to the Soviet Union.

General von Seeckt, Chief of the German General Staff, had attempted to make contact with the Soviets before the Treaty of Versailles, but Hilger places the first cooperation at 1921, originating with a Junkers request for assistance from the German government in the establishment of an aircraft plant in Russia. Special Group R of the German War Ministry was established for military collaboration and gave the necessary political guarantees and financial assistance to Junkers. A branch office of Group R was established in Moscow and known as Zentrale Moskau; it operated under 'Neumann', a pseudonym for Major Oskar Ritter von Niedermayer.[22] The latter was head of Zentrale Moskau until 1932 and passed a stream of military information back to Germany, as he was far less restricted than the official military attaché

[17] Department of Justice letter to Military Intelligence (U.S. State Dept. Decimal File, 316–164–271).

[18] U.S. State Dept. Decimal File, 316–164–256.

[19] U.S. State Dept. Decimal File, 316–164–283.

[20] U.S. State Dept. Decimal File, 316–164–317.

[21] U.S. State Dept. Decimal File, 316–164–250.

[22] Hilger, *op. cit.*, p. 194. The German Foreign Office used a supersecret classification 'Z' for all documents in contravention to the Versailles Treaty.

at the German Embassy. The latter, according to Hilger 'had no opportunity to talk to the constant stream of German Army personnel passing through . . . on their way to or from different places within the Soviet Union.'[23] Hilger, as economic attaché, may have been in a similar position of isolation, because he contributed very little to our knowledge of the extensive economic transfers of the 1920s.[24]

THE RED AIR FORCE, 1929

Total personnel in the Red Air Force in 1929 numbered approximately 30,000. Purely military aircraft numbered 1,200, of which 160 were with the Red Navy. Table 15–2 summarizes Red Air Force and Navy equipment, and its origin.

Table 15–2   RED AIR FORCE EQUIPMENT AND WESTERN ORIGIN, 1929

Type of plane	*Origin*
Observation	Soviet-made R-1, copy of British De Havilland.
Attack	Fokker D-XI and D-XIII, imported
	French Nieuports.
Bombers	Farman-Goliath (80) and a few Rohrbachs, imported.
Navy (Black Sea)	Fokkers D-XI (Holland).
	Ballilo (Italy).
	Dornio-Wal (Italy).
Navy (Baltic fleet)	Junkers J-20 (from Sweden).
	Fokkers D-XI (Holland).
Aircraft engines	
R-1 observation	M-5, made with German assistance.
	Some imports from Bayerische Motor Werke.
Attack	450 h.p. Hispano-Suiza and German makes.

Source: U.S. Military Intelligence Report, *Combat Estimate: Russia.*

Table 15–2 can be summarized briefly. The only complete aircraft built in the U.S.S.R. was the R-1 light observation plane. All other aircraft and engines were imported—from every country manufacturing aircraft. In other words, the Soviets were able to compare, test, select for purchase, and at some point manufacture the best features from planes manufactured in all Western countries.

RUSSIAN-GERMAN TRAINING CENTERS

The main German air base in the Soviet Union was at Lipetsk. It was initially funded in 1924 by an appropriation from the German war budget and

[23]   Hilger, *op. cit.,* p. 179.
[24]   The United States received excellent information from its Riga Consulate.

further funded by an appropriation from the Ruhrfond (Relief Fund for Ruhr Workers). This fund was administered by Group R. Lipetsk was used as a base for final pilot training, and the testing and development of new planes by both the Germans and the Russians. Nearly everything was shipped from Germany, either by Derutra or Russgertorg by a circuitous rail route. Only very basic materials such as wood and stone were supplied by the Soviet Union. At the end of 1924, there were about 60 German pilots and another 75–100 technical personnel stationed at Lipetsk. This group was known as the Fourth Squadron of the Red Air Force.[25]

Clause two of the German-Russian Military agreement required dispatch of German naval instructors to Russia to train the Red Navy. In mid-1923 an intercepted telegram from Moscow to Berlin ordered the 'military attaché' in the Soviet Berlin Trade Delegation to arrange for the transfer of 1,200 German naval instructors.[26]

BERSOL POISON GAS PRODUCTION

A considerable amount of work was done on poison gases under the tsar. Liquid chlorine, the major poison gas used in World War I, was made in eight different plants. The difficult technical problems involved in handling chlorine gas—especially liquefaction—were solved by Russian chemists, 'since the methods and techniques used in Western Europe were unknown to us.'[27] Production was so successful that a chlorine over-supply developed, and by summer 1917 there was a tank reserve of 100,000 poods. Phosgene was produced at five plants under the supervision of Professor E. I. Spitalsky. Apart from use as a poison, gas was useful in synthesis of organic pigments and drugs. The work was done under the supervision of the Commission on Poison Gases, which also established an experimental factory under the directorship of I. Klimov, who continued as director after the Revolution.

Ipatieff was for a while chairman of the Russo-German commission which negotiated production of explosives and poison gases in the U.S.S.R. by German companies. A mixed commission of three Russians and two Germans carried out the agreement. The tsarist poison gas factory at Samara had been only partly built by the time of the Revolution, and Ipatieff was sent to

---

[25]   G. Freund, *Unholy Alliance* (New York: Harcourt, Brace & Co., 1957), p. 205 *et seq.*

[26]   U.S. State Dept. Decimal File, 340–5–670 (intercepted telegram, June 1923).

[27]   V. I. Ipatieff, *op. cit.*, pp. 212–235. It is noteworthy that tsarist Russia had little help from the Allies in the development of gases or gas masks. The Kumant-Zelinsky gas mask was a purely Russian development, and although it had defects it was more effective than the French mask and equally as effective as the German and British. The tsarist Chemical Committee supplied some 15 million of this type of mask. (Ipatieff, *op. cit.*, p. 225.)

evaluate the plant for purposes of the German agreement and to determine its use in the production of both chlorine and phosgene. Ipatieff received instructions not to underestimate the plant's value, since the greater the original value, the more the Germans would have to invest in the agreement. Although Ipatieff felt the plant valueless, he assessed it at six million rubles. The German valuation quite naturally was considerably less. The contract was awarded by the German government to Stolzenberg, owner of a Hamburg gas factory making phosgene, chlorine, and ammonium chloride. The Samara plant was renamed the Trotsky and rebuilt by German engineers. Other institutions and schools were formed to handle other aspects of poison gas production and use.[28]

Soviet interest in gases was intense. A special military agent was maintained within the Berlin Trade Delegation solely for the purpose of collecting foreign information on poison gas and allied materials. Ipatieff recounts how a Dutch engineer offered to bring the Soviets a new substance effective against all smoke and poison gas vapors. Reports were sent back on German attempts at Essen to manufacture a gasproof fabric.[29]

Not much appears to have been achieved. The Trotsky plant was a failure. In 1927, Voroshilov commented that 'our entire chemical industry for military purposes has yet to be built up. . . .' However, he placed great emphasis on chemical warfare and aviation as the weapons of the future and wanted to equip 'every laborer and every toiler' with a gas mask.[30]

PRODUCTION OF SHELLS, ARTILLERY, AND SUBMARINES FOR THE RED ARMY AND NAVY

The third major task of GEFU was supervision of factories at Tula, Leningrad, and Schlesselburg for production of artillery shells at the rate of 300,000 per year.[31] In 1927 it was reported that seventeen plants for the construction of artillery were being built by Krupp in central Asia.[32] The existence of such a large number of shell and artillery plants is credible in the light of the Soviet recoil to the German *Barbarossa* attack of 1941. The Russian counterattack in the winter was made before Western aid flowed in quantity and was made by utilizing large massed fronts of artillery and tanks of a single model.

---

[28] *Ibid.*, p. 385.

[29] *Ibid.*, pp. 459–60.

[30] *Izvestia*, No. 97, April 30, 1927.

[31] A booklet entitled *Sowjetgrenaden*, based on interviews with workers at the shell plants, was issued by the Social Democratic Party in 1927.

[32] U.S. Embassy in Stockholm, Report 66, August 12, 1927. (316-60-1003.)

Submarine construction is less well documented. It is known that Krupp estimated construction of submarine pens at Leningrad.[33] Bailey holds that U-boats were built at both the Leningrad and Nikolaevsk yards by German companies.[34]

EQUIPMENT OF THE SOVIET ARMED
FORCES IN 1929

In 1929 the Soviet army comprised 1.2 million men. It was largely equipped with prewar or foreign weapons. The standard rifle issue was the 1891 Russian .30 supplemented by Browning automatic pistols and a mixture of Russian, French, German, and British hand and rifle grenades.[35] The one-pound guns used in infantry regiments were MacLean or German makes. Heavy machine guns were either Maxim or Colt. Light machine guns were either Browning, Chaucgat, or Lewis. Artillery was comprised of the 1902 Russian 76 mm, the 4.5-inch English howitzer, and 1909 model Russian 4.8 howitzer. The basic anti-aircraft equipment was the 1916 Russian 76 mm and the Vickers 40 mm.[36] Tanks were the Renault, built with technical assistance at Fili, and a Russian-built copy of the British Mark IV. A few Fiat tanks had been purchased from Italy.

Military strength in 1929 was, then, based entirely on foreign weapons and military production technology. Further development, at least at any acceptable rate, was possible only with Western assistance. Without it, self-generating economic development would have been prohibitively slow. Russia was without an automobile industry, without a useful aviation industry, without modern iron, steel, and metalworking facilities, and much else with which to forge a military structure. But, as the Military Intelligence estimate pointed out, 'if her economic and military recovery continue at the present rate in a few years she will be a formidable enemy.'[37]

---

[33]   See chap. 14.
[34]   G. Bailey, *The Conspirators* (New York: Harper, 1960).
[35]   The Russian 1891 3-line model rifle was the subject of Clause 1 of the 1922 German-Russian military agreement.
[36]   Military Intelligence Division U.S. War Dept., *Combat Estimate: Russia* (1929).
[37]   U.S. State Dept. Decimal File, 316–110–347.

CHAPTER SIXTEEN

Soviet Trading Companies and the Acquisition of Foreign Markets

ACQUISITION of Western technology and skills required, of course, a source of finance. Some large-scale inter-government loans were made; of these, the 1925 German loan of 100 million marks and the 1926 loan of 300 million marks were the largest. Unpublicized private business loans and credit were much more common and more important. Export of gold was not at first considered a generator of foreign exchange. After 1925, coincident with the Lena Goldfields agreement, the export of gold became a valued means of acquiring foreign technology. Further, the extensive collections of confiscated platinum, silver, rare metals, tsarist crown jewels, plateware, and ikons gathered up by the Bolsheviks were sorted and catalogued by yet another Western expert, H. J. Larsons, Deputy Chief of Currency Administration, and then exported.[1]

The primary source of foreign exchange during the 1920s was export of raw materials—especially petroleum products, furs, minerals, and foodstuffs. Export of food to regain prewar markets was implemented even while American relief was importing supplies into Russia for the famine areas. In one case, the Soviets were loading a boat with Ukrainian wheat for export to Germany, while alongside was a boat from the United States unloading American wheat for the famine areas to the north of the Ukraine. The chicken industry was nationalized at an early date and eggs assembled for export to Europe by Russot and other mixed Type II concessions.

These markets were entered by using mixed joint-stock companies which specialized in trading. The Soviets normally held a 50 percent interest and the foreign partner the other 50 percent. Germany, Austria, and the United States each had two of these general trading companies in the early 1920s.

[1] H. J. Larsons, *An Expert in the Service of the Soviets* (London: Benn, 1929).

Turkey, Poland, Italy, and Persia had one company each. The foreign firm advanced credits to the Soviet organizations, found the buyers and arranged transportation and storage. In some cases the foreign partner undertook assembly within the Soviet Union. In addition to these general trading companies, there was a more numerous group of specialized trading companies with agreements covering trade in specific commodities. In both cases the Soviets profited by the skilled knowledge and trading skills of the Western partner until such time as they were able to organize their own institutions for foreign trade.

By far the more important of the United States general trading companies was Allied American, with its Berlin subsidiary, Alamerico. Simon Sutta was a much smaller and short-lived arrangement.

ALLIED AMERICAN CORPORATION (ALAMERICO)

The Hammer family held three concessions in the Soviet Union. One covered the Alapievsky asbestos deposits; the second, granted in July 1923, was a general trading concession,[2] and the third was the pencil and stationery concession. The Hammers had been trading with the U.S.S.R. under a Soviet trading license, since 1918; the concession gave them the right to establish an office in Moscow and represent a number of large American companies. Previous to the grant of the concession, Hammer had been described as the 'Soviet trade representative in the United States.'[3]

The Hammer trading concession represented thirty-eight large American companies. These had an aggregate capitalization in excess of one billion dollars, and included Ingersoll-Rand, American Tool Works, Heald Machine, Ford Motor Company, U.S. Rubber, U.S. Machinery, and other companies of similar stature.[4]

Hammer also made contracts in the United States for the sale of Soviet raw materials. The right was granted to conduct operations independently of the government trade monopoly: quite a remarkable situation, given the vehemence with which the Soviets normally defended their monopoly on trading rights. The only limitation on Hammer operations was that imports into the Soviet Union could not exceed exports. It appears that the Hammer concession was represented within the U.S.S.R. by Soviet organizations. For example, in the Northwestern oblast, the concession was represented by the Northwestern Trade Association, 'which institution will carry out all the transactions of the Company.'[5] The concession was financed by the U.S.S.R.

[2]   *Ekonomicheskaya Zhizn*, No. 51, March 3, 1926 (advertisement).
[3]   *New York Times*, November 6, 1921, p. 23, col. 3.
[4]   *New York Times*, July 9, 1923, p. 3, col. 3.
[5]   *Pravda* (Petrograd), No. 189, August 24, 1923.

and 50 percent of the profits accrued to the Soviet Union. It was rare at that time for the Soviets to finance operations originating outside the Soviet Union and operated by foreigners; the only other example was the Swedish locomotive firm of Nyquist and Holm, which received significant financial aid in its program of locomotive production for the U.S.S.R. However, as has been pointed out, Andersson, the director of the plant, had a special relationship with the Soviet Union.

The Board of Directors of Alamerico contained a Russian member, G. L. Rappaport, a member of the People's Commissariat of Foreign Trade.[6] A rather curious letter appeared in the *New York Times* shortly after the agreement, maintaining that the concession was neither a concession nor a mixed company but 'a temporary commercial agreement.'[7] As events turned out, Alamerico was precisely that: a temporary commercial agreement. The motivation for the letter and the source of the information can only be guessed. One might infer that it was inspired by Vneshtorg to avoid a conflict with Glavkontsesskom.

Alamerico filled the gap for the Soviets between the demise of the Soviet Bureau in New York and the establishment of Amtorg; as Amtorg found its feet, Alamerico faded into the background, and in 1926 the agreement was not renewed. In a six-month period in 1925-6, Alamerico exported $221,000, only twice the amount of the purchases of Lena Goldfields concession in the United States in the same period.[8] Clearly the Soviets were never hampered by lack of United States recognition insofar as having a trade organization in the United States; they were able to operate through individual American companies in a way denied the United States in the Soviet Union.

A formal trade agreement of a specialized nature was the mixed Type II joint-stock company which operated under the name of the Russian-American Engineering and Trading Company (RAITCO), formed in mid-1923 by Allis-Chalmers Manufacturing Company, the Bucyrus Company, and the Sullivan Machinery Company in the United States and the People's Commissariat for Foreign Trade (Vneshtorg) in the Soviet Union.[9]

Clause II of the agreement described the objectives of the concession as to import into the Soviet Union from the United States articles required for 'equipment and supply of agriculture and all kinds of industrial construction work,' and to introduce 'American working methods' and 'projects.' Clause III described the ways by which these objectives might be achieved: by representation of American firms—in particular, industrial, construction,

[6] *Ibid.*
[7] *New York Times*, July 18, 1923, p. 14, col. 6.
[8] *Amerikanskaia torgovlia i promyshlennost'* (Amtorg Trading Company, 1926).
[9] The agreement is in the U.S. State Dept. Decimal File, 316–131–70/84.

engineering, and financial firms—by organization of a staff of experts, and by the import of articles required for the equipment of Russian industry. The company was to submit proposals and initiate discussions with the necessary Soviet institutions, and for this purpose might establish offices, warehouses, and branches within the Soviet Union. The capital stock was divided equally, and each party was represented by an equal number of directors.

The first 10 percent of profits went into a reserve fund to sustain possible losses. The balance (not to exceed 40 percent of the capital stock) was to be divided equally among the parties. Of the excess, 75 percent was to go to the Soviet government and 25 percent to the group of firms. Altogether there were 24 clauses detailing precisely the methods and conduct of the business.

From the viewpoint of the Western firms this was a logical move to protect their markets in the Soviet Union, given the continued operation of the International Harvester plant in Moscow. Indeed, the Soviets may well have had such a reaction in mind.[10]

UNITED KINGDOM TRADING COMPANIES

Arcos (the All Russian Cooperative Society, Ltd.) was formed in London on July 11, 1920 with a nominal capital of £15,000, allegedly to act as the representative of Russian cooperatives in the U.K., to carry on business as an export-import merchant, and to provide all services, in the broadest sense, necessitated by these functions. Of the stock, 65 percent was personally held by Leonid Krassin, the Soviet trade representative. This agreement was followed by another all-Soviet undertaking, the First All Russian Import and Export Company, Ltd., also a trading company. Then followed a series of trading companies in joint ownership with British and other foreign shareholders.

There was considerable criticism in the British press concerning the validity of Arcos calling itself a cooperative society when 485,996 of the 500,000 shares issued were held by Krassin and his deputy, Klisko. It was argued that Arcos was in effect the Russian Trade Delegation in the United Kingdom and had no connection with the Russian cooperatives. The position was confused by the appearance of a second company also claiming to represent the Russian cooperatives. Subsequent events proved the criticisms correct. Arcos became the focal point of Soviet trade (and subversion) in the U.K. but the subterfuge was used to gain entry, in the same way that Amtorg on entry into the United States denied that it had connections with Soviet trade organizations and argued that it was solely a business organization.

---

[10]   International Harvester's plant was expropriated for the first time in 1924, *after* the signing of the agreement with Allis-Chalmers, Bucyrus, and Sullivan.

In 1921 capital in Arcos was raised to £100,000, and Arcos began to sell Russian goods as well as to buy British manufactured goods. In 1922 capital was increased to £500,000 and in 1923 to 10 million gold rubles. The London office then employed some 500 people, about one-third of them Russians. Branches were scattered throughout the U.K. and Europe, as well as Russia. The guise of a cooperative representative was dropped when it appeared that deportation proceedings would not be continued—one of the dangers avoided by entering under the shield of a mixed company including foreign partners. By 1925 the company described itself as follows: 'The commercial organization of Arcos, Ltd. is of such a manifold and flexible character that it is able to carry out the most diverse transactions for the importing and exporting bodies of the Soviet Union.'[11]

Four years after its rather tentative entry into the United Kingdom, Arcos was handling 86 percent of all Soviet purchases in the U.K. 'made by all the companies, economic bodies and trading organizations carrying on Anglo-Soviet trade.'[12] Only 13.7 percent of the exports from the Soviet Union were being handled by Arcos. Its successful establishment was followed by a host of mixed and Soviet-owned companies in the U.K., predominantly for the sale of Russian raw materials. When these mixed companies, with foreign partners, were no longer needed, they were dropped.

THE RUSSO-BRITISH GRAIN EXPORT COMPANY

Exports of Russian grain began again in 1922 and gained new impetus in 1923. Russia had been the world's largest exporter of grain in tsarist times, and the Soviets naturally wanted to regain 'their' share of the market. One of the first agreements in the grain trade was completed in October 1923 between Centrosoyuz, Arcos, and Khlebexport on the one hand and a group of English companies on the other (the Cooperative Wholesale Society; Shipton, Anderson, Laurence and Company; and Furness Withy). As a result, the Russo-British Grain Export Company was formed. The English and the Soviets were represented equally on the board. The company had the support of British banks who provided from the outset a line of credit amounting to £1 million sterling at any one time to cover Russian grain at seaboard, in port, or afloat.

The willingness of leading banks and commerical institutions to finance trade operations in the U.S.S.R. on ordinary commercial terms, even when the question of expropriation was still far from negotiation, contributed greatly to the success of these early efforts; without such financial aid they

[11]   *Commercial Year Book of the Soviet Union, 1925*, p. 250.
[12]   *Ibid.*

would never have been realized. The proceeds of these grain sales were used to purchase manufactured goods in the U.K.[13]

Another Type II mixed company was formed in December 1923 between the Commissariat of Foreign Trade and Dava-Britopol (the Danzig-Warsaw British-Polish Company) called Ruspoltorg. This company had the prime objective of exporting timber, bristles, horsehair, and medical herbs. To assemble, store, and prepare these materials for export, it invested in the Soviet Union. The capital of Ruspoltorg was one million rubles invested equally by the founders, but it also had a line of credit amounting to four million rubles from a group of Polish financiers, and some additional United Kingdom backing.

Table 17–1   SPECIALIZED TRADING CONCESSIONS (TYPE II)

Lumber	Petroleum Products	Transport	Dairy Products
Russangloles (U.K.)	Persaneft (Persia)	Russtransit (Germany)	Eggexport (Germany)
Russhollangloles (U.K.-Holland)		Russcapa (Canada)	Union Cold Storage (U.K.)
Russnorvegloles (U.K.-Norway)	Deruneft (Germany)	Deruluft (Germany)	Siberian Co. (Sibiko) (Denmark)
Mologa-Waldindustrie (Germany)		Derutra (Germany)	G. H. Truss (U.K.)
Dvinoles Export, Ltd. (U.K.)		Ocean Travel Bureau (U.S.A.)	
Repola Wood, Ltd. (Finland)			
Deruwa (Germany)			

Cotton and Silk	Foodstuffs	Animal Products	Miscellaneous
Persholk (Persia)	Russot (45 percent International)	Kossayger	Persshold
Perskhlopok (Persia)	Russperssakhar (Persia)	A. Roesch (Germany)	Russian-Asiatic Stock Co.
Kazuli (Greek)		Iva (Germany)	Shark
Turksholk (Turkey)		Wostwag (Germany)	Sovmong
		Koshsuryo	Derumetall

The company paid all Soviet taxes, imposts, and duties, and an additional 10 percent of annual profits to the Soviet government. Exports amounted to about $1 million per year.[14]

GERMAN TRADING COMPANIES AND THE U.S.S.R.

In late 1921, Centrosoyuz concluded an agreement with a German trading company, Nord-Ost, for exchange of Russian raw materials for German

[13]   *Manchester Guardian*, October 18, 1923.
[14]   *Ekonomicheskaya Zhizn*, No. 366, December 20, 1924.

manufactured goods. The company opened a line of credit of 500 million marks, and goods were valued at prices prevailing on the Hamburg Exchange at the time of the offer.[15] In the following year, the Ukrainian Centrosoyuz signed an agreement with the Dutch firm of Amexima of Amsterdam, under which all exports of the Ukrainian Centrosoyuz to Holland were handled through Amexima, which had the exclusive right to supply the former with imported goods.[16]

By far the largest of the German trading companies was Russgertorg (Russische-Deutsche Handels A-G) a Type II concession, owned jointly by the Soviets and the Otto Wolff interests, which represented a number of large German firms, including Phoenix, Rheinische-Stahlwerke, Rheinmetal, and Zippen and Bissener. It was signed in October 1922 and at a later date included some United States firms who were unwilling to deal directly with the Soviet Union. The company was jointly capitalized at 175 million marks. It functioned as an import-export company. The Soviets determined the nature of the imports (mainly equipment for Soviet plants), and exports had to be coordinated with Vneshtorg. Russgertorg also handled shipments made under the military agreement with the Soviet Union.

Otto Wolff provided working capital of £750,000 plus a revolving credit of £500,000 and a further credit equal to the income from half of the orders placed with the company by the Soviets. The board of directors was selected equally from each side. The company established itself very quickly—Hilger suggests too quickly for its own good. In the second year of operation it was handling one-fifth of all Soviet imports—essentially machinery and industrial equipment. In the first eight months of 1925, its business doubled to over 20 million rubles, of which three-quarters was financed by the seller and did not require the company's working capital.[17]

Although there are reports that Rusgertorg made a comeback, it probably did not survive beyond 1925. It was 'extremely profitable' for both parties while it lasted. It was, however, too successful from the Soviet viewpoint, and within a short time it so dominated Soviet domestic and foreign trade that 'the Government regarded its continued existence as a threat to its interests and to its own governmental trade organizations.'[18] The company did receive

[15]   *Pravda* (Petrograd), January 26, 1922.
[16]   U.S. Consulate in Helsingfors, Report 2110, May 15, 1922. (316–107–763.)
[17]   U.S. State Dept. Decimal File, 316–131–89/102. See also Troyanovsky, *op. cit.*, pp. 895–7.
[18]   'The case of Russgertorg was a typical example of the way in which the Soviet Government made use of its foreign partners as long as it derived benefits from such contracts, and dropped them as soon as the conditions under which the contracts were concluded had changed.' (Hilger, *op. cit.*, pp. 172–3.)

a house-building concession in late 1928 but reportedly could not raise sufficient capital for operations.[19]

Derutra (Deutsche-Russische Lager und Transport m.b.H) had a virtual monopoly of Soviet-German land transportation, but not ocean freight, between 1923 and 1926. It was a joint-stock Type II concession owned jointly by the Hamburg-Amerika line and Vneshtorg. The concession had great difficulties from the beginning, and Hilger suggests this was partly because of the clumsy Soviet economic system and partly because of Soviet distrust. An official reason for its dissolution was never given but the 'obvious reason was that the Hamburg-Amerika Line . . . had a closer view of Soviet economic conditions than Moscow desired.'[20]

Whereas Russgertorg was mainly involved with manufactured imports and Derutra with transportation, the Type II concession Wostwag was organized in 1923 for exporting raw materials—mainly furs, casings, bristles, caviar, horsehair, potash, and oil. It established a network of workshops in the U.S.S.R. for the 'working up' of bristles. Its functions were much more circumscribed than those of Russgertorg, and it was limited to a precise list of imports and exports. Furthermore, the trade in any one item in any one year could not amount to less than 1.2 million gold rubles. Profit was divided equally with Vneshtorg, and Soviet representatives sat on the board of directors.[21]

Whereas most trading concessions were of the mixed Type II variety, Rueben and Bielefeld was a pure concession in which the Soviets held neither management nor legal rights. It was concluded in 1923 to enable the firm to buy fish products within the Soviet Union and export these products. The U.S.S.R. collected 50 percent of the profits as a fee in lieu of taxes.[22] Another Type II concession was Derumetall (Deutsche-Russische Metallverwertungs G.m.b.H.), which joined the Berlin firm of N. Levy with Metallotorg to export scrap metal. This must have been a sizable business, in the early years Derumetall employed some 66 ships in removing scrap from the Soviet Union to Germany.[23] In addition there were several minor concessions, such as Rusot, operating in the oilseed and oil cake field.[24]

RUSSO-AUSTRIAN TRADING COMPANY (RUSAVSTORG)

The Russische-Oesterreichische Handels und Industrie A-G was a mixed Type II concession linking Vneshtorg to a group of large Austrian firms. The

[19]   U.S. Consulate in Riga, Report 5789, December 28, 1928.
[20]   Hilger, *op. cit.*, pp. 177–8.
[21]   *Izvestia*, No. 126, June 9, 1923; and *Ekonomicheskaya Zhizn*, No. 102, May 10, 1923.
[22]   *Izvestia*, No. 108, May 17, 1923.
[23]   U.S. State Dept. Decimal File, 340–5–566.
[24]   *Ekonomicheskaya Zhizn*, No. 105, February 7, 1924.

capital stock was owned jointly by the Soviet government and the firms, but the Austrians actually purchased 75 percent of the stock and donated 25 percent to the Soviet government; the other 25 percent of the Soviet share was paid out of accumulated profits and not subscribed at time of formation. In addition, the Austrian firms granted a credit of $1.6 million to the mixed company and a $1 million credit directly to the Soviet government. The profits were divided: 10 percent went to the Soviet government, and the balance (up to 40 percent of the capital stock) was divided equally between the Soviet government and the Austrian firms. Of the profits in excess of 40 percent, 60 percent went to the Soviets and 40 percent to the Austrians. The Soviets had the deciding vote and in effect controlled the company.[25]

The second Austrian trading concession was Ratao (Russische-Oesterreichische Handels A-G) a mixed joint-stock company one-half of whose capital was held by two Austrian firms and the balance by the Soviet Union.

COMPAGNIA INDUSTRIALE COMMERCIO ESTERO (CICE)

This was a jointly owned Type II trading concession handling all import and export between Italy and the U.S.S.R. The company had its head office in Milan and a branch office in Moscow and other cities throughout Europe. It was capitalized at fourteen million lire and provided exclusive representation for major Italian metalworking, leather, textile, and chemical companies, including the Fiat company, which had extensive sales and technical-assistance agreements in both automobiles and aircraft.

The transport and handling of commodities and equipment from Italy to the U.S.S.R. was handled by Società Mista Italo-Russa di Commercio e Transporti, with agents and correspondents scattered throughout Europe and Russia.

By 1924 the Soviets found they had exhausted the possibilities of the mixed Type II trading concession. Originally formed to attract capital and get into direct contact with foreign suppliers and customers, the mixed companies achieved both aims. The Soviets did not hide their reasons for dropping the foreign partners. An article in *Ekonomicheskaya Zhizn* points out they were no longer necessary: capital had been acquired and more could now be obtained by direct contact with the foreign suppliers; there was now no problem in getting in touch with foreign businessmen. It was proposed that trading companies should now become 'producing and trading companies' and that this would 'appeal to those who are really specialists in a given branch of the export industry and not merely middlemen and traders.' The example

[25] *Izvestia*, No. 148, July 5, 1923.

of the German firm, Seyfurt, egg assemblers and producers in the Soviet Union under concession, was given.[26]

What had the trading concessions achieved?

First, they had gained entry for the Soviet Union into foreign markets; this was vital for the sale of Russian raw materials to generate foreign exchange for imports of the technical means for economic development. This could not have been achieved without foreign help. Once entry had been gained then the sequence of orders could be maintained without too much skill.

Second, the use of trading companies with foreign partners effectively maintained the trade monopoly in Soviet hands. In the early years the Soviets did not appreciate the value of a trading monopoly, but once the value became obvious they defended it with vehemence. The mixed joint-stock companies, in which final control remained with the Soviets, in effect extended the trading monopoly into areas where the foreign firms might join together to establish a joint selling and buying company as a bargaining unit in the path of Vneshtorg. The trading concession performed the supremely valuable function of maintaining the trade monopoly for the Soviets until such time as they could establish their own overseas branches.

CREDIT FROM WESTERN FIRMS

It is generally believed that the Soviets received no credit during the early phases of their development. This view has been propagated by the Soviets themselves. Even well-informed writers have maintained this point.[27] There were, it is true, few government-to-government credits of any size. There were two sizable German loans and a few smaller direct loans from Austria and Czechoslovakia. However, irrespective of non-recognition, numerous firms, both American and foreign, were willing either to advance credit to the Soviet Union or to aid in the acquisition of funds through intermediaries. By the end of the decade the Soviets were no longer complaining about lack of credit; there was more than enough. They were, however, complaining about payment of interest and the fact these firms did not treat the U.S.S.R. as a 'first-class customer.' In brief, Soviet development was in no way restricted by lack of finance capital, although the proof of existence of this financing has had to be pieced together from numerous sources.[28]

---

[26] *Ekonomicheskaya Zhizn*, No. 127, March 4, 1924.

[27] For example, see F. D. Holzman, 'Financing Soviet Economic Development,' in M. Abramovitz (ed.), *Capital Formation and Economic Growth* (Princeton: Princeton University Press, 1955), p. 55.

[28] See Note A to chap. 7 for agricultural equipment credits.

Given the risks involved, the amount of financing forthcoming was surprisingly large. The files of the United States War Trade Board indicate that American import-export companies advanced credit for Soviet purchases on the heels of the Revolution. One firm, Foreign Products Company, bought $670,000 of clothing and condensed milk in March 1920, before trade restriction with Bolshevik Russia were lifted, on the basis of an order and a small deposit. The company then applied for export permits. This application was rejected, but the company replied 'We insist upon passing of the above mentioned applications.' Some products were getting through the blockade through foreign firms operating under various names. One such was Niels Juul of Christiania (Oslo), Norway, which, according to the War Trade Board, 'used a number of cover names and in every way had a bad standing.'[29]

Beginning in about 1921–2, credits began to flow from manufacturing companies of some size and standing. Avery and Moline, and Sullivan Machinery in the United States, the Clayton Company in England, Pamp in Sweden, the Russian-European Company in Germany, and others in Finland and Austria were advancing credit in 1922–3. From a position of 'no credit' the United States moved to one of long-term loans and security issues within a period of eight years, in a graduated erosion of executive interpretation and under constant pressure from the Soviets and American financial and manufacturing houses. The two major breaches of 'no-longterm loans' policy were the American Locomotive Sales case of 1927 and the Harriman bond issue case in 1928. By the end of the decade, more than 200 American firms were advancing credit for up to three years at quite reasonable interest rates.[30]

Chase National Bank and the Equitable Trust Company were leaders in the Soviet credit business. For some years this was handled on the basis of platinum credits, as the State Department requested return of gold shipped from the Soviet Union. In time this position also changed.[31] Some financial houses, notably Blair and Company, had a decidedly bad reputation within the State Department.[32]

Credits to the Soviet Union were supposedly against State Department policy in the mid 1920's. The German Foreign Ministry Archives has reports however of an International Harvester credit of $2.5 million for 18 months

---

[29] United States Export Control regulations were not always treated seriously. One shipper, on being informed by Customs that a load of coal to Murmansk required a permit, said, 'Hang the license, I will ship to Norway and then re-ship to Murmansk.' Customs reported this was not uncommon. (Memorandum, Dickson to Merle-Smith, October 29, 1920, U.S. War Trade Board files.)

[30] Bron, *op. cit.*, p. 57.

[31] U.S. State Dept. Decimal File, 316–136–471.

[32] Memorandum, Division of Russian Affairs (316–137–404).

Table 17-2   CREDITS ADVANCED TO THE SOVIET UNION
BY WESTERN FIRMS

Country	Year	CREDIT GRANTED		
		Thousands of Rubles	Percent of Purchases	Average term in months
Germany				
1st 3 quarters	1925/6	19,176	72.6	6.7
1st 3 quarters	1924/5	16,748	56.0	5.8
Italy				
1st 3 quarters	1925/6	11,987	99.7	7.7
1st 3 quarters	1924/5	651	55.6	6.2
England				
1st 3 quarters	1925/6	6,452	71.7	6.5
1st 3 quarters	1924/5	9,832	60.8	4.8
United States				
1st 3 quarters	1925/6	3,283	43.2	9.1
1st 3 quarters	1924/5	8,419	72.5	5.2
France				
1st 3 quarters	1925/6	3,598	91.9	15.7
1st 3 quarters	1924/5	519	31.9	4.4
Sweden				
1st 3 quarters	1925/6	3,233	92.1	12.1
1st 3 quarters	1924/5	1,963	87.0	9.6
Czechoslovakia				
1st 3 quarters	1925/6	3,329	99.9	7.7
1st 3 quarters	1924/5	1,091	14.0	6.4

Source: U.S. State Dept. Decimal File 661.1115/466½

in 1925; this was overshadowed by the $30 million revolving credit advanced by Chase National in 1926.[33] It has already been mentioned that American banks involved themselves in making purchases on behalf of the Soviet Union. Chase tried to buy Liberty engines.[34] The Equitable Trust Company financed a group of Bolivian tin producers to supply the tin requirements of the Soviet Union.[35]

Credits from Germany up to 1925 were limited by Germany's own economic position, by the necessity to pay reparations, by some doubt as to Soviet intent or ability to repay loans and to some extent by the necessity to avoid offending the Allies by making advances to the U.S.S.R. The first credits were on a barter basis. German reconstruction and operation of the Ukraine sugar refineries was paid for in sugar. A similar arrangement was made with grain in 1923.[36] This was followed by the October 12, 1925 short-term loan of 100

[33]   German Foreign Ministry Archives, Roll 3033, Frame H109454.
[34]   See chap. 15.
[35]   U.S. Consulate in La Paz, Bolivia, Report, December 26, 1929.
[36]   Hilger, *op. cit.*, pp. 184–6.

million marks at 8.5 percent. The loan was hailed by Solnikov, the Finance Minister, as the first breach in the financial blockade of the Soviet Union. It was handled jointly by the Deutsche Bank and Reichs Kredit Gesellschaft A-G and repayable in bills on New York.[37] In 1926 came the 300 million mark credit by German business firms, guaranteed by the German government to the extent of 35 percent in case of default. The German *lander* accepted another 25 percent guarantee. The loan was restricted to the purchase of equipment for specific industries.[38]

The International Union of Cooperatives was more skeptical. A joint meeting with Centrosoyuz in Moscow in 1922 did not impress the European delegates. It was suggested that the Moscow Co-operative Bank become a member of the International Co-operative Bank, but when it was indicated that the Moscow Bank would have to take up shares in proportion to its claimed membership, it was suggested that the international cooperative movement should meet Russia halfway because of her difficult economic position. The foreign delegates were not impressed and put off the question of credits to the international conference to be held at a later date in Milan. The point never came up for further discussion.[39] One surprising conclusion from this study has been that organizations which are often thought to be somewhat socialist in character, such as cooperative and trade unions, have consistently refused to have anything to do with the Soviet Union in the matter of credits, aid, trade, or technical assistance. The few exceptions, such as Haywood and the Amalgamated Clothing Workers, make the overall coolness of these movements very obvious. On the other hand, the industrial and financial elements in all Western countries have, in the final analysis, provided more assistance for the growth of the Soviet Union than any other group.

[37] This provision is intriguing. The Soviets were heavy buyers of American cotton at this time. One wonders where the U.S. dollars were being obtained. The Chase credit may have some connection with repayment of the German loan.
[38] Hilger, *op. cit.*, pp. 184–6.
[39] IS Report, April 1, 1922. (316-107-748.)

PART TWO

The Significance of Foreign Concessions and Technological Transfers

CHAPTER SEVENTEEN

The Foreign Firm and the 'Arm's Length Hypothesis'

THE compilation of data which forms Part I of this study yielded several supplementary hypotheses in addition to support for the basic hypothesis that Soviet economic development for 1917–1930 was essentially dependent on Western technological aid.

The most significant supplementary hypothesis is termed the 'arm's-length hypothesis.' In some concessions and agreements, the Western partner had noneconomic links to the Bolshevik cause; this particularly applies to early concessions. In other words, from the Soviet viewpoint the invitation to foreign capital was hedged, and initially limited to the more 'reliable' foreign capitalists. One such arrangement sprang directly from the New York-based Soviet Bureau of Martens before his deportation; but although the bureau had been financed by numerous American businessmen, only a few of these could be called ideological sympathizers.

The hypothesis is that some concession holders were in effect in arm's-length relationship with the Soviet government, and their contribution to the revolutionary cause was to lead the way and instill confidence in the Soviet government in the hope that other businessmen would follow.

Quite clearly all agricultural communes, the American Industrial Colony (AIK) in the Kuzbas, the Russian-American Steel Works, the Russian-American Instrument Company, the Third International Clothing Factory, and the Haywood concession (the Russian-American Industrial Corporation) were inspired by ideological fervor. The operators were either Communist Party members expelled from or emigrating from the United States and other Western countries or, as in the case of Haywood, sympathizers. That they were sadly disillusioned does not alter the fact that the initial desire was to support the Revolution; they clearly fall within the scope of the hypothesis. Others require further explanation.

CHARLES HADDELL SMITH OF THE INTER-ALLIED RAILWAY COMMISSION IN SIBERIA[1]

According to the State Department, Charles H. Smith, formerly United States representative on the Siberian Railway Commission and member of the Soviet Peasant International, was 'more or less' an agent of the Soviet government.[2] The name threads throughout the history of U.S.S.R.-United States trade relations in the 1920s.

There is evidence that Smith used delaying tactics[3] while he was American member of the Inter-Allied Railway Commission of Siberia. On April 25, 1919 the State Department sent a telegram, 'Urgent for Smith . . . please advise what materials Committee proposes to purchase in the United States.'[4] At the same time, Stevens, the Chairman of the Technical Committee of the Commission, was urgently requesting railroad materials: track motors, air brakes and high-speed tool steel.[5]

On May 2, Smith replied as follows to the urgent State Department telegram: 'Technical Board has not had time to study railway needs carefully.' Smith appended a list of items based on 'past information' and adds, 'Do not think rails and track fastenings are needed just now. . . .'[6]

By June 18, no orders had been placed, although Stevens was still requesting material urgently. By August 25, Smith had apparently been removed from the sphere of ordering supplies and now it was found that 200,000 tons of rails with 3A fastenings were needed.

The impression from the flow of telegrams from the Consul's office in Vladivostock to the State Department is that Stevens, President of the Technical Committee, was competent, active, and anxious to start work, and was requesting necessary supplies. These were delayed by inaction, and misinformation.[7]

After leaving the Railway Commission, Smith was active in the Far East, generating support and winning influence for the Soviet Union, and trying

---

[1] The U.S. State Dept. Archives refer to Charles Haddell, Charles H., Charles W., and Charles S. Smith, sometimes preceded by 'Colonel.' According to file notations they are one and the same. (See 316–130, 316–131, 316–136, and 316–176.)

[2] U.S. State Dept. Decimal File, 316–131–1/2. Covering letter from Consul states, 'Mr. Smith is more or less an agent of the Soviet Government, and it is to his interest to publish propaganda of this sort.'

[3] 'Delaying tactics' as a weapon were formulated by Representative Walter Judd. The Harry Dexter White case and the takeover of China by the Communists is another example. See A. Kubek, foreword to *Morgenthau Diary (China)*, Vol. I, U.S. Senate Committee on the Judiciary, February 5, 1965.

[4] U.S. State Dept. Decimal File, 316–163–442.

[5] U.S. State Dept. Decimal File, 316–163–452, 316–162–454, and 316–162–456.

[6] U.S. State Dept. Decimal File, 316–163–460.

[7] U.S. State Dept. Decimal File, 316–163–440/677.

to introduce foreign capital into the Far Eastern Republic. He was connected with the Far East Exploration Syndicate (also known as the Far Eastern Prospecting Syndicate) and various proposed lumber and mining concessions. Soviet reporting explained that Smith was 'a capitalist not under the control of the United States Government'[8] and a 'breakaway.'[9]

Part of Smith's activity involved propaganda in favor of the Soviets. Smith pleaded, for example, with Senators Borah and Johnson, on their visit to the Far East, to press for recognition of the U.S.S.R. and for the return of the Chinese Eastern Railway to Russian hands:

> As always the Chinese Eastern Railway is a key to the solution. The sooner the Russians would get it back, the better would it be for all nations except Japan. . . . We who represent America here used to say that this is a Russian railway and it must remain in Russian hands.[10]

Letters and memoranda in the U.S. State Department files testify to his consistent pro-Soviet activities. Part of this activity was in concert with another suspected Soviet agent, Lively, who represented the United States Department of Agriculture in the Far East and China.[11]

Smith turns up later in the decade as vice-president of the American-Russian Chamber of Commerce (which had such well-known members as International Harvester, General Electric, Westinghouse, American Car and Foundry, and Guaranty Trust) and Moscow representative of the Chamber.[12]

THE HAMMER FAMILY AND SOVIET OPERATIONS

Dr. Julius Hammer (born in Russia in 1874, died in the United States in 1948) was a member of the steering committee which founded the Communist Party of the United States at the First National Left-Wing Conference of the Socialist Party, held in New York City in June 1919. The Hammers were then trading under license with the U.S.S.R. They continued to trade until 1923 when they operated, jointly with the Soviets, the Allied American Corporation (Amerikanskoi Ob'edinennoi Kompanii), sharing both capital and profits on a 50:50 basis.

The secretary of Allied American Corporation was Armand Hammer;[13] who also managed the Alapievsky asbestos concession,[14] while Dr. Julius

[8] *Ekonomicheskaya Zhizn*, No. 24, October 28, 1923.
[9] *Far Eastern Times*, November 22, 1923.
[10] U.S. State Dept. Decimal File, 316–131–1/2.
[11] U.S. State Dept. Decimal File, 316–130–1259, 316–176–409 and 316–176–838.
[12] See page 289.
[13] Armand Hammer, *Quest of the Romanoff Treasure* (New York; Payson 1936). Armand Hammer is currently President and Chairman of the Board of Occidental Petroleum Corp., Los Angeles.
[14] See chap. 6.

286 Western Technology and Soviet Economic Development, 1917–1930

Hammer, his father, was serving a term in Sing Sing for criminal abortion. Later in the 1920s Armand Hammer operated the American Industrial Concession, for pencil factories in Moscow.[15]

Upon grant of the Alapievsky asbestos concession, the *New York Times* reported F.B.I. investigations had ascertained that Dr. Hammer 'had for many years been prominently identified with the Socialist movement in this country and became a Lenin-Trotsky propagandist.' Dr. Hammer had then become associated with the Soviet Bureau in New York and acquired affluence. When he was sentenced to Sing Sing it appears that Martens 'and other representatives of the Soviet Government in this country had taken an active part in the effort to prevent the physician from being sent to Sing Sing.'[16]

Smith and Hammer therefore appear to fall within the 'arm's-length hypothesis.' There may be others. In 1920–1 the Robert Dollar company handled $7 million of the total $15 million worth of United States exports to the U.S.S.R. The company's Moscow representative was Jonas Lied, who had, according to the State Department, an 'interesting dossier' in the Department of Justice (i.e., the F.B.I.) and intelligence in the State Department.[17] Like other Western traders with the Soviet Union, Dollar was reluctant to say very much except to blast the 'radical element in the country (which) should not be allowed to block trade.'[18]

One of the partners in Bryner and Company, operators of the Tetiukhe metals concession in the Far East, 'was suspected of espionage for the Soviets.'[19] J. Finger and Professor Johnson of the Joint Distribution Committee (Agro-Joint) gave glowing reports of the 'new Russia.'[20]

Although the German ex-Chancellor Wirth, operator of the Mologa concession, has been described by some writers as a 'Communist sympathizer,' there is no evidence, and Hilger is probably correct in denying the charge.[21]

In brief, there is supporting evidence for the 'arm's-length hypothesis.'[22]

---

[15] See chap. 13.

[16] *New York Times*, November 4, 1921, p. 1, col. 2; November 6, 1921, p. 23, col. 3; November 7, 1921, p. 10, col. 2; and November 24, 1921, p. 12, col. 4.

[17] U.S. State Dept. Decimal File, 316–109–1375.

[18] *Memoirs of Robert Dollar* (San Francisco, 1925), III, p. 34. Out of a three-volume *Memoirs*, Dollar devotes only one and a half rather general pages to his Russian trade activities.

[19] U.S. State Dept. Decimal File, 316–136–1254.

[20] U.S. State Dept. Decimal File, 316–108–652.

[21] Hilger, *op. cit.*

[22] According to documents at U.S. State Dept. Decimal File, 316–139–28/9, there were also 'leaks' from the State Dept. to Moscow. Coleman suggested his reports be kept under close control and limited distribution, as the contents were finding their way to his opposite number in Riga and he feared for the security of American couriers.

Companies such as Westinghouse and International Harvester, who operated their prewar plants for some years, do not fall within the 'arm's-length hypothesis.' Westinghouse, International Harvester, Singer, and other American companies are still awaiting settlement for expropriation of their plants. Swedish General Electric, the Swedish Separator Company (manufacturers of dairy equipment) and SKF all domiciled in Sweden, had concessions, but there is no evidence that they fall within the scope of the hypothesis. In fact the unfavorable treatment of these companies when compared to those firms that do fall within the scope of the hypothesis confirms rather than denies the hypothesis.

Swedish General Electric, Swedish Separator, and SKF made considerable profits from their concessions but were blocked from transferring these profits out of the U.S.S.R.[23] Although profit figures for concessions are hard to find, it appears that Hammer and Eitingon-Schild were the only concessionaires to make substantial profits and export them. Amtorg reports that the 22 principal concessions made 6.5 million rubles profit in 1926–7 and 12 million in 1927–8, but nowhere indicates how much of this profit was transferred out of the U.S.S.R.[24]

As Paul Scheffer put the case, 'Concessions in Russia are a sort of sport for rich people who can afford to pay dearly for their experience. . . .'[25]

AMERICAN ORGANIZATIONS FOR PROMOTION OF TRADE WITH THE U.S.S.R.

American organizations with the objective of promoting Soviet-American trade were formed on the heels of the Revolution, unlike those of Britain and France, where organizations to gain recompense for expropriated capital were stronger and more vocal than those designed to promote trade.

Prerevolutionary foreign investment had been heavily concentrated under French (33 percent) and British (23 percent) control. About 20 percent was German, but only 5 percent came from the United States. Consequently there was comparatively less ex-shareholder pressure in the United States against trading with the Soviet regime.[26]

The American pressure organizations were linked directly and indirectly to the U.S.S.R. and numerous American firms.

The American Commercial Association to Promote Trade with Russia was founded in 1919 by a group of American manufacturers, including the

---

[23] U.S. State Dept. Decimal File, 316–131–661.
[24] Amtorg, *op. cit.*, IV, 179. SKF alone made 2.8 million rubles in 1928 and reported that exports of these proceeds were being blocked.
[25] *Berliner Tageblatt*, January 11, 1929.
[26] U.S. State Dept. Decimal File, 316–107–1323.

LeHigh Machine Company, Bebroff Foreign Trading Company, New Hide Manufacturing Company, Fairbanks Company, Morris Company of Chicago, and perhaps 100 other firms and some well-known representatives of the financial world. The first tasks of the association were to get the licensing requirements enforced by the War Trade Board removed and to press for removal of restrictions on financial transactions with the U.S.S.R. The association, according to claims of its president, Emerson P. Jennings, succeeded in both objectives. Other objectives included a writ of mandamus to release ships held in United States ports with goods for the U.S.S.R.[27]

Probably the most important of its actions (although certainly not its most highly publicized) was the financing of Ludwig C. A. K. Martens's Soviet Bureau in New York. Jennings states that this was the work of a group of American businessmen anxious to trade with Russia, rather than a plot financed by 'Soviet gold,' as ran the current hue and cry.[28]

Not only did the association finance the Soviet Bureau but it also maintained communications. The chairman of the Resolutions Committee was Martens's attorney.[29] Congressman James P. Mulvihill, who represented the New Hide Company in the association, was in contact with Heller, of the Commercial Department of the Soviet Bureau.[30] In brief, the association, comprised of American businessmen, was also intimately connected with the operation of the Soviet Bureau.

The attachment was the result of political naïveté rather than ideological obeisance to the cause of the Revolution. In the fall of 1921, Emerson P. Jennings spent a few months in the U.S.S.R. to drum up trade for members of the association. As soon as he reached Reval, Estonia, on his way back to the United States, he commenced one of the bluntest condemnations of the Soviet Union on record. While in Reval, Jennings wrote a six-page bitter denunciation of the U.S.S.R., complaining of the complete and utter unworthiness and untrustworthiness of the Bolsheviks. 'Pikers,' 'fakers,' and 'babies,' are some of the epithets used. Nevertheless, he concludes by making a plea

[27]   American Commercial Association to Promote Trade with Russia, *Bulletin*, February 1920.

[28]   Emerson Jennings, *Report to the Association* (American Commercial Association to Promote Trade with Russia, 1921). The Soviet Bureau had both trade and propaganda functions. For example, see A. A. Heller, *The Industrial Revival in Soviet Russia* (New York: T. Seltzer, 1922). Heller was commercial attaché to Martens and the Soviet Bureau, and liaison with the U.S.S.R. He was arrested and deported in May 1921 to Riga, Latvia, for these activities and became the Vesenkha representative in the United States. The book was an attempt to disguise the pitiful state of Russian industry at that time. [Memorandum, Poole to the Secretary of State (316-129-633).]

[29]   American Commercial Association, *Bulletin*, February 1920.

[30]   L. I. Strakhovsky, *American Opinion about Russia 1917–1920* (Toronto: University of Toronto Press 1961), p. 85, fn. 9.

for the United States government to advance credits to the Soviet Union for the benefit of American manufacturers.[31]

THE AMERICAN-RUSSIAN CHAMBER OF COMMERCE[32]

The American-Russian Chamber of Commerce was comprised of a group of major United States manufacturers and financial institutions interested in trading with Russia, and was a factor in the pressure for recognition of the Soviet Union and resumption of full trade with credits. In a letter to the Secretary of State (February 27, 1922), the chamber pressed for a policy statement 'announcing under what conditions you would be glad to cooperate with all nations in relation to the economic development of Russia,' and utilizing the alternative of German political domination as a pressure point.[33]

The president of the chamber was Reeve Schley, a vice president of the Chase National Bank, which was in the forefront of financing United States trade with the U.S.S.R. and reluctant to follow State Department policy.[34]

In 1926 the chamber decided, in view of its failure to persuade the State Department to send a commission or a representative to Russia, to send its own representative to 'open an office in Moscow and generally obtain information which will be of assistance to its members.'[35] The representative was Charles Haddell Smith, previously described by the State Department as being in the employ of the Soviets and a member of the Soviet Peasant International.

In 1928 'Colonel' Smith was appointed vice-president of the Chamber and toured the United States speaking in favor of increased trade with the U.S.S.R. This brought forth protests from organizations and individuals who viewed trade with the Soviet Union in a rather different light. Matthew Woll, for example, vice-president of the American Federation of Labor and president of the National Civic Federation, sent an open letter to the American-Russian Chamber of Commerce complaining of its activities and particularly called upon it to use its influence to stop Soviet propaganda and subversive activities

---

[31]   *Report to the Association*, Emerson Jennings, August 31, 1921.

[32]   The board of directors of the chamber represented many companies associated with Russian development: Deere & Co., Worthington Pump, Russian Singer, Mercantile Trust, International Fur Exchange, International Harvester, Lucey Manufacturing, American Locomotive, International General Electric, Guaranty Trust, Westinghouse Air Brake Co., and American Car and Foundry. (316–107–451.) The chamber was founded in 1916 to 'foster trade, encourage and generally promote the economic, commercial and industrial relations between the United States of America and Russia.' A Moscow office was established in 1927. By 1931 its publications were reflecting many of the propaganda shibboleths of Soviet regime.

[33]   Letter from American-Russian Chamber of Commerce to U.S. State Dept., February 27, 1922. (U.S. State Dept. Decimal File, 316–107–451.)

[34]   U.S. State Dept. Decimal File, 316–109–1424.

[35]   U.S. State Dept. Decimal File, 316–107–451.

in the United States. Perhaps unfortunately, Matthew Woll suggested that the presence of Smith in Moscow as representative of the Chamber 'furnished additional grounds for the belief that the Bolsheviks would heed any requests or demands made by your body.'[36] If such a request had been made by the Chamber (it was not), its handling by Smith would have been a most interesting episode.

AMERICAN BANKS AND SOVIET SECURITIES

A number of American banks were partners in a Soviet attempt to float a bond issue on the American market. The Chase National at first refused to break off the relationship, using its past banking services for the U.S.S.R. as the reason.

On January 19, 1928, the State Bank of the U.S.S.R. placed an advertisement in the *New York Times* to the effect that the bank had guaranteed the principal and interest of a 9-percent Soviet railway loan and that coupons might be presented for payment at the Chase National Bank, the Amalgamated Bank of Chicago, and the Bank of Italy in San Francisco. The advertisement also contained the address of the State Bank in Moscow where 'further information' could be obtained.

Two weeks before the advertisement, a $30 million railway bond issue had been authorized in Moscow. The certificates permitted payment of interest and principal to the holder *in dollars*, thus in effect converting the bond issue to a dollar loan—flatly prohibited by the State Department. The issue was to be sold by mail in the United States, and it was estimated that at the time of the advertisement about $100,000 of such bonds had been sold, mostly to one of the fur concession holders; in other words bona fide sales were insignificant. The coupon advertisement was justifiably interpreted as an offer for sale of Soviet bonds, and this interpretation was made plain to the associated banking houses in letters from the State Department.[37]

Among other things, Chase National was called an 'international fence'[38] acting to compromise American foreign policy. It was said that they were 'a disgrace to America. . . . They will go to any lengths for a few dollars profit.'[39]

---

[36]   U.S. State Dept. Decimal File, 316–110–268.

[37]   The documents are in U.S. State Dept. Decimal File, 316–110–250. Letters from corporations and other interested parties in the files suggest that the State Dept. was by no means alone in its interpretation of the action of the State Bank and Chase National. See the three-page telegram at 316–110–259/61, from New York Life Insurance Co.

[38]   By the National Civic Federation (representatives from business, labor unions and the public). (U.S. State Dept. Decimal File, 316–110–266.)

[39]   By the Allied Patriotic Societies (U.S. State Dept. Decimal File, 316–110–284). The letters from private citizens were even more specific.

The Bank of Italy announced immediately that it would have nothing further to do with the loan and specifically that it would not honor the bond coupons. Other banks (the Chicago Amalgamated and Chase) were more reluctant. The Chase made a step-by-step withdrawal. One reply (February 5) stated that it wanted to conform to government policy but would continue to pay the coupons. The second step of the retreat came after the State Department bluntly pointed out that the payment of coupons would facilitate Soviet financing and was against government policy. The third letter from Chase indicated they had advised the U.S.S.R. State Bank 'that until further advice of any change in policy by the Department of State we must decline to make payment of any such coupons.'[40]

There is no doubt that stepped up purchases of American equipment and technical assistance motivated this attempt with the aid of American banking companies to break United States policy. The contracts with Dupont, Ford, Kahn, McCormick, and many others were being signed, and dollars were required for payments. The denial of the railway bond issue was followed by a substantial increase in Soviet gold deposits in the United States.[41]

The amount of pressure placed by American firms individually and through their associations on cabinet officials is very difficult to gauge. Samuel Gompers, President of the AFL, thought it was sufficient in 1923 to make a strong attack on Mr. Hearst, former Secretary Fall of the Interior Department (of Teapot Dome notoriety), the Sinclair and Barnsdall organizations, Senator King, and Senator Ladd, together with 'international bankers, oil magnates and concession hunters' all of whom he accused of placing pressure on the cabinet for trade with Russia.[42]

When the desk level in the Division of East European Affairs suggested that it would be 'unwise to *initiate*' an investigation of Harriman's negotiations with unofficial representatives of the Soviet Union, one can only infer that pressures above the desk level were at work.[43] It was widely felt that General Electric brought political pressure to bear in 1928 for permission concerning its credit agreement with the U.S.S.R. for supply of electrical equipment.[44] The American Locomotive case was decided at the presidential level, and the files certainly suggest interest by parties outside the executive branch.

American big business was almost unbelievably naïve politically concerning the Soviet Union. Standard Oil of New Jersey, for example, negotiated oil

[40]　Letter from Chase National to U.S. State Dept. (Decimal File, 316–110–341.)
[41]　With the collapse of the bond scheme, a shipment of $6 million in gold was made from the U.S.S.R. to the Chase National and the Equitable Trust Company. (U.S. State Dept. Decimal File, 316–110–337.)
[42]　*New York Times*, November 23, 1923.
[43]　See chap. 6.
[44]　U.S. State Dept. Decimal File, 316–131.

development simultaneously with the Soviets and the White Russians.[45] Many major American firms, including Standard Oil of New York, Bethlehem Steel, Armour and Company, and the Pennsylvania Railroad, were represented by Ivy Lee, a well-known public relations agent. For much of the 1920s, Standard of New York was battling with Royal-Dutch Shell over Soviet oil; in 1926–7 Standard of New York decided to build a kerosene refinery for the Soviets at Batum and lease it back to supply Standard Near and Far East markets. Ivy Lee had the job of selling the switch to the American public, and after a quick trip wrote of the U.S.S.R. as follows:

> I had heard that the Russian Government, the Communist Party and the Communist International are all combined in a conspiracy against mankind, particularly *capitalist* mankind. I was anxious to find out, by first hand examination, just what is the nature of that conspiracy and how it is functioning.[46]

Quite predictably, 180 pages later, Lee concludes that the communist problem is merely psychological. By this time he is talking about 'Russians' (not Communists) and concludes 'they are all right.' He suggests the United States should not engage in propaganda; makes a plea for peaceful coexistence; and suggests the United States would find it sound policy to recognize the U.S.S.R. and advance credits.[47]

Walter Duranty felt, probably with accuracy, that the Rockefeller oil interests were playing both ends of the game. Standard Oil of New Jersey wanted compensation for its expropriated petroleum holdings, while Standard Oil of New York was buying oil in Russia and had therefore leased back the Standard-built kerosene refinery in 1927 at Batum. Duranty quotes *Izvestia:*

> While the Standard Oil of New Jersey is talking about moral reasons for refusing to do business with the Soviet Union, Ivy Lee who handles the Rockefeller propaganda recently visited the Soviet Union and carried on an unobtrusive press campaign for the improvement of trade relations between the United States and the U.S.S.R.[48]

EUROPEAN TRADE WITH THE SOVIET UNION

Promotion of trade with the U.S.S.R. became the objective of Parliamentary delegations in a number of countries. In the United Kingdom, members of

---

[45] U.S. State Dept. Decimal File, 316–137–83/126, 131–343/5.

[46] Ivy Lee, *U.S.S.R.: A World Enigma* (London: Benn, 1927), p. 9.

[47] *Ibid.* William White acted as interpreter for Ivy Lee in his interviews with Rykov, Sokolnikov, Karahan, Radek, Hinchuk and Piatakov. 'Mr. White stated that the interviews which he attended were extremely inane in character but that because of his Standard Oil connections Mr. Lee seemed to stand A-1 with the Soviet authorities.' [U.S. Embassy in Berlin, Report 5099, November 26, 1929 (U.S. State Dept. Decimal File, 316–110–1391).]

[48] *New York Times*, July 25, 1927, p. 33, cols. 1, 2 (quoting *Izvestia* of July 24, 1927).

Parliament sympathetic to the 'new Russia' made the usual trips and published glowing reports on their return suggesting that the Soviets had demonstrated their 'fair-minded treatment of concessionaires,' and that this removed the need for 'excessive caution' on the part of foreigners as the 'new Russia' could be relied upon to give a 'square deal to foreign capital.'[49]

On the other hand, associations devoted to émigré and prerevolutionary owner interests in France were almost equally injudicious in other respects. Émigré businessmen resident in Paris had several vocal associations, including the Association Financière, Industrielle et Commerciale Russe, which issued memoranda and booklets concerning the economic position of Soviet Russia. For these groups nothing could possibly be right nor could any development possibly take place without the return of former owners.[50]

In Germany, attempts to trade with the U.S.S.R. began in 1919, and in late 1920 German firms interested in resuming trade with the Soviet Union formed a Research Association for the Resumption of All Trade with the East (Studiengesellschaft für die Aufnahme des gesamten Handels mit dem Osten).[51] After the Treaty of Rapallo, which contained economic and commercial protocols, relations with the U.S.S.R. developed very rapidly. An all-German section of the All-Union Chamber of Commerce of the U.S.S.R. was formed, and this became the focal point for industrialists and German Embassy officials in discussion concerning the reconstruction of both Germany and the U.S.S.R. —until, as Hilger points out, the Embassy was blocked off by the Soviets from either assisting or communicating with German companies working in the U.S.S.R. The Soviets also utilized the meetings of the German section to move German industrialists along 'more desirable' lines, to reassure them that imports of German machinery would not lead to dumping, and to complain that the Americans 'do not guard manufacturing secrets so jealously.'[52] However, the U.S.S.R. found continued resistance by some German companies, especially I. G. Farben, to the transfer of technology.

On the other hand, Dr. Otto Deutsch, managing director of A.E.G. (Allgemeine Elektrizitäts Gesellschaft), was most interested in resumption of trade with the U.S.S.R. and became a member of the German commission established to further this objective. His basic arguments were that the U.S.S.R. was a vast market which could not be ignored and that, as the

---

[49] Anglo-Russian Parliamentary Committee, *Possibilities of British-Russian Trade* (London, 1926), p. 67. The booklet argued that the Lena and Harriman concessions 'illustrate sufficiently clearly our . . . contention.' They were both expropriated within the next few years.

[50] *La Situation Economique et Juridique de la Russie Sovietique* (Paris: Association Financière, Industrielle et Commerciale Russe, 1924).

[51] Hilger, *op. cit.*, p. 29.

[52] *Ekonomicheskaya Zhizn*, No. 225, September 29, 1929.

U.S.S.R. could not pay cash, concessions and credits would be necessary.[53][54] In 1928 during the 'Shakta Affair' when A.E.G. engineers were arrested and charged with sabotage, the initial A.E.G. reaction was to pull all their engineers out of the U.S.S.R. After a few days contemplation of the number of outstanding contracts and the losses involved, the German General Electric (A.E.G.) company decided to continue working.[55]

CONCLUSIONS

In brief, the 'arm's-length hypothesis' that some firms had noneconomic links to the Soviet Union, applies to early concessions, and these were of great importance; they were 'pour encourager les autres.'

The pressure in the United States for trade with the U.S.S.R. began while the Revolution was still in progress and was fostered by several active organizations.

Later in the decade, industry pressure was placed on the executive branch of the government to facilitate credit in trade with the U.S.S.R. and modify the State Department position of denying credits to the U.S.S.R. The latter policy was gradually eroded under pressures originating above and outside the 'desk level' of the Department.

On the other hand, German trade with the U.S.S.R. was placed on a formal basis by the government in 1921–2, and the Soviets had no need to use intermediaries to break down an unfavorable economic policy.

[53] *Mittelungen der Handelskammern*, February 1922.
[54] 'European industrial progress cannot be restored without the active participation of the 160,000,000 purchasers in Russia. I do not defend the Russian regime as we know it, but to wait until it is transformed into something more pleasing is an idle fancy. Despite what it is today, the situation in Russia does not prevent the operation of commerce on condition that one takes reasonable precautions.' (Otto Deutsch, *New York Times*, November 13, 1927, p. 4, col. 3.)
[55] 'The directors of the AEG in the first flush of indignation had initially declared that they would immediately withdraw all their engineers who were in Russia mounting machinery, regardless of existing contracts. A few days later, however, they seem to have regretted their impetuosity; they withdrew their initial declaration, obviously afraid of the losses that would occur because of the non-fulfillment of contractual agreements.' (Hilger, *op. cit.*, p. 221.)

CHAPTER EIGHTEEN

Organized and Disorganized Governments: The State Department and the Acquisition of Technology

WESTERN GOVERNMENT ASSESSMENT OF SOVIET INTENTIONS

ALTHOUGH the transfer of technology involved all those Western countries with any degree of industrialization, it essentially included Germany in the 1920s, and then the United States, as German credits ran out and the U.S. State Department increasingly relaxed its stand against credits to the U.S.S.R. Another factor was the gradual acceptance of American techniques in preference to European. It was the mass production technique of Ford rather than the more conservative production horizon of European producers that at first mystified and ultimately attracted the Soviets.

At the beginning of the decade, Western governments were in substantial unity concerning the aims of the Soviet Union. Certainly the State Department in 1923 had accurate ideas of Soviet intent in so far as trade and credit were concerned. A very clear statement formed part of a 'confidential' report, no doubt for circulation to friendly governments, by New Scotland Yard in London. The relevant part of the report reads:

> Concessions are offered, and foreign capital is sought with the object of restoring the collapsed industries of Russia in the interest of the Communist State. It is calculated that in some years foreign industry and enterprise will have revived these industries which then, more firmly established and efficient than ever before, will revert to the State, which will then be able, fortified by experience and the method of foreign participants to resume the Marxist experiment. Nor need one believe that any conditions subscribed to by the Soviet Government will be faithfully observed. The capitalist and the private owner have no inherent rights. Faith need not be kept with them. Cozened into the open by their capitalist greed they will be overwhelmed when the great advance is resumed.[1]

The State Department did not hesitate to subscribe to this analysis. A memorandum from Evan E. Young, Chief of the Division of Eastern European Affairs, to the Secretary of State comments:

> I have read the report with care and attention, and while it contains no new information, it is to me of especial interest and importance in that the report agrees, in all respects and in every particular with our information and our position.[2]

However, there does not appear to have been unanimity on the question of Soviet trade, concessions, or technical assistance within the United States Administration. Arguments for resumption of trade began while the Bolshevik Revolution was still in progress. It was suggested by Mr. Edwin F. Gay at a meeting of the War Trade Board, December 1918, that the policy of economic isolation of the areas under Bolshevik control was not the best means of bringing about a stable government:

> . . . if the people in the Bolshevik sections of Russia were given the opportunity to enjoy improved economic conditions, they would themselves bring about the establishment of a moderate and stable order.[3]

EROSION OF UNITED STATES POLICY ON SOVIET TRADE CREDITS

The basic policy of the State Department in the 1920s was that the United States government would neither support nor intervene in individual or business relations in trade with the Soviet Union. In other words, it was a policy of noninterposition or 'hands off.' The individual or firm was entirely on its own, and could expect no diplomatic or consular help in the event of trouble with the Soviet government.

Toward the end of 1920, there were world-wide rumors concerning a gigantic billion-dollar concession alleged to have been obtained by a man named Washington B. Vanderlip for the development of Siberia and Kamchatka. There is some possibility that Vanderlip represented himself to Lenin as another Vanderlip, banker and friend of Senator (later President) Harding. The syndicate behind Vanderlip contained a number of substantial Southern California citizens: Harry Chandler (of the Los Angeles *Times*), E. L. Doheny,

---

[1] *Present Position and Policy of Soviet Russia*, U.S. State Dept. Decimal File, 316–108–699.

[2] U.S. State Dept. Decimal File, 316–108–697. There are numerous indications of the State Dept. views in the files; this example was chosen because of its succinctness, clarity, and agreement with the view of a major European government.

[3] *Minutes of the War Trade Board*, V, 43–4, December 5, 1918. After Mr. Gay's argument, the Board adopted a motion recommending to the Dept. of State that a policy of economic isolation and blockade ' . . . is one calculated to prolong the control of the Bolshevik authorities . . .' (p. 7). This is the earliest statement of the 'bridge-building' argument.

the Union Oil Company, Merchants National Bank, Braun and Company, and other California firms and institutions. Vanderlip's negotiations, while General Wrangel was still fighting in the South, were not well received by the United States or the British governments. In the end, although the affair took up 100 or so documents, now in the Archives, nothing was achieved, and the concession faded into thin air.[4]

It can be argued, with substantial evidence from State Department files, that the pressures in the 1920s for expanded trade with the U.S.S.R. came from business firms and promoters such as Vanderlip and Farquhar, as well as from within the State Department itself.

The American Locomotive case of 1927 was one of the turning points in erosion of United States policy. The American Locomotive Sales Corporation inquired in October 1927 concerning sales of railroad material to the U.S.S.R. on long-term (more than five years), credit. The company argument was that it was extremely desirable 'to obtain foreign orders in view of the Depression'; that bankers and manufacturers had found that the Soviets lived up to their short-term commitments, and that German sales were being financed anyway by American banks. Then could sales of United States equipment be financed on a long-term basis by American banks, preferably by the sales of securities to the American public?[5]

In the next month, two memoranda were written by R. F. Kelley, Chief of the Division of Eastern European Affairs. These indicate that the State Department had not previously objected to short-term credits incidental to current commercial transactions, but also that only one such transaction had ever been presented to the Department for approval.[6] The Department had previously objected to bank credits and loans designed to finance the sale of German manufactures to Russia. The memorandum then quotes the denial to W. Averell Harriman in 1926 concerning a scheme to float a loan of 25 to to 35 million dollars on the American market, the proceeds of which were to be used to extend credit to German industrialists in order to sell goods to the Soviet Union. It also mentions the New York Trust Company and the Farquhar denials.[7]

---

[4] U. S. State Dept. Decimal File, 316–132–148. The State Dept. files connect Vanderlip with Martens and the Soviet Bureau in New York.

[5] Letter from American Locomotive Sales Corp. to U.S. State Dept. October 17, 1927 (316–124–0026).

[6] Kelley Memorandum, October 28, 1927 (316–124–0031). This was in 1925 when the Chase National Bank had informed the State Dept. it was arranging a cotton credit. The State Dept. did not object, as the arrangement was 'considered as incidental to ordinary current commercial intercourse.'

[7] U.S. State Dept. Decimal File, 316–124–0031.

The memorandum makes the following very pertinent commentary:

> . . . if the object of the Department's policy with regard to Russian financing is to exercise pressure on the Soviet regime to the end that this regime may eventually come to realize the necessity of abandoning its interference in the domestic affairs of the United States and of recognizing the international obligations devolving upon it with respect to the indebtedness of Russia to the United States and its citizens, and with respect to the property of American citizens in Russia,—if such is the Department's aim the logic of the situation would seem to demand that the Department view with disfavor all financial arrangements, whether in the form of bond issues or long term bank credits and whether designed to facilitate American exports to Russia or to serve other purposes which would result in making financial resources available to the Soviet Government.[8]

In brief, the Kelley argument was that *any* financial arrangement was going to be of assistance.

The decision, made at the Presidential level after consultation with Mellon and Hoover, was to allow American Locomotive to extend long-term credit to the Soviet Union for the purchase of railroad equipment.[9]

The Soviets kept pressing foreign firms. They finally succeeded in breaching the long-term loan situation in 1928–9 by holding Harriman and Company and the State Department 'over a barrel.' Harriman had been forced out of his manganese concession[10] and the Soviets offered compensation in the form of long-term bonds. Harriman accepted bonds at an interest rate of 6 percent. This was gleefully hailed by the Soviets as the first American loan to the U.S.S.R.[11]

When the Harriman bonds were received by the Chase National Bank in New York there was no mention on the face of the certificates of the fact that they were for any specific purpose. Vice-President Schley informed the State Department as follows:

> I do not look upon the transaction in any way as an attempt to float any securities in this country, but as an obligation given in payment of a single business transaction, and I trust that the Department will view it in the same light.[12]

---

[8]   U.S. State Dept. Decimal File, 316–124–0032.

[9]   Marginal notation on letter to American Locomotive, U.S. State Dept. Decimal File, 316–124–0027. It might be added that in August 1927 a rumored Dillon Reed loan of $30 million to develop the Solikamsk potash deposits and other projects had been quashed by the U.S. State Dept., acting apparently on its own initiative.

[10] Harriman says he left by agreement (see page 91). This explanation is not at all consistent with the contemporaneous newspaper or archival material. He was forced out by interference, by high costs, and generally by what Walter Duranty called an 'utterly inept' agreement.

[11] 'This is actually the first American loan received by the Soviet Government.' (Amtorg, *op. cit.*, IV, No. 16–17, 298.)

[12] U.S. State Dept. Decimal File, 316–138–296/7.

The subsequent State Department memorandum noted that the bonds received by Chase National totalled $4.45 million, whereas the Harriman investment had only been $3.45 million. The memorandum comments:

> It would appear therefore that Harriman and Company has advanced to the Soviet Government a sum of approximately $1,000,000. . . .[13]

The memorandum goes on to suggest that this was probably a *quid pro quo* for compensation for expropriation and that:

> No useful purpose would be served by placing difficulties in the way of Harriman and Company from recovering the money invested in the concession. . . .

The memorandum then argues that the additional $1 million was not really a loan but part of the original concession. The Riga Consul (Coleman) was less vague and called the whole Harriman transaction a 'loan.' This statement, however, was given the classification (in the department) of 'confidential.'[14]

It is amply clear, in retrospect, that the Harriman 6-percent 20-year bonds were a long-term loan and effectively breached the last remnants of United States credit policy vis-à-vis the Soviet Union.[15]

THE STATE DEPARTMENT AND PATENT PROTECTION

A Soviet decree of September 12, 1924 gave patent rights, under certain conditions, to inventors for a period of fifteen years. Article 2 of the original decree stated that no invention would be considered novel if, prior to the date of application, it had either in the U.S.S.R. or abroad been 'described fully or with substantial particulars so openly as to be capable of being reproduced by experts.' This was subsequently amended to read 'described fully . . . or *applied*.' (Italics are added.) In brief, if the invention had been described or *used abroad* then protection would not be given under Soviet law.[16]

Irrespective of written law, which gave scant enough protection to foreign inventions, Bolshevik practice gave no protection whatsoever. Law and the judiciary in Leninist political theory exist only to further the ends of the state. Consequently, true patent protection, in the sense that we understand it in

---

[13]   U.S. State Dept. Decimal File, 316–138–299.

[14]   U.S. State Dept. Decimal File, 316–138–289.

[15]   It will be remembered that previously the U.S. State Dept. had been unwilling to '*initiate*' an investigation into Harriman's conduct of negotiations with unofficial representatives of the Soviet Union in the United States. It is sensed, but without conclusive evidence, that the State Dept. could not become involved in a stand on principle at this point. If the documents in the United States and German Archives are viewed in toto, they give the distinct impression that political pressures well above the desk level of the department were at work.

[16]   A. A. Santalov and L. Segal, *Soviet Union Yearbook, 1926.* (London: Allen and Unwin, 1926), p. 477.

the West, could in no way be construed to exist, *whatever* the written content of the decree. This was in fact the initial interpretation and conclusion of the State Department.

The Columbia Graphophone Manufacturing Company was informed by the State Department in 1921 'that the Bolsheveki had nationalized all private and industrial property in Russia and that it could therefore be inferred that any individual rights—such as patent and trademark protection—could not be secured during their regime.'[17] This was confirmed in 1922 upon a second inquiry by Columbia. This interpretation is confirmed by history as there is considerable evidence, even without the Archives, that the Soviets were indeed sequestering patents and anything else of a technical nature in the 1920s—as they do even in the present day.[18] That this confiscatory policy was widely known is suggested by the numerous letters of inquiry in the State Department decimal file.[19]

In any event, caution was indicated by a quite separate chain of happenings. In 1919 the United States had deported, as an undesirable alien, Ludwig K. Martens, organizer of the Soviet Bureau in New York and hardly a friend of the United States, although Martens had been assisted in the organization and financing of the Soviet Bureau by a number of American companies. On November 12, 1924, Martens was appointed by the Soviet of Labor and Defense as Chairman of the Committee on Inventions.[20]

In 1925 or thereabouts, there was a definite change in the administration of American policy in relation to patents. Rather than the early doctrine of noninterposition, a doctrine of positive encouragement of Soviet trade was substituted, but partially clothed in the words of noninterposition. Where caution was indicated, active and positive suggestions were made in response to inquiries for advice on patent and other matters. This change cannot be traced to any specific Congressional action, and, there is no evidence to suggest pressure from above the 'desk level' of the State Department. It predates by a year or so the changes in credit and loan policies discussed above.

---

[17] U.S. State Dept. Decimal File, 316–108–679/680.

[18] See the report of H. L. Roosevelt of RCA on negotiations with the U.S.S.R. for a long-range radio transmitter: 'The Soviets desired . . . strangely enough, the right to use Radio Corporation patents for manufacturing purposes. The latter request had somewhat amused Mr. Roosevelt as he found the Soviets brazenly copying many foreign products.' [U.S. Consulate in Stockholm, Report 248, April 10, 1928 (U.S. State Dept. Decimal File, 316–108–791).] In October 1924, the Norton Company complained that the Ilytch works in Petrograd was marketing a grinding wheel under the name of NORTON. (316–108–815.)

[19] For examples see U.S. State Dept. Decimal File, 316–108. Also, see *Ford Delegation Report (1926)*.

[20] *Izvestia*, No. 273, November 29, 1924. That patents were not protected, even for Russians, is confirmed by V. N. Ipatieff, *op. cit.*, p. 287, who noted that his patent for 'Ipatite,' a gas-absorbent material, was immediately turned over to the Revolutionary War Council.

An internal indicator of the change is treatment of an official Soviet notice on patents issued in June 1925. The United States Commissioner of Patents and the United States Department of Commerce questioned the State Department as to whether the notice on patents received by them should be published in the Official Gazette at all 'in view of the fact that this circular is published by or in the interest of the Soviet Government.' The State reply to the memorandum was simply to enclose a draft of the phraseology to be employed in publishing the notice without directly answering, either way, the substance of the questions.[21]

In advising American firms, after about 1926, on the patent position in the U.S.S.R., a policy of active encouragement was followed. In September 1927 the State Department received a letter from Gleason, McLanahan, Merritt, and Ingraham, attorneys at law, which indicated that a client had an 'invention of international importance' which he wanted to protect. Further, they said that 'we fear that if the process should become public in Russia and no protection can be secured, much of the value of our invention may be lost.' To be consistent with previous replies and the policy of noninterposition, the State Department reply should have indicated that it could not intervene, that there were neither diplomatic nor trade relations between the two countries and therefore that no protection could be given to a United States citizen.

The actual State Department reply gives the address of the Leningrad patent office (Ulitza Herzena, 24, Leningrad) and then adds:

> In as much as there are no official representatives of the Soviet regime in the United States, documents required for the registration of patents in Russia should be certified in the United States by the diplomatic officers of a nation with which the Soviet regime has diplomatic relations. Among such countries are Germany, France, Italy and Poland. . . .[22]

Instructions then follow on the procedures to be followed with the Soviet authorities after the necessary signatures have been obtained. There is nothing in the reply that would suggest for all practical purposes a patent could not be protected, as we know it in the West, under Soviet law and practice.

The Automatic Damper Company sent a scribbled, almost illegible, half-page note requesting general information on Soviet patent laws, obviously with the intent of patenting one of its devices.

The Automatic Damper Company must have been pleasantly surprised with the detailed two-page reply which indicated precisely how to go about patenting a device and gave two addresses in the U.S.S.R. One of these was

[21] U.S. State Dept. Decimal File, 316–108–683/6.

[22] U.S. State Dept. Decimal File, 316–108–691/3. Also see Lacey and Lacey inquiry, October 6, 1927 (316–129–687/8).

the Inventions Bureau (TsBRIZ), under the control of Martens Committee.[23] One wonders if the State Department realized that all stoking appliances, including dampers, were being produced by the Richard Kablitz concession and that this was an area where purely Russian technology was nonexistent. Work in this field was dependent on Western equipment. For example, the report of Professor L. K. Ramzin at the meeting of the 1930 World Power Conference in Tokyo covers his experiments utilizing Moscow brown coals, which have a moisture content of 32 percent. Ramzin reported that predrying had been a failure but that these coals could be completely burnt with the aid of hot-air draught as follows: 'The fuel was ground in a high speed Atritor mill of Messrs Alfred Herbert and the aerated dust was blown into two long flame burners located in the upper arch of the furnaces, the flames then being diverted downwards and forming a U. The bottom of the furnace was fitted with a Babcock and Wilcox water screen. . . .'[24]

In short, a policy was instituted of suggesting how to overcome absence of diplomatic relations and ensuring that patentable techniques would, in fact, be transferred to the U.S.S.R. without protection. If the reader is dubious, then indication of the treatment afforded another type of patent inquiry— those from individuals in trouble and requesting help—will complete the picture.

On November 21, 1928, Rector, Hibben, Davis, and Macauley, attorneys in Chicago, requested advice on behalf of the Burroughs Adding Machine Company, which

> has been requested to furnish . . . all sorts of publications describing the products of the Burroughs firm . . . we hesitate to advise the Burroughs Company to furnish the information without a little more accurate advice as to what is really going to be done with the information after it is obtained.[25]

The firm had been told by the Soviets that the information would be used in considering applications for patents, but obviously both Burroughs and Rector were skeptical. The State Department reply was that it had no information, and no means of ascertaining the purpose for which such publications might be desired and 'cannot advise you in the matter.'[26]

An appeal for help from B. Singer, a specialist in trademark and patent law who represented clients with patents registered in the U.S.S.R., was rejected. A number of patent applications had been filed through a Soviet citizen, Blau, who had been arrested by the GPU and whose office had been closed.

---

23   U.S. State Dept. Decimal File, 316–108–694/6.
24   *Engineering*, CXXX (February 7, 1930), 184.
25   U.S. State Dept. Decimal File, 316–108–690.
26   *Ibid.*

Singer requested the good offices of the State Department to facilitate the transfer the Blau's office records to a new associate, one Feldman. The reply curtly indicated regret but inability to help Singer in any way 'as this Government has not recognized the regime now functioning in Russia.'[27]

Thus, the State Department was willing to aid the transfer of patent information, or tacitly encouraged Soviet acquisition of information (Burroughs), but not willing to warn of possible confiscation, which was known to the department, nor outline the Soviet record or philosophy. Formal statements of noninterposition in trade relations were followed by advice or suggestions running counter to the implementation of a doctrine of noninterposition.[28]

The promotion of Soviet technical data acquisition by the State Department is particularly curious in the light of the fact that knowledge of expropriation was widely known in industrial and commercial circles, and one presumes that State Department had access to the same knowledge.

For example, the 1926 *Ford Delegation Report* makes the following pertinent comment. After pointing out that the Soviet Union has a patent law, the report adds:

> This law does not seem in any way to hinder the reproduction in Russia of foreign patented products. In the automotive line the Fordson tractor is reproduced in Leningrad under the name of the 'Red Putilov' Tractor. The Italian Fiat 1½ ton truck is reproduced in Moscow under the name AMO and the Bosch spark plug is reproduced in Leningrad by the Avtopromtorg organization.[29]

The U.S. Consul in Riga, among other U.S. representatives abroad, pointed this out on a number of occasions. It is a reasonable presumption that the State Department was encouraging transfer of technical information knowing that the result would be expropriation without compensation or permission. The reasons behind such a policy are beyond the confines of this study.

---

[27] U.S. State Dept. Decimal File, 316–108–763.

[28] This raises the question of the extent to which the State Dept. is able or required to go in order to protect United States citizens. In another context, State Dept. letters suggest it was not aware of any dangers for engineers or firms entering the U.S.S.R., but usually added that it could not provide protection in the absence of diplomatic relations. The State Dept. was aware in May 1928 that Rykov had ordered three German engineers involved in the Shakhta affair to be shot. This had been stricken from the official record of the Rykov speech. Yet the engineers may have been sentenced to death because Rykov was compromised by the Shakhta affair in the eyes of Stalin. It appears to the writer that United States firms are entitled to knowledge of the likelihood of this type of arbitrary action. The Baaghorn and Mott cases are more recent examples.

[29] *Ford Delegation Report (1926)*, p. 38.

THE MONOPSONISTIC POWER OF THE SOVIET TRADE ORGANIZATION

Foreign trade was a state monopoly under Vneshtorg from the beginning, and superb use was made of this monopoly in trade relations with the West, especially in playing one company, or country, off against another.

Little thought was given to this process of 'divide and conquer'; the Soviets stumbled onto it in their pragmatic search for foreign assistance.

There is an interesting report, of uncertain origin (probably written in the German Foreign Ministry in 1928), which provides a clear discussion of this problem and the pressures and counterpressures that a united front of Western firms and countries would encounter.[30] In essence the report proposed concerted action by Western powers in relation to trade with the Soviet Union. The writer expresses surprise that a decade of trade with the monopoly trade organization of the Soviet Union had elapsed before discussion of 'organized counteraction.'[31] Brief examination of the factors making for diversified rather than a unified approach leads the writer to the conclusion that the

> Soviet government in a masterly fashion took advantage of these conflicts of interest between the powers, for a consolidation of the monopoly of foreign trade. . . .

The author argued that little good could come of carefully worded articles and treaties with the U.S.S.R. Monopoly of foreign trade was one of the 'commanding heights' of the Soviet economy; and attempt to create an international 'united front' had been met with claims of an 'anti-Soviet front.' In 1928 only the German and French chemical industries were able to agree with the Soviets on prices and joint deliveries. Finally, the author suggested that such international cooperation would have to take the initial form of uniform credit and delivery conditions.

Hilger suggests that neither the Germans nor the Soviets were aware in 1921–2 of the potential power of a trade monopoly, and that the opportunity of meeting the Soviet trade monopoly with a central German business organization was missed 'because of the tenacity with which the predominantly Socialist Government of Germany stuck to the principles of free enterprise.' Later Germany formed the Russian Committee of the German Economy (Russland Ausschuss der Deutschen Wirtschaft) to provide advice and orientation on German-U.S.S.R. business. Hilger comments that, once the Soviets

---

[30]   U.S. Consulate in Riga, Report 5156, March 26, 1928 (316–109–579).

[31]   The author of the report would be even more surprised to learn that in 1966, almost fifty years after the Bolshevik Revolution, there was still no unified counteraction, although NATO, SEATO, and CENTO are the military and political equivalents of such counteraction.

realized the importance of the trade monopoly, they were suspicious of any attempt to impede its value and began to block embassy aides from aiding German firms in negotiations, especially with the Main Concessions Committee.[32]

The Soviet Union, supposedly the opponent of monopoly, has in fact been the greatest recipient of monopsonistic profits in the history of industrialized society. Neither has it been slow or backward in recognizing and protecting the value of this monopoly.

THE BOLSHEVIK ATTITUDE TOWARD THE FOREIGN FIRM

Bolshevik unity was split by Lenin's concession policy. The rank and file Bolshevik questioned the wisdom of, and the necessity for, the return of the capitalist—after all, had not the Revolution just ejected him? The Party had difficulty in convincing its ranks that foreign capitalists were a necessary evil. In particular, the OGPU, charged with the purity of the Revolution, was dubious concerning foreign elements. Whenever it had the chance, as in the Shakhta affair, the OGPU exercised punitive measures with great zeal. The pleas to the Party faithful to accept foreign capitalists and engineers give the clue that Communist intent was to absorb capital, skills, and technology, and then, 'when the lemon was sucked dry,' to discard it. There are numerous speeches and articles in contemporary Soviet literature which suggest both the captive nature of the concession and, on the other hand, the necessity for the concession in the reconstruction and development of a socialist society.[33]

The Urquhardt negotiations in 1922, although a failure, are interesting in this regard. Urquhardt was president of Russo-Asiatic Consolidated, Ltd., which had held very large concessions in tsarist Russia. Negotiations with Urquhardt for operation of his former properties, then lying idle, would have led the way for other entrepreneurs. Although Urquhardt was well aware of Bolshevik strategy, he made a concession agreement with Krassin in 1921; the latter then went to Moscow for ratification by Lenin and Trotsky. Before this could be obtained, word leaked out and the hue and cry within the Party forced Lenin to scuttle the agreement, using British activities in the Middle East as a pretext.

---

[32] Hilger, *op. cit.*, pp. 166–67. This may have colored Hilger's interpretation of the value of concessions. If the embassy was denied data, they could have assumed a minute impact of the concession.

[33] See Volume II. Not all the clumsiness was on the part of Western businessmen. In a conversation between Mr. Arlt of the Königsberg Chamber of Commerce and a 'high Soviet official' the latter, in reply to a question concerning the safety of German investments in Russia, said, 'Until Germany goes through a successful World Revolution they will be safe. If Germany goes Bolshevist, however, it will make little difference to German industrialists whether their possessions are expropriated in their own country or in Russia.' (316–133–140.)

Some early Bolsheviks were clearly aware of the necessity for foreign help. Krassin had formerly been managing director of Siemens Schukert in Petrograd. He then became a revolutionary, and in 1920–1, as Soviet Trade Representative in London, he argued that

> Russia . . . cannot without assistance organize her trade. She cannot bring together her resources in a productive manner and she must rely upon capital, the experience and initiative of foreign capitalists. . . .[34]

An article by Arsky in *Krasnya Gazeta* in 1921 in effect clarifies this policy: 'The question of concessions has been under discussion for the last half year but so far it has mostly been in the air . . . nothing has been done.'[35] The writer then describes the proposed Northern Telegraph concession, argues its advantages as a generator of foreign exchange, and the alternative of not being able to use the line at all. 'As a result of this treaty,' he writes, 'we shall get a repaired telegraph line and hundreds of millions of francs in gold to carry on trade with abroad.'

Arsky then discusses a Kuban sulphates concession in the same glowing terms: 'Of course the concessionaires will profit hugely but let them do so for it will bring wealth to us and we must pay for that.' Finally, considering a Baku forest concession, Arsky argues that, although the concessionaire will profit, 'as Lenin foretold we shall have to pay a high price to foreigners for their help, science and energy in enterprise.' He then adds that in any event there are not enough skilled Soviet workmen, nor could the Soviets feed them, nor will they be able to in the near future—'*We must seize the moment.*' The Soviets, he says, are well able to take care of their own interests, certainly in the matter of concessions: 'They will demand from those who get them the maximum of profit for the country and its re-establishment.'

The Party line had to be sold to the rank and file, and it would appear that the closer the explanation got to the factory and farm level the less circumscribed was the description of the fate awaiting the foreign specialist. For example, Ipatieff quotes a collective farm chairman, Kopylov, in a speech at Tikhonova Pustyn in Kaluga Province:

> Of course we need bourgeois specialists for a short time. As soon as Party members learn what these specialists know we'll get rid of the specialists fast enough. Right now we must treat and feed them far better than ourselves; but their time will come, just as it did for the rest of the bourgeoisie.[36]

[34]   *New York Times*, June 12, 1921, p. 2, col. 3.

[35]   *Krasnya Gazeta*, September 3, 1921. Arsky was, at least, able to look after his own interests; by 1924 he had acquired 30,000 shares in Moskust, a joint-stock company in Moscow.

[36]   Ipatieff, *op. cit.*, p. 486.

The opposition to foreigners at the plant level became overt on numerous occasions, but it is not always clear whether this was due to ideological dislike, counter-revolutionary activity or just plain antipathy for those who came along to improve plant discipline. It is reasonably likely that the majority of Party members were kept in line by Party discipline, whatever they thought. It is more likely that the opposition came from non-Party bureaucrats and perhaps counter-revolutionary segments, except where discord was created on direct orders of the Party, as part of a campaign to eject a specific concessionaire. It is entirely conceivable, on the other hand, that the OGPU overtly attempted to scuttle the introduction of foreign elements in the name of protecting the Revolution. Douillet, Belgian consul in Russia, relates how the OGPU arrested and jailed an Austrian aircraft worker at the Junkers plant and a diesel specialist in Shelkotrust. They were retained without charges and then expelled.[37]

The Americans at the Kuzbas project (the American Industrial Corporation) had clearly ideological opposition. The newcomers were classified as either Communists or sympathizers and neither was particularly popular among Kuzbas coal miners. McDonald, an engineer with a technical-assistance agreement with Uralmed, met opposition from Soviet engineers, whom he accused of 'seriously interfering with the progress of important work.'[38] This is rather similar to the opposition met by Ruykeyser at Uralasbest—fear that technical inadequacy might meet dismissal, or worse.

By the end of the decade opposition had become serious, especially at the Dniepr generating plant, the largest in the world, being built by American and German engineers. There was a rather natural conflict between the two foreign groups, but there was also an 'unfriendly attitude' on the part of the local workers serious enough to warrant the attention of V. V. Kuibyshev in a speech to the Supreme Soviet:

> But, have these foreign and alien hands not been brought by the proletarian state, and is the transplantation of foreign technique not necessary in order to enable socialist technique . . . first to overtake and then excel European capitalist technique? Without resorting to foreign assistance on a still greater scale, this is impossible. The application of foreign technique is one of the keys to hasten the tempo of our development. . . . Such

[37] Douillet, *op. cit.*, pp. 74, 76.

[38] *Pravda*(Moscow),No.239, October 16,1929. Similar cases were reported in a special supplement on foreign specialists in *Ekonomicheskaya Zhizn*, No. 243, October 20, 1929; for example, German engineer Scheibil at the Karl Liebknect works of Ugostal was 'abused and persecuted.' Another engineer (Mashik) at the Tomsky plant of Ugostal was subjected to an 'inquisition' and put to work in a shop (316-130–927/8). Two German engineers at the Komintern pottery works under reconstruction were isolated because one of them (the technical director) gave 'strong orders' to the workers (*Ekonomicheskaya Zhizn*, No. 245, October 23, 1929).

assistance is absolutely necessary in the ferrous and non-ferrous coal and chemical industries.[39]

Kuibyshev then went on to add that in the non-ferrous, ferrous, and pottery industries there were cases of hostility to foreign workers.

Hilger, economic attaché at the German Embassy in Moscow, confirms that resistance to concessions and foreign aid came from the lower levels of the Communist Party, the bureaucracy, and the OGPU.[40] He also suggests that the Soviet leaders intended duplicity in the long run and that 'it was never more than a retreat,' although he quite correctly points out that it is difficult to distinguish cause from effect. In retrospect, it seems that the Soviets were never honest in their concessions operations. Hilger avoids, or perhaps momentarily forgets, the numerous references in Lenin's speeches in which concessions were held to be temporary and destined for expropriation when their purposes had been achieved.

BOLSHEVIK LEADERS AND THE JOINT-STOCK COMPANIES

Some of the Bolshevik leaders found this a suitable time to improve their personal fortunes and a number had holdings in private enterprises and mixed companies.

Moskust, one of the most important stock companies, controlled a cloth mill and paper, shoe, tarpaulin, glass, and leather factories. Trotsky owned 80,000 chervontsi shares, while Arsky held 30,000, Sklyansky 45,000, and Muralov, the Commander of the Moscow Military District, an unknown number. It was believed other leaders participated through relatives.

Zinoviev was interested in Arcos and the Leningrad Tobacco Trust and owned 45 percent of the Volkhovstroi stock company. Chicherin held an interest in the mixed company Turksholk (Turkish silk), and Dzerzhinsky was chairman and held 75,000 chervontsi shares in the Coal Mines Exploitation Joint-Stock Company.[41]

Krasnatchokov, former Chicago lawyer and President of the Far East Republic (later absorbed into the Soviet Union), rose to become a member of Vesenkha and President of Prombank. While in the latter position he made a

> . . . rather liberal contract with a Russo-American concern, with which he was personally connected, and from which his wife drew monthly assignments payable in the United States.[42]

[39] Speech at Sixth Plenary Session of the Supreme Soviet, October 1929.
[40] Hilger, *op. cit.*, pp. 170–1.
[41] U.S. State Dept. enclosure to U.S. Consulate in Riga, Report 2394, September 24, 1924 (316–129–1229). Ipatieff comments acidly on the behavior of Party functionaries attached to the Berlin Trade Delegation and Purchasing Commission. (*Op. cit.*, pp. 408–9.)
[42] Scheffer, *op. cit.*, p. 129.

Although these cases may prove shocking to the ideological purist who considers the Marxist to be above personal gain, they are insignificant, considering the opportunities available in a complete dictatorship, and are certainly less than the personal empires built up by Stalin and his henchmen in more recent times.

CHAPTER NINETEEN

The Necessity for Foreign Technology and the Process of Acquisition

THE IMPACT OF REVOLUTION ON THE INDUSTRIAL STRUCTURE

IT has been assumed almost axiomatically that World War I, the revolutions, the Intervention, and the Civil War created the catastrophic collapse of the industrial and agricultural sectors in 1922.[1]

The basic cause for the collapse was the economic illiteracy of an ideology which had neglected to think out its economic counterpart and drove a viable growing economy into a shambles. The campaign to inflate the ruble to zero value, the demobilization of industry, the policy of 'free' transport, utilities, and other services, the massive decline in labor productivity, coupled with doubled and tripled wages, were contra-developmental in effect.

In the first year of the war, the Russian economy had changeover problems which persisted until industry was on a war production basis; then growth, as measured in terms of output and employment, resumed. The industrialization mobilization campaign of 1916 created significant growth. New industrial centers were created at Nizhni-Novgorod, Rybinsk, and Samara, in addition to the expansion of existing centers in Moscow, Petrograd, and earlier industrial areas. One result was an increase in the demand for raw materials, and the

---

[1] The following is a typical statement: 'Russian industry, agriculture and transportation declined greatly during the war, and by 1917 were in a condition approaching collapse. The civil war served to accelerate economic disruption, with the result that by 1920-1 industry was practically at a standstill while agriculture was fast approaching the condition which, coupled with a severe drought, precipitated the famine of 1921-22.' [American-Russian Chamber of Commerce, *Economic Handbook of the Soviet Union* (New York, 1931), p. 7.]

This myth has been compounded by using 1913 as a comparative statistical base. In fact, some industries had a 1916 output twice that of 1913. Some chemical products (such as benzene, toluene, and zylene) not produced at all in 1913 were produced in quantity between 1914 and 1917. (Ipatieff, *op. cit.*, p. 210.)

excess of imports over exports in 1916 was due to this upsurge in activity. *Between January 1, 1916 and January 1, 1917, industrial employment increased by 8.9 percent.*[2]

The greatest increase was in metallurgy and food products. Agricultural implement works were turned over to munitions production: 'there was hardly a repair shop of any size connected with the textile, confectionery, macaroni or other industry which was not assigned to the manufacture of grenades, mines, field kitchens, or other war materials.'[3] In a few industries output declined due to enemy action: most sugar refineries were in occupied territory, cement production declined because of a shortage of hoop iron for barrels, and there was a shortage of spare parts. But on balance, in the year before the revolutions, Russia had resumed her economic growth, new industries were being created, and industrial employment was greater than ever.

The first revolution was a shock to this expanding structure. The Ministry of Trade and Commerce undertook a survey which covered five months between the Kerensky Revolution and the Bolshevik Revolution. Between March and July, 568 industrial enterprises were closed down and 104,000 employees lost their employment. Almost one-third of the enterprises closed were engaged in manufacture of food products, with textiles and metalworking next in importance. The most important single reason for failure was lack of fuel. Less than 10 percent closed for lack of orders, a condition which could well have come about as a secondary result of lack of fuel and supplies elsewhere. Excessive demands of workmen and financial difficulties comprised a very small proportion of failures, considering that this was a period of revolutionary unrest. Most firms closed were small and unable to plan against these factors. In spite of this decline in industrial activity, concentrated in smaller enterprises, all the larger and important plants were operating at the time of the Revolution; nor is there a reported case in the two major industrial centers of Moscow and Petrograd of a large plant looted, burned or destroyed by the Revolution itself.[4]

The largest single blow to the structure of industry was a decree issued by the Soviet Commissariats of Labor and War on December 21, 1917, calling a halt to all military production and dictating a return to peacetime activities

---

[2] *Report of the Ministry of Trade and Commerce*, August 1917 (316–111–1015).
[3] U.S. Military Intelligence Report, *Russian Industries*, October 1918 (316–129–25).
[4] There are reports in the U.S. State Dept. Archives which mention 'looting' of plants, but this always refers to removing specific items of value (especially brass or copper) and not to physical destruction of the plant or its equipment. Overt destruction was limited to institutional symbols of the tzars. For examples, see the Sokoloff collection of photographs at the Hoover Institution, Stanford University. In 1920 Petrograd was deserted but intact. For instance, in photograph No. 24, taken on the Neva, large plant buildings and smoke stacks are still standing, but idle.

within *one month*. Industry at this time was working at full capacity on war material and had no alternate plans for consumer products. This simple order had a major adverse effect. One month was, of course, an insufficient time to change course completely. Not one factory was able to start peacetime production by January 21, 1918, and most were forced to close. The only exceptions were those plants where workers insisted on fulfilling military contracts as an alternative to closure. The resultant chaos compounded an earlier problem. The Bolshevik Revolution had caused most foreign and numerous Russian skilled workers to flee abroad along with the managers and engineers. The 'instant demobilization' decree hastened the exit of skills, but workers now went to the villages.[5] In brief, this single decree robbed the industrial structure of that skill and technical component which had not already left. This structure, which, despite supply difficulties, had been operating reasonably well, and in 1916 was giving definite signs of renewed growth, was now placed on the road to collapse.

The period of War Communism was entered with neither technical nor administrative apparatus, under a government of Soviets which had neither plans nor solutions for the chaos. Feeble attempts at planning civilian production were made by some worker's committees; this led to duplication of effort, and, in any event, neither financial nor technical problems were overcome. The Soviets then tried centralization, but lack of knowledge and information led to conflicts among makeshift managements. Concurrently came a major decline in productivity as the discipline of a market system collapsed. Inflation led to payment in kind rather than in depreciated paper money. Lack of goods was instrumental in creating self-supply organizations in factories, until the principal task of the factory became feeding and clothing its own workers. Resultant losses were made up by state subsidy, thus furthering the inflation.

The decline in production of one of the largest Moscow machine shops, which was producing iron and steel castings and forgings, was reported to the State Department. In January 1917, just before the Revolution, the index of production was at a base of 100. The difficulties of the inter-revolutionary period are reflected by a decline in the index to 76. By the following January, just after the 'instant demobilization decree' the index had fallen to 45. By August 1918, reflecting attempts at stabilization, the index had fallen only to 37. Data from other sources supports this chain of events. On the Northern Railways there was 0.67 a laborer per verst of line in 1913 and 5.8 laborers in 1919; on the Moscow-Kursk line there were 6.48 laborers per verst in 1913 and 18.9 in 1919. Railroad work was a preferred occupation as it gave access to food supplies in the villages.

[5]   Rykov, in a speech before the Third Congress of the People's Council in January 1920, indicated that 90 percent of skilled workers left the factories at this time.

The labor supply position in the large plants confirms that skilled workers left in droves while the plants themselves were intact. In 1920 about 30 factories in Petrograd were attempting to work for the Red Navy. The major problem was lack of skills. The Baltic plant employed 3,500 and required another 5,800. The Franco-Russian factory had no workers and was looking for 1,500. The famous Putilovets had only 350 workers and wanted another 1,100. The Petrograd Metal Works employed 150 and was looking for another 1,000. In the 30 or so works listed, a total of 11,000 people were employed and a total of 22,000 additional workers were required. This counters the myth that the plants lacked equipment. The plants lacked skilled labor and management, both of which had been dispersed by the Bolshevik Revolution.[6]

In brief, as we already know, there was a complete collapse under War Communism. This collapse had little to do with the Civil War. It was created at the very beginning of the period of War Communism by dispersion of skills, absurd decrees, and the removal of disciplinary market forces.

THE TROUGH OF THE INDUSTRIAL DECLINE

In many sectors, production declined to almost zero by 1922. Cast iron reached less than 1 percent, cotton yarn 1.5 percent, rubber galoshes about .33 percent, and gold about .5 percent of 1913 production. Food products, especially if processed, fell to less than 5 percent. Per capita production of sugar was less than 1.5 pounds per year, and vegetable oils about .33 pound per year.[7] The accepted explanations for these abysmal declines were the war, revolutions, the Civil War, and the blockade. Actually production increased during the war, and the revolutions did little physical damage to production facilities. General Wrangel still occupied the Crimea, but this was a small part of the vast Russian geography. The allied blockade had been raised in 1921 and foreign products began to flow in larger quantities. The decline continued after these 'reasons' had ceased to exist. The real cause must be sought elsewhere than in political and military factors; the decline was essentially caused by economic factors.

THE NEW ECONOMIC POLICY (NEP)

NEP was introduced to offset the economic problems caused by Bolshevik economic policy. Nonpayment for work removed incentives. Nationalization, when there was no managerial talent available, was suicidal. NEP was a temporary move to utilize the knowledge and experience of the capitalist class

[6]   U.S. State Dept. Decimal File, 316–111–1157.
[7]   See Report by Vesenkha to IX Congress of Soviets.

to revive the economy, 'This is not an attempt to restore the capitalist class but to adapt it to our constructive work.'[8] The major impact of NEP was in the spheres of trading and small manufacturing, although it has also been seen as an accommodation to the reluctant peasant. Implementation turned nationalized enterprises back to private operations. This was somewhat more widespread than Dobb has suggested.[9] *Pravda* (January 18, 1922) gives a summary by region of the number of enterprises remaining under government supply and finance after the initial NEP reorganization.

Table 19–1   REGIONAL DISTRIBUTION OF ENTERPRISES
UNDER GOVERNMENT AND PRIVATE CONTROL
AFTER NEP REORGANIZATION, 1922

Region	PRIVATE			STATE		
	Number of Factories	*Number of Workmen*	*Average Workers per Plant*	*Number of Factories*	*Number of Workmen*	*Average Workers per Plant*
Moscow	477	118,457	248	110	78,375	710
Vladimir	118	7,262	61	74	13,487	182
Ivanov	45	7,887	175	10	1,746	174
Tver	59	1,173	20	47	5,199	111
Valuga	54	3,929	73	n.a.	517	n.a.
Riazan	23	2,242	97	16	3,436	215
Total	776*	140,950	182	257	102,760	400

Source: Adapted from *Pravda*, January 18, 1922, p. 2.
* 775 in original text in *Pravda*.

A decree in *Krasnya Gazeta* for August 13, 1921 signed by Lenin divided all industrial enterprises into two groups: the first included those large enterprises to be supplied with raw materials and operated by the state, and the second group included factories leased to private individuals and foreign concessions. All other plants were closed and the workers transferred to operating factories. It will be noted that those enterprises retained under state control were almost always the largest, irrespective of regional distribution. The clash between the data in table 19-1 and in Dobb turns on a point of definition. Dobb argues that few were turned back to private *ownership* but that numbers were turned over to groups of workers including artels. The

[8] *Krasnya Gazeta* (Petrograd), December 20, 1921.
[9] ' . . . there was a certain amount of denationalization. . . . The extent of this . . . should not be exaggerated; and its economic significance was nothing like as great as foreign commentators at the time were inclined to suppose.' (Dobb, *op. cit.*, p. 142.) Dobb then adds that private enterprise covered only 12.5 percent of workers in the 1923 census, but he does not mention the limits of the 1923 census, which only covered part of the industrial structure.

enterprises listed in table 19–1 are those in which supply of inputs and finance is from private sources. It implies nothing about ownership, an academic question since 1917; the important point is the mechanism for overcoming deficient working capital and input supplies. It was to private mechanisms that the Soviet government turned. Any statement concerning ownership under a Soviet regime is illusionary.

Bogdanov, President of the Supreme Economic Council, stated emphatically on December 20, 1921, that large scale industries could only be re-established by foreign investment and technology (i.e. by private mechanisms):

> The investment of foreign capital is absolutely unavoidable as the equipment of whole branches of our industry depends upon foreign countries in so far as they were never created and supported in Russia by our own resources. It will be necessary to support these branches of industry in the future for a certain time by means of foreign capital and the introduction of foreign technical equipment.[10]

This capital and technology, added Bogdanov, were to be admitted in a controlled manner, 'only . . . where it is absolutely necessary, i.e., exploitation of new mines.' NEP had succeeded, he said, in moving industry from 'almost a standstill' in June 1921 to 'very, very slight' progress; but then he added a warning against optimism and suggested the road would be a long one, although the turn had been made. The policy of decentralization—i.e., the improvement in supply conditions by private trade and small plant leasing —was the factor behind the reversal in fortunes. NEP had a limited objective—to arrest the decline. In this it had been successful. The next step was reconstruction—restarting the numerous large and intact tsarist plants.

CONCENTRATION, TRUSTIFICATION, AND CONTRACTION

After several alternate solutions had been tried, it was decided to shrink the economic system by abandoning those plants making losses, grouping the remaining plants into trusts, and turning smaller or inoperable units back to domestic or foreign private enterprise.

The trust was designed with the introduction of foreign technical assistance in mind. The declared intent was to make the trust the vehicle for the transfer of foreign capital and technology demanded by Bogdanov. Examination of those trust agreements that are available confirms this objective. As reported in *Krasnya Gazeta*,[11] the twin aims of all trusts were, to obtain capital and assistance from abroad, and to retain chief controlling interest in the hands of the Soviets. One presumes the order of ranking was not accidental. The original

---

[10]   U.S. State Dept. Decimal File, 316–107–661.
[11]   January 26, 1922.

intent was to encourage foreign participation only in those trusts with dormant plants which were backward technically or which required large injections of capital. In practice most of the trusts looked to the West for assistance.

In the electrical and petroleum industries, technological progress was impossible without Western assistance, and so even comparatively well-run trusts looked westward. Trustification moved along fairly rapidly in late 1921 and 1922 but did little to improve the economic situation. Industrial production continued to slide downhill at an alarming rate and reached a nadir in the summer of 1922. The adopted countermeasure was the 'contraction of industry' policy. In order to reduce government subsidies, it was proposed by Vesenkha to select and close down nonessential industries.[12] A curious rationalization of this policy, made by Jacub, was that a socialist economy has alternate booms and slumps: 'each autumn and winter industry expands, while each spring it undergoes a crisis and contracts.' This statement was made in mid-summer and ignored the almost continual decline, winter and summer, which had been underway since the Bolshevik Revolution. Jacub viewed a condition of permanent crisis and suggested that a temporary contraction was not enough:

> There are only two ways to go—either pronounce our industry incurable . . . and close it down entirely, or else adopt measures, not for its contraction, but to keep it operating at capacity.[13]

In other words, technical and managerial rationality had to be injected into the shambles that the Bolsheviks had created from a buoyant, viable economy.

The end was reached in August 1922. There is a report in the State Department files concerning a meeting at Vesenkha. Bogdanov made the opening address and again stated in the bluntest language the condition of industry organization: it had 'reached its limit.' The situation was 'appalling and desperate.' The only hope, concluded Bogdanov, was the receipt of foreign capital and a good harvest coupled with complete denationalization.[14]

THE TREATY OF RAPALLO (APRIL 16, 1922)

After the collapse of the Genoa Conference, the Soviets and the Germans signed the Treaty of Rapallo, under which they reciprocally renounced all war claims and war losses. Germany also agreed to renounce compensation for nationalized property in the U.S.S.R., 'provided that the Soviet Government

---

[12] This policy is described in the four issues of *Ekonomicheskaya Zhizn*, Nos. 122–5, for June 2, 4, 7, and 8, 1922. Engineer Jacub read the report before a joint meeting of Gosplan and Vesenkha. Judged from the amount of space devoted to it, the report seems to have had top-level backing, but a lowly engineer was selected to present the total admission of failure.

[13] *Ekonomicheskaya Zhizn*, No. 125, June 8, 1922.

[14] IS Report (316–107–727).

does not satisfy similar claims of other States.' Diplomatic and consular relations were resumed, the most favored nation principles applied mutually, and the basis was established for resumption of trade and economic relations.

Rapallo laid the groundwork for economic recovery. American and European relief stemmed the famine. The military agreement of 1922 was the basis for development of the Red Army, Navy and Air Force, and gave the Soviets the benefit of German military technology. The long-denied economic protocols were the basis for German economic and technical assistance and gave the Soviets sufficient breathing space to consolidate the Revolution and turn to other members of the Western world for capital and technical assistance. It was a successful three-pronged policy and brought the U.S.S.R. back from the brink of complete collapse.

The State Department files contain a remarkable summary of the Communist viewpoint of Rapallo from a top-level source:

> . . . we are still the gainers from the Rapallo Treaty. Apart from the fact that our industry will be restored with the aid of German experts, our political activity and importance through the medium of Germany will increase very rapidly. . . . German specialists therefore are being welcomed into all branches of our State life and have already penetrated into the most important branches of industry. General Bauer's Commission now in Moscow is acquainting itself with all sides of our military life and advising the General Staff, although its official mission is merely to improve our aviation.[15]

With Rapallo and its important military and economic protocols came the International Barnsdall agreement which effectively halted the decline of Baku and modernized production techniques to make this area the most important earner of foreign exchange. By late 1922 the Soviets felt sufficiently strong to recommence exports of grain and renationalize privately operated organizations. The turning point of Soviet fortunes was mid-1922 and was dependent on the Rapallo protocols.

RECONSTRUCTION AND THE SECOND BOLSHEVIK REVOLUTION

Reconstruction as used in this era does not mean physical reconstruction but the revival of dormant enterprises. The revival of trade and distribution, together with the limited contribution of NEP, enabled a return to the Bolshevik road. The growth of small retail and manufacturing enterprises

---

[15] U.S. State Dept. Decimal File, 340–7–10. The document originated with IS and was marked 'CONFIDENTIAL For Secretary and Under Secretary.' See Appendix A for reliability of IS. The above extract comprises about one-third the total report, so that, on the basis of space, the impact of German assistance should be considered as a prime objective of the Soviets.

was choked off in 1924 as reconstruction by German technicians placed the Soviets into a stronger overall economic position. Over 300,000 private enterprises were closed within a few months.[16] An article in *Ekonomicheskaya Zhizn* entitled 'Results of the struggle against private capital' summarizes these major changes. Such a revolution would not have been dared unless Vesenkha felt confident about the possibilities of economic revival. In textiles, 44 percent were produced by private means in the first quarter of 1923–4 and only 14 percent in the last quarter. In flax, the percentage declined from 11 to 6 percent, and in woolens from 7 to 2 percent. The sugar trust had early German help and reported 27 percent in the first quarter and only 5 percent in the last. The salt syndicate, also with German aid, reported a decline from 40 percent to 10 percent. Both the sugar and salt trusts benefited from American machinery, for example, the Fulton Iron Works made extensive shipments of sugar machinery in 1922–3.[17]

The early Soviet economy was full of paradoxes, not the least of which was the source of the strength enabling the Second Bolshevik Revolution. Destitute in 1922, they were back on their feet in 1924. As individual trusts gained strength, private Russian elements were eliminated and replaced once again by the Soviet state. The foreign elements, however, were still needed. Their turn was to come at the end of the decade.

THE PROCESS OF ACQUIRING FOREIGN TECHNOLOGY

The Bolsheviks were revolutionaries *par excellence*. But revolutionary dogma contained no hints on the operation of a socialist economy. On this subject Marx, Engels, and Lenin were silent.

In spite of this silence, there was a clear recognition of the place of technology. The machine was the Marxian engine of progress. Given ignorance of the functions of the entrepreneur, it is not surprising that 'industrialization' and its superficial symbols, the tractor, the automobile, and machines in general, were seen as the high road to plenty. The assessment was superficial. It was assumed that the machine would work as well in a socialist environment as in a capitalist environment. The concepts of scarcity, rationality, and choice in relation to technology and innovation did not penetrate Leninist thinking. The end result was technological naïveté, and this was compounded by an overriding concern with things political.

Exhortations, slogans, shock methods, and ideological purity were seen as the solution to all problems, including machine and production problems. The collapse after the Revolution was a blow to the ideologues and was

---

[16]   Scheffer, *op. cit.*, p. 174.

[17]   U.S. State Dept. Decimal File, 661. 1115/484. See *New York Times*, November 16, 1921, p. 13, col. 2, for German assistance to the salt industry.

explained away on the basis of exogenous conditions and enemies of the Revolution rather than a deficiency in the political ideology applied to economic fact. It was not Lenin who saw the solution; it was Krassin, ex-director of Siemens-Schukert A-G in Petrograd—capitalist turned revolutionary. Lenin had the pragmatic wisdom to adopt the Krassinist solution.

Introduction of NEP, concessions, and foreign skills and technology did not completely inhibit experimentation with a 'socialist technology.' Attempts were made to develop an indigenous technology to reduce reliance on the West. No attempt in the 1920s was successful, unless one counts the 2 percent of drilling by the turbine method (an indigenous development). If we place to one side the technical incompetence of the trust personnel, the root cause for failure was the superficial political view of technology and the denial of the necessity for choice among innovations. Choice became a political decision. The attempt to manufacture the GNOM, a small Soviet-developed tractor was a complete failure. Machinery was purchased in Germany and installed in the old Balakov factory. No tractors were ever produced. There were two fully equipped automobile plants (the AMO and the Russo-Baltic); neither produced an indigenously designed automobile. The comic opera production of the Putilovets tractor (a copy of the Fordson) prompted Sorensen to suggest blowing the plant out of its misery. The 700 'tractors' produced held together only a few weeks. The German and American engineers who tried to re-design and re-start the Kertsch steel works complained of political interference in decision-making. And so on. In the face of these failures, complete reliance was placed upon Western help, a solution rationalized as the necessary prelude to 'socialist construction.' The reliance became so great that the Five-Year Plan did not get off the ground until after contracts had been placed with Western companies and stiff penalty clauses inserted for failure to meet construction deadlines.

THE GERMAN 'SECRET' ENGINEERING DEPARTMENTS

The protocols to the 1921 trade agreement and the Rapallo Treaty with Germany were the foundation for the transfer of massive German technical aid. Inconclusive references to this transfer can be found throughout the State Department and German archives; nothing of substance has appeared in Western news media or books on Soviet development. This transfer has been as deeply buried as it was extensive.

It has been extraordinarily difficult to quantify the transfer. The data is exceedingly fragmented—much more so than that for any other aspect of this study.[18] A number of lists of German firms marked 'Streng vertrauchlich,'

[18] Material on German engineers in the U.S.S.R. is scattered throughout Microcopy T-120, Serials L293, L308, and L391 to L395.

for the attention of Minister Wallroth, were found in the German archives. Two of the lists were dated the 14th and the 19th of August 1922: a significant fact, as this was exactly the point at which Bogdanov proclaimed 'the end.' Material in the State Department files backs up the belief that when 'the end' was reached, massive German assistance moved in to restart the closed plants. In some cases the lists make reference to specific projects, such as Carbo II and some Agrar projects which have not turned up elsewhere and which cannot be identified.

The 2,000 or so German engineers and technicians who moved into Soviet industry after Rapallo were replaced by a greater number of American engineers after 1927–8. These were employed by almost all trusts, including Giprotsvetmet, Selmashtroi, Steklostroi, Giproneft, Gipromez, Resinotrest, Tsentroboom, RKI, AKO, Zernotrest.[19] The most noticeable feature, apart from their numbers, was the fact that they were spread across the face of the Soviet economy (see table 20–3). They were employed by all design and construction bureaus. The only gap was in the furniture industry. Large numbers of American specialists were concentrated in 'key' activities. For example, in 1929 there were 66 foreign engineers in the three trusts Tokmekh (instruments), Mosstroi (Moscow Building Trust), and Khimtrust (the Chemical Trust).[20] The range of employment went from water irrigation projects to candy manufacture. Nor were the Soviets reticent in admitting their acquisitive dragnet (although in more recent times they appear to have gone to great lengths to reduce dependence on Western skills):

> In matters of technical assistance we follow neither an English, nor a German nor an American orientation. Our orientation is a Soviet orientation. In every country we are ready and willing to learn in those areas in which that country is most advanced. When we had the problem of modernizing the petroleum, automobile and tractor industries we turned to the United States, as America is the leading country in these industries. When it came to the chemical industry we asked for German help and it is no fault of ours if we were forced to go elsewhere for part of our technical assistance. . . .[21]

Planning and administrative posts were handed over to foreigners. H. J. Larsons was Deputy Chief of Currency Administration; Alcan Hirsch was Chief Engineer at different times for Chemstroi, Chemtrust, Giprokhim and Giproazot, as well as Chief Consultant to the heavy chemical industry;

---

[19]　See Bron, *op. cit.*, pp. 145–6, for a more complete listing.

[20]　*Torgovo-Promyshlennaya Gazeta*, No. 166, July 23, 1929.

[21]　*Ekonomicheskaya Zhizn*, No. 225, September 29, 1929. Compare this Soviet statement, which is clear enough, to the numerous statements in Western literature which argue that the Soviets developed without any foreign assistance. (See Holzman, *op. cit.*, L. Fischer, *op. cit.*, and M. Dobb, *op. cit.*)

Littlepage was chief engineer, later Deputy Director of Soyuszoloto. Downs was Technical Director of the Altai Polymetal Trust and so on. Even the sacred post of planning director at Gosplan was at one time reportedly held by a Swede.[22] That these individuals were needed is reflected in Party speeches and articles. Rykov, speaking before the First Moscow Oblast Soviet Congress in October 1929, related that the U.S.S.R. had had considerable success with foreign technology and the use of foreign techniques and that this had overcome technical backwardness and the shortage of engineering cadres. He indicated the practice was to be extended, and mentioned cases in which Soviet institutions had been working 'a great length of time' on projects when foreign consultants had checked and found the plans and construction deficient, which had necessitated starting again.[23] Ruykeyser's experience at Uralasbest confirms this possibility. One problem was that the proportion of technical personnel to factory workers in the more advanced countries of the West was about 10–15 percent, while in the Soviet Union it was not more than 2 percent. Of this 2 percent, only half had more than an elementary education. Of the plant directors in 770 works, 3.5 percent had no school education whatsoever, 71.6 had an elementary education, and the rest a high school education.[24] Given this shortage, it is not surprising that large numbers of Russians were sent abroad for training. All technical-assistance agreements and most equipment-purchase agreements contained clauses enabling the Soviets to have groups of their personnel trained abroad. This training was normally a few months, and no case has been uncovered where it ran longer than one year. In 1925–6 about 320 Soviet engineers were sent abroad; this rose to more than 400 in 1927–8 and to more than 500 in 1928–9. These were individual training visits in addition to the much greater number of technical delegates who went abroad for exploratory purposes.

Although there were ways of ensuring that these engineers returned to the U.S.S.R., it was more difficult, but not impossible, to retain Western engineers against their will. There are however some cases of the latter.[25]

The concession itself was a method of technological transfer. All such agreements required the transfer of the latest in Western technology, and some of the trading agreements (such as RAITCO) appear to have been much more

22 U.S. State Dept. Decimal File, 336–129–99.
23 U.S. Consulate at Riga, Report 6496, October 22, 1929.
24 U.S. Consulate in Vienna, Report 2158, April 9, 1929 (316–110–1079.)
25 For example, see Fred E. Beal, *Proletarian Journey* (New York: Hillman Curk, 1937). Beal met H. N. Swayne (an American) in Fergana, Uzbekistan. 'He was supervising the building of a gin mill for the Uzbekistan Soviet. He had two co-workers in this enterprise, an Englishman and a German. All of them were kept in the district against their will. How? The Russians couldn't find their passports....' (P. 254.) Beal was a Communist Party member.

vehicles for the transfer of Western technology than means for the Western partner to 'trade' with the U.S.S.R. When the transfer was completed, the concessionaire was expropriated, as Leninist dogma dictated. There were few cases of compensation and these (Mologa and Harriman) were for tactical reasons involving the possibility of acquiring other fields of Western skills. After 1925, news of concessions was heavily restricted and in 1927 made an act of espionage.

Foreign companies did little to enlighten the Western public, and indeed there are reports that the companies themselves put effective clamps on news concerning concessions.

After 1927 the Type III technical-assistance agreement was widely used. Where assistance had previously been tied to the purchase of equipment on a 'turnkey' basis, it was now the subject of separate agreements. At the same time, the emphasis moved away from Germany and toward the United States, although the Soviets still had great interest in acquiring the fruits of German scientific endeavors. From January 8 to 15, 1929, a German 'Technical Week' was held in Moscow, and a series of lectures was presented by German professors and experts who came (all expenses paid) for the occasion. The lectures included several by technical directors of German firms such as Telefunken Radio, A.E.G., and Frederich Krupp, and directors of technical institutes such as the Mulheim Coal Mining Institute and the Chemical Research Institute. The theme was the transfer of German work to the Soviet Union in the 'search for peace.'[26]

The Smolensk archives contain an example of the efficiency of the internal distribution of Western technology within the U.S.S.R. The State Institute for Foreign Technical-Economic Information published a monthly entitled *Fruitgrowing Economy* (presumably one of a series of such journals). This was a mimeographed circular which detailed in a summary manner the current results of Western research. It abstracted such obscure journals as the *Agricultural Gazette of New South Wales*, which would be difficult to locate in even a well-stocked Western library. Matching dates of the original articles with date of publication shows that the time difference was only a matter of months.[27]

PROBLEMS IN THE ACQUISITION OF FOREIGN TECHNOLOGY

The transfer was by no means smooth and efficient. *Ekonomicheskaya Zhizn* made a survey of the inefficiencies resulting from use of foreign technology.[28]

[26]   U.S. Consulate at Riga, Report 5869, February 2, 1929. (340–6–499.)
[27]   Smolensk Archives, Microcopy T 87, Roll 31, File WKP 264.
[28]   *Ekonomicheskaya Zhizn*, No. 57, March 7, 1928; No. 72, March 25, 1928; and No. 83, April 7, 1928.

Enormous wastage of funds was found. This was partly due to lack of foresight, partly to inexperience and lack of coordination, and also to lack of funds at strategic moments.[29] Many British and German firms may have supplied inferior equipment, although this may be a Soviet rationalization of inability to cope with more advanced technical systems. However, it is difficult to see what protection was available if foreign manufacturers for one reason or another wished to foist second-rate and inferior equipment onto the Soviets. In the absence of an indigenous technology, they could compare performance only to their own antiquated plants or to other foreign purchases. There were no impartial arbiters built into the economic system.[30] It is also difficult to see how they could adapt a technology developed for another and presumably different set of relative factor scarcity patterns.

There were many cases of machinery being bought before the plant had been erected, so that complete factories were left standing, often with inadequate protection, until plants were erected. There were cases of plant and equipment not suiting each other. Given the very precise civil engineering tolerances required in modern construction, this is not too surprising. A paper factory in Leningrad had a building ready but only part of the equipment, 'and even this [could not] be assembled before the arrival of special foreign technical personnel who [were] having difficulties in obtaining visas.' Lack of coordination between foreign suppliers of equipment for the same plant was quoted as a major delay. A textile mill with a capacity for 127,000 spindles had only received 15,360. Equipment for a power station in the Don was lying on the ground, as the project had been abandoned. There were no funds available to install equipment at the Marti plant in Nikolaev; two plants of Ugostal (Petrovsk and Lenin)—the railroad workshops at Dniepropetrovsk and the Ukrainian Silicate Trust—had the same problem. The Komintern locomotive plant at Kharkov changed its plans and would not use equipment imported for its use. Other equipment valued at almost 400,000 rubles at the same plant was idle because there was no electrical power for installation. Transportation, communications, and similar problems were delaying and confusing, and diverted quantities of imported materials.

This problem of unused foreign equipment appears to have been widespread. *Izvestia* (March 31, 1928), in an article entitled 'Problems with imported equipment,' reported that Khimugol had imported 1.3 million rubles worth

---

[29] Barmine and Kravchenko both made this point.

[30] For example, in 1931 the Soviets bought one-third of the output of Ruston-Bucyrus (U.K.), a manufacturer of mechanical shovels. 'The Soviet purchases . . . not only helped to improve our earnings record, but also enabled Ruston-Bucyrus to clear out most of its stocks of obsolete Ruston and Hornsby models.' *Designed for Digging*, p. 260.

of equipment which could not be used for at least two years. Similar delays were reported for the Kharkov locomotive works, the Krivoi Rog power station, and a bolt-making works. Curiously enough, on the same day *Pravda* ran an article entitled 'Methods of transferring foreign techniques,' which described the channels to be used: first, sending Soviet engineers abroad; second, importing foreign engineers; and third, utilizing technical-assistance contracts. The actual ranking order of use appears to have been the reverse. This article laid the blame for mistakes on the procurement organs of the government and especially their failure to use up-to-date catalogs. There were cases of machinery imports in which the design was of 1890 vintage.

Restoration and modernization of the electrical equipment industry was almost entirely dependent on imported machinery, and in 1930 this represented 90 percent of all boilers, turbines, and generators installed. It was the resultant wide diversity of models which resulted 'in complicating the design, erection and construction of generating installations to a large extent.'[31] The balance of 10 percent was produced within the U.S.S.R. with foreign technical assistance and further compounded the diversity problem. Further problems arose because the Soviets insisted on non-standard features in turbine development; these turbines were produced at the U.K. works of Metropolitan-Vickers, and, if the Soviets are to be believed, some 25 of these turbines were giving trouble by about 1930–1.[32]

The uninhibited copying of Western products may not always have been the outright gift it superficially appears. Sorensen, of the Ford Motor Company, comments on this:

> What the Russians had done was to dismantle one of our tractors . . . and their own people made drawings of all the disassembled parts. I visited a department where the rear axle and the final drive were being assembled . . . a lot of trouble with the worm drive . . . it was apparent that, while the Russians had stolen the Fordson tractor they did not have any of our specifications for the material that entered into the various parts. And you can't find that out merely by pulling the machine apart and studying the pieces.[33]

Sorensen probably understates the problems. Even if a qualitative analysis was made, for example, on the axle steel, and a specification produced, the grade still had to be manufactured. The heat-treatment problems alone would be a major headache. Many Soviet products reported as of poor quality are probably no more than imperfect copies of Western products. Production of quality required concomitance of design, development, and production.

[31]   *Electric Power Development in the U.S.S.R.* (Moscow: INRA, 1936), p. 101.

[32]   *Correspondence Relating to the Arrest of Employees of the Metropolitan Vickers Company at Moscow*, Command Paper 4286. (London: H.M.S.O., 1933), p. 9.

[33]   C. E. Sorensen, *op. cit.*, p. 202.

THE SHAKHTA AFFAIR

In 1928 the Soviets staged the first of their show trials involving foreign engineers. The Shakhta affair concerned five German engineers of A.E.G. working in the Shakhtinsky coal mines in the Don region.[34] The official charge was discovery of 'a counter-revolutionary plot to destroy and disorganize the coal industry.'[35] The engineers were accused of having links with former mine owners and the Polish counter-espionage service. It was said they had started fires, created explosions, wrecked coal-cutting machines, broken-down shafts, and generally created mayhem in the mines. In sum, they were accused of sabotaging 'socialist construction.' The burden of the accusation was placed on the foreign engineers as individuals and not on the foreign companies. Rykov carefully avoided accusing the firms of improper behavior.[36] The timing of the arrests, just as a German-Soviet treaty was to be negotiated and when the Soviets clearly needed German help, mystified most observers. U.S. State Department archives contain a number of foreign government reports, and their concensus is that the real reason for the arrests was the dominant place achieved by the Germans in Russian industry. They had become too powerful and threatened the hold of the Party. The move was against the 'united front' of specialists, old-time Russian engineers, trade unions, many of the workers, and some of the 'red' plant directors.[37]

The specialists controlled operation of many of the most important plants. They had supported and been supported by the old-time Russian engineers, not only because of similarity of political thinking but also by common background training and experience. The trade unions supported the foreign specialists as a means of getting production; many workmen viewed the foreign engineers with respect and the new 'red' engineers with derision. Many 'red' directors were interested primarily in output, recognized that the foreign specialists could get output, and placed day to day operations in their hands.[38]

Remaining Trotskyites used the question of specialists to 'prove' the Stalinist clique bourgeois; the latter then had common cause with the OGPU to attack this threat to Stalinist power. Terrorism via mass arrests was used to

[34] About 35 German engineers were jailed at this time on various charges, but only five as a result of Shakhta; and two of these were immediately released. The number in prison is an interesting indicator of the large number of German engineers in the U.S.S.R.

[35] *Izvestia*, No. 60, March 10, 1928.

[36] *Izvestia*, No. 61, March 11, 1928.

[37] U.S. State Dept. Decimal File, 316.6221/13 (Polish Foreign Ministry, Report); 361.6221/25 (German Foreign Ministry, Report); and 316-6221/28 (Greek Chargé d'Affaires in Moscow, Report).

[38] *Sevodnia* (Riga), March 21, 1928 [article by 'KC' (Moscow)].

frighten the foreign elements and their Russian allies. Choice of Shakhta was not accidental. Here the conflict between the 'red' and the foreign engineers was acute. Lambert, formerly a Belgian consul in Moscow, argued that the choice of the Ukraine was part of a reaction to Ukrainian nationalism which had sent many Muscovites back to Moscow and promoted native Ukrainians.[39] The Polish Foreign Office pointed out that it was noticeable that the many Belgian, Austrian, English, and American engineers were not molested. The Ministry argued this was one major aspect of an attack on *German* engineers. Further they were to be seized as scapegoats for the general inefficiency.[40]

[39] U.S. State Dept. Decimal File, 316.6221/32.

[40] U.S. State Dept. Decimal File, 361.6221/13, Report 1671, April 10, 1928. In view of the advice given to American firms in 1928 that it was 'safe' to enter the U.S.S.R., the following facts should be noted: (1) There was no shred of evidence of sabotage against the Germans. None was produced at the trials and none has ever been produced since 1928. They were 'acquitted' by the 'court.' (2) They were imprisoned in conditions described by the German Embassy representative Legationssekretaet, Dr. Schliep, as 'incredibly horrible,' while one of the unfortunate Germans was suffering from pneumonia (U.S. State Dept. Decimal File, 361.6621/13, Report 3403, April 13, 1928).

This once again raises the question whether the U.S. State Dept is justified in giving advice to United States firms and individuals which is contrary to the interests of these parties in the light of evidence with Departmental files. One presumes the function of the State Dept. is to protect American citizens, and yet today (1966), after the Baaghorn and Mott cases (among others), the State Dept. is still encouraging travel by tourists in the U.S.S.R.

CHAPTER TWENTY

The Western Contribution to Soviet Production and Productivity, 1917-30

THE CONTRIBUTION OF THE EARLY CONCESSIONS

THE original intent of the concession was to acquire both foreign finance and technology; both were deemed equally necessary. As it turned out, only technology was acquired, but this was facilitated by sufficient private credits to enable the transfer to take place in a reasonably satisfactory manner. It is misleading to argue that economic development depends only on finance capital; the latter is only a vehicle for the transfer of technology. It is also misleading to argue that, because there were no government-to-government financial transfers, the Soviet Union developed without Western assistance. The major factor in development is technical progress. The key question to be asked in the case of Soviet development is, from what did its technology derive? From internal resources, or from external transfers?

Examination of the role of the early concessions suggests that they played an important part in reversing the industrial decline and establishing the base for development. International Barnsdall introduced modern American methods of rotary drilling and deep-well pumping with results described in chapter 2. The lumber industry was wholly dependent on the transfusion introduced by the operating sections of the mixed companies Russangloles, Hollandoles, and Norvegloles. All transportation was dependent on early German concessions (Russtransit, Derutra, etc.). The locomotive repair program was undertaken abroad. Most modernization work in textiles and clothing originated with the Sidney Hillman concession. Foreign markets were developed by Type II mixed company concessions. These early concessionary arrangements (not numerous, but located in strategic sectors of the economy), when coupled with the post-Rapallo assistance from Germany, helped the Soviets to turn the corner.

There was an interval in 1921–2 when contemporary sources were reporting industrial revivals in some sectors and shutdowns in others. These parallel but opposite movements are related precisely to foreign assistance and the concessions. McKeevsky was reporting its mines were closing down while the Kuzbas coal mines were responding favorably to the work of the American Industrial Corporation. In 1923 shafts in the Don were reduced from 202 to 176, while AIK doubled Kuzbas output. While Embaneft and Grozneft were declining, Azneft was picking up new life with International Barnsdall.

In sum, the upswing may be linked precisely to the introduction of the first concessions and German technical assistance. No case of an upswing was uncovered which was not so linked.

SECTORAL IMPACT OF CONCESSIONS ON THE EARLY SOVIET ECONOMY

The proposition that every industrial sector of the early economy had foreign technical assistance, specifically in the form of pure Type I, mixed Type II, or technical-assistance Type III contracts, has been examined in detail. The proposition is much too important to be dismissed with the verbal generalizations typical of much discussion of Soviet development. The next pages contain an empirical demonstration of the validity of the argument that every corner of the economy was penetrated by Western technology between 1917 and 1930.

The structure of the inherited tsarist economy was sufficiently broad that it can be spanned with the Standard Industrial Classification.[1] This economy contained in embryonic form representatives of most modern industries. The SIC is an identification code for the modern American structure, but the components of today's structure can be traced clearly to the first two decades of this century. All sections of the modern SIC were represented by at least one plant in tsarist Russia, and this was the structure inherited by the Soviets. The structure included aircraft and automobile manufacturing. The advantages of using the SIC code are that we may be sure that every sector in the economy presents itself for examination, that we are sure of discussing the whole economy, and that we do not dismiss some sectors because they happen to be inconvenient for the hypothesis. It has been, for example, inconvenient for the Soviets to admit there were aircraft and automobile technologies (of an indigenous nature) in tsarist Russia.

---

[1]   *The Standard Industrial Classification (SIC)* (Washington, D.C.: Bureau of the Budget, 1957). Manufacturing is divided into 43 sectors, numbered 0 to 49. (Numbers 03 to 06, 18, and 43 are not used by the Bureau.) Sector 50 has been added by the writer to include trading.

Tables 20–1 and 20–2 classify concessions by country of origin and relate these to major groups in the SIC. Table 20–1 covers Type I (pure) and Type II (mixed) concessions while table 20–2 covers Type III or technical-assistance agreements. Where a concession has been identified and described in the text for a specific sector, its name has been inserted into the relevant portion of the matrix. In some sectors more than one concession existed but the extent of duplication is not indicated and can be determined from the text. A later set of tables examines the depth of technological impact within each sector. It should be added that the identification of concessions is still incomplete; it is estimated that less than 70 percent have been described and listed in this study. The remaining 30 percent will not come to light until the Soviets decide to release their archival data.

After compilation, the tables were scanned to determine the concession type and country making the greatest contribution to the Soviet industrial

Table 20–1 SECTORAL IMPACT OF FOREIGN CONCESSIONS
(TYPES I AND II)

Standard Industrial Classification (Major Group)	Industry	Source of Concessions Skill and Capital		
		United States	Germany	Others
01*	Commercial farms	Ware	Druag	Cannon (U.K.)
02	Noncommercial farms	Communes	Communes	Communes
07	Agricultural services	Hudson's Bay (Canada)	Druag	Vinge (Norway)
08	Forestry	—	Mologa	Russangloles (U.K.)
09	Fisheries	—	Hochseefisch erein	Romanoff Caviar
10	Metal mining	Harriman	Rawack & Grunfeld	Tetiukhe (U.K.)
11	Anthracite	RAITCO	—	Lena Goldfields (U.K.)
12	Bituminous coal	AIK	—	Grumant (U.K.)
13	Crude oil	Int'l Barnsdall	—	Gouria (U.K.)
14	Quarries	Int'l Mica	Krupp	Lena Goldfields (U.K.)
15	Building, general	ARK	Kossel A-G	Geoffrey & Curting (U.K.)
16	Building (not housing)	Ragaz	Krupp	—
17	Special trades	ARK	Russgertorg	Kablitz (Latvia)
19	Ordnance	—	GEFU	—
20	Food	Morris	Seyfurt	Union Cold Storage (U.K.)
21	Tobacco mfr	—	—	Lopato (China)
22	Textile mills	RAIC	—	Altman (Austria)
23	Apparel	RAIC	Stock	Trilling (Poland)
24	Wood products	—	Mologa	Dava-Britopol (U.K.)

Table 20-1 Continued

Standard Industrial Classification (Major Group)	Industry	Source of Concessions Skill and Capital		
		United States	Germany	Others
25	Furniture	—	—	—
26	Paper products	—	—	Raby Khiki (Japan)
27	Printing	—	Berger & Wirth	—
28	Chemicals	—	Bersol	—
29	Petroleum refining	Standard of New York	—**	—
30	Plastics	Kahn	—	S.I.M.P. (France)
31	Leather products	Eitingon-Schild	Wostwag	—
32	Stone, glass	AIK	Krupp	AGA (Sweden)
33	Primary metals	Russian-American Steel	Bergman	Lena Goldfields (U.K.)
34	Fabricated metal	—	Derumetall	Raabe (Finland)
35	Machinery (not electrical)	Westinghouse Brake Works	Leitz	SKF (Sweden)
36	Electrical equipment	International General Elect.	—	Swedish General Electric (Sweden)
37	Transportation equipment	International Harvester Co.	Junkers	Fiat (Italy)
38	Scientific instruments	Russian-American Instrument	—	Sovmetr (France)
39	Misc. mfg.	Alamerico	Block & Ginsberg	Schulmann (Latvia)
40	Railroads	—	Mologa	Lena Goldfields (U.K.)
41	Local transit	—	—	Cunard Line (U.K.)
42	Motor freight	—	—	—
44	Water transport.	—	Hamburg-Amerika Line	Norway-Russian Navigation (U.K.)
45	Air transport.	—	Deruluft	—
46	Pipelines	—	—	—
47	Transportation services	Russcapa	Derutra	Irtrans (Italy)
48	Communications	RCA	—	Great Northern Telegraph(Denmark)
49	Utility services	—	Hecker A-G	—
50	Trading	Alamerico	Russgertorg	Rusavstorg (Austria)

* All sectors in the SIC have been listed. Some numbers were not used in the original classification. This accounts for number gaps above.

** File 312 of the Bureau of Foreign and Domestic Commerce indicates the Germans obtained 'operating privileges' in the Maikop oil fields under the Rapallo Treaty protocols. No other data is known nor have other German Type I or II concessions been unearthed for this activity.

structure (i.e., which type is represented in most sectors). The type with the largest number of representations was United States Type III technical-assistance agreements, of which there were 36. This is consistent with our argument that United States technology was the preferred technology. Out of a total 43 sectors[2] that could have received concessions and the transfer of Western skills and technology we identified 36, or 84 percent. As the early economy consisted of only a few plants of prerevolutionary origin in each sector, the transfer could be rapidly spread within the sector. The agreements were made with either the trust overseeing the plants or with the best equipped and largest member of the trust group. Consequently, identification of even one technical-assistance agreement with a member of a narrowly defined industry with only a few plants implied that the transfer could be rapidly spread. Bogdanov indicated that the trusts were created with the prime purpose of transferring foreign technology; in practice they were well suited for this purpose.

It is interesting to note the contiguity of trusts and the SIC classification groupings; it is almost as if Lenin had the SIC Manual in front of him when he drew up the contours of the trusts. Crude oil (SIC 13) plus petroleum

Table 20–2   SECTORAL IMPACT OF FOREIGN TECHNICAL
ASSISTANCE AGREEMENTS (TYPE III)

Standard Industrial Classification (Major Group)	Industry Name	Source of Technical Assistance		
		United States	*Germany*	*Others*
01	Commercial farms	None outside	Type I and II concessions	
02	Noncommercial farms	Campbell	Druzag	Truss (U.K.)
07	Agricultural services	Sullivan Machinery	Wostwag	Langmann (U.K.)
08	Forestry	—	—	Harry Ferguson, Ltd.
09	Fisheries	—	—	—
10	Metal mines	Oglebay, Norton	Rawack & Grunfeld	—
11	Anthracite	Stuart, James and Cooke	Steinback & Taube	—
12	Bituminous coal	Allen & Garcia	Knapp A-G	—
13	Crude oil	Int'l Barnsdall	Machinenbrau	Mitsub'shi (Japan)
14	Quarries	General Engin. Co.	Deilmann Bergbau	—
15	Building-general	Longacre	Humboldt	—

[2] Table 20–2 consists of 43 sectors, as commercial farms were not relevant for the U.S.S.R., but table 20–1 includes 44 sectors, as there were concessions operating commercial farms. In any event, it makes little difference to the basic argument.

Table 20-2 Continued

Standard Industrial Classification (Major Group)	Industry Name	Source of Technical Assistance		
		United States	Germany	Others
16	Building (not housing)	Koppers	Koppers	Karlsrads Mechaniska
17	Special trades	Austin	Gefrierscha chbau	—
19	Ordnance	—	Krupp	Fokker (Holland)
20	Food	McCormick	Harberger	Maatschappij (Holland)
21	Tobacco mfr	—	—	—
22	Textile mills	Lockwood, Green	Kohorn	Soieries de Strasbourg (France)
23	Apparel	RAIC	—	—
24	Wood products	—	—	—
25	Furniture	—	—	—
26	Paper products	Hardy, Ferguson	—	—
27	Printing	Fulton Iron	—	—
28	Chemicals	Dupont	I. G. Farben	Casale (Italy)
29	Refining	Graver	Wilke & Pinsche	Vickers (U.K.)
30	Plastics	Seiberling	—	—
31	Leather products	—	Steinert	—
32	Stone, glass	Thomas Co.	—	Vakander (Sweden)
33	Primary metals	Freyn	Demag	SKF (Sweden)
34	Fabricated metal	McDonald	Faudewag	RIV (Italy)
35	Machinery (not electrical)	Mechanical Mfg.	Deutz	Separator (Sweden)
36	Electrical equip.	GE	A.E.G.	Metropolitan-Vickers (U.K.)
37	Transportation equipment	Koehring	Hohern zollern	Armstrong-Whitworth (U.K.)
38	Scientific instruments	Sperry Gyroscope	A.E.G.	Compagnie Générale de TSF (France)
39	Misc. mfg.	Underwood	Messer	—
40	Railroads	Baltimore & Ohio	Siemens Bau	Brown-Boveri (Switzerland)
41	Local transit	Seabrook	Siemens Bau	—
42	Motor freight	Ford Motor	—	—
44	Water Transport	Moissieff	Friedlam	—
45	Air Transport	Irving Chute	Junkers	—
46	Pipelines	J. I. Allen Co.	Mann	Crossley (U.K.)
47	Transportation services	Davis, Bishop	Derutra	—
48	Communications	RCA	Telefunken	Ericsson (Sweden)
49	Utility services	J. G. White	Siemens Schukert	Werksaden Kristine-gamm (Sweden)
50	Trading	Heller	Derumetall	Johnson, Mathey (U.K.)

refining (SIC 29) equals the Neftsyndikat, comprising Azneft, Grozneft and Embaneft. Anthracite mining (SIC 11) plus bituminous coal mining (SIC 12) equal the coal trusts (Donugol, etc.). Ordnance (SIC 19) equals the military trust. Scientific Instruments (SIC 38) equals Tokmekh; SIC 30 equals Resinotrest; SIC 33 equals Ugostal; and so on. There are two possible explanations. First, when the trusts were being designed with the objective of technological acquisition as their prime purpose, they may have been grouped in order to facilitate the transfer. Second, there is an internal logic to the structure of modern industrialization, and the early Soviet economy had the same structure as the early American economy, although the similarity has not persisted. In other words the grouping may have been obvious on grounds of logic.

Examination of the 36 (out of a possible 43) sectors covered by United States technical agreements and the 7 sectors not covered by such agreements suggests that, in fact, coverage was greater than 84 percent and was virtually complete. In other words the Soviets transferred United States technology to every sector.

Of the seven listed as not receiving technical assistance, several received *informal* aid as a by-product of purchases of large installations. Purchases of sawmill equipment included equipment installation. Fisheries received indirect aid from Pacific Coast manufacturers in the construction of large crab and salmon canneries. Even SIC 19 (ordnance) received indirect aid through the purchase of Curtiss engines. This problem is overcome in table 20-7, which examines the degree of impact and includes two types: direct and indirect technical impact.

The second largest group of concessions is the 'other country' Types I and II category (table 20-1). These comprise pure and mixed concessions with countries other than the U.S. and Germany. Out of 44 possible 'other country' sectors, these concessions were identified in 33 sectors, or 75 percent. They were concentrated in raw materials development. The category contains Lena Goldfields, Ltd., Tetyukhe, Kablitz, Trilling, the Japanese Sakhalin concessions, SIMP, ASEA, SKF, Union Cold Storage, Altman, Raabe, and so on. Pure 'other country' concessions were comparatively rare in the industrial and transportation fields. When they were granted, they were limited in scope, occupied prerevolutionary plants in decrepit condition, and were granted a technological area in which the limited company was an acknowledged world leader such as AGA, SKF, and the Cunard Line.

There were no 'other country' pure concessions in the fields of ordnance, chemicals, petroleum refineries, and, generally, transportation. These were strategic sectors requiring the transfer of German or United States technology.

The third largest group is German technical-assistance contracts. There were 32 sectors with identifiable agreements of this type, or 74 percent. This group contains many of the largest and best-known German companies: Demag, Koppers, Humboldt, Krupp, A.E.G., Siemens, Junkers, and so on.

The fourth largest group comprised German pure and mixed concessions representing work in 29 sectors, or 66 percent. This group also contained well-known German firms; Leitz, Krupp, Hamburg-Amerika Line, etc.

The fifth group comprised United States pure and mixed concessions and is represented in 27 sectors, or 61 percent. This included also some well-known names: Harriman, International Oxygen, International Harvester, and Standard Oil of New York.

The last and smallest group comprised the 22 'other country' technical-assistance agreements, represented in 51 percent of the economy. This small group confirms the argument that the desirable technology was from Germany and the United States. When it was transferred from one of the 'other countries' it was always in a highly specialized and narrowly defined area, such as ball bearings, synthetic nitrogen, radio apparatus, telephone equipment, dairy apparatus, and artificial silk technology. In sum, the Soviets went to countries other than the United States and Germany when there was a decided superiority in the technology in question.

Table 20-3 SUMMARY STATEMENT OF SECTORAL IMPACT
OF TYPES I AND II CONCESSIONS

	Types I and II Concessions Associated With:		
	United States	*Germany*	*Other countries*
Sectors with Type I & II concessions	27 (61 percent)	29 (66 percent)	33 (75 percent)
Sectors without Type I & II concessions*	17 (39 percent)	15 (34 percent)	11 (25 percent)
Total sectors**	44 (100 percent)	44 (100 percent)	44 (100 percent)

* This is a conservative statement, as less than 70 percent of operating concessions have been unearthed.
** Summary regardless of geographic association:
  95.0 percent of all sectors had concessions (42 sectors)
  5.0 percent of all sectors did not have concessions (2 sectors)

There is another way of looking at tables 20–1 and 20–2 and the summaries contained in tables 20–3 and 20–4. How many sectors of the early Soviet economy received concession agreements? Of the 44 sectors of the economy open for Types I and II concessions, 42 sectors, or 95 percent, actually received them. Of the 43 sectors open for Type III technical-assistance agreements, some 40 sectors or 93 percent received them.

Table 20–4 SUMMARY STATEMENT OF SECTORAL IMPACT
OF TYPE III TECHNICAL ASSISTANCE AGREEMENTS

| | Technical Assistance Agreements Associated with: | | |
	United States	Germany	Other countries
Sectors with t/a agreements	36 (84 percent)	32 (74 percent)	22 (51 percent)
Sectors without t/a agreements	7 (16 percent)	11 (26 percent)	21 (49 percent)
Total sectors	43 (100 percent)	43 (100 percent)	43 (100 percent)

Note: Summary regardless of geographic association:
93 percent of all sectors had technical assistance agreements (40 sectors).
7 percent of all sectors did not have technical assistance agreements (3 sectors).
Source: Table 20–2.

Finally, if we assume that the technical transfers take place irrespective of legal ownership or operational status (i.e., that we do not distinguish between concession types), *then only one sector out of the 44* (furniture and fixtures) did not receive a concession and thus had no opportunities for technological transfer. Of the total sectors 98 percent took advantage of foreign technology, and this was supplemented by indirect transfers.

Table 20–5 SUMMARY STATEMENT OF THE SECTORAL IMPACT
OF ALL CONCESSIONS, IRRESPECTIVE OF TYPE

| | Concessions Associated with: | | |
	United States	Germany	Other countries
Sectors with concessions	38 (86 percent)	38 (86 percent)	39 (89 percent)
Sectors without concessions	6 (14 percent)	6 (14 percent)	5 (11 percent)
Total sectors	44 (100 percent)	44 (100 percent)	44 (100 percent)

Note: Summary regardless of geographic association:
98 percent of all sectors had some form of concession (43 sectors).
2 percent of all sectors had no form of concession (1 sector).
Source: Tables 20–1 and 20–2.

SECTORS WITHOUT IDENTIFIABLE CONCESSIONS

To this point discussion has been concerned with sectors possessing identifiable concessions. The results imply an infusion of Western skills and technology. As Krassin foresaw, 'Each concession (would) . . . infuse a spark of vitality into the country's industrial life and would be in itself a training ground for Russian technical specialists and workmen.'[3] Use of the SIC code ensured that all sectors came up for consideration in an impartial

[3] Krassin, *op. cit.*, p. 184.

manner and that any possible biases on the part of the researcher would be eliminated. Possible criticism of the use of the SIC is far outweighed by the impartiality obtained.

Examination of sectors without concessions indicates the thoroughness with which the Soviets undertook this program. It is difficult to see how the canard of 'no large number of concessions' arose and spread to the point of becoming part of State Department advice to a well known scholar.[4] It is interesting to note that the handful of books written in 1928–9 on the impact of concessions universally reduced its importance, and nothing has been written since that time.

Of 44 sectors, only one had no identifiable concession. This is SIC 25 (furniture and fixtures): hardly surprising, as furniture making is a small scale industry with a static technology. Further only two sectors (apart from furniture) had fewer than two concessions: tobacco manufacturing and motor freight transportation, each of which had one concession. Given the extensive makhorka industry, the former exception is not surprising. The lack of motor buses until 1924 and absence of roads makes the latter exception understandable. There was no Soviet automobile industry until the Ford-Fiat agreements of 1928–9. All other sectors had concession agreements with two or more countries. Reliance was not placed on one source of technology. The net was spread wide enough to capture all the benefits of Western technology wherever they originated.

THE DEGREE OF TECHNOLOGICAL IMPACT WITHIN SPECIFIC SECTORS

It now remains to estimate the degree of impact within each sector. Table 20–6 estimates the direct and the indirect impact of Western technology upon each of the sectors discussed in Part I.

Table 20–6 DIRECT AND INDIRECT IMPACT OF WESTERN TECHNOLOGY BY SECTOR AND SUBSECTOR

Industry	Estimated Direct Impact	Estimated Indirect Impact
Oil industry (chap. 2)		
Exploration technology	Complete	Not applicable
Drilling technology	Complete	Not applicable
Pumping technology	Complete	Not applicable
Oil-field electrification	Complete	Not applicable
Pipeline construction	Complete	Not applicable
Refinery construction	Complete	Not applicable
Market acquisition	Complete	Not applicable

[4] See page 10.

Table 20-6 Continued

Industry	Estimated Direct Impact	Estimated Indirect Impact
Coal and anthracite mining (chap. 3)		
Coal fields: Donetz	Heavy	Significant
Kuzbas	Complete	Not applicable
Moscow	Heavy to complete	Not applicable
Far East	Complete	Not applicable
Sakhalin	Complete	Not applicable
Shaft development	Complete	Not applicable
Mine mechanization	Complete	Not applicable
Ferrous metallurgy (chap. 4)		
Iron-ore mining	Heavy	Limited
Blast-furnace repairs	Limited to significant	None
Blast-furnace new design	Complete	Not applicable
Steel-plant construction	Complete	Not applicable
Rolling-mill construction	Complete	Not applicable
Nonferrous Metallurgy (chap. 5)		
Zinc mining	Significant	Limited
Zinc smelting	Complete	Not applicable
Lead mining	Significant	Limited
Lead smelting	Complete	Not applicable
Copper mining	Significant	Limited
Copper smelting	Complete	Not applicable
Silver mining	Complete	Not applicable
Silver smelting	Complete	Not applicable
Manganese production	Complete	Not applicable
Manganese markets	Complete	Not applicable
Miscellaneous mining and smelting (chap. 6)		
Gold mining	Complete	Not applicable
Platinum mining	None	Heavy
Platinum markets	Heavy to complete	None
Bauxite exploration	Heavy	None
Pilot aluminum smelting	Complete	Not applicable
Mica mining	Complete	Not applicable
Asbestos mining	Heavy to complete	Not applicable
Asbestos mill technology	Complete	Not applicable
Asbestos shingles manufacture	Complete	Not applicable
Agricultural technology (chap. 7)		
Wheat farming	None	Significant
Seed growing	Limited	Limited
Cotton growing	Limited	Limited
Merino flocks	Complete	Not applicable
Dairy industry	Significant	Limited
Egg and butter markets	Complete	Not applicable
Tractors	Complete	Not applicable
Other agricultural equipment	Limited	Limited

Table 20–6   Continued

Industry	Estimated Direct Impact	Estimated Indirect Impact
Other food industries (chap. 8)		
Fishing	Limited	None
Fur collection	Limited	None
Fur sales	Heavy	None
Fish canneries	Heavy	Limited
Lumber industry (chap. 9)		
Forestry production	Heavy	None to limited
Lumber markets	Complete	Not applicable
Pulp and paper mills	Not applicable	Complete
Machine construction (chap. 10)		
Locomotive construction	Heavy	Not applicable
Machine building	Heavy to complete	Not applicable
Ball bearings	Complete	Not applicable
Steam boilers	Heavy	Not applicable
Precision engineering	Complete	Not applicable
Electrical equipment industry (chap. 11)		
High-tension equipment	Complete	Not applicable
Electrical motive equipment	Complete	Not applicable
Low-tension equipment	Complete	Not applicable
Accumulators	Complete	Not applicable
Turbines and generators	Complete	Not applicable
Hydroelectric technology	Heavy	Limited
Chemicals, compressed gases and dyes (chap. 12)		
Synthetic ammonia	Complete	Not applicable
Nitric acid	Complete	Not applicable
Superphosphates	Complete	Not applicable
Sulphuric acid	Complete	Not applicable
Coke oven by-products	Complete	Not applicable
Oxygen and hydrogen	Complete	Not applicable
Basic and intermediate dyes	Complete	Not applicable
Glass technology	Complete	Not applicable
Rubber technology	Heavy	Limited
Clothing, housing, and food (chap. 13)		
Textiles	Heavy	Limited
Clothing manufacture	Limited	Limited
Artificial silk	Complete	Not applicable
Buttons	Limited	None
Food processing	Significant	Limited
Construction industry	None to limited	Limited
Misc. small items	None to limited	Limited

Table 20-6 Continued

Industry	Estimated Direct Impact	Estimated Indirect Impact
Transportation and transportation equipment industries (chap. 14)		
Railroad operations	None to limited	Heavy
Railroad electrification	Complete	Not applicable
Telegraphic communications	Heavy	None
Radio communications	Complete	Not applicable
Automobile construction	Complete	Not applicable
Truck construction	Complete	Not applicable
Shipping	Heavy	Limited
Shipbuilding	Heavy	None
Port construction	Significant	None
Freight transportation	Limited	None
Military technology (chap. 15)		
Airplane construction	Complete	Not applicable
Pilot training	Complete	Not applicable
Poison gas production	Heavy	None
Artillery and shells	Complete	Not applicable
Armored cars and tanks	Complete	Not applicable
Trading companies (chap. 16)		
United States markets		
United Kingdom markets	All trading companies had heavy assistance	
German markets	in the early years of the decade.	
Austrian markets		
Italian markets		

Note: This table summarizes the evidence presented in Part I concerning the degree of impact of Western technology on the Soviet economy. The 'direct impact' treated in column 2 refers to identifiable technical associations between Western firms and Soviet institutions. This involves not only Soviet adoption of Western processes *in toto* but also the employment of foreign engineers in the U.S.S.R. for production or training of Soviet engineers.

The 'indirect impact' treated in the last column refers to the acquisition of Western equipment not, however, operated by a foreign company. Such instances are comparatively rare in this period, but they become more common in the periods to be covered by later volumes. The characteristic distinguishing the two types of influence is the supply of supplementary services; training, installation, break-in operations and servicing. The degrees of impact are defined as follows:

Complete	80 percent of all new capacity
Heavy	60 to 80 percent of all new capacity
Significant	40 to 60 percent of all new capacity
Limited	20 to 40 percent of all new capacity
None	0 to 20 percent of all new capacity

Thus, in a sector such as oil-field rotary drilling, there was a complete and direct impact. The adopted technology was almost completely Western, and the equipment was installed and initially operated by a Western company.

THE CONTRIBUTION OF IMPORTED TECHNOLOGY TO SOVIET PRODUCTION

In 1921 production was zero or rapidly approaching zero. Large segments of the industrial structure were in a state of 'technical preservation.' The first task was to get these plants started; the second was to repair plants damaged or in disrepair; and the third was to modernize. Although each industry solved its problems in a slightly different manner, the importation of foreign skills was common to all of them.

The description in the preceding pages indicates that foreign technology had both an extensive coverage within the economy and a significant impact within each sector. No other factors were capable of bringing about the same end result. If internal skills or internal capital accumulation had existed then perhaps the answer would not be as obvious. As the facts stand, the conclusion is quite clear. The rapid growth of the 1920s was dependent on foreign operative and technical skills. Electrical energy grew more rapidly than any other sector; from a base of 100 in 1913 the index grew to 412 in 1929. There is no reason to doubt the basic accuracy of these figures. The assistance given Soviet trusts, together with the equipment known to have been imported, could have accomplished this increase, even allowing for the previously mentioned problems and inefficiencies in the transfer. By the end of the decade, Lenin's dictum that socialism equals electrification was well on the way to implementation. This was heralded as a triumph of socialist construction, but unless one defines the latter as Western enterprise operating in a socialist economy, it should be hailed as a triumph of Western private enterprise working under enormously difficult technical and political conditions. Western engineers were aghast, as their writings show, at the interference from political 'straw bosses' whose contribution to construction was purely verbal, generating great heat in a show of ideological fervor. The remarkable growth of production in the 1920s is in those sectors which received the greatest Western aid; coal, oil, pig iron, and rolled steel. Those sectors without a great deal of aid barely improved their position during the course of the decade.

The Western contribution to Soviet production between 1917 and 1930 was total. *No important process has been isolated which was not a West-to-East transfer.* The Soviets quite rationally made no attempt whatsoever to develop completely new processes; even experimentation was limited and soon abandoned. They concentrated on acquiring new Western processes, training cadres of politically reliable engineers and establishing numerous basic and applied research institutes. The question was not *whether* to transfer Western technology but *which* process to transfer. Decisions were made on the basis of Western factor resource patterns and these may, or may not, have been applicable to the U.S.S.R. There are a few signs that the Soviets were aware of this problem and induced Western companies to undertake the necessary research and development work.

CHAPTER TWENTY-ONE

The Significance of Foreign Technology and Concessions for Soviet Exports

THE COMPOSITION OF SOVIET EXPORTS

THE Bolsheviks were realists. There was little hope that largescale Western government credits would be forthcoming. World revolution was being actively promoted, and great things were expected daily from the German proletariat, for instance. It could not be assumed that even the most naïve of Western Governments or the most grasping of capitalists was going to subsidize its own downfall on credit terms. The alternatives were concessions, gold, or exports.

The concessions policy was closely related to the drive for exports. A decree signed by Lenin in August 1921 established an Extraordinary Export Commission to assemble, process, and store raw materials for export. The Commission had the right 'to impose fines and inflict punishment on persons guilty of delays.'[1]

Table 21-1   CAPITAL GOODS AS PERCENTAGE OF
U.S.S.R. TRADE, 1920 TO 1930

	Capital Goods		Raw Materials, Foodstuffs	
	% Imports	% Exports	% Imports	% Exports
1920	39.7	—	60.3	100.0
1921–2	45.6	—	54.4	100.0
1922–3	76.2	—	23.8	100.0
1923–4	82.7	0.1	16.3	99.9
1924–5	68.5	0.3	30.8	99.7
1925–6	82.6	0.1	16.2	99.9
1926–7	89.5	0.1	9.3	99.9
1927–8	86.4	0.1	12.5	99.9
1928–9	88.4	0.3	10.2	99.8
1929–30	88.1	0.2	9.8	99.8

Source: Alexander Baykov, *Soviet Foreign Trade* (New Jersey: Princeton, 1946).

[1] *Ekonomicheskaya Zhizn*, August 26, 1921.

After this decree, a number of concessions were concluded under which foreign companies entered the Soviet Union to handle the assembly and export of animal products (eggs, butter, casings, fish and similar products). In 1920, imports were primarily food and raw materials; by 1923 imports were primarily capital goods. The first function of the concession was to help solve the supply crisis and then develop materials for export. After 1923, exports were between 99.7 and 100 percent raw materials and foodstuffs.

Table 21-1 suggests the significantly high proportion of Soviet imports which consisted of capital goods. This is consistent with our hypothesis of complete technological dependence on the West. The counterpart was a very high proportion of raw material and foodstuffs exports. The U.S.S.R. was exchanging consumer goods and raw materials for capital goods. This is not just the mere exchange of resources; the gains from trade were far more effectively captured by the Soviets as a result of their monopsonistic trading organizations facing atomistic Western sellers. Further, even with equality of bilateral bargaining, the Western investment in research and development could not be recouped in sales to the U.S.S.R. Only if the Soviet Union were to export freely its own technological advances would the balance be approximately even.

Very early trading efforts by the Soviets suggests that they did not then appreciate the advantages of a monopoly trading organization, but after about 1923, any attempt by Western sellers to form a buying group was met by vehement opposition and any concession (such as Russgertorg) which appeared to be gaining bilateral bargaining strength was quickly disbanded or had its wing clipped. Certainly the monopoly profits earned by the U.S.S.R. in the fifty years following the Bolshevik revolution far exceed that of the 19th century American trusts and 'robber barons' dealt with by the Sherman Act of 1890.

In sum, trade was used as a development mechanism. Manganese, oil, lumber, gold and butter developed by concessions operating inside the Soviet Union were sold on the Western markets by other concessions in which the Soviets held a controlling interest. The foreign exchange generated was used for purchase of capital equipment for the expansion and modernization of the industrial structure.

THE SIGNIFICANCE OF PURE AND MIXED CONCESSIONS IN RAW MATERIAL DEVELOPMENT

The concession may be related directly to the development of exports. Table 21-2 takes the twelve leading exports and lists the related importance of the concession as it has been detailed in Part I of this study.

Table 21–2 LEADING SOVIET EXPORTS AND SIGNIFICANCE
OF CONCESSIONS

Rank Order	Exports (1927–8)	Value of Exports thousand rubles	Percent of Total Exports	Significance of Concessions[1]		
				Type I	Type II	Type III
1.	Oil	124,090	19.1	X	X	X
2.	Furs	119,207	18.3	X	X	—
3.	Lumber	118,540	18.2	X	X	X
4.	Clothing	103,163	15.9	x	x	x
5.	Eggs	40,462	6.2	—	X	X
6.	Butter	39,120	6.0	x	X	x
7.	Sugar	33,803	5.2	X	X	X
8.	Flax	25,893	4.0	x	—	—
9.	Manganese	13,781	2.1	X	X	X
10.	Wheat	11,210	1.7	x	—	x
11.	Casings	10,659	1.6	—	X	—
12.	Fish	10,367	1.6	x	X	x
		650,295[2]	99.9 percent			

Notes: [1] X = major significance
x = minor significance
[2] Percent of all exports: 80.9 percent

These items include just under 81 percent of all Soviet exports. Oil, furs, and lumber contributed just less than 20 percent each (together 55.6 percent) of this total; each activity was completely dominated by foreign assistance supplied through concessionary arrangements.

CHAPTER TWENTY-TWO

Conclusions

THE industrial structure of the Soviet Union between 1917 and 1930 was the reorganized tsarist structure. This consisted of several hundred medium-to-large manufacturing enterprises located in urban centers, notably Petrograd and Moscow. This manufacturing complex was supplemented by numerous self-contained mining enterprises in the Donbas and the Urals which were centers of incipient industrialization. Some of these plants were large by any standards. The International Harvester plant at Omsk for example was the largest in the company's world-wide network. The first major conclusion is that the tsarist industrial structure was not at all negligible. To say that 'Russia prior to 1917 was not unlike a country such as India on the one hand or large areas of southeastern Europe on the other,'[1] is rank absurdity. Airplanes and automobiles *of indigenous Russian design* were produced in quantity before the Bolshevik revolution. Although industrialization was restricted to a few population centers, it utilized modern, efficient plants operating on scales comparable to those elsewhere in the world. Further, there were obvious signs of indigenous Russian technology in chemicals, aircraft, automobiles, turbines, and railroad equipment.

The second major conclusion was that this structure was substantially intact after the Bolshevik Revolution. Intervention did not affect the main *manufacturing* areas. There was damage to the railroad system, particularly in the Donbas and Siberia, and the Port of Petrograd was heavily damaged and mined. Petrograd industry, however, was basically in operable condition. Industrial damage was concentrated in the Ukrainian sugar industry and in the Ural and Donetz Basin mines.

What, then, created the economic debacle of 1921–2?

It was not brought about by absence of operable production facilities. While plants were in a state of 'technical preservation,' work discipline collapsed,

[1] M. Dobb, *op. cit.*, p. 11.

and skilled workers, engineers, and managers fled into the villages or abroad. The distribution system was abandoned as unnecessary in a socialist economy. Productivity consequently sank to abysmally low levels, and the 'supply crisis' followed on the heels of the rejected distribution system. Systematic destruction of a viable economy was aided by the inflation of the ruble to zero value (on the basis that money was not needed in socialism), the 'instant demobilization of industry' decree, 'free' public services, and the replacement of skilled managers with unskilled proletarians. By August 1922 the Soviet economy was at the point of collapse. This is not deduction. Lenin, Bogdanov, Arsky, Krassin and others have made the point clearly. The end had come. As Krassin phrased the problem, 'Anyone can help pull down a house; there are but few who can re-build. In Russia there happened to be far fewer than anywhere else.'[2]

The economic decline which directly followed the Revolution is unparalled in the history of industrialized society; however, the Soviets not only survived, but in 1924 were able to institute the Second Bolshevik Revolution and return to the path of State control of industry. The factors behind the miraculous recovery are detailed in the text.

In mid-1922 Soviet industry was at a standstill. Soviet inability, for lack of skilled engineers and workers, to restart the tsarist plants is well illustrated by the Russo-Baltic plant at Taganrog, moved during the war from Reval. Four massive buildings were visited (and photographed) by the 1926 Ford Delegation. The plant had furnaces, hammers, hydraulic presses, and a power station, as well as approximately 2,000 machine tools. These had been idle since 1917, although coated with oil to keep the tools in some sort of preservation. The photographs indicate the gigantic size of the plant, idle for at least nine years. It was operable although perhaps technologically out of date compared to the rapidly developing industries in the West. The urgent needs were two-fold: to restart the silent plants and modernize the equipment. The trust was the organizational vehicle adopted for these objectives. As Bogdanov pointed out, the primary aim of the trust was the transfer of foreign skills and technology to fulfill both these urgent requirements.

Trustification and technical transfer were achieved step by step. First, a selection from among important industries was made. Choice was on an ideological basis. Railroads, mining, and machinery sectors were selected on the basis of political, not economic, choice; they were only coincidentally key sectors in the economy. In the process of selection, several key economic activities, such as gear-cutting (Citroen plant) and air-brake manufacture (Westinghouse Air Brake Company) were left in foreign hands. The pragmatic

[2] Krassin, *op. cit.*

Communists understood their own inability to run these rather complex enterprises. After selection, the remaining operable units were isolated from the inoperable, and the latter were left outside the trust structure. The inoperable units were offered to foreign firms as concessions (the Berger and Wirth dye plant, the Bergman ferrous metallurgy plant, the Kablitz boiler-making operation, the AIK textile plants, the Lena and Kemerovo mines, etc.). In sum, the isolation procedure eleminated two categories of economic activity from the trusts: first, complex operations requiring lengthy foreign assistance, and second, those units requiring substantial modernization. These were leased directly to foreign operators as pure concessions.

The remaining or operable units were then grouped into trusts. Most were either dormant or working on an intermittent basis; given technical and managerial skills, they were operable. The names were 'proletarianized' and attempts were made to restart. In some plants 'white' engineers took over from unskilled 'red' directors—notably in the electrical and machinery sectors. But in all cases operation without the discipline of the market system led to hopeless inefficiency. The answer to a massive loss was a massive subsidy. These got out of hand by 1923 and were countered by the 'contraction of industry' policy.

Contraction (i.e., elimination of the most heavily subsidized plants) was concurrent with the injection of foreign assistance. Although this began as early as 1919–1920, it received a strong assist from the German Trade Agreement of 1921 and the Rapallo economic, military, and trade protocols. Extensive documentation in the German Foreign Ministry Archives attests to the thoroughness and completeness of German economic and technical help after 1922.[3] Such assistance was at first almost completely German, in fact. The Shakhta affair reflects the influence of Germany in the U.S.S.R. The Soviets were concerned about the massive infiltration and influence of German specialists in Soviet industry. They had penetrated most large industrial and mining enterprises, and in many cases had formed understandings with the prerevolutionary engineers. Whatever the judicial failings of the Shakhta 'trials,' the OGPU was probably correct in recognizing a threat to the Revolution. As late as 1928, Soviet industry was run by a partnership of German and prerevolutionary engineers independent of nominal Party control.

The tendency at the end of the decade was to turn increasingly toward American technical leadership. Of the agreements in force in mid-1929, 27 were with German companies, 15 were with United States firms and the remain-

---

[3] The writer examined rather cursorily more than 25,000 documents, including a small group of Russian documents relating to this cooperation and the work of the various committees and sub-committees formed to channel the assistance. Committees IV and V were mainly concerned with the economic and technical aspects.

ing ones were primarily with British and French firms. In the last six months of 1929, the number of technical agreements with U.S. firms jumped to more than 40.[4] It is this change which forms a logical break in the examination of Soviet technology and industrial development. The usual break point—1928 (the beginning of the first Five-Year Plan)—is meaningful only in propaganda terms; the Plan was implemented *after* a sequence of construction and technical-assistance contracts with Western companies had been let.

The Freyn-Gipromez technical agreement for design and construction of giant metallurgical plants is economically and technically the most important.[5] Despite the German work, the metallurgical industry was on a 1913 technical level. It had not incorporated current advances in rolling techniques such as the American wide strip mill or the powerful, heavy blooming mills developed in the mid-1920's. The A. J. Brandt-Avtotrest agreement for reorganization and reconstruction of the prerevolutionary car plant (the AMO) was overshadowed by the 1930 Ford Motor Company agreement to build a completely new integrated plant for the mass production of the Model A, the 2.5-ton Ford truck, and buses using Ford patents, specifications, and manufacturing methods. The plant was erected by Albert Kahn, the builder of River Rouge and so enabled the Soviets to duplicate the immense advances of American automobile engineering within a few years of inception in the United States. Two agreements with Orgametal by other American companies completed assistance in the heavy engineering field. The electrical industry had the services of International General Electric (in two agreements), the Cooper Engineering Company and RCA for the construction of long-range powerful radio stations. The Stuart, James and Cooke, Inc., contracts with various coal and mining trusts were supplemented by specialized assistance contracts, such as the Oglebay, Norton Company aid agreement for the iron ore mines and the Southwestern Engineering agreement in the non-ferrous industries. The chemical industry turned to Dupont and Nitrogen Engineering for synthetic nitrogen, ammonia, and nitric acid technology; to Westvaco for chlorine; and to H. Gibbs to supplement I.G. Farben aid in the Aniline Dye Trust. This was supplemented by more specialized agreements from other countries: ball bearings from Sweden and Italy; plastics, artificial silk, and aircraft from France; and turbines and electrical industry technology from the United Kingdom.

---

[4] Bron, *Soviet Economic Development and American Business.*
[5] The U.S. State Dept. Decimal File contains a rather curious exchange of letters between Freyn Engineering and the State Dept. Obviously there had been a major communication of ideas and attitudes between both parties. Both sides, however, refrained from placing the understanding on paper; or at least an understanding has not been traced within the Archives. Those documents in the files suggest that Freyn was powerfully influenced by the State Dept. viewpoint. (See U.S. State Dept. Decimal File, 661.1116/62.)

The penetration of this technology was complete. *At least 95 percent of the industrial structure* received this assistance. To demonstrate this, all sectors of the economy have been examined impartially.

We may conclude therefore, that the basic Soviet development strategy was to learn from that country considered to have the most advanced processes within a given field of technology and to leave no industrial sector without the benefits of this transfer process. In 1929–30, some 40 million rubles were spent for technical-assistance agreements alone. When it is considered that the marginal costs to the Western supplier were very small, that this ensured extremely low purchase prices for technology (in the light of opportunity costs), and that much of the transfer was done informally at no cost as a part of equipment-supply agreements, then the magnitude of the benefits becomes very clear. The greater part of this sum was spent in the U.S.; 'In America,' it was said, 'they do not guard manufacturing secrets so jealously.'[7]

The success of this strategy was not lessened by the fact that political interests always dominated economic requirements. When individual concessions threatened the hold of the Party even remotely, the reaction was sharp and ruthless. The Shakhta affair was an example of Leninist terror used to bring a 'united front' into line, whatever might be the economic consequences. The move from German to American technology was partially dictated by the probability the American engineers were less likely to get tangled in the meshes of counter-revolution, which had its origin in Europe rather than the United States. Import of equipment always reflected the domination of the political. One of the first imports from the U.S., after the lifting of the blockade, was 1,300 printing presses from the Fulton Iron Works. Production of long-range radio stations went ahead rapidly with the help of RCA and International General Electric, at the time when the State Department files had ample evidence of subversion (see, for example, Microcopy 316, Roll 141 for Soviet activities in the Dutch East Indies in 1928, the cracking of the Bolshevik code and instructions to Soviet agents at precisely that time at which permission was given to RCA and IGE to export radio stations to Soviet Russia). One at least understands why RCA checked and then double-checked with the State Department on permission to export high-powered radio stations.

The dominance of the political aspects over the economic did not restrain development; the Soviets correctly foretold the inaction of major Western

[6]   To place U.S. technical aid to the U.S.S.R. in perspective, the reader is referred to *Current Technical Service Contracts* (U.S. Dept. of State, 1966). Brazil is the largest country in this listing. Pages 62–6 list AID technical-assistance projects in Brazil. Comparison of these with U.S. aid agreements in the U.S.S.R. in 1928–9 will convey the enormous size and scope of the latter. There is nothing comparable to the Ford Motor Co. agreement, for example.

[7]   *Ekonomicheskaya Zhizn*, No. 225, September 29, 1929, p. 3.

governments during the transfer of technology. The Soviets were determined and based their moves on accurate information. Western governments failed to cooperate one with another and made policy determinations inconsistent with material on file.

The concessions policy itself had two aspects. On one hand the Soviets described to the Western businessman the profitable opportunities awaiting entrepreneurs in the U.S.S.R. These were presented in hopeful little booklets, backed up by trade journals and trade delegations. On the other hand, the Soviets had only limited interest in the concession hence their eventual expropriation of the Western entrepreneur naïve enough to invest in the Soviet economy. There was no danger to the Revolution, said Lenin: 'They are a foreign thing in our system . . . but whoever wants to learn must pay.' The West was needed to build up socialism, did it matter if the Soviets gave away a few tens of millions in resources? As Lenin said, 'afterward we shall get it back with interest.'[8] The closer the explanation got to the rank and file, the more explicit were the Communists in describing the fate awaiting the Western businessman. It was unlikely that W. Averell Harriman was reading *Komsomolskaya Pravda*, and on this the Soviets guessed correctly. It is less credible that the State Department did not investigate the ample data at its disposal—data backed by very accurate field reports—to determine the fate of investors in the U.S.S.R.

As the lesson penetrated Western business circles, the pure and mixed concessions were replaced by the technical-assistance agreement, under which the assistance was either bought outright or was included as part of a large equipment order. After the 1928 Gillette Razor Blade concession, no further pure concessions were concluded. Mixed companies persisted for a few years. The technical agreement remains and is currently in use.

---

[8] *Komsomolskaya Pravda*, October 9, 1928.

APPENDIX A

A Guide to Sources of Material

ALMOST all of the material used in this study, including the microfilmed copies of State Department and other records, has been deposited with the Hoover Institution on War, Revolution and Peace, at Stanford University.

THE STATE DEPARTMENT DECIMAL FILE

The National Archives has published much of the State Department Decimal File for 1910–30 on microfilm. Microcopy 316 is the main source for this study, particularly Rolls 107 to 143. Wherever possible, references are given to the National Archives microfilm copy, not to the original Decimal File copy.

The first three figures of such a reference consist of the Microcopy number (usually 316); the second group of figures refers to the roll number in the microcopy, and the last group refers to the frame number.

Thus, 'U.S. State Dept. Decimal File, 316–131–228' means that the source is the Decimal File and the reference may be found in National Archives Microcopy 316, Roll 131, Frame 228.

Some Decimal File records have not been microfilmed; these are referred to by the original Decimal File number (i.e., 361.6221/1). They may be specially ordered on microfilm, or the original documents may be examined at the National Archives.

For readers in Washington, D.C., wishing to see the original document (not the microfilmed copy), the National Archives has finding aids which make it possible to trace the Decimal File number from the Microcopy-Roll numbers given in the text.

Documents of the Bureau of Foreign and Domestic Commerce are referred to by file number only. No roll and frame identification exists.

For German Foreign Ministry records references are to National Archives Serial, Roll and Frame numbers. Thus, 'German Foreign Ministry, T120–3032–H108752' refers to Microcopy T120, Roll 3032, Frame H108752.

RELIABILITY OF DATA ORIGINATING
INSIDE THE U.S.S.R.

Archival material from United States and German sources was assessed according to the reliability given by the respective foreign offices. During the 1920s the United States had excellent sources of information inside the Soviet Union. Two agents (IS and IS/2) provided much political and economic material. IS was especially prolific and passed over many hundreds of documents. These were assessed by the State Department as reliable, and a number were marked for the attention of the Secretary and Assistant Secretary. The writer checked a selection of IS material against later events and found it to be very precise. No case was found where IS was wrong in an important fact.

List of Operating Concessions, 1920 to 1930

TYPE I (PURE) CONCESSIONS

Name	Country of Origin
Aktiebolaget Svenska Kullagerfabriken (SKF)	Sweden
Aktiengesellschaft für Bauaufurungen	Germany
Alftan Concession	Lithuania
Allezundsky Union	Germany
Allgemeine-Warren Treuhand A-G	Austria
Allied American Corp. (See Hammer, Julius)	
Allmanna Svenska Elektriska A/B (ASEA)	Sweden
Altebauag	Germany
Altman	Austria
Aluminum Company of America (ALCOA)	United States
American Asbestos Co.	United States
American Industrial Colony	United States
American Industrial Concession	United States
American Model Industrial Corp.	United States
American-Russian Constructor Co. (ARK)	United States
Anglo-Russian Grumant Co., Ltd.	United Kingdom
Aschberg Concession (Russian Bank of Commerce)	Germany
Ayan Corp. Ltd.	United Kingdom
Beloukha Corp.	United States
Berger and Wirth A-G	Germany
Bergman A-G	Germany
Block and Ginsberg	Germany
Boereznsky	Lithuania
Bolton, August	Germany
Brand, Leo	Germany

Name	*Country of Origin*
Brock A-G	Germany
Bryner & Co., Ltd.	United Kingdom
Cannon Co. Ltd.	United Kingdom
Caucasian-American Trading and Mining Co.	United States
Chatkeiama Gomei Kaisha	Japan
Chatma Co.	Greece
Christensen Concession	Norway
Control Co.	Unknown
Czestochova Concession	Poland
Deutsch-Russische Agrar Aktiengesellschaft	Germany
Deutsch-Russische Film Allianz A-G (Derufa)	Germany
Deutsch-Russische Saatbau Aktiengesellschaft	Germany
Dyer Concession	United States
Ericsson A/B	Sweden
Estonian-American Oil Co.	United States
Euroamerican Cellulose Products Corp.	United States
Far Eastern Prospecting Co., Inc. (Far Eastern Syndicate)	United States
Farquhar, Percival	United States
Gaso-Accumulator A/B	Sweden
German Fishing Union (Hochseefischerein)	Germany
Gesellschaft für Wirtschaftliche Beziehungen mit den Osten (Eastern Relations Society)	Germany
Gesellschaft zur Förderung gewerblicher Unternehmungen (Gefu)	Germany
Gillette Co.	United States
Gouria Petroleum Co., Ltd.	United Kingdom
Great Northern Telegraph Co. (Det Store Nordiske Telgraselskab)	Denmark
Hagakeyama Gomeikaisha	Japan
Hammer, Julius (see American Industrial Concession, etc.)	United States
Hammerschmidt, D. A.	United States
Harriman, W. A. Manganese Concession	United States
Haywood Concession	United States
Heller, L., and Son, Inc.	United States
Hillman Clothing Concession	United States

Name	*Country of Origin*
Hokushinkai	Japan
Holland-Ukraine Syndicate	Holland
Holter and Borgen	Norway
Holz Industrie Aktiengesellschaft Mologa	Germany
Hudsons Bay Co., Ltd.	Canada
Iasima Chatchiro	Japan
Igerussko (I. G. Farben)	Germany
ILVA Alti Forni e Acciaierie d'Italia s.p.a.	Italy
Indo-European Telegraph Co., Ltd.	United Kingdom
International Barnsdall Corp.	United States
International Harvester Co.	United States
International Mica Co., Inc.	United States
Italian Kuban Concession	Italy
Junkers-Werke	Germany
Kablitz, Richard (Gesellschaft für Okonomie der Dampferzeugungskosten)	Latvia
Kahn, Montefiore	{ United States, Germany
Kita Karafu Tau	Japan
Marchand et Cie.	France
Netherlands Spitsbergen Co.	Holland
Nichiro-Giogio Kabusiki-Kaisha	Japan
Otopitel (Refrigeration)	Unknown
Polar Star Concession	Unknown
Priamur Mines, Ltd.	United Kingdom
Prikumskaya (See Russian-American Agricultural Corp.)	United States
Raabe A/B	Finland
Resch Concession	Germany
Rheinbaden	Germany
Rorio Rengion Kumai	Japan
Rorio Rengio Rumian	Japan
Ruben and Bielefeld A-G	Germany
Russian-American Agricultural Corp. (Prikumskaya)	United States
Russian-American Engineering and Trading Co. (Raito)	United States
Russian-American Industrial Corp. (Raico)	United States
Russian-American Mining and Engineering Corp.	United States
Russian-American Steel Works	United States
Russian Mining Corporation	United Kingdom

Name	Country of Origin
Separator A/B	Sweden
Serkovsky, Yan	Poland
Shirak Oil (see Società Minere)	
Shova Kiuka Kabushiki Kaisia	Japan
Shulmann, Elia	Latvia
Siemens-Schukert	Germany
Sinclair Exploration Co.	United States
Singer Sewing Machine	United States
Skou-Keldsen	Germany
Società Minere Italo-Belge di Georgia	Italy, Belgium
Société Industrielle de Matières Plastiques (SIMP)	France
Spies Petroleum Company, Ltd.	United Kingdom
Stock A-G	Germany
Storens, F.	Norway
Tetuikhe Mining Corp., Ltd.	United Kingdom
Tiefenbacher Knopfabrik A-G	Austria
Trans-Siberian Cables Co.	Denmark
Trilling, O.	Poland
Tschemo A-G	Germany
Tsukahara	Japan
Union Minière du Sud de la Russie	France
United German-American Corp.	United States
Vega	Norway
Vinge and Co.	Norway
Vint Concession	United States
Ware, Harold (see Russian-American Agricultural Corp.)	United States
Westinghouse Air Brake	United States
Windt	
Wirtschaftliche Verband der Deutschen Hochseefischerein	Germany
Yasimo Hachiro	Japan
Yasimo Tanaka	Japan
Yotara Tanaka	Japan
Zatbaugesellschaft	Germany
Zellugal	Germany
Zhest-Western	Austria

TYPE II (MIXED COMPANY) CONCESSIONS

Name	*Country of Origin*
Alamerico (Berlin)	United States
Allied American Corp.	United States
American Foreign Trade Corp.	United States
American Industrial Corp.	United States
Amexima	Holland
Arbor Co.	Estonia
Baltische Russische Transport und Lager A-G (Baltrustra)	Germany
Bersol A-G	Germany
Brenner Bros.	United States
Compagnia Industriale Commercio Estero (CICE)	Italy
Cunard Line	United Kingdom
Dava-Britopol (Ruspoltorg)	{ Poland, United Kingdom
Deruluft	Germany
Deruneft	Germany
Derutra (Deutsch-Russische Transport u. Lager Gesellschaft)	Germany
Deruwa (German-Russian Merchandise Exchange)	Germany
Deutsch-Russische Metallverwertungs Gesellschaft m.b.H. (Derumetall)	Germany
Duverger Concession	France
Dvinoles Export, Ltd	United Kingdom
Eggexport	Germany
Eitengon-Schild	United States
Exportles	United Kingdom
French Steamship Lines	France
German Orient Line	Germany
German-Russian Krupp Manushka Co.	Germany
Hamburg-Amerika Line	Germany
Holland-Amerika Line	United States
International Oxygen Corp. (see Ragaz)	United States
Internationale Warenaustauschgesellschaft (IVA)	Germany
IRTRANS (Società Mista Italo-Russa di Commercio e Transporti)	Italy

Name	*Country of Origin*
Kazuli Co.	Greece
Kossayger	International
Kossel, P., A-G	Germany
Kossuryo	International
Krupp'sche Landconcession Manytsch G.m.b.H.	Germany
Narova Co.	Estonia
Nord-Ost	Germany
Norway-Russian Navigation Co., Ltd.	{ Norway, United Kingdom
Ocean Travel Bureau	United States
Persaneft (Persian-Azerbaidjian Naphta Co.)	Persia
Perskhlopok	Persia
Persshold	Persia
Perssholk	Persia
Raby Khiki Kansha	Japan
Ragaz (Russian-American Compressed Gas Co.)	United States
RAIF Iron Co. for aid to Volga Colonists	Germany
Ratao (Russische-Oesterreichische Handels A-G)	Austria
Rawack and Grunfeld A-G	Germany
Repola Wood, Ltd.	{ United Kingdom, Finland
Royal Dutch Shell	{ United Kingdom, Holland
Ruben and Bielefeld	Germany
Rugerstroi (see Kossel, P., A-G)	
Russangloles, Ltd.	United Kingdom
Russavstorg (Russisch-Oesterreichische Handels und Industrie A-G)	Austria
Russgertorg (Russische-Deutsch Handels A-G)	Germany
Russhollandoles, Ltd.	{ United Kingdom, Holland
Russian-Asiatic Stock Co.	International
Russian Bristles Co.	United Kingdom
Russian-Canadian Navigation Co. (Russcapa)	Canada
Russian Land Concession Manytsch, Ltd.	United Kingdom
Russian Wood Agency, Ltd.	United Kingdom
Russnorvegloles, Ltd.	{ Norway, United Kingdom

Name	*Country of Origin*
Russo-British Grain Export Co. (Russobrit)	United Kingdom
Russo-Latvian Co.	Latvia
Russ-Norwegian Navigation Company, Ltd.	United Kingdom, Norway
Russot	International
Russotgorn	Turkey
Russo-Turkish Export-Import Co. (Russo-Turk)	Turkey
Russperssakhar	Persia
Russpoltorg	Poland
Russtransit (Russo-German Trading and Transit Co.)	Germany
Sale and Company, Ltd.	United Kingdom
Seyfurt A-G	Germany
Sibiko (Danish-Siberian Co.)	Denmark
Società Mista Italo-Russa di Commercio e Transporti (IRTRANS)	Italy
Société Russo-Anglaise des Matières Premières (Raso)	United Kingdom
Sorgagen A-G	Germany
Sovmetr	France
Sovmong	Mongolia
Standard Oil of New York	United States
Stern	United Kingdom
Suomen Nahkatehtaitten Osakeyhtio	Finland
Sutta, Simon	United States
Sveaexport	Sweden, Finland
Truss, G. H. and Co., Ltd.	United Kingdom
Turksholk	Turkey
Ukrainian Brewing Co. (Okman)	Estonia
Union Cold Storage, Ltd.	United Kingdom
United States Lines	United States
Vlessing	Holland
Warren, G. and Co., Inc.	United States
West-Oestliche Warenaustausgesellschaft (Wostwag)	Germany
White Sea Timber Trust, Ltd.	United Kingdom
White Star Line, Ltd.	United Kingdom

TYPE III (TECHNICAL-ASSISTANCE AGREEMENT) CONCESSIONS

Name	*Country of Origin*
Allen, J. I., and Co.	United States
Allen and Garcia, Inc.	United States
Allgemeine Elektrizitets A-G	Germany
Allis-Chalmers Manufacturing Co. (see RAITCO)	United States
Akron Rubber Reclaiming Co.	United States
Aufbau Trade and Industrial Co.	Germany
Austin Co.	United States
Badger, E. B., and Co.	United States
Baldwin Locomotive Works	United States
Birmingham Small Arms Co.	United Kingdom
Borsig, A. G.m.b.H.	Germany
Brandt, Arthur J., Inc.	United States
Brown Lipe Gear Co., Inc.	United States
Burrell-Mase Co., Inc.	United States
Compagnie de Produits Chimiques et Electrométallurgiques S.A.	France
Campbell, Thomas	United States
Casale Ammonia S.A.	Italy
Caterpillar Tractor Co.	United States
Chase, Frank, Inc.	United States
Cheretti i Tonfani	Italy
Compagnie Générale de TSF	France
Cooper, Hugh L., and Co., Inc.	United States
Davis, Arthur P., Lyman Bishop, and Associates	United States
Deilmann Bergbau u. Tiefbau Ges.	Germany
Demag A-G	Germany
Deutz Motorenfabrik A-G	Germany
Deutsch Tiefbohr A-G (Deutag)	Germany
Du Pont de Nemours and Co.	United States
Electric Autolite Co.	United States
Electrokemisk	Norway
Ferguson, Harry S., Ltd.	United Kingdom
Ford Motor Co.	United States
Foster-Wheeler Corp.	United States

Name	*Country of Origin*
Fröhlich und Knüpfel Maschinenfabrik	Germany
Freyn Engineering Co., Inc.	United States
Gasmotoren-Fabrik Deutz A-G	Germany
Gebrüder Sulzer A-G	Germany
General Engineering Co.	United States
Geoffrey and Curting, Ltd.	United Kingdom
Harry D. Gibbs	United States
Goodman Manufacturing Co., Inc.	United States
Graver Corp.	United States
Harburger Eisen und Bronzewerke A-G	Germany
Hect-Feifer A-G	Germany
Henshien and Co., Inc.	United States
Hercules Motor Co., Inc.	United States
Hilaturas Casablancas S.A.	Spain
Higgins, John J., Co.	United States
Humboldt-Deutz Motoren A-G	Germany
International General Electric Co.	United States
Irving Air Chute Co., Inc.	United States
Albert Kahn, Inc.	United States
Karlstad Mechaniska Verkstaden A/B	Sweden
Kohorn, Oscar A-G	Germany
Koppers Construction Co.	United States
Frederick Krupp A-G	Germany
Lockwood, Green and Co.	United States
Longacre Engineering and Construction Co.	United States
Lurgie Gesellschaft für Chemie und Hüttenwerke m.b.H.	Germany
Maschinenfabrik Augsburg-Nürnberg A-G (MAN)	Germany
Maschinenbau A-G	Germany
Maschinenbau-Anstalt-Humboldt	Germany
Maatschappij Tot Exploitatie von Veredlinsprocedes	Holland
McCormick Co.	United States
McDonald Engineering Co.	United States
McKee, Arthur T., and Co., Inc.	United States
Mechanical Manufacturing Co., Inc.	United States
Messer A-G	Germany
Metropolitan-Vickers Electrical Co., Ltd.	United Kingdom
Multibestos Co.	United States

Name	*Country of Origin*
Neumeyr A-G	Germany
Newport News Shipbuilding and Drydock Co.	United States
Nitrogen Engineering Corp.	United States
Officine Villar Perosa (RIV)	Italy
Oglebay, Norton & Co., Inc.	United States
Penick and Ford, Inc.	United States
Pierce, Charles and Co.	United States
Pflanzennamme G.m.b.H.	Germany
Radio Corp. of America (RCA)	United States
Radiore Co., Inc.	United States
Reidinger, A-G	Germany
Roberts and Schaefer, Inc.	United States
Scintilla A-G	Switzerland
C. F. Seabrook Co., Inc.	United States
Seiberling Rubber Co.	United States
C. V. Smith and Co., Ltd.	Canada
Frank Smith Co., Inc.	United States
Société de Prospection Electrique Procédés Schlumberger	France
Société du Duralumin S.A.	France
Société Française Anonyme Lumière S.A.	France
Soieries de Strasbourg S.A.	France
Southwestern Engineering Corp.	United States
Sperry Gyroscope Co.	United States
Standard Oil Co. of New York	United States
Stein A-G	Germany
Steinert, C. T.	Germany
Stuart, James and Cooke, Inc.	United States
Sullivan Co. (see RAITCO)	United States
Szepesi, Eugene, Consulting Management Engineers	United States
Telefunken Gesellschaft für Drahtlose Telegraphie	Germany
Thyssens A-G	Germany
Timken-Detroit Axle Co.	United States
Torfplattenwerke A-G	Germany
Underwood Typewriter Co.	United States
Union Shoe	Austria

Name	*Country of Origin*
Vakander A/B	Sweden
Vattenbyggnadsbyran A/B	Sweden
Verein Deutscher Werkzeugmaschinen Fabriken Ausfuhr Gemeinschaft (or Faudewag)	Germany
Vereinigte Carborundum und Elekritwerke A-G	Germany
Vereinigte Kugellager Fabriken A-G	Germany
Warren, G. W., Co.	United States
Webber and Wells, Inc.	United States
Westinghouse Company (see Metropolitan-Vickers)	
Westvaco Chlorine Products, Inc.	United States
Wheeler, Archer E., and Associates	United States
J. W. White Engineering Co.	United States
Winkler-Koch Engineering Co.	United States
W. A. Wood Co.	United States

Selected Bibliography

Aksamitnyi, Anatolii Sergeevich, *Die Wolga-Don Grosswasserstrasse*, Moscow, 1929.

Amalgamated Clothing Workers of America, *Bibliography of the Amalgamated Clothing Workers of America*, New York, 1929.

Amalgamated Clothing Workers of America, *Report of the General Executive Board, Sixth Biennial Convention*, Philadelphia, May 1924.

American Association to Promote Trade with Russia, *Reports* to the Association and *Bulletins*, New York, 1920–1.

American Bankers Association, *Commerce and Marine Commission, Russia: A Consideration of Conditions as Revealed by Soviet Publications*, New York, 1922.

American Industrial Colony, *Kuzbas*.

American-Russian Chamber of Commerce, *Economic Handbook of the Soviet Union*, New York, 1931.

Amtorg Trading Company (New York), *Amerikanskiai torgovlia i promyshlennosti*, New York, 1926.

Amtorg Trading Company (New York), *Economic Review of the Soviet Union*, New York, 1926–30.

Association Financière, Industrielle, et Commerciale Russe, *La situation économique et juridique de la Russie soviétique*, Paris, 1924.

Bank for Russian Trade Review, Moscow Narodny Bank Ltd., London, 1928.

Bernstein, S. A., *The Financial and Economic Results of the Working of Lena Goldfields Limited*, Blackfriars, London and Leicester, n.d.

Bron, Saul G., *Soviet Economic Development and American Business*, Horace Liveright, New York, 1930.

Burrell, George A., *An American Engineer Looks at Russia*, Stratford, Boston, n.d.

Butkovski, V. I., *Inostranye Kontsessii v Narodnom Khozyetve S.S.S.R.*, Moscow, 1928.

Clark, W. Gardner, *The Economics of Soviet Steel*, Harvard, Cambridge, 1956.

Commercial Yearbook of the Soviet Union: 1925, Allen and Unwin, London, 1925.

Conolly, V., *Soviet Trade from the Pacific to the Levant*, Oxford, London, 1935.

Conover, Helen F., *Selected List of References on Diplomatic and Trade Relations of the U.S.S.R., 1919–35*, U.S. Library of Congress, Washington, 1935.

Dobrovol'skii, Boris Nickolaevich, *The Nizhne-Tagil Car Building Works*, Moscow, 1929.

Egorov, Pavel Ivanovich, *The Magnitogorsky (Magnet Mountain) Metallurgical Works*, Moscow, 1929.

Engineering and Mining Journal, New York, 1925–36.

Ford Motor Company, *Report of the Ford Delegation to Russia and the U.S.S.R. April–August 1926*, Detroit, 1926, Ford Motor Company Accession Number 49.

Foreign Claims Settlement Commission of the United States, *Report*, Washington, 1959.

General Electric Company, *The Monogram*, Schenectady, 1943.

Geologicheskii komitet, *Godovoi obzar mineral'nykh resursov S.S.S.R. za 1925–6, gg.*, Leningrad, 1927.

Gerschuni, G., *Die Konzessionspolitik Sowjetrusslands*, Berlin, 1927.

Gershenkron, A., *A Dollar Index of Soviet Machinery Output, 1927–8 to 1937*, RAND Corp., Santa Monica, 1951.

Glavnyi Kontsessionnyi komitet, *Documents Concerning the Competence of the Arbitration Court Set Up in Connection with the Questions Outstanding Between the Lena Goldfields Company Limited and the U.S.S.R.*, Moscow, 1930.

Goulevich, A. de, 'Les concessions et les sociétés mixtes en Russie soviétique,' *Révue Économique Internationale*, Brussels, 1925.

Great Britain, *Correspondence Relating to the Arrest of Employees of the Metropolitan-Vickers Company at Moscow*, Command Paper 4286, London, 1933.

Great Britain, Anglo-Russian Parliamentary Committee, *Possibilities of British-Russian Trade*, London, 1926.

Hammer, Armand, *The Quest of the Romanoff Treasure*, Payson, New York, 1932.

Hilger, G. and Meyer, A. G., *The Incompatible Allies*, Macmillan, New York, 1953.

Hillman, Sidney, *Reconstruction of Russia and the Task of Labor*, New York, 1922.

Hirsch, Alcan, *Industrialized Russia*, Chemical Catalog Company, New York, 1934.

Hoover Institution on War, Revolution and Peace (Stanford University), *The Percival Farquhar Papers* (4 boxes).

——, *American Engineers in Russia.* Special Collection.

Indo-European Telegraph Company, Ltd., *Annual Reports*, London, 1927–8.

Ipatieff, V., *Life of a Chemist*, Stanford, 1946.

Izdaniye Iitizdata NKID, *Annuaire politique et économique: 1925–26*, Moscow, 1926.

Jen, Hwang, *Le régime des concessions en Russie soviétique*, Gamber, Paris, 1929.

Karty kontsessionniky ob'ektov S.S.S.R., Moscow, 1926.

Keller, Werner, *Ost minus west = null*, Droemersche Verlagsanstaldt, Munich, 1960.

Kelley, H. G., *General Report on Ekaterina Railway, Donetz Railway*, New York, 1926.

Kostrov, Ivan Nikolaevich, *The Nadejdinsky & Taganrog Metallurgical Works*, Moscow, 1929.

Krimmer, Alexandre, *Sociétés de capitaux en Russie impériale et en Russie soviétique*, Librairie du Recueil Sirey, Paris, 1934.

Kruglyakova, V. I. (ed.), *Sbornik statisticheskikh svednii po gornoi i gornozavodskoi promyshlennosti S.S.S.R., za 1927–8 gg.*, Moscow, 1930.

Kukel'-Kraevskii, Sergiei Andreevich, *The Svir Hydro-Electric Station for the Leningrad District*, Moscow, 1920.

Larsons, H. J., *An Expert in the Service of the Soviets*, Benn, London, 1929.

La Vie Économique des Soviets, Éditions de la Représentations Commerciale de U.R.S.S., Paris, 1927–30.

Le Pétrole Russe, supplement to *La Vie Économique des Soviets*, 1927–30.

Lee, Ivy, *U.S.S.R.; A World Enigma*, Benn, London, 1927.

Lewery, Leonard John, *Foreign Capital Investments in Russian Industries and Commerce*, Washington, 1923.

Liberman, L., *Trud i byt gorniskov Donbassa*, Moscow, 1929.

Littlepage, J. D. and Bess, D., *In Search of Soviet Gold*, Harcourt Brace, New York, 1938.

Mamonov, P., *Forest Concessions*, Khabarovsk, 1925.

Mautner, Wilhelm, *Der Kampf um und gegen das Russische Erdol*, Vienna, 1929.

Melville, C. F., *The Russian Face of Germany*, Wishart, London, 1932.

Monkhouse, A., *Moscow 1911–1933*, Little, Brown, Boston, 1934.

The Nation, New York, 1922–3.

Nutter, G. Warren, *The Growth of Industrial Production in the Soviet Union*, National Bureau of Economic Research, Princeton, N. J., 1962.

Perin and Marshall (engineers), *Report on Improvement of the Ugostal Steel Plants of South Russia*, New York, 1926.

Pim, A. and Bateson, E., *Report on Russian Timber Camps*, Benn, London, 1931.

Russian Yearbook 1912, Macmillan, New York, 1912.

Ruykeyser, W. A., *Working for the Soviets*, Covici-Friede, New York, 1932.

Santalov, A. A. and Segal, L. (eds.), *Soviet Union Yearbook: 1925*, London, 1926 (also 1926–1930 inclusive).

Shimkin, Demitri B., *Minerals: A Key to Soviet Power*, Harvard, Cambridge, 1953.

State Law Publishing House, *Wrecking Activities at Power Stations in the Soviet Union*, Moscow, 1933.

Swianiewicz, S., *Forced Labour and Economic Development*, Oxford University, London, 1965.

Thompson, A. Beeby, *The Oil Fields of Russia*, Lockwood, London, 1908.

Troyanovsky, A., *Eksport, import i kontsessii soyuz S.S.S.R.*, Moscow, n.d.

U.S. State Department, Decimal File 1910–1929 (available at National Archives, Washington).

U.S.S.R. Chamber of Commerce, *Economic Conditions in the U.S.S.R.*, Vneshtorgizdat, Moscow, 1931.

Vysshii sovet norodnogo khoziaistva, *Concession Agreement Between the Government of the U.S.S.R. and W. A. Harriman and Co., Inc. of New York*, Moscow, 1925.

Zinghaus, Victor, *Die Holzbearbeitungsindustrie der Union der Sozialistischen Sowjetrepubliken (Ud S.S.S.R.)*, Gustav Fischer, Jena, 1929.

Zuev, P., *Ugol'nya Promyshlennost' ee Polozhenie*, Moscow, 1921.

Index

www.ingramcontent.com/pod-product-compliance
Lightning Source LLC
Chambersburg PA
CBHW060324100426
42812CB00003B/875